...re a Governor of Fort ...tory & please...t to me ...iously repa... ...person for whom ...good will an so ...e. But he never will ...fects of this Govt ...o & skillful hand, ...onal authority. ...is uncertain; but I ...never under any ...nd Clive to Bengal; ...n will fall to ruin.

Two Views of British India

Frederick Hager
Guy Fawkes' Day 1970.

Two Views of British India

THE PRIVATE CORRESPONDENCE OF MR DUNDAS AND LORD WELLESLEY: 1798–1801

EDITED WITH AN INTRODUCTION BY

Edward Ingram

Assistant Professor in the History of the British Empire
at Simon Fraser University

ADAMS & DART

© 1970 Edward Ingram
First published in 1970 by
Adams & Dart, 40 Gay Street, Bath, Somerset
SBN 239 00032 3
Printed in Great Britain by W & J Mackay & Co., Ltd

Preface

These are the private and confidential letters of the two most celebrated figures in the history of the Raj. For seventeen years, from 1784 until 1801, Henry Dundas, first Viscount Melville, ran the board of control for India. For the last three of them, he was partnered by Richard Colley Wellesley, second earl of Mornington and Marquis Wellesley, governor-general of Bengal from 1798 until 1805. They wrote to one another long, outspoken, and revealing letters. The letters are in two series. Dundas wrote to Wellesley thirty-three *private* letters, and Wellesley wrote thirty-four back. Wellesley also wrote to Dundas fourteen *secret and confidential* letters, and Dundas replied to them when necessary. Intermingled in the two series are many 'separate' *private* letters and 'unnumbered' *secret and confidential* ones. Some of them have already appeared in *The Despatches, Minutes, and Correspondence, of the Marquis Wellesley, K.G., during his Administration in India*, published by Montgomery Martin, under Wellesley's own supervision, in 1836 and 1837. They contain repeated minor alterations, and frequent major omissions; and to remedy them these letters are published from the original manuscripts, wherever possible taking Dundas' letters from Wellesley's papers, and Wellesley's from Dundas'. They are numbered, however, as they were numbered by the writer. The numbering is not always identical: Wellesley's numbering of Dundas' letters gives the impression that some of them are missing.

From this collection there are three letters missing. Dundas' *private* letter number 26, of 18 April 1800, merely enclosed a letter to the chairman of the East India Company, and is supplied by an abstract. The two missing letters by Wellesley are more important. No copy was taken of his *secret and confidential* letter number 10, of 1 August 1799, but only the briefest abstract, because his private secretary, his brother Henry, was away at Seringapatam. This letter criticized the court of directors, and their methods of appointment. Three *secret and confidential* letters, numbered 8 to 10, are missing from Dundas' papers; but the other two are supplied from copies taken for Pitt. Finally, neither collection contains the *private* letter in which Wellesley recommended Dundas to attack the Spanish Indies.

The letters are published without their enclosures, which are very bulky and much less interesting. To the more interesting ones, references are supplied. Where this is to Martin's edition, it is to be remembered that it is probably an extract. The letters are also published chronologically. As they are not usually replies to previous letters, this does not lessen their impact, it heightens it; because it reveals what two men were thinking about the same questions, at the same time, half the world apart.

The editor wishes to thank the trustees of the British Museum and the National Library of Scotland, the keeper of the Public Record Office, and the librarians of the John Rylands Library and the India Office Library, for permission to publish extracts from their collections; and particularly to thank Mrs G. B. Sanderson, of Keltie Castle, Dunning, Perthshire, for permission to publish extracts from the Melville Castle Muniments on loan to the Scottish Record Office.

Barford,   EDWARD INGRAM
All Saints' Day, 1969.

I am a dreadful tyrant; arbitrary, jealous of power, sovereign lord and master, and impatient of all control in India, excepting that of my own sense of right and wrong. If you do not like me so, pray recall me.

WELLESLEY

Contents

The endpapers are reproduced from an original letter to Henry Dundas from Lord Wellesley by kind permission of Mrs G. B. Sanderson

ABBREVIATIONS

Add. MSS.   Additional Manuscripts, British Museum, London.
Buckingham   Duke of Buckingham, *Memoirs of the Courts and Cabinets of George III* (London, 1852–5).
Bucks.   Buckinghamshire Record Office, Aylesbury.
Dropmore   Historical Manuscripts Commission: *The Manuscripts of J. B. Fortescue, Esq., Preserved at Dropmore* (London, 1892–1927).
Film. Mss.   Microfilmed Manuscripts, India Office Library.
I.O.   India Office Records, India Office Library.
I.O.L.   India Office Library, London.
Parlt. Hist. *Parliamentary History of England*, ed. W. Cobbett (London, 1820)
P.R.O.   Public Record Office, London.
S.E.E.R.   *Slavonic and East European Review*, London.
S.R.O.   Scottish Record Office, Edinburgh.
Wellesley   *The Despatches, Minutes, and Correspondence of the Marquess Wellesley, During his Administration in India*, ed. M. Martin (London, 1836–7).
W.O.   War Office Records, Public Record Office.

NOTE ON THE REFERENCES

The chairmen and deputy chairmen of the East India Company are not identified every time they are mentioned in the text. They held office for a year; and it was the custom for the deputy to become chairman the following year. Between 1798 and 1801 the chairmen were:

1798 Jacob Bosanquet and Stephen Lushington.
1799 Stephen Lushington and Hugh Inglis.
1800 Hugh Inglis and David Scott.
1801 David Scott and Charles Mills (until September).
1801 Charles Mills and John Roberts (from September).

TWO VIEWS OF BRITISH INDIA

Dundas is more active and diligent than any other, but also selfish and Scotch. [His interest is] pillage and patronage: pillage by conquest and patronage at home.

CANNING

The rapidity with which Lord Wellesley changed the political face of India, has begot in him a taste for conquest and aggrandizement.

CHARLES RICKETTS

INTRODUCTION

These appear to be the letters of two men who agreed both upon the aims and principles of British policy in India and upon the best way to apply them. Certainly they wrote as if they agreed. 'I cannot describe the satisfaction I feel', Wellesley told Dundas in November 1798, 'in having so happily conformed to your opinion.' 'Our ideas were so much in unison', replied Dundas in December, 'as to leave me no doubt that your conduct would be precisely what I could wish.' Within three years it was clear that Wellesley's conduct was not at all what Dundas could wish, and that it never had been. The difference between them was hidden so long and so successfully because of one event they rarely discussed, the French expedition to Egypt.

Wellesley was chosen by Pitt, not Dundas, and his appointment was not straightforward. His predecessor, Sir John Shore,[1] had quarrelled with the governor of Madras, Lord Hobart.[2] Hobart had gone out to India to succeed Shore; but both their characters and their policies were radically different, and Hobart, who rapidly became furiously impatient waiting for Shore to leave, bombarded Dundas with letters demanding his recall. Dundas, who gave up reading these letters, was wearied by Hobart's accusations. He decided to ask Lord Cornwallis[3] to return to India to succeed Shore, to recall Hobart, and at Pitt's suggestion to ask Wellesley to succeed him. Wellesley's subsequent injured protestations of friendship for Hobart are belied by the memorandum in which he recommended his recall. Wellesley had been a member of the board of control for some years, but this was not a particularly good training for governing India, because Dundas refused to allow his colleagues to do anything. Wellesley would agree to go to Madras only if Cornwallis went to Bengal; and provided, if Cornwallis changed his mind, that he should go to Bengal instead. Dundas tried to resist this demand, but with the support of Pitt Wellesley had his way. In July 1797, when Cornwallis did change his mind, Wellesley was appointed in his stead.

The British possessions in India in the late eighteenth century were grouped around the three presidency towns of Calcutta, Bombay, and Madras. The Bengal presidency, with its government at Fort William, consisted of Bengal itself, Bihar, Benares and Ghazipur, part of Orissa, and Chittagong. The Bombay presidency was virtually only the two islands of

---

[1] Sir John Shore (Lord Teignmouth, 1798) (1751–1834); governor-general, 1793–8.
[2] Robert, Lord Hobart (4th earl of Buckinghamshire) (1760–1816); governor of Madras, 1794–8; secretary for war, 1801–4.
[3] Charles, 1st Marquis Cornwallis (1738–1805); governor-general, 1786–93, 1805; lord-lieutenant of Ireland, 1798–1801.

Bombay and Salsette, and about two hundred miles of the Malabar coast north of Cochin. At this period Bombay was not the pre-eminent port it later became. The Madras presidency, with its government at Fort St George, consisted of various scattered territories, held on various tenures, in various parts of the peninsula. On the east coast, in addition to the territory surrounding Madras itself, the British controlled a large territory north of Masulipatam, called the Northern Circars, on a lease from the nizam of Hyderabad. Finally, until Wellesley's arrival in 1798, these three presidencies were politically, as well as geographically, distinct. Their relations resembled the relations of friendly states; and this became very plain when they were occasionally in violent disagreement.

Bengal was administered under a system known as the Permanent Settlement. Whatever the merits of this system, it brought great fame to the three men who introduced it, Cornwallis, Shore, and Sir George Barlow.[1] The Permanent Settlement recognized that the zamindars were not merely the officials of the state, employed to collect the revenues of all the land which belonged to it, but were themselves hereditary owners of the land. In return for this recognition, the zamindars were to pay to the state ten-elevenths of their income; and the British agreed not to attempt either to farm the land taxes or to collect them themselves. At the same time the presidency was subdivided into thirty-six districts, each with a collector to supervise the revenues, and a magistrate to supervise the civil courts. Originally, criminal justice was left to the natives, but in 1790 the British replaced the native courts by four provincial courts of circuit and appeal with British judges. Finally, at the head of the judicial system were the supreme court, for trying Englishmen, and the sudder dewany and nizamut adaulat, respectively the highest courts of civil and criminal justice for the natives. It was this system which Wellesley and Dundas debated introducing in Madras.

To the north-west of Bengal was Oudh, enlarged in 1774 by the addition of Rohilkhand. Much of its income was spent on a British subsidiary force, the British were responsible for defending it, and in 1798 Shore had not hesitated to depose one vizier and to appoint another. To the north of the Oudh lived the Mogul Emperor, who was a pensioner of the Marathas, and further still lived the Sikhs, a confederacy of chieftains, of whom the British knew little. Most of the peninsula was divided between three states. In the middle was the nizam of Hyderabad, gradually growing weaker since his defeat by the Marathas at the battle of Khardla in 1795. Either he would pass under the suzerainty of the British or of one of the

---

[1] Sir George Hilaro Barlow, Bart. (1762–1846); secretary to the supreme government, 1796–1801; member of the supreme council, 1801–5; governor-general, 1805–7; governor of Madras, 1807–12.

two more powerful native states on either side, Mysore to the south and the Maratha Confederacy to the north and west. Mysore was antagonistic to the British, because of the astringent terms of peace imposed by Cornwallis in 1792 at the end of the Second Mysore War. The Maratha Confederacy was in disarray. Only this disarray preserved the semi-independence of Hyderabad. The peshwa of Poona, responsible for the confederacy to his titular overlord, the rajah of Satara, was overshadowed by Sindhia of Gwalior and Ujjein, who was himself in danger of being overshadowed by the French officers who trained and commanded his armies. Nevertheless, Sindhia was the most powerful prince in India. There were three other princes in the confederacy. Holkar of Indore was temporarily virtually powerless. In the west the gaekwad of Baroda was prepared to be friendly with the British. In the east was the territory of the rajah of Berar. His attitude was important to the British because his territory separated the Circars from Bengal. Technically, the British relations with these states were governed by a treaty of 1790, between the British, the nizam, and the peshwa on behalf of the Marathas, which protected all of them against an attack from Mysore. According to Wellesley, however, it was doubtful whether the nizam would be able, or the Marathas inclined, to abide by it.

Wellesley had reached this conclusion before he arrived in India, at the Cape of Good Hope. His first solution was to strengthen Hyderabad by disbanding the divisions of the nizam's army which were commanded by Frenchmen, and by substituting a larger British subsidiary force. The subsidiary alliance was one of the symbolic features of British India. Provided their allies would allow them to control their foreign policy, the British would provide them with a force of sepoys and British officers, more efficient than any they could train themselves. Originally, the allies had paid annually in cash; but Wellesley, in both Hyderabad and Oudh, insisted instead upon a permanent cession of territory. The advantage of this system was that it extended British influence without contravening the act of Parliament which forbade extensions of territory. The East India Company, who did not control Indian politics, did not want to have to pay for them. However, subsidiary alliances, whatever they might state to the contrary, were also a satisfactory means of gaining control over the internal affairs of allied states, without being officially responsible for them. The British have always preferred to limit their imperial liability. Wellesley was perfectly frank about this. In a passage carefully removed from his published correspondence, he dismissed the alternative solution of trying to strengthen the nizam's own army, because that 'might render it more efficient for *his* purposes, whatever they may be'. A subsidiary force, by contrast, 'would tend to strengthen him for *our* purposes only, and would give him no additional means, but rather weaken him, in any contest with us'.

3

Before he reached India, therefore, Wellesley was determined to carry out a vigorous policy of expansion. Dundas appeared to be; but in fact he was not. Throughout the war Dundas was principally anxious to protect British India from all the dangers he saw looming, and particularly from the French. His own strategy required Britain to concentrate upon capturing all her enemies' overseas possessions: 'It is laid down as an *axiom* applicable to the conduct of extensive warfare by this country', he told Wellesley, 'that our principal efforts should be to *deprive our enemies of their colonial possessions.*' Reasonably enough, as they had been battling for empire for half the century, he could not believe the French would not do the same. As Dundas was particularly nervous in 1798, his schemes of defence often closely resembled Wellesley's schemes of offence, but their motives were different. This was most apparent in their attitudes towards Mysore. The Third Mysore War was the most important, and most frequently discussed issue of their correspondence. It was also Wellesley's most successful and applauded performance, which was why he talked about it so much. Dundas' reasons for applauding, however, were different, for in the summer of 1798 he and Wellesley gave different emphasis to the two events which determined, or at least justified, their policy.

On 1 June, Dundas learned that the French expedition had sailed from Toulon. He feared that it would go to Egypt or to Syria. This fear was confirmed, on 14 June, when he learned that the governor of Mauritius had publicly announced the offer of an alliance from Tipu Sultan.[1] Dundas promptly arranged to reinforce the Indian army, and told Wellesley that, if Tipu Sultan had, in fact, offered the French this alliance, he was to attack him. What mattered to Dundas, who believed that they could invade India from the near east, was the French threat. He reacted in the same way towards the annual invasions of Zeman Shah.[2] What made them dangerous was the chance of French co-operation. The chairman of the East India Company held a more extreme version of this view. Because the French, not the native states, were the threat to British India, he wanted the governor-general to accommodate Tipu Sultan until the French had been destroyed. He did not expect that Tipu Sultan ever would be accommodated; but because he was antagonistic to the British did not mean that he would necessarily attack them.

Wellesley received these two pieces of information in the opposite order. He learned of Tipu Sultan's offer to France on 8 June; but not until 18 October did he learn of the French landing in Egypt. He knew that the French expedition had sailed eight weeks previously, but he did not believe

---

[1] Tipu Sultan (1753–99); succeeded his father, Hyder Ali, the usurper of Mysore, in 1782.
[2] Zeman Shah Abdali, amir of Afghanistan, 1793–1801.

that they would go to Egypt. Wellesley told Dundas in November that 'my opinions entirely agree with yours with regard to the possibility of the success of the late French attempt to penetrate to India through Egypt'. Actually, they entirely disagreed. In Wellesley's opinion the French could only attack British India by sending a fleet round the Cape of Good Hope. Therefore, throughout the summer of 1798, Wellesley had to find enough local Indian justification for attacking Tipu Sultan. This was why he placed much greater emphasis than Dundas on Tipu Sultan's approach to the governor of Mauritius, and asked Dundas how many French troops must actually land to justify a declaration of war. Of course, he proposed to go to war anyway, and by October he had received Dundas' permission to do so.

Wellesley's need to find Indian justification for his attack on Mysore also explains another of the most frequent topics of his letters in 1798 and early 1799, his abuse of the government of Madras. As soon as Wellesley heard of the embassy to Mauritius he decided to attack Mysore. He soon realized that he would be unable to do so; because nobody could raise the money, because the monsoon in the south would make the roads impassable, and because neither the nizam nor the peshwa would provide any assistance. Therefore, on 6 July he told Dundas that the attack would be postponed. As these were also the arguments subsequently put forward by the government of Madras, it would be difficult to understand Wellesley's great anger, except that their premise was different. Throughout 1798 and 1799 Wellesley had to write as if Tipu Sultan was about to attack the British: in fact the British were about to attack him. It was particularly necessary to provide great provocation, because when the war was fought the British would immediately have to take the offensive. The premise behind all the reasoning at Madras was that however antagonistic Tipu Sultan might be, and, as he had lost half his territory in 1792, he was bound to be antagonistic, he was not planning to attack the British. Whatever the appearances, Madras argued that Tipu Sultan's policy was defensive, and that he would be provoked to attack only if the British made their preparations too obviously offensive.

Dundas was prepared to approve an attack on Mysore. His principal interest in doing so was to obtain control of the entire west coast of India; and it is clear that he thought—if he thought ahead at all—that this would settle the question of the balance of power there. He was also prepared to approve a new subsidiary alliance with Hyderabad. Wellesley's argument about the danger to British interests in India from the French divisions in the armies of the native states is equally revealing of his aggressive intentions. Wellesley argued that they challenged the British indirectly, in peace as well as in war, because they undermined the native states. The

5

lands assigned to provide for their troops would become, when fortified, virtually private principalities. If they co-operated, the effect might resemble the British subsidiary system. Without ever conflicting directly with the British, they might in time become an alternative paramount power. This argument, however, only reinforces the conclusion that Wellesley's talk of strengthening the allies was only designed to hide taking them over. How dangerous and how Jacobinical Wellesley claimed these divisions to be depended upon how anxious he was to take over any particular state. In 1798 he argued ceaselessly about the danger of the French divisions in the nizam's army; while completely ignoring those in Sindhia's, because it was Hyderabad at this stage on which he wished to impose his will. Wellesley successfully disbanded these French divisions in 1798, but this still did not provide a satisfactory basis of relations. Once Tipu Sultan was destroyed, Hyderabad was no longer a useful buffer between the Marathas and Mysore, and would become merely another Maratha plundering-ground, unless the British made it clear that they would not tolerate this. By Wellesley's reasoning, therefore, conquering Mysore merely brought the British face to face with a new contest with the Marathas over the control of Hyderabad. In 1800 Wellesley negotiated a final subsidiary alliance with the nizam, by which, in return for a large permanent cession of territory, the British guaranteed his remaining possessions against an attack by the Marathas; but he had tried unsuccessfully for two years to negotiate what he considered to be a satisfactory settlement with them.

Wellesley's conception of an ideal state of the Maratha Confederacy, as he explained to Dundas from the Cape of Good Hope, was rearranging the balance among the five chieftains, so that no one would be strong enough to mould the others into an efficient and hostile power, while leaving the peshwa enough influence to be a useful ally when necessary. This scheme was not even theoretically possible in 1798, because the peshwa was over-shadowed by Sindhia, who had for some years been living at Poona, although why it is difficult to determine. Wellesley's aim was to persuade Sindhia to return to Hindustan by offering him an alliance against Zeman Shah; and at the same time to consolidate British influence with the peshwa by offering him a subsidiary alliance. At first Wellesley treated the Maratha princes as virtually independent of each other. Later he changed his method. The treaty of Bassein implied that the decision of the peshwa committed them all. Wellesley's aim, however, remained the same: he wanted to control the relations not only between the Marathas and the British but between the Marathas themselves. He became increasingly displeased with the resident at Poona, and eventually removed him, because he could not persuade the peshwa to agree to this subsidiary alliance. Wellesley failed to realize that the peshwa would never agree to it until he was forced to do so to keep his throne. The native princes were perfectly aware of the implications of allying with the British.

Neither could Wellesley persuade Sindhia to return to Hindustan. The native princes were also perfectly aware of the extent of the danger from Zeman Shah. Wellesley chose to take this danger seriously because it suited him to do so. It justified his interference in Oudh. Here again Wellesley acted with Dundas' approval, but again for different reasons, for Dundas had thought for a long time that if any European power did wish to attack the British in India they would be wiser to concentrate their attention not on the peninsula but on the Indus basin. Therefore, satisfactory relations with Oudh were particularly necessary; and both Dundas and Wellesley wished to disband the vizier's army entirely, and to replace it by a subsidiary force from the Company, in order to strengthen the British north-west frontier. Only Wellesley, however, wished to take over Oudh altogether. The occasional references to Oudh in this correspondence also reveal another of Wellesley's more offensive habits. He tried continually to pass off the vizier's resistance to some new demand as an uncooperative refusal to abide by the terms of some old agreement. Wellesley was angered because the vizier never would admit that Zeman Shah did threaten Oudh, and, therefore, that he could be expected to contribute a larger sum to its defence. The same method of reasoning was apparent in Wellesley's relations with the nabob of Arcot; but with greater justification. The British were responsible for the defence both of Oudh and the Carnatic. However disorganized his finances, the vizier had always paid his subsidy—he was one of the Company's best allies, which was why Wellesley was so angry with him—; the nabob had not. Wellesley wished to take over the Carnatic. There was every reason why he should wish to, because it was notoriously badly governed. For nearly forty years the nabob of Arcot, who lived in a sumptuous palace in the suburbs of Madras, had been borrowing large sums of money at exorbitant rates of interest from most of the Company's servants there, and pledging as his security the land revenues of the Carnatic. While the British were responsible for the defence of the Carnatic, they had no control over its government, and could not obtain any financial assistance from the nabob in times of stress. The nabob absolutely refused to reform and was encouraged to refuse by the large numbers of men who profited from his debts. One of the disputes between Shore and Hobart was whether or not the British should coerce him. Hobart wished to, but Shore refused. Wellesley agreed with Hobart and produced the most spurious justification for doing so. Using the device of an examination conducted by the governor of Madras, Lord Clive,[1] he argued that some

[1] Edward, 2nd Lord Clive (earl of Powis, 1804) (1754–1839); governor of Madras, 1798–1803; married Lady Antonia Herbert, daughter of the last Herbert earl of Powis.

7

letters found at Seringapatam proved that the nabob had been negotiating with Tipu Sultan. As the letters in question appeared to be on quite other matters, in order to argue this he had to suggest that their ostensible substance was a fraud, designed to cover up their actual anti-British purpose. There were good reasons why the British should annexe the Carnatic, but their grounds for doing so were fabricated.

Dundas and Wellesley did not clash about Wellesley's political activity, because everything Wellesley did before 1801 could reasonably be argued to be defensive. The difference between them was implicit, however, in Wellesley's reaction to Dundas' instructions of October 1800 to send an army to Egypt. Wellesley had to obey, of course, but he did not wish to, and by this time Dundas knew it. Wellesley wanted to keep the Indian army in India, in case his expanding subsidiary system, and especially his proposed alliance with the peshwa, provoked a war with the Marathas. When the chance of this alliance seemed slight Wellesley wanted to attack first Mauritius and then Batavia; because these were the two principal bases for the French privateers in the Indian Ocean; and because, in Wellesley's view, these were the only two advanced bases from which the French could mount an attack on India. The French expedition to Egypt was not a danger to India, and there was, therefore, no Indian reason for driving them out.

How far Dundas disagreed with Wellesley became apparent not on questions of politics, but on questions of finance; in particular on the size and cost of the army. For while Wellesley was most interested in expanding Britain's territory and influence in India, Dundas was most interested in reducing her debt there. It would be incorrect to suggest that Dundas never advocated schemes of expansion. In the autumn of 1799 he advocated the most grandiose scheme of all. His subsidiary alliance with the Marathas would have extended British influence to the Indus. The subsidiary force, however, was to be stationed in Guzerat, revealing once again that Dundas was principally attempting to make British India impregnable against a European attack. The scheme was the result of the temporary allied successes in Europe. Their subsequent defeats left Dundas increasingly cautious and preoccupied with expense. Regardless of the merits of his innovations, he told Wellesley in September 1800, 'in the present moment, I am sorry to add, we must look accurately to expense'.

Dundas was preoccupied with reducing the Indian debt, which had reached the figure of £14,000,000. He had hoped for a long time to reduce this by what he called his plan of remittance. Dundas argued that the debt should be funded and transferred to Britain. The Company would then gradually pay it off out of the profits of increasingly large sales of goods, themselves paid for by increasingly large surplus revenues in India. In

8

1793 Dundas was still talking about surplus revenues of £500,000 a year. The debt was to be remitted by the Company's servants. Dundas hoped they would fund the debt by buying bonds, paying five per cent interest, and redeemable from the Company in London, as a means of transferring their fortunes to Britain. The plan did not work. Partly, the terms of remittance were not attractive enough. The Company's servants could obtain a better return on their money by investing in neutral shipping. Partly, while the Indian governments always held out hope of surplus revenues, during the war there never were any. To increase the size of the investment, therefore, Dundas temporarily agreed to allow the Company to borrow money in India; but he rapidly became alarmed at the result of doing so, and turned the whole system around. Dundas told Wellesley that he was not to borrow money to provide for the investment, and that any surplus revenues should be used to pay off the debt, 'for the East India Company shall either curtail their trade, or they shall find resources at home for carrying it on'. Dundas insisted that the Company should send out bullion from England for their investment; and he warned Wellesley that under no circumstances should he divert this money from commercial to political purposes. Wellesley, however, ignored the warning, and the more money the Company sent out the more Wellesley spent on his wars. This was one of the principal causes of the clash between Wellesley and the court of directors; and by the time Wellesley was recalled in 1805 he left government credit exhausted and much of the army unpaid.

Wellesley bitterly protested against this prohibition; but on the other method of increasing the investment he and Dundas were agreed. This was the question of the private trade, and as usual their motives were different. One of Dundas' original aims, particularly during his early period of hostility to the Company, had been to encourage foreign trade with India. This had grown enormously; but what displeased the Company most about it was that their servants in India invested in this trade as a way of remitting their fortunes to Europe. They preferred to invest in neutral rather than Company shipping, because although the Company was required to provide 3,000 tons annually for the private trade on their own ships, usually they sent these at awkward times of year and charged high rates of freight. To undermine the foreign trade, Wellesley engaged India-built shipping and allowed the owners to sail when they would and charge what rates they would. His principal interest, however, was political: he wanted to drive the foreign factories out of India, to increase the British pre-eminence amongst the natives. Dundas privately supported Wellesley's policy, but for financial not political reasons, and encouraged him to bring it before the court of directors. Dundas, however, was too optimistic about the chances of persuading the directors to agree. In the spring of 1800 he was encouraged to make the attempt, because Hugh Inglis[1] and David Scott,[2] his two most vigorous supporters in the Company, were elected chairman and deputy. They could not, however, carry the court against Dundas' most persistent opponents, the Shipping Interest.

While Dundas and Wellesley were in agreement about the merits of encouraging the private trade, they were not in agreement about the extent to which retrenchment in India could contribute towards a surplus revenue. The question at issue between them was the size of the Indian army. Wellesley demanded that the Indian army should increase in size as the British took over more territories; and that the King's army should also increase in size to continue in the correct proportion to the Company's. In the summer of 1800 Wellesley argued that he needed 30,000 European infantry. Dundas could not provide a force of this size for Britain's European campaigns, to assist the Portuguese, to co-operate with the Austrians in northern Italy, or to invade Egypt. Moreover, he argued that it was absurd to increase the size of the army every time the British defeated a dangerous enemy. He calculated that the actual strength of the army in India had risen from 69,111 in 1793 to 111,840 in 1799, and could be reduced to 82,676 with perfect safety. To Dundas the financial calculation was simple: only curtailing the military establishments would provide surplus revenues in India. This was partly why Dundas agreed to Wellesley's subsidiary alliances. If large detachments of troops were stationed with the allies, at their expense, particularly in Oudh, they protected the British frontiers, and would permit the British to keep far smaller numbers in their own territories. Dundas, unlike Wellesley, did not think of the army as a political tool of an expanding empire, responsible for policing the Company's own subjects, as much as defending them against foreign aggression. His calculation continued that only surplus revenues would pay off the debt, and unless the debt was paid off 'all our boasted prosperity and splendour are mere bubble and delusion and will vanish on the first severe struggle'.

There were, however, more general reasons why Dundas tried to restrain Wellesley. Dundas had great difficulty in his relations with the East India Company, once it was controlled by the Shipping Interest; and he had decided views of his own about India's value to Britain. The Shipping Interest was the most powerful group in the Company throughout these years. Their power was particularly obvious in 1801, when they forced David Scott to resign the chair. They made their fortunes from paying for, building, or sailing, the Company's ships: and in consequence

[1] Sir Hugh Inglis, Bart.; director, Indian interest; chairman, 1797, 1800, 1812.
[2] David Scott of Dunninald; director, Indian interest; chairman, 1796, 1801; a great friend of Dundas.

were the men most interested in maintaining the Company's commercial privileges. They also made their fortunes in Britain, and were more interested in profitable sales in London than expensive schemes of reform at Calcutta. They resisted Dundas' scheme to open the trade of India to private shipping; and they also resisted his scheme to disband the Company's European army. They did not want to lose this valuable patronage. Dundas had always to avoid an outright collision with the Company, because Pitt's government had always relied on their support. It was no longer essential, but it remained very useful. Dundas' own political position also relied on their support. Considering his background, Dundas' eminence in British politics was astonishing. One of the principal reasons for his success was his successful management of Scotland, and his successful management of the Company. Sometimes, indeed, Canning's[1] jibe appears to be not unfair, that to Dundas India was merely something to be managed. Dundas was tired by 1798: during the war he had been asked to do too much. He had not been able to concentrate enough attention either on the Company or on the war, relying too heavily on Scott on the one hand and William Huskisson[2] on the other; he was embittered by the criticism of his handling of both; and he wanted to be rid of both. Frequently he offered to resign the war department, and had not the whole government resigned in 1801 Dundas had already told Pitt that he was going to resign the board of control.

Wellesley by contrast was younger, brash, and eager to make his name and fortune. It was the thought that Wellesley would have the future chances he would now miss which so annoyed Hobart. This accounts both for Wellesley's aggressive policy and for the emphasis with which, like Cicero in Rome, he continuously repeated how he alone had defended British India from dire peril. He bitterly resented the slightest check and immediately threatened to resign. Partly this was the traditional battle, begun by Warren Hastings[3] and Edmund Burke, between demands for unlimited authority and demands for responsible control; but partly it was the result of Wellesley's character. These letters reveal that Wellesley was a bad-tempered and overbearing man. Even allowing for the exaggeration of eighteenth-century writing, they also reveal that he was ungenerous. Much has been written of the bright young men trained by Wellesley in India; and many later innovations have justly been attributed to his influence. There is, however, a less deserving aspect of this, for these were junior men. Wellesley liked bright young men who would carry out his instructions with vigour, alacrity, and admiration. He would allow them a

---

[1] George Canning (1770–1827); under-secretary (south) for foreign affairs, 1796–9; member of the board of control, 1799–1801.
[2] William Huskisson (1770–1830); under-secretary for war, 1795–1801.
[3] Warren Hastings (1732–1818); governor-general, 1774–85.

great deal of latitude in the execution of his instructions; but he would tolerate no debate about the policy on which those instructions were based. 'My recognition of his extraordinary judgement, no less than my own sense of duty,' remarked John Malcolm,[1] one of his most famous young men, to Samuel Manesty, the resident at Basra, 'has always led me . . . to be more solicitous about executing his orders than investigating their propriety.' 'Really great men,' replied Manesty, 'listen to all suggestions with attention, and frequently benefit very essentially from the wisdom of their conduct in doing so.' This Wellesley could not do. One whole series of his correspondence with Dundas would appear to be a systematic denigration of anybody who could reasonably claim, because of his office, to influence British policy, whether the commander-in-chief, the chief justice, or the governors of Madras and Bombay. Partly Wellesley objected to their powers as much as their characters. His attitude towards Lord Clive was notorious and eventually rebounded against him. Having demanded Clive's recall on the grounds of his complete incompetence, Wellesley later equally forcefully demanded he should be appointed his successor, to forestall the appointment of anybody with different ideas. Clive he could accept because he was subservient. However, it was this subservience which persuaded the directors to remove some of the members of the government of Madras, in the hope of provoking Clive to resign. They did not wish the governments of India to speak on every subject with only one voice. Had Wellesley been a man of outstanding ability, his criticism might have been palatable. His term as foreign secretary proved that he was not; that he was incapable of working with his peers. Dundas' irritation with these letters is increasingly apparent, and bursts forth in his outspoken reply to Wellesley's threat to leave India early in 1801.

Finally, Dundas and Wellesley disagreed about the role of India in relation to Britain. Wellesley, if the phrase is permissible, was morally neutral: unlike Cornwallis and Shore, his politics did not imply any superiority to the natives. When Shore talked of the weakness of the native princes, he meant that they were depraved: when Wellesley did, he meant that they were powerless. Wellesley thought strictly in terms of power. He suggested that he was interested in improving the lot of the inhabitants of Oudh: he was merely finding another argument to justify the annexation. Unlike Dundas, who hoped that increased prosperity and goodwill would improve the revenues, Wellesley did not deceive himself about the extent to which the British could attract the loyalty of the natives. The British conquest of India was merely another military conquest; and like all the others it would rest on force. Loyalty would never replace the army. The

---

[1] Captain John Malcolm (1769–1833); assistant resident at Hyderabad, 1798–99; envoy to Persia, 1799–1801; governor of Bombay, 1827–31.

head of an old family from the Pale, he was just moving from one conquered country to another: British attitudes to Ireland were even more unyielding than their attitudes to India.

Dundas did not want to conquer India, he wanted a source of tribute; and he was the more optimistic because his attitude did contain an assumption of racial or at least European superiority. British rule would conciliate the natives because it would promote security, prosperity, and trade. However, he was less interested in the prosperity or the trade than the remission of surplus revenue to Britain. The prospect of this was one of the grounds he had put forward in 1793 for renewing the Company's charter; and why he put forward the suggestion of an Indian income tax. Whatever happened, and this was where Dundas parted from Wellesley—perhaps as Rosebery parted from Joseph Chamberlain—India must not be a source of expense. Nothing must be done which 'would be to make India a burden upon Britain. Such a result of the conquest of Seringapatam . . . would be mortifying and afflicting to the public, who have been taught to expect better things from India.' This was why Dundas was so sensitive to the danger of invasion. It would not be impossible to defeat an invading army in battle. The difficulty would be political and financial; for the native states would join the invader, making 'it a tedious conflict, and attended with such an enormous expense, as to have rendered it very doubtful whether this country was equal to it either in point of inclination or ability'.

Finally, the most typical feature that is apparent in this correspondence was how determined was Dundas that nobody should settle in India. They should trade and leave. It was settling, in Dundas' opinion, which ruined the Portuguese. He sympathized with Wellesley's demand to send home anybody he wished; and he would not support the college at Fort William because it would appear too settled. Education must be provided in Britain. Official India was renowned in the late nineteenth century for the disdain with which it treated private Englishmen. This had started early; the result of Dundas' concern with profit and Wellesley's with conquest.

It hardly needs saying that Dundas did not make his profit. There were no surplus land revenues; the debt continued to increase; and Wellesley continued to make war. By the time the French army evacuated Egypt, Wellesley had taken over Mysore, Tanjore, the Carnatic, Hyderabad, and Oudh, and was getting close to his subsidiary alliances with Poona. The map of India was dramatically changed. Wellesley had been fortunate. He had gone out to India determined to expand. The Egyptian Expedition had enabled him to do so with the approval of the Company, where he might have expected their opposition. He had used the threat of invasion which he did not fear, but they did, to conquer Mysore; and he had used the threat of a French alliance with Zeman Shah, which he did not fear, but

Dundas did, to take over Oudh. With the defeat of the French the illusion was exposed. His policy in Oudh and the Carnatic was severely criticized: his Maratha policy was countermanded. Wellesley knew that this was so. 'It is evident,' he told the new prime minister, Henry Addington,[1] in October 1801, 'that I no longer possess that degree of credit in the opinion of the court of directors, or of Mr Dundas, which is necessary to inspire confidence . . . in the discharge of my duties.' He did not resign, but the lines of battle were drawn.

[1] Henry Addington (Viscount Sidmouth) (1757–1844); speaker of the house of commons, 1789–1801; prime minister, 1801–4.

THE PRIVATE CORRESPONDENCE OF
MR DUNDAS AND LORD WELLESLEY
1798–1801

[Wellesley's] schemes are so vast that they exceed the compass and reach of ordinary understandings, and certainly some which will not admit of higher qualification will be employed in cavilling at and paring down works which they want the power to comprehend.

DARTMOUTH

I

The Rt Hon. Henry Dundas to the Earl of Mornington

30 January 1798, Whitehall
Private: no. 1

My dear Lord

Enclosed you will receive a copy of a letter from the secret committee to your government directing you to secure the person of Mons[ieur] de Baumez, and to send him to Europe by the first ship that should sail from your presidency after the receipt of these orders.

The above letter, having been written at my suggestion, was, on account of the hurry with which the ships were dispatched, sent off without submitting the same to me. On considering the subject, it appears to me that the sending home M. de Baumez, without a strict inquiry whether his conduct has been such as to merit so harsh a measure, is certainly improper. Therefore, previous to taking such a step, it certainly must strike your Lordship to direct such inquiry to be made, and to act in the manner that shall appear most proper to your Lordship from the result of the investigation.

I shall communicate the substance of this letter to the chairs for the information of the secret committee.

I am, . . .

HENRY DUNDAS

II

The Earl of Mornington to the Rt Hon. Henry Dundas

23 February 1798, Castle of Good Hope
Private: no. 1

My dear Sir

Among the subjects which you recommended to my early consideration upon my arrival in India, you particularly urged the necessity of my attending with the utmost degree of vigilance to the system, now pursued almost universally by the native princes, of retaining in their service numbers of European or American officers, under whom the native troops are trained and disciplined in imitation of the corps of sepoys in the British service.

By accident I found at this place, on account of his health, Major Kirkpatrick,[1] lately resident at the court of Hyderabad, and formerly at that of Sindhia, and I have endeavoured during the period of my detention here to collect from him whatever information he could furnish respecting the European or American officers and the corps commanded by them in the service of the nizam.

For this purpose after several conversations on the subject, I requested Major Kirkpatrick to return detailed answers in writing to several questions which I drew, with the intention of bringing under your observation not only the actual strength, but the original object of this part of the nizam's military establishment, its rapid increase, the consequences to be expected from its continuance or further growth, as well as the means which either had been or might be suggested for averting any danger which those consequences might threaten to our interests in India.

I transmit with this letter a copy of my questions and of Major Kirkpatrick's answers,[2] and although I am aware that the substance of both must be familiar to you, yet imagining that it may hitherto have come under your notice only incidentally in detailed dispatches and advices from India, I think it may be useful to lay before you in a more regular and connected form a view of this most material and (in my judgement) formidable branch of the system to which you have directed my attention.

In this letter, I shall endeavour to recapitulate the most important facts stated by Major Kirkpatrick, adding such observations as have occurred to me upon them, in the hope of receiving from you at an early period your

---

[1] Lt-Col. William Kirkpatrick (1754–1812); military secretary to the governor-general, 1798–9; acting private secretary to the governor-general, 1799–1801.
[2] *Wellesley*, ii, 637.

16

instructions upon such points as the materials before you enable you to determine.

It appears that the nizam has recently at different periods retained in his service, exclusive of our detachment, three distinct corps of sepoys under the command of European or American officers; one commanded by a Frenchman by the name of Raymond,[1] another by an American of the name of Boyd, and the third by an Irishman of the name of Finglass, for some time a quarter-master in the 19th reg[imen]t of dragoons. There is a fourth corps commanded by a Frenchman of the name of D'Agricourt in the service of Umjid ud Daulah at Hyderabad. This corps is paid by the state. It consists of fifteen hundred men. The commander is a determined Jacobin. The corps of Boyd and Finglass were taken into the service of the nizam during the residence of Azim ul Umra[2] at Poona, at the suggestion of our resident at that court, acting under the sanction of the government of Bengal. This measure was taken by our resident and by that government principally with a view of forming a counterpoise to the corps of Raymond.

Boyd's corps consisted of about 1,800 men, it is no longer in the service of the nizam, and has probably passed into that of the Marathas. Finglass' corps still remains at Hyderabad, but consists of only one battalion of about 800 men. Both these corps appeared to be well affected to our interests, as may be judged by their willingness to assist our detachment in repelling an expected attack from the corps of Raymond.

The corps of Raymond had been in the service of the nizam before the last war with Tipu Sultan, and in 1792 its strength was not more than 1,500 men at the highest estimation. At the battle of Khardlah in 1795 its strength amounted to no less than *eleven thousand* men, it now consists of *ten thousand* men, and the order has actually been given for augmenting it to the number of fourteen thousand men. Attached to this corps is a train of artillery of about 30 field pieces, and a troop of 60 native dragoons. The discipline of the corps does not appear to be by any means good, and accordingly it has never yet rendered any distinguished service in the field.

The pay of the corps is now secured by the assignment of a large district of country, part of which borders the Carnatic. At this particular station is a fortified post, and constant communication is maintained between it and the port of Narpilly, as well as with Ongale and other parts of the territories of the Company and of the nabob of Arcot. The corps is recruited, in the proportion of one third of its total numbers, from our territories and those of the nabob of Arcot,[3] and partly from deserters abandoning our service.

[1] Michel Joachim Raymond (1775–98); had commanded a corps for the nizam since 1785. Succeeded by Piron.
[2] Azim-ul-Umra; principal minister to the nizam of Hyderabad.
[3] Umdut-ul-Umra, nawab of the Carnatic, 1795–1801; in succession to his father, Mohammed Ali Khan Walajah; better known as the nabob of Arcot.

The chief officers are Frenchmen of the most virulent and notorious principles of Jacobinism; and the whole corps constitutes an armed French party of great zeal, diligence, and activity. The efforts of this party are continually directed to the object of magnifying the power, resources, and success of France in the eyes of the court of Hyderabad, and of depreciating the character, force, and credit, of Great Britain by every possible means.

The detachment of this corps stationed on our frontier has been very assiduous with great success in seducing from their duty our sepoys quartered in the neighbourhood. A considerable desertion lately took place in one of our native reg[imen]ts on its march from Masulipatam to the southward, and many of the deserters on that occasion are to be found in Raymond's corps.

No positive proof has yet appeared of a direct correspondence between the leaders of this corps and the French government, but it seems to be unquestionably certain that they communicate with Tipu Sultan and with the French corps in his service.

Whatever may be the discipline or military skill of this corps, it now forms by far the most considerable part of the nizam's military establishment. In this corps consists the main strength of the army of our ally; and it possesses the influence which usually belongs to an army in the councils of the native princes of India. This influence seems to have alarmed Azim ul Umra, the first minister of the nizam.

Neither the origin nor the subsequent augmentations of this corps appear to have been at all connected with any hostile dispositions in the court of Hyderabad towards the British interests. The institution of the corps proceeded from an admiration of the successful policy of Mahadaji Sindhia,[1] and the subsequent augmentation was directed principally if not solely against the Marathas. There is reason to believe that the orders lately given for a further increase of the corps to the number of 14,000 men arose from a desire, in the mind of Azim ul Umra, of drawing us into a more intimate connection with the nizam by exciting our jealousy of the growing influence of the French party at Hyderabad.

Such is the state of the leading facts communicated by Major Kirkpatrick.

The result in my mind is a decided opinion that the continuance, and still more the further growth of the corps of Raymond ought to be prevented by every means within our power, consistent with the respect due to the court of Hyderabad, and with the general principles of moderation and justice, which ought to form the rule of our conduct in India. The dangers to be apprehended from the existence of this corps are not to be estimated

---

[1] Mahadaji Sindhia, rajah of Gwalior, 1759–94; succeeded by his great-nephew, Daulat Rao Sindhia.

by a consideration of its actual state of discipline, or even of its actual numbers, or degree of present influence over the councils of the nizam. I consider it as the basis of a French party in India, on which (according to the opportunities of fortune, and the variation of events) the activity of the enemy may found a strength of the most formidable kind either in peace or war. If we are to look to the settlement of peace, can it be possible to provide a more ready channel for the intrigues of France, than would be offered by the existence of a body of ten thousand men, united by military discipline, and stationed in the dominions of one of our principal allies, and on the borders of our own? If the war is to continue in Europe without extending to the continent of India in the first instance, the danger of French intrigue acting with such an instrument as I have described would be greatly aggravated. But if the war should extend to the continent of India, and if we should be under the necessity of calling forth the strength of our allies to assist us in any contest with Tipu, what assistance could we expect from the nizam, the main body of whose army would be officered by Frenchmen, or by the agents of France, and the correspondents of Tipu himself? In such a situation it would be difficult to determine whether our danger would be greater from an entire desertion of our cause by the court of Hyderabad, or from our acceptance of the only species of support which its military force could offer us in the field.

But I confess I carry my opinion upon this subject still farther. I have no doubt that the natural effect of the unchecked and rapid growth of such a party at the court of one of our principal allies must be in a very short period to detach that court entirely from our interests, and finally to fix it in those of our enemy, to subject its councils to their control, and its military establishments to their direction. However despicable the corps of Raymond may now be in point of discipline or effect in the field, would it be wise to leave such a large body of men in readiness to receive whatever improvements the ability, assiduity, and zeal of French officers, sent from Europe for that express purpose, might introduce into the constitution of a corps, so prepared by corresponding principles and objects to meet the most sanguine expectations of their new leaders? Under these circumstances, the corps, which perhaps now has little more efficiency than that of a political party, might soon become in the hands of our enemy as efficient a military force, as it is now, in that view, wholly useless to the nizam or to us. I desire to add one more consideration. Must not the continuance of such a corps in the service of our ally tend to raise the hopes of Tipu, and in the same proportion to disparage us in the eyes of all the native princes of India? That it has tended to encourage Tipu, I have no doubt, and his correspondence with the leaders of the corps will sufficiently show in what light he views them. Perhaps I have dwelled too long on this part of the subject, where the proof of the weak policy of suffering such an evil, as I have described, to increase without check or disturbance seems to require no labour of argument.

A more interesting and difficult consideration will be to devise some form of remedying this evil, some means which shall not expose our interests to as great a danger as that which we wish to avoid. In the paper transmitted with this letter four distinct measures are proposed for consideration with a view to the desirable object of subverting the French party at the court of the nizam.

The first is to introduce British subjects, or others (being the subjects of friendly powers), into the military service of the nizam, for the purpose of forming a balance against Raymond's corps. This measure has already been partially attempted by the introduction of the corps of Boyd and Finglass at Hyderabad, but it has failed of success in the case of Boyd, who upon some quarrel with the court has left the service of the nizam. I do not think this measure likely to be effectual to any good purpose, and it might even aggravate the evil which it is proposed to remove. A party so consolidated and united as that of Raymond, which has been strengthening itself for a period of several years at Hyderabad, and has established the means of recruiting and augmenting its numbers, will not be counteracted by the irregular and desultory opposition of such adventurers as might be induced by our encouragement to seek employment in the service of the nizam. Persons of this description (and we cannot expect that any other will engage in such an undertaking) would want the system and concert necessary to give vigour to their operations. It is also difficult to suppose that the nizam would at once retain in his service such a number of these persons as could in any degree enter into competition with the numerous corps of Raymond and his adherents. But even if these objections did not exist against the introduction of a crowd of European adventurers at Hyderabad, there would remain a difficulty which appears to me insuperable; the impossibility of finding a sufficient number of such adventurers on whose principles any reliance could be placed. In such circumstances, our attempt to subvert the French party at Hyderabad might only serve to furnish it with additional recruits of other nations; and I much fear that many British subjects might be found in India whose spirit of adventure would rather direct them to seek a new order of things, than to contribute to the maintenance of our power. Lord Hobart[1] has declared his objection to this measure, but, as well as I recollect his letter, his principal ground is the danger of improving the military discipline of the armies of the native princes by furnishing them with European officers. Unfortunately, this objection now comes too

---

[1] 'A temporary expedient pregnant with mischief', Hobart called it. To Shore, 31 July 1797, Bucks. Hobart MSS. India/A.

late. The system, which Lord Hobart very justly dreads, has been suffered gradually to gain such strength, that there is scarcely a native court in India without its establishment of European officers.

The second measure proposed in the annexed paper is nothing more than that we should endeavour by representation and demand to induce the nizam to disband Raymond's corps. I recommend Major Kirkpatrick's observations on this head to your particular attention. Certainly no representation from one friendly state to another could ever be more solidly founded than ours might be to the nizam in the case before us. But besides that Major Kirkpatrick expects no benefit from representation and demand, unconnected with the offer of some advantage to the nizam, I doubt whether our manifesting in the first instance the extent of our anxiety for the dismission of Raymond's corps, might not embarrass us in the progress of the most effectual measures for that desirable end. At present the court of Hyderabad seems willing to purchase a closer connection with us by great sacrifices, and if that connection should not appear objectionable on other grounds, it may probably take place on much more advantageous terms to us, if we grant it as a matter of favour to the solicitation of the nizam, than if we commence the negotiation by demanding the dismission of any part of the nizam's military establishment. This observation will be better understood when I come to take notice of the fourth measure proposed by Major Kirkpatrick. Before I leave this article, I must however remark that I should not be satisfied by obtaining the modification hinted by Major Kirkpatrick in this article, namely, 'That the French officers or other Europeans in Raymond's corps should be dismissed, and their places filled by British subjects nominated by us.' This modification would leave the corps precisely in its present form with the exception of the European officers only. Although the European officers are certainly the most objectionable part of the establishment, it may be doubted whether the habits and dispositions of the native officers and sepoys formed under their French leaders would be at once broken by a mere change in the command, while every other circumstance of the corps remained the same. A further objection to this modification is, that it would furnish the nizam the means of improving his own troops, whereas our policy should be to give him no additional strength which could in any case become exclusively his own. The same remark applies also to Major Kirkpatrick's first proposal of introducing British adventurers into the nizam's army. The effect of such a measure, if successful, must be to improve the discipline of his army, and to render it more efficient for all *his* purposes, whatever they may be. A body of our own troops, receiving the pay of the nizam, would tend to strengthen him for *our* purposes only, and would give him no additional means, but rather weaken him, in any contest with us.

21

Seeing then no prospect of success from official representation or demand alone, and thinking it imprudent to anticipate the expected application of the court of Hyderabad for a more intimate connection with us by urging to them at this period any proposition, the concession of which they might deem as a favour, I proceed to examine Major Kirkpatrick's third suggestion. This he states to be of a nature justifiable only by the case of an actual rupture with the nizam, or of open violence on the part of Raymond against us. The measure is no other than to induce Raymond's officers by pecuniary compensation to abandon the corps. Of this measure it is unnecessary to say anything, because the cases alone to which it is meant to apply neither have existed, nor are now likely to happen. I own that I should never think it worth while, even in the cases supposed of a rupture with the nizam, or of an attack from Raymond, to repel the aggression by corrupting the officers of the hostile army. I trust that in either case, we should soon find a more certain, as well as a more honourable mode of effectually destroying this French party and its adherents.

The fourth proposition contained in Major Kirkpatrick's paper is that to which I wish to call your most particular attention.

The desire of the court of Hyderabad to obtain from us an increase of our detachment now serving the nizam, and also an extension of the power of employing the force furnished by us, has appeared on several occasions, and you will find allusions to this disposition in the last secret dispatches from Bengal. There seems to be no objection to the first part of this proposition, provided our consent to it shall secure to us equivalent concessions on the part of the nizam. In another letter which I shall forward to you on the general subject of the political state of India in the present moment, you will find my reasons for entertaining an opinion that it would be a wise policy for us to check by timely aid the rapid declension of the nizam's weight among the powers of Hindustan. This could be done in no manner so effectual or unobjectionable as by furnishing him with a large increase of our force now in his pay; the pay of the augmented force to be secured in the manner best calculated to prevent future discussion and embarrassment. In granting this force to the nizam, we ought not only to stipulate for the disbanding of Raymond's corps, but we ought to take care that the officers should be immediately sent out of India. There are perhaps other points which on this occasion might be obtained from the court of Hyderabad.

The great difficulty which would obstruct such an arrangement would be that the nizam would be probably be unwilling to part with Raymond's corps, which he has the power of employing against any enemy, unless he could obtain powers equally extensive with respect to the employment of any force furnished by us. You are aware that the British detachment now in the pay of the nizam is not only restricted from acting against the Marathas in any possible case, but also from acting against certain Polygars tributary both to the Marathas and to the nizam, and even from passing, without a formal permission, certain parts of the Maratha territory which are intertwined with the dominions of the nizam. The object of the court of Hyderabad would of course be to obtain our guarantee of its possessions generally against the Marathas, accompanied with the assistance of a large force, to be employed with the same or nearly as extensive powers as now apply to the corps of Raymond. For this object, I have little doubt that the nizam would sacrifice the whole French party at his court, and even the peishcush now paid by us on account of the Northern Circars. But such an alteration of our connection with the nizam would naturally raise the jealousy of the Maratha powers, and might involve us in discussions of a very disagreeable nature, if not in a war with them. The result, therefore, of this view of the subject would lead us to inquire whether some arrangement might not be framed, founded on a modification of the views of the court of Hyderabad, and comprehending certain favourite objects of the Maratha states, which, while it secured for us the destruction of the French party at Hyderabad, should tend to restore to the nizam his due weight among the Indian powers, without exciting the animosity of the Marathas against the British government.

It appears to me that the only effectual mode of eradicating the French party at Hyderabad would be to furnish to the nizam such a force as should be a just equivalent to Raymond's corps. Considering the superior discipline of our sepoys, I believe that three thousand men under British command, not only would be, but would be deemed by the court of Hyderabad, a force fully equal to that of Raymond in its present state.

The restriction, by which our detachment is prevented from acting (as the troops of the Marathas and of the nizam now act) against the Polygars, who pay joint tribute to the two powers, might probably be removed by a full previous explanation with the Marathas; as this restriction does not appear to be founded on any solid principle, nor could the removal of it open the way to any real inconvenience or danger to the interests of the Maratha state.

The power of mutually passing their intermixed boundaries is now constantly exercised by the troops both of the Marathas and of the nizam; and there is no reason to suppose that a formal permission would have been refused to our detachment for the same purpose, had it ever been demanded. But the nizam never would allow any application to be made for a permission to do that which he held to be his right, and which was constantly done without question both by his own army and by that of Poona. It is very improbable that we should find great difficulty in engaging the

23

Marathas to place our detachment in this respect on a footing with the other branches of the nizam's military force, and with their own; nor can I foresee any tenable ground of argument on which this point could be maintained against us.

The settlement of these two points only would, I understand, be considered as a great acquisition by the nizam, and would go a great way towards inducing him to substitute a British force in the room of Raymond's corps.

The third point is of much more importance and of much greater delicacy and danger. I speak of the desire of the court of Hyderabad to obtain our guarantee of their possessions against the Marathas as well as against Tipu, together with a right of employing defensively the troops furnished by us against the former, as well as against the latter, of those powers. This point perhaps might be reconciled with the interests of the Marathas, if it were thought prudent to enter into similar engagements with them, or, in other words, to guarantee their possessions against any attack from the nizam. The effect of such an engagement with both powers would be to place us in the situation of arbitrators between them; and perhaps their mutual apprehensions of our interposition in the case of any aggression on either side might tend to restrain the resentment and ambition of both. In this view, such a system of treaty with the Marathas and with the nizam, so far from being liable to the objection of an undue interference in the disputes of the native powers of India, or of that description of officiousness and intriguing spirit which tends to foment divisions, and to occasion war, might be deemed the best security for the maintenance of the peace of India, as well as the strongest pledge of our disposition to preserve it from disturbance. It would also tend to preserve unimpaired the strength and resources of the two powers, on whose co-operation we must depend for assistance against any future attempt on the part of Tipu. It cannot be a wise policy to suffer the nizam and the Marathas to weaken themselves by repeated contests, while Tipu remains at rest; and any measure deserves attention, the tendency of which is to restore to the Marathas and to the nizam their relative consideration and power, as they stood at the conclusion of the treaty of Seringapatam.

You will find by the last secret dispatches from India, that some opening has been given for our arbitration in settling the disputes between the several Maratha chiefs, and that the government of Bengal has agreed to undertake the mediation proposed, under the condition of a previous formal agreement, signed by all parties, binding themselves to accept our award as final and conclusive upon their respective claims. If any such proceeding should take place, it will give a natural opening to such further engagements as may appear advisable.

The same dispatches will inform you of the anxiety of the Marathas to obtain our agreement to a general defensive treaty against Zeman Shah. The government of Bengal have postponed the consideration of this proposition to a period of time which I confess I should think the most unfavourable for the examination of this difficult question, and still more unseasonable for the negotiation of a treaty with such a power as the Maratha states. This period of time is no other that the moment 'when Zeman Shah shall again approach the frontier of Hindustan'. Without giving any decisive opinion on the wisdom of entering into the treaty proposed, I shall certainly think it my duty upon my arrival in India to proceed without the delay of one moment to the examination and decision of the proposal made by the Marathas. If it should appear expedient to engage with them in a defensive system against the threatened invasion of Zeman Shah, there is no doubt that such a measure would tend greatly to reconcile to them any propositions which we might wish to offer with respect to the arrangements at the court of Hyderabad.

The inclination of my opinion at present rather leads me to think that a general defensive treaty of all the existing powers of Hindustan (Tipu perhaps alone excepted) against the expected invasion of Zeman Shah, would not only be the best security against the success of such an invasion, if attempted, but might have the effect of deterring that prince from an undertaking, which must end in his own disappointment and ruin, if our governments in India and our allies do not neglect to make seasonable preparations of defence. If a treaty can be framed at an early period so as to unite the Maratha powers with us in a cordial and systematic plan of vigorous opposition to the supposed projects of Zeman Shah, without binding us to advance farther from our own frontier than the real exigency of the case may appear to demand upon his approach, I should think such a treaty a solid acquisition of strength in the present critical situation of India. There is one consideration (which I have omitted to state) that would probably induce Azim ul Umra, the minister of the nizam, to agree to the dismission of Raymond's corps, and accept ours in the place of it, almost without any other condition. That consideration would be our engaging to support the nizam's nomination of a successor. Azim ul Umra will certainly induce the nizam to name Secundar Jah, the eldest son, who is married to Azim ul Umra's daughter. If the Marathas could be brought to concur with us in support of Secundar Jah's succession, such a co-operation would greatly facilitate our arrangements at Hyderabad, and at the same time frustrate any views which Tipu may entertain of governing by intrigue or force the succession to the throne of the nizam.

You will observe from this detail that I consider the fourth measure suggested by Major Kirkpatrick to be the only one from which it is reasonable to hope that the effectual destruction of the French army at Hyderabad can be accomplished, but that I view that measure as connected with considerations of the most serious nature, and involving consequences of the utmost delicacy and importance. I have laid before you the whole train of my thoughts on the subject, as I shall think it my duty to do on every question affecting those interests, which I know to be not only highly valuable in your estimation, but the most particular and anxious objects of your unremitting solicitude and care. I will conclude this long letter by stating the precise questions on which I wish to receive your instructions, and by submitting to you the plan of measures which I propose to pursue with relation to this subject in the interval which must elapse before I can receive your opinion.

In the first place, I wish to be informed whether you think a closer connection than at present subsists between us and the nizam advisable for our interests on general grounds, provided such a change of our engagements with the nizam can be rendered acceptable to the Marathas?

Secondly, whether you would approve of our entering into treaties with both the Marathas and the nizam guaranteeing the dominions of each power respectively against the aggression of the other?

Thirdly, whether you would approve of our taking measures for acting in concert with Azim ul Umra in support of the succession of Secundar Jah, the eldest son of the nizam; whether we should endeavour to obtain the co-operation of the Marathas in securing this succession; and what should be our conduct, if the Marathas should differ from us in the choice of the successor to the nizam?

Fourthly, whether you would approve of a general defensive treaty against any invasion from Zeman Shah, and what limitations would you propose to the powers which the other allies might require of employing our troops beyond our own frontier?

You will observe that the determination of all these questions is necessary, in my view of the subject, in order to enable me to carry into effect the only measure which I can rely upon as a sufficient check to the growth of the French interest at the court of Hyderabad, and as a permanent barrier against any future revival of that interest in the same quarter.

But I am aware that I cannot receive your opinion for a long time. In that interval circumstances may compel me to decide some of these important questions upon my own judgement. My wish, however, is to reserve them all for yours; and with this view I propose to pursue a system of measures, which, while it shall leave all the most delicate parts of the situation of affairs in India open to your decision, shall tend to curb in some degree the progress of the French party at Hyderabad, and to furnish me with such materials as shall enable me to form a competent opinion of the effects to be expected from any decision of the points reserved for your judgement.

I propose to direct the resident at Hyderabad to suffer no augmentation of Raymond's corps to take place, if it can be prevented by the strongest and most pointed representations. This step may probably check the increase of the corps, although from this step alone I cannot hope for its final annihilation.

I mean also to direct that any proposals from the nizam's ministers for an increase of our detachment shall be favourably received; and I shall increase the detachment accordingly on the first practicable occasion. But I shall stipulate that for every man we grant, there shall be a proportional reduction made in Raymond's corps. This proportion shall be calculated upon the relative estimation of our sepoys (in the opinion of the ministers of the nizam themselves) when compared with Raymond's corps; and I believe that on this ground I shall not find it difficult to contend that a reduction of three thousand men should be made for every thousand men granted by us. In reducing the army of Raymond, I shall endeavour in the first instance to disband the most obnoxious and dangerous officers with their corps.

I have reason to believe that I may be able to effect this species of partial reduction of Raymond's corps, without entering upon any of the difficult points involved in the general question stated in this letter. In the meanwhile, however, I shall direct the resident at Hyderabad to ascertain the temper of that court upon every one of those points without delay.

The residents at Poona and with Sindhia will be directed to ascertain as speedily as possible the views and dispositions of those powers with respect to the same points, and especially with respect to any alteration of our connection with the nizam, to the support of his eventual successor, and to the proposed defensive engagements against Zeman Shah.

In submitting the whole of this extensive subject to your consideration, I have been obliged to leave many parts of it open to doubt, for want of the information which may be expected from the residents with Sindhia and at Poona. I believe, however, that it will not be difficult for you to answer the questions which I have proposed, framing your answers in such a manner as may admit of any variation of opinion, which the information from those courts may require.

The state of the military establishments of the Maratha powers did not properly come under Major Kirkpatrick's view. And I propose to transmit to the residents at Poona and with Sindhia a copy of my questions to Major Kirkpatrick, with such alterations as the several cases may require, in order to obtain for you a full statement of the corps disciplined by European or Americans in the service of the Marathas. I am at present able to give you no fuller information on this part of the subject than that Sindhia employs about twenty thousand sepoys disciplined by Europeans or Americans. The commander is named Perron, a Frenchman; most of the officers are British subjects. The discipline of this corps is said to be superior to that of Raymond's, but the disposition of its officers to be much more favourable to the British than to the French interests. This was De Boigne's[1] corps, whose history you probably know; De Boigne was lately in London. If he should not have left it, he can give you the fullest information of the state of Sindhia's army. There was a small corps of about two thousand men commanded by European officers in the service of the peshwa, and another of about the same number in that of Tuckoji Holkar. They are both inconsiderable, if they still exist; and the dissensions, which have broken out between Holkar's two sons since the death of their father,[2] have left that branch of the Maratha power in a situation from which little danger is to be apprehended.

I am, . . .

MORNINGTON

The rajah of Berar is said to have a corps in his service commanded by British officers. It is said not to consist of above two thousand men.

In disbanding the whole, or any part of the corps of Raymond, care will be taken to send the officers out of India.

III

The Earl of Mornington to the Rt Hon. Henry Dundas

28 February 1798, Castle of Good Hope
Private: no. 2

My dear Sir

During my detention at this place the ships of which I enclose a list arrived with dispatches from Bengal. My anxious desire to learn the actual state of affairs in India from the most authentic source induced me to open the public and secret packets, the contents of which I have examined with great attention and care. I flatter myself that this step, proceeding from a wish to enable myself to do justice to their service, will meet with the

[1] Benoit, comte de Boigne; commander of Sindhia's army in Hindustan, 1784–96; succeeded by Pierre Perron.
[2] Tuckoji Holkar, ruler of Indore, 1768–97; succeeded by his son, Kashi Rao, 1797–1801, who was deposed by his illegitimate brother, Jeshwant Rao.

approbation of the court of directors, and that they will be satisfied with the reasons which I have offered in my letter to them on this subject. The inspection of the dispatches has so far answered my purpose in opening them, as to have furnished me at this early period of time with a full knowledge of many details, which I must have studied at Calcutta, amidst all the pressure of the current business of the day, before I could have formed a competent judgement on many points of urgent importance. I have thought it worth my while to remain here for some days longer than the repair of the *Virginie* required, for the express purpose of giving to the dispatches the most full consideration, and of communicating to you my sentiments upon their contents, connecting the whole with the opinions and instructions which I had already received from you on the subject of the political state of India. My continuance here will in all probability not at all retard the time of my arrival in India, as the season will from day to day become much more favourable for the passage round the Cape and up the bay of Bengal; and the week, which I have passed here in reading the dispatches from India, and in committing my thoughts to paper for your further instructions, must have been passed at sea in struggling against contrary winds, without any prospect of accelerating my passage to Madras. Feeling it to be of importance that the dispatches which I have read from on board the *Houghton* should reach England as soon as possible, and having every reason to believe that the arrival of the *Crescent* frigate, returning home with Admiral Pringle,[1] would be much earlier than that of any of the Company's ships, I have requested the captain of the *Houghton* to deliver his dispatches to Admiral Pringle, who has been so good as to undertake the charge of them as well as of my letters.

The contents of these dispatches have led me to a very serious review of the opinions which I had formed under your direction with regard to the relative situations of the several native powers of India, and to the system to be pursued with respect to their interests by the government committed to my charge.

The leading principle of your instructions to me, as applicable to our external policy in India, was, that I should endeavour as nearly as possible to preserve the balance of power between the native princes upon the same footing on which it was placed by the treaty of Seringapatam.

It would be a waste of your time to state at any length the precise nature of the relative conditions of those states, whose interests were affected, and whose power was ascertained by the operation of that treaty. It will be sufficient to remark that one part of the policy of the treaty was, by strengthening the Marathas and the nizam to the extent and in the manner provided

[1] Rear-Adm. Thomas Pringle; flag officer in command, Cape of Good Hope, 1796–8.

29

by the articles of the treaty, to establish an efficient check upon the future ambition or resentment of Tipu, and to secure to us an efficient support against him, whenever we might have occasion to call for it.

The plain question to which my attention has been directed by the inspection of the late dispatches is this. Are the Marathas and the nizam now in the same condition in which the treaty of Seringapatam left them, and can we now look to both, or either of these powers for that degree of support against Tipu, which it was the intention of that treaty to provide? I am afraid that a very short examination of the present position of the Marathas and of the nizam will furnish ample proof that neither of those powers remain in the same state in which they stood in 1793, either with relation to each other, or to the general balance of power in India; and above all, that their means of assisting us against Tipu are considerably diminished.

Since the conclusion of the peace of Seringapatam, the credit and resources of the court of Hyderabad have been constantly declining. The disgrace which fell upon the nizam's army in the unfortunate contest with the Marathas at Khardlah reduced the military character of the court of Hyderabad to the lowest point of degradation. The treaty in which that defeat terminated completed the humiliation of the nizam. You will remember that he was compelled to sacrifice a large portion of territory, to engage to pay a fine of three crores of rupees, and to submit to the captivity of his minister Azim ul Umra, who was carried to Poona. Azim ul Umra resided at Poona during the late convulsions in the Maratha government, and bore a very distinguished part in supporting Nana[1] through the various revolutions which followed the sudden death of the Peshwa Madhav Rao.[2] For these services, Nana had agreed to sacrifice all the benefit acquired for the Maratha state against the nizam by the treaty of Khardlah. But the event has been that Nana has insisted on the cession of one fourth part of the territory, and on the payment of one fourth part of the fine stipulated by that treaty. So that the final result is a considerable diminution of the territory and resources of the nizam, added to all the effects which might naturally be expected to be produced upon his domestic peace and foreign consideration by so heavy a loss both of power and honour. The two rebellions of the nizam's son Ali Jah, and of the son of Dara Jah, are stated to have arisen from the contempt into which the nizam's authority had fallen at home; and although those rebellions have been quelled, the collections of the revenue have been so severely affected, as well by them as by the detention of Azim ul Umra at Poona, that the resources of the country are not likely to recover the shock for some time.

[1] Nana Fadnavis (1741–1800); minister to the peshwa, 1774–1800.
[2] Madhav Rao, Peshwa of Poona, 1772–94; succeeded by Baji Rao II, after a struggle with his brother Chimna Appa.

The effect of these causes has been very much to lower the value of the nizam's power in the scale of the neighbouring states. He has been obliged to submit implicitly to the will of the government of Poona; the rajah of Berar has exacted large contributions from his territory; and Tipu (although endeavouring to gain him as an ally) has omitted no occasion of expressing the utmost contempt for his abject situation.

But the most striking feature of [the] change in the state of the nizam's affairs since 1793 is the alteration which has taken place in his military establishment. This at first view might appear an improvement of his political strength; but whatever may be your judgement upon that question in a general view of it, you will, I am persuaded, concur with me in opinion that the alteration which has taken place in the nizam's military establishment since the peace of Seringapatam has nearly disqualified him from co-operating with us as an ally in the cases for which that treaty meant to provide.

The nizam since the peace has greatly reduced his cavalry and other troops, and in the meanwhile has considerably augmented the corps of Raymond, of the nature and principles of which I have given a description in my letter *no. 1*. The corps of Raymond now forms the great force of the nizam's army, and although very deficient in point of discipline and skill, when compared with our troops, is stated to be more capable of performing useful service in the field than the whole army furnished to us by his Highness in the late war with Tipu. On the other hand, perhaps the existence of this corps, united as it is in the cause of France, connected with Tipu, and animated by that spirit of intrigue, which would lead it to mix in every distraction of the state, if not to disturb the internal peace of the country by originating the causes of confusion, may be considered as a circumstance of positive weakness in the frame of the government. Azim ul Umra has certainly felt the force of this argument, and, by consenting to the introduction of the corps of Boyd and Finglass, appeared to be aware that the corps of Raymond might eventually gain an ascendancy, which it might be difficult to reduce within any bounds of moderation, and which might hereafter overthrow the power of a minister, or dictate the succession to the throne itself.

But with respect to our alliance, and to the value of the guarantee under the treaty of Paangul, the altered state of the nizam's army places him in a condition worse than that of absolute inefficiency. In a war with Tipu, or in the still more aggravated case of a war with him and France, the forces of the nizam must become useless (if not dangerous) to us, precisely in proportion to the exigency of the case in which our cause should demand the aid of our allies. I have stated this argument already in my letter *no. 1*, to which I refer you, with this additional observation; that I cannot conceive the case in which we could take the nizam's French troops into the field with us, without the utmost hazard of treachery, nor the case in which we could leave them behind us, without providing an equal force to watch their movements. Recollecting that this corps is the only military force of any kind of efficiency which we can expect from the nizam in the event of war with Tipu and France, you will judge without difficulty what answer should be given to the question which I have proposed upon this part of the subject.

I have already observed how much the posture of the nizam's affairs is altered with relation to the balance of power between him and the Maratha states, and how much he has been weakened and degraded by the treaty of Khardlah, and by the manner in which it has been carried into execution. In this view, it has been a favourable circumstance to the nizam (and is perhaps that cause to which alone he is indebted for the preservation of any degree of strength or even of his throne) that the distractions of the Maratha empire have so shaken the power of the peshwa and disturbed the unity of the confederation of the principal chiefs, as to have very much impaired their means of carrying on any considerable military operation. Notwithstanding this circumstance, I still consider the nizam to be in a much weaker state even with relation to the Marathas, divided and broken as their power now is, than he was at the conclusion of the peace of Seringapatam.

This leads me to submit to your consideration my ideas on the actual condition of the Maratha empire. I am aware that some opinions have been thrown out from very respectable quarters, the tendency of which appears to lead towards a sentiment approaching to satisfaction in the dissensions and divisions which have lately taken place among the Marathas. I always considered the precise situation in which the Maratha empire stood after the peace of Seringapatam as the most favourable to our interests. The powers of the different coestates were then sufficiently balanced amongst each other to prevent any danger of that degree of union which could at any time bring the whole of their force to operate in one consolidated mass against the British possessions. On the other hand, the influence of the peshwa or head of the coestates, and of his minister Nana, were such as to enable them to bring into the field a respectable force, whenever their engagements with us might require such an effort. This appears to me to be the position in which we ought to endeavour to maintain the Maratha states; in which no one branch of the empire should obtain such an ascendancy as might enable it to concentrate the formidable strength of the whole against us; while the head of this great body should still preserve such a degree of power over several of the leading chiefs as to become a respectable ally to us in the moment of necessity. The present posture of the Maratha power is directly the reverse, in one respect, of that which I have described. Fortunately no one of the coestates, nor the head of the empire, has yet acquired the means of wielding the united force of the whole body. But while some of the chiefs have made great and valuable acquisitions of dominion, and considerably increased their military strength, the authority and influence of the peshwa has rapidly declined; and it could not now be expected that any respectable body of the chiefs would be disposed to prosecute under his direction any common view or joint operation with any degree of zeal or vigour. This has been the effect produced by the late series of revolutions at Poona. Looking to the most important question for our consideration, namely, the extent of the assistance which we may expect from the Marathas, if we should have occasion to call for their aid under the engagements subsisting between us, I have viewed those revolutions with great regret; and I cannot now see their consequences in any more favourable light, as far as they regard us, than that of a positive diminution of the strength of those barriers which it was the policy of the treaty of Seringapatam to raise against the power of Tipu. I have avoided entering into a detailed account of the respective positions of each of the great Maratha chiefs, wishing to call your attention to the more essential and pressing part of the subject. But I believe you will find the circumstances of each branch of the Maratha power to have varied since the year 1793 nearly according to the following statement.

Sindhia has made large acquisitions of territory, and improved the discipline of his troops. He has also acquired great influence at Poona, but it may be doubted whether the death of Mahadaji Sindhia has not been a greater loss to the power of this branch of the empire than will be compensated by any of these advantages. The character of Daulat Rao Sindhia and of his ministers is such as to render the power of this branch much less formidable than it was in the lifetime of Mahadaji.

The rajah of Berar has made some progress in power since the peace of Seringapatam at the expense of the peshwa, of the nizam, and of some Pathan princes in Malwa. His strength and consideration are said to be upon the increase.

Tuckoji Holkar's power was on the decline even before his death. Since that period the political weight of this family has been greatly diminished by intestine divisions between the successors of Tuckoji.

The chiefship of Pursuram Bhow is extinct, and that of Hurry Pundit has lost the greater part of its credit and power.

I have already spoken of the peshwa. The events which have reduced his importance are familiar to you. I will only add this remark, that the jealousy which must necessarily subsist between the present peshwa and his minister Nana (who at one period of the late revolutions at Poona supported Chimna Appa, the younger brother of Baji Rao the present peshwa) is a circumstance likely to present additional obstacles to any vigorous exertion of the force of the government of Poona, if it does not produce some new convulsion in its frame. I believe it may justly be said that, since the foundation of the government, the power of the peshwa never was so inconsiderable in the general scale of the Maratha states as it is at this moment.

Having thus stated to you my reasons for apprehending that the efficiency of both the allies on whom we are to depend for aid in any future contest with Tipu is so much impaired since the year 1793, that we could not look to them at this juncture for the same degree of assistance (whatever that may have been) which Lord Cornwallis derived from their co-operation in the late war with that prince; I now beg leave to call your attention to certain circumstances in our own situation, intimately connected with our political weight in India, and with our means of encountering again at any early period the pressure of war. The dispatches which accompany this letter will inform you of the death of the Nawab Vizier Asuf ud Daulah, and of the very extra-ordinary scenes which have passed in Oudh since that event. The event itself I should have considered in the abstract as highly favourable to our interests; being persuaded that under the reign of Asuf ud Daulah it would ever have been impracticable to have carried into permenent effect any reform in the disordered finances and undisciplined army of that province. With the assistance of Tofuzil Hussein Khan, the new minister of Oudh, it might have been hoped that the succession of a new prince might have opened more favourable prospects. But the strange and unfortunate circumstances attending the succession of Vizier Ali[1] seem to lead to a situation of affairs in Oudh which for some time must impair the strength of that frontier, and render the country more open to the impression of a foreign enemy. Almas Ali is said to be ready to take the field with a very respectable force, and the Rohilla chiefs, of whose persevering spirit we have had a recent experience, are also mentioned as being upon the point of insurrection. The whole country is represented to be in a state to require the presence of a large military force for the maintenance of internal peace and good order. This state of our affairs in Oudh must be deemed a positive diminution of our actual force. I trust that the activity (perhaps even the mere presence of our troops) may reduce the insurgents to submission; but while any ambiguity remains respecting the permanency of the settlement made in favour of Vizier Ali, and while the same turbulent spirit shall exist among the Rohillas, and the military power of Almas Ali continue undiminished, it can never be safe to withdraw our

---

[1] Vizier Ali Khan; adopted son of Asuf-ud-daulah, who died in 1797; was deposed in favour of his uncle, Saadat Ali Khan, vizier of Oudh, 1798–1814.

troops. And it must be remarked that the danger of withdrawing them would be increased exactly in proportion to the pressure of the necessity of employing them against any foreign enemy. You will find that the governor-general states his conviction without reserve that the approach of Zeman Shah towards the frontier of Oudh would become the signal of general revolt and plunder in that province.

In the meanwhile I cannot consider the call for the employment of our troops in quelling the spirit of insurrection in another quarter to be yet so little urgent as to leave us free to act against an enemy on that side without apprehension of our own subjects. I allude to the present state of the coast of Malabar. I find that a treaty has been signed with the Pyche Rajah; but as far as I can collect from the dispatches it does not appear to me that his submission has been so complete, or his power so broken, as to warrant a sense of security either in his weakness or in his sincerity. This circumstance again must operate as a diversion of our force in the event of war.

With respect to our financial resources I refer you to the same dispatches for an account of the general embarrassment both of public and private credit, and of the difficulty of raising money for public purposes, even at the exorbitant interest of twelve per cent with the combined advantage of a remittance. The great expense of the long-intended and suddenly-relinquished expedition to Manila[1] must of necessity increase both the difficulty and the exigency of raising further loans.

To this view of our situation must be added the state of our dependencies of Arcot and Tanjore, as represented by the Madras government, both with respect to the disaffection and refractory spirit of the nabob and rajah, and to the decline of the permanent sources of public revenue.

I hope I shall not be suspected of wishing to draw a gloomy or exaggerated picture of the altered aspect of our affairs since the peace of Seringapatam. My only wish is to fix your attention, as I have fixed my own, on the true points of our weakness for the purpose of considering the speediest means of recovering our strength. I know that the fortunate events of this most glorious war have given us an ascendancy over every European nation in India such as we never before possessed. But I cannot shut my eyes to the diminution which our weight in the scale of the country powers has suffered, and is likely to suffer still more, if the means of checking the progress of the evil be much longer neglected. Nor can I refuse my assent to the truth of a proposition, which I now think it my duty to urge to you with great earnestness, that unless effectual and vigorous measures be taken for quelling the disturbances in our own provinces and in those of our dependencies, I do not see how we can again be prepared to

---

[1] Abandoned by Hobart on 28 August 1797, after news of the Austro-French preliminaries of Leoben.

meet an enemy of any respectable force in the field. To the distress of our finances I am persuaded your most serious attention will be given without delay, and you may rely on receiving from the most ample communications on that subject upon my arrival in India.

In reviewing our political situation in India, particularly with regard to our comparative power of curbing the attempts of Tipu, I ought not to omit the consideration of the relative strength of that prince as it exists in the present moment, and as it stood as the conclusion of the peace of Seringapatam.

Since that period of time he has enjoyed perfect internal tranquillity. While our allies all around him have been distracted and exhausted by domestic rebellions, successive revolutions, and mutual wars, he has been employed in recruiting the sources of his strength, improving his revenues, and invigorating the discipline of his armies. It is true that he must now have nearly lost all hope of assistance from France, or from any other European power: but that hope was long cherished by him, and it encouraged him to the great exertions which have unquestionably added to his military strength. He has been very active for some time past in his applications to the courts of the native powers, endeavouring to stir them up against us. He certainly applied for that purpose to the nizam, and (during the absence of Azim ul Umra at Poona) he made a very strong impression upon the politics of the court of Hyderabad, where he now has a vakil, and where he certainly has many partisans as well in the corps of Raymond as in the service of Umjid ud Daulah, a chief of a considerable faction called the *Paugah Party*,[1] and in that of Imtiauz ud Daulah, nephew to the nizam. Tipu has also sent vakils to Poona with the same object of raising a spirit of hostility against us. His success, I believe, has not answered his wishes in that quarter.

But the most remarkable step which Tipu has lately taken is his communication with Zeman Shah. The declared projects of Zeman Shah, added to the attempts which he has recently made towards carrying them into execution, must in their general impression and effect be considered as an accession of strength to the cause of Tipu. If an invasion of Hindustan should ever seriously be attempted by Zeman Shah, the diversion of our force which would be occasioned by such an event would offer the most favourable opportunity to an attack from Tipu on our possessions in the peninsula. No mode of carrying on war against us could be more vexatious or more distressing to our resources than a combined attack upon Oudh and the Carnatic. It is not improbable that the late intercourse between Tipu and Zeman Shah had for its object, on the part of the former at least, some such plan of joint operation. I know that it is the fashion to treat the

[1] The party grouped around the head of the nizam's household troops.

projects of Zeman Shah very lightly. In the dispatches you will see an account of his force, and you will find a detail of all the intelligence obtained respecting his future intentions, as well as of the causes likely to obstruct their execution. The result of an examination of these materials upon my mind is a conviction that Zeman Shah has not abandoned his project of invading Hindustan, and that the safest means of rendering that project abortive will be to consider it as practicable, and to take the best precautions against it which the advantages of our situation and the interval of time can furnish. The fact is that Zeman Shah was able to advance to Lahore without opposition from the Sikhs: whatever circumstances recalled him to his own dominions, the above-mentioned fact well deserves attention, because it contradicts all the conjectures and opinions which had been so confidently formed with respect to the obstacles which Zeman Shah would meet on his march from his own dominions to our frontier. The nation of the Sikhs was said to form the first barrier against him, and it was asserted that this obstruction alone would be insuperable. He contrived, however, to pass through the country of the Sikhs unmolested; and if I am rightly informed, he has since endeavoured, not without success, to negotiate a treaty with some of the leaders of the various factions, which distract that nation. Should he succeed in establishing an amicable intercourse with any large body of the Sikhs, it would greatly facilitate the success of his supposed project of invasion. Between the country of the Sikhs and the frontier of Oudh no obstacle remains but the Maratha power. It is perfectly well known that when Zeman Shah reached Lahore, the Marathas were by no means in a condition to check his progress. They had no army in that quarter which could have been opposed to him in the field. Sindhia was at that time at Poona with the greater part of his force, deeply engaged in the intrigues and revolutions of which that place has been so long the scene. If Zeman Shah had not been recalled by some domestic cause (of which the true nature does not seem to be yet thoroughly understood), there cannot be a doubt that he might have penetrated through the possessions of Sindhia in the neighbourhood of Delhi and Agra without difficulty, if not without opposition. From the accounts which I have received of the military force of Sindhia, I do not believe that he alone would be equal to cope with the army of Zeman Shah; and therefore I do not feel that we should be secure at any time if we relied on his single efforts to check the approach of the invading force.

With the experience of this critical state of affairs in my mind, I cannot consider the idea of an invasion from Kabul as a mere visionary danger. It does not appear to have been so considered by the present government of Bengal, who have stated it as one of the leading circumstances which called for an augmentation of their native infantry.

To recur, therefore, to the view of the political balance of power in India which I was endeavouring to submit to you, I think myself compelled to estimate the force of Tipu with reference to the projects of Zeman Shah, and to the possibility of their (at least limited) success; and on this ground I must conclude that Tipu's consideration has received additional weight since the year 1793. If the facts be true which I have stated on both sides of this enumeration of the comparative circumstances of our situation in India, and of those which affect the situation of Tipu, it must be admitted that upon the whole he has rather gained than lost weight in the period of time described, and that the consequence, unity, and efficiency, of our side of the balance has suffered no inconsiderable degree of diminution.

In my letter *no. 1* from this place I have opened to you some parts of the general outline of those measures which appear to me to be best calculated to restore the native powers of India and ourselves to the same position in which we stood in 1793, as far as the change of times and circumstances will admit. So far from viewing any plan tending to this object as an innovation upon our system of Indian government, I feel it to be my duty to state such a plan, in conformity to the instructions which I had received from you at my departure, and to every principle which I have formerly imbibed from you on this interesting subject. The balance of power in India no longer exists upon the same footing on which it was placed by the peace of Seringapatam; the question, therefore, must arise, how it may best be brought back again to that state, in which you have directed me to maintain it?

My present view of the subject is that the wisest course would be to strengthen the Marathas and the nizam, by entering into a defensive alliance with the former against Zeman Shah, and by affording to the latter an addition of military force and the means of extricating himself from the control of the French party at Hyderabad.

In framing a treaty of defensive alliance against Zeman Shah, the object to be sought would be, the securing an efficient force to be in the field in due time to check the progress of Zeman Shah in the Maratha territory of Delhi, or at least of Agra; the danger to be avoided would be, the drawing our troops farther beyond the line of the frontier of Oudh than might be necessary for securing the fair common objects of the alliance. To this treaty I would make the nizam a party. The treaty should not contain a hostile word against Zeman Shah, excepting only with reference to the single case of his projects of invasion; and it should be communicated to him, with assurances of our determination never to molest him in his own dominions, nor to suffer him to approach ours.

I have sufficiently stated all that relates to the nizam in my letter *no. 1*; to which I refer you also for my opinion of the possibility of removing the grounds of jealousy between him and the Marathas, or at least of checking the hostile attempts of either party upon the power of the other.

You will perceive that the course of my opinions would also lead me to take every step, consistent with the rules of caution and moderation, for restoring to the peshwa such a degree of power as might render him able to fulfil the subsisting engagements between us and the Maratha empire.

The most pressing part of the whole subject seems to be the state of Oudh, of the coast of Malabar, of the Carnatic, and of Tanjore.

With respect to the disturbances in Oudh, I trust that the exertions of Lord Teignmouth and of Sir Alured Clarke[1] will have done a great deal before my arrival. I think this the occasion to remark to you, that I have met no person who does not complain of the insufficiency of our force of cavalry in Bengal and Oudh. Our new regiments are yet scarcely formed, and there is but one regiment of European dragoons in that quarter, which also is nearly inefficient, from having been imprudently and unnecessarily exposed to the violence of the heat. There is a very good and more than complete reg[imen]t of dragoons here, the 8th, which having been here for near two years is well seasoned for the Indian service. It would be a very acceptable guest in Bengal, and might become very useful not only in the event of any attempt of Zeman Shah, but also in quelling the disturbances in Oudh, and in serving as a model to our newly raised native cavalry. I confess that under all the present circumstances of India, I should be glad to see one or two more King's regiments of infantry in Bengal. There is a very fine regiment now here, the 84th, which has been thoroughly seasoned, and is extremely strong in point of numbers. At all events I hope you will reinforce our cavalry without delay, and at the same time send us some good cavalry officers to form the new corps.

With respect to the coast of Malabar I shall never think our affairs safe in that quarter, until the whole tribe of peculators and plunderers has been severely punished, and until the Pyche Rajah has been reduced to unconditional submission. I do not know whether your idea is to fill the chair at Bombay with some person of more animation than Mr Duncan.[2] He is, I believe, a very able and upright public servant in the department of revenue, but he does not seem to think himself qualified for his present station, which requires spirit, vigour, and decision. Our possessions on the coast of Malabar will become an incumbrance to us, if they are not speedily brought into some condition of order. A more active and vigorous control is necessary, as well over the corruptions of our own servants in that province as over the refractory spirit of the native princes and landholders.

[1] Lt-Gen. Sir Alured Clarke; commander-in-chief, Madras, 1796–7; commander-in-chief, India, 1797–1801.
[2] Jonathan Duncan (1756–1811); governor of Bombay, 1795–1811.

Mr Duncan, I believe, would be a great acquisition to the council of Bengal.

I cannot speak of Arcot and Tanjore until I have been upon the spot. You will find by the dispatches that, in consequence of a failure in the payment of his kists, a part of the rajah's country is fallen into our hands. The present state of India does not perhaps upon the whole offer the most favourable occasion for the new settlement of the musnud of Tanjore. If I should see cause for delay, I shall not hesitate to postpone the deposition by the discretionary power vested in me by the orders of the secret committee.

The only point which remains for consideration is the conduct to be observed towards Tipu. You will find in the dispatches, that the supreme government still retain their opinion respecting our right to the district of Wynaad: but as they have directed that an amicable inquiry should take place on that question, the execution of your orders will become more easy.

I have adverted in this letter to the increased assiduity with which Tipu has endeavoured to raise animosities against us among the native powers, and to his intercourse with Zeman Shah. I wish to know from you whether we ought to suffer without animadversion and spirited representation such open acts of hostility on the part of Tipu? My ideas on this subject are, that as on the one hand we ought never to use any high language towards Tipu, nor ever attempt to deny him the smallest point of his just rights, so on the other, where we have distinct proofs of his machinations against us, we ought to let him know that his treachery does not escape our observation, and to make him feel that he is within the reach of our vigilance. At present it appears to me that he is permitted to excite ill will against us, wherever he pleases, without the least attempt on our parts to reprehend either him for the suggestion, or the court to whom he applies for listening to it.

This examination of the political state of India leads me to look at the situation in which we should find ourselves in that quarter in the event of the speedy conclusion of a peace with France.

The best peace we can expect will restore to the French all, and to the Dutch (whom I consider as French under another name) a great part of their former possessions in India. The condition of the several native powers, both with relation to each other and to our interests, is more favourable to the success of French intrigue than it has been at any period since the peace of Seringapatam. We must therefore expect to be assailed on all sides by the combined operations of every species of instrument, which can be set to work, for the purpose of undermining the foundation of our credit, character, and power. You can best judge whether it may be possible to introduce into the treaty of peace any restrictions which shall tend to check in any degree the violence of this evil. But if there be truth in the view which I take of the state of India, and of the probable conduct of the French whenever they shall again obtain their former footing in that country, how powerful an argument arises against permitting them to receive any addition of strength which might render them more respectable in the general scale of Indian power. I am persuaded that the possession of Ceylon,[1] either in the hands of France or of her bondslave Holland, would enable the French interests in India to rise within a very short period to a degree of formidable strength, never before possessed by them. On this subject I find no difference of opinion in the minds of any persons acquainted with India. The possession of Ceylon is universally held to be indispensable to the preservation both of our power on the continent and of our commerce on the seas of India.

I am led by this observation to add a very few words with relation to this place.

Before my arrival here I had formed very high ideas of the intrinsic value of the Cape as a colony, but I had not estimated so highly its value with reference to the defence of our trade to the east, and of our territories in India.

You will have received from Lord Macartney[2] such ample details with respect to the real value of this colony in point of revenue and of every species of resource, that I shall say no more than that I am convinced it would require a long tract of time to render the Cape an object of any consideration in this view. You must consider it as a possession which cannot furnish the means of maintaining its own expense; and you must look for its value in the positive advantages which it would afford to the enemy as a military and naval station for offensive purposes against you, and in the relative advantages which you would derive from it for the purposes of defence. As a military station I believe it to be one of the most advantageous which can be imagined to a power compelled to maintain a large European force in India. The climate is remarkably healthy; so much so that the appearance both of the officers and soldiers stationed here bears striking testimony to the fact. You will hardly see regiments in England of so healthy an appearance as those which have been here for any time. The heat is however frequently very severe, so that a soldier who has been here for a year or two is well accustomed to be exposed to a very ardent sun, and receives a sort of preparation for the climates of India. The advantage of this circumstance has lately been proved in India, where the regiments, which had passed through the seasoning of this climate, have arrived and continued in much better health, than those which proceeded thither

---

[1] Britain had captured the Dutch colonies of Ceylon and the Cape of Good Hope in 1795. Between 1798 and 1802 Ceylon was administered by the East India Company.
[2] George, earl of Macartney (1737–1806); governor of Madras, 1781–4; governor of the Cape of Good Hope, 1796–8.

directly from Europe, or which remained here but for a very short period of time. As a depot, therefore, for the maintenance of a military force in India, the Cape is invaluable; and to the enemy is this view it would furnish easy means of pouring in troops either upon the coast of Coromandel or of Malabar in such a state of health as to be able to encounter all the inconveniences of an Indian climate. With this opinion you may judge with what serious apprehension I should see this place in the hands of the enemy, to whose political consideration in India such a possession would always be a powerful accession, but at no time so formidable as in the present disturbed state of the native powers.

As a naval station I look upon the Cape to be still more important. Many ships in the Indian and China trade make the land upon the outward, and all upon the homeward passage, and the course of those even which keep farthest to the southward never is more distant from the Cape than two or three degrees of latitude. An enemy's squadron stationed at the Cape could not fail to intercept the greater part of our trade to and from the East, without being under the necessity of making any very distant cruises. We should find it impossible to check the operations of such a squadron, unless we could contrive to send out with every trading fleet from Europe a convoy of such considerable force, as must compel us greatly to increase our present naval establishments. The expense of sending out such large fleets of ships of war, victualled and stored for the whole voyage to India or China, would be enormous. And here in my opinion is the point of the question upon which the whole argument must turn: which would be the heavier expense, to retain the Cape keeping up a large naval and military establishment here, and using it as an outpost to your Indian empire, or to leave the Cape in the hands of the enemy, and by so doing to incur the necessity of increasing to a vast amount the protecting naval force requisite for the defence of your Indian and China trade? The expense of the Cape in our hands, however large, must not be estimated as so much positive loss. There are two points of view in which that loss may be considered to be compensated by a proportional diminution of expense in other establishments. The army stationed at the Cape might always be looked upon as a part of the Indian force; and a corresponding saving might be made in your European army in India. Your Indian and China ships might, under proper regulations, be victualled at the Cape at a much cheaper rate than in Europe; consequently their valuable cargoes both outward and homeward might be increased in proportion to the smaller quantity of tonnage occupied by their provisions. Instead of taking six months provisions from Asia or Europe, they need not take more than three, and the vacant tonnage might serve for an augmentation of their cargoes of merchandize. In this view, a great advantage would result to the East

India Company from the possession of the Cape. The whole of this comparative statement might be reduced to calculation, and it would not be difficult for you at once to estimate the several articles of expense which must be incurred by the public in either event, of retaining the Cape, or of abandoning it to France.

But I doubt whether, with the Cape in the hands of the enemy, it would be possible for you to maintain your Indian trade or empire, unless you could acquire some other settlement on the southern continent of Africa. This I know to be Lord Macartney's opinion; and if this opinion be just, the question of the expense of retaining the Cape will be materially varied.

To bring back this discussion to the point from which it proceeded; I trust you will always bear in mind the state of the native powers in India at this moment; and recollecting, that the greatest advantage which we now possess, in the present deranged condition of those interests, which had been so wisely and judiciously balanced by the treaty of Seringapatam, is the utter exclusion of any preponderant European power from the scale of Indian politics, you will contend strenuously against any concession in the peace with France, which may place the security of our Eastern trade and empire at her mercy.

Believe me, . . .

MORNINGTON

I wish to point out to your attention that passage in the governor-general's minute relating to Zeman Shah which describes the several powers in his neighbourhood likely to become a check upon his motions; and I recommend it to you to consider whether something might not be done in Europe to induce the Russians to leave Persia in such a state, as that it might be a restraint hereafter upon the ambition of Zeman Shah.

I am also desirous of learning from you, whether in the event of any negotiation with the Marathas, the exchange of any part of our possessions on the coast of Malabar for the district of Cuttack would appear to you an advisable measure.

I have annexed to this letter a paper delivered to me by a very able navigator of the Indian seas on the subject of the naval protection of our oriental commerce.

On reading over my letter, I find that I have omitted to state one consideration relating to the value of the Cape as a military station. I believe the necessity of retaining Ceylon is now admitted universally: with the Cape in the hands of an enemy, would it be possible to retain Ceylon for any long period of time?

IV

The Earl of Mornington to the Rt Hon. Henry Dundas

7 March 1798, Castle of Good Hope
Private: no. 3

My dear Sir

I have been detained here much longer than I expected or wished by a variety of circumstances. The *La Virginie* was in such a state upon her arrival here as to require considerable repair; the difficulty of obtaining proper stores, the want of small craft in Table Bay for conveying the necessary articles to the ship, and the uncertainty of the winds in this climate, which at least for five days in the week blow such a hurricane as renders all communication between the ships and the shore impracticable, have contributed much to my detention. The ship was a month employed in doing that which under other circumstances might have been done in a fortnight. The arrival of the fleet from Bengal induced me to delay my departure for motives stated in my letter *no. 2* to you, and in my letter to the court of directors. And since I have closed my letters for Europe, I have been detained several days by the adverse state of the wind and weather. I now expect to sail tomorrow morning.

No advices from Europe have reached this place of a later date than the time of my departure. This has been a disappointment to me.

I enclose an extract of a letter, which I thought it necessary to address to the chairman of the court of directors on the subject of the supply of this place with India goods. I request that you will give your early attention to this question, and forward your instructions to me.

I cannot speak too highly of the kind reception which I have met from Lord Macartney, whom I find a most amiable man, and admirable public officer. Mr Barnard and Lady Anne[1] have lodged me in their house during the whole time of my continuance here with such circumstances of attention and kindness as I can never forget. I find that Mr Barnard is a very intelligent man, and goes through the business of his office with great diligence and assiduity. Pray remember me very kindly to Lady Jane[2] and to all your family. I have seen a great deal of General Dundas,[3] and dined twice with him at his country place, which is delightful. He is very well, and in

---

[1] Andrew Barnard; secretary to government, Cape of Good Hope, 1796–1803; married, 1793, Lady Anne Lindsay, daughter of the 5th earl of Balcarres, who had refused Dundas.

[2] Lady Jane Hope, daughter of the 2nd earl of Hopetoun, married Dundas in 1793; his second wife.

[3] Maj.-Gen. Hon. Francis Dundas (d. 1824); commander-in-chief, Cape of Good Hope, 1797–1803; Dundas' nephew.

good spirits. I must add his name to the list of my hospitable friends at the Cape. You shall hear from me whenever I reach Madras.

One channel of intelligence informs me that Lord Teignmouth will certainly have left Calcutta before my arrival, another that he will certainly wait for me. At present I am rather inclined to believe the latter report, ten days ago I believed the former.

Believe me, . . .

MORNINGTON

A report has reached this place, by a Danish ship, of a revolt in China, which had gone to very great and alarming excess, previous to the departure of the Dane from Canton. As this ship carries dispatches from the supra-cargoes at Canton to the court of directors, I conclude the particulars of the revolt will be stated in those dispatches.

V

The Earl of Mornington to the Rt Hon. Henry Dundas

8 May 1798, Fort St George
Private: no. 4

My dear Dundas

I arrived here on the 26th of April, and found General Harris[1] in the government. Notwithstanding every possible effort, and to all appearance the most favourable impressions which I could desire, the main object of my mission to this presidency has not been accomplished. I shall communicate the fullest details of my proceedings by the first safe conveyance; when you receive them, I hope you will think that nothing has been left untried within the extent of my powers, and something gained in point of impression, which may form an advantageous basis for a future negotiation.[2] I have much to submit to your consideration with respect to the state of this presidency. One point it is quite safe to entrust to this conveyance. The army here is in the finest condition, and one of the noblest bodies of men in the world. Every circumstance seems to promise the continuance of peace in this quarter.

I am delighted with the magnificent appearance of this country, but it

---

[1] Maj.-Gen. George Harris (1746–1829) (Lord Harris, 1815, having refused an Irish title in 1800); commander-in-chief, Madras, 1797–1800.
[2] Mornington is referring to his negotiations with the nabob of Arcot.

must be confessed that the climate is very hot. Tomorrow I take my departure for one still more oppressive. My health, however, has not yet suffered, although I have been employed from morning till night since I have been here. The only circumstance which distresses me is my separation from my family. Sir John Shore sailed from Calcutta the 10th of March, and Lord Hobart from this place the 20th of February. I am much pleased with Harris, who I think would make a very good commander-in-chief in Bengal, if anything should happen to occasion a vacancy there. Pray inform Lord Cornwallis of my arrival in India. Remember me kindly to Lady Jane, and all the Wimbledon gang.

Yours very sincerely,

M[ORNINGTON]

Tomorrow I sail for Fort William from whence you shall receive full details of the state of affairs.

VI

The Rt Hon. Henry Dundas to the Earl of Mornington

16 June 1798, Wimbledon
Private: no. 2 (Secret)

My dear Lord
Having been unwell for a considerable part of the spring, and particularly distressed with a weakness in my eyes, I have been obliged chiefly to make use of a secretary's hand. Perhaps you may tell me that this does not require much apology.

The subject of this letter arises from recent dispatches from the Cape of Good Hope, and the state of affairs in the Mediterranean, in consequence of a French fleet, and a great armament, being fitted out from Toulon and having actually sailed upon some secret expedition, under the conduct of their favourite, General Bonaparte. The intelligence we have received from the Cape must have reached you either from the Mauritius itself, or from the Cape of Good Hope, long before you can receive this. I think it however right to send you the copy of a proclamation said to be issued by the governor of Mauritius,[1] and if it speaks true we are probably by this time at war with Tipu Sultan. If we are not, it must have arisen either from

---

[1] Anne Joseph Hippolyte Maurès, comte de Malartic; governor of Mauritius, 1792–1800.

his name being introduced into the proclamation without authority, or from his having, in consequence of proper representations from our government in India, disclaimed and disavowed the whole in such a manner as to set your mind at ease upon the subject. When I speak of disclaiming what is imputed to him, I mean that his conduct should be such as to evince the sincerity of his professions, for if he contents himself with a mere denial, and is at the same time, by preparations and hostile movements, demonstrating his real intention of breach of treaty with this country, your Lordship's wisdom and vigilance will not be lulled asleep or trifled with, but will, when you think it the proper moment for doing so, bring him to an explanation in the only way such conduct merits. And I am persuaded, that it will be your peculiar care, so to act with regard to our allies as to induce them to co-operate with us in chastising so notorious a breach of faith, not only to us, but also to all those who were united together in that war which led to the peace concluded under the auspices of Marquis Cornwallis.

I likewise send to your Lordship the most secret intelligence we have received relative to the expedition fitted out in the Mediterranean.

For a long time it was thought that Bonaparte was intended to lead the threatened invasion against Great Britain and Ireland, but whether it has proceeded from the irresistible superiority of our fleet, or from the great preparations which the zeal and loyalty of his Majesty's subjects has enabled him to make throughout the kingdom, I cannot pretend with certainty to know; but it does appear of late they have been more reserved in their menaces, and less forward with their preparations in the ports opposite to our coasts, and the great exertions of the Republic appear to have been made to fit out the present armament from the ports of the Mediterranean. The destination of this expedition has been matter of various conjecture. It was sometime supposed to be destined against Naples or Portugal, or, under cover of the latter, to lay the foundation for revolutionizing the Spanish monarchy. By the latest intelligence, transmitted to me by Lord Grenville,[1] the copies of which are herewith enclosed, it would appear that Egypt and India are the ultimate objects of this great preparation. We have intelligence of the armament having sailed upon the 19th day of May, and we entertain sanguine hopes that whatever the destination of it may be, the design of the enemy will be frustrated, and the armament itself destroyed, by a powerful squadron acting in the Mediterranean under the command of Sir Horatio Nelson,[2] the object of which is to watch and to pursue it, wherever its course may be directed. If it actually is destined for Egypt, it appears to me to be a great and masterly stroke, and if

[1] William Wyndham Grenville, Lord Grenville (1759–1834); foreign secretary, 1791–1801.
[2] Rear-Adm. Sir Horatio Nelson (Lord Nelson, 1798) (1758–1805); flag officer in command, detached squadron, Mediterranean, 1798–1800.

successful would be attended with very perilous consequences to the interests of this country. In order to avoid entering into a long detail at present upon that view of the subject, I shall content myself with sending to your Lordship a copy of a letter written to Lord Grenville two days ago,[1] in consequence of the intelligence communicated to me by his Lordship. We expect soon to receive certain advice both of the object of the expedition from Toulon, and of the success of the force which has been detached to counteract it; but with the intelligence before us, to which I have referred in this letter, his Majesty's servants would be culpable in delaying a moment to inform you of what is at present known to them, and of the measures which they have in consequence resolved upon.

It is intended with as little delay as possible to send a very respectable reinforcement of European force for the service of India. First, a body of about 1,500 troops from the Cape of Good Hope; that settlement to be strengthened by other force as soon as circumstances will allow of it. Secondly, it is proposed to send 1,500 newly recruited troops to the garrison of Gibraltar, and to forward from thence an equal number of troops which have been seasoned there. And lastly, there are above 1,500 European troops now serving in Portugal, which it is likewise intended to order to India. These different detachments, from the flower of the British army, will tend to put his Majesty's European forces in India upon a respectable footing. By the arrangement with the East India Company, his Majesty's European regiments of infantry are to be 1,200 strong. His Royal Highness the duke of York[2] will accordingly issue his orders to the commanders-in-chief at the different settlements to draft the regiments into each other in such a manner as not to increase the expense agreed upon in the arrangement with the Company, and this operation will of course produce a great number of supernumerary King's officers in India.

This circumstance has suggested to my mind a mode of employing them, to which, as it has only occurred to me this morning, and I have not yet had an opportunity of stating the idea to the duke of York, no attention will of course be paid, unless special directions are transmitted by his Royal Highness to the respective commanders-in-chief for carrying it into execution. I have for some time past observed with considerable regret a practice growing in India of the native powers having considerable numbers of troops in their service disciplined and commanded by European officers, some of them of a description by no means favourable to the interests of Britain in India. This is particularly the case at the nizam's court, and the same practice prevails to a certain extent in other parts of India. I know

---

[1] *Wellesley*, i, 688.
[2] Frederick Augustus, duke of York (1763–1827); commander-in-chief, 1798–1809; commander-in-chief, Holland, 1799; 2nd son of George III.

that there is a great difference of opinion existing how far it is eligible to employ British officers in the service of the native powers of India. I do not think it necessary at present to form any decisive judgement upon that subject as a general system; but I am decidedly of opinion that at the present moment, when a dangerous combination is forming against the British power in India, it is our duty to collect strength in every shape and mode that can tend to resist such a combination. It is obvious that if such a combination does actually exist and is acted upon, the fate of India must depend upon the exertions made either upon the Coromandel and Malabar coasts in contest with Tipu Sultan, or within the dominions of Oudh, if an attempt is made by Zeman Shah, by the Sindian government, or any other of the Indian powers to the northward of our most valuable possessions. In all these quarters, therefore, it would be of the highest importance if, instead of the rabble in the service of our allies, large corps of native infantry could be formed, disciplined, and commanded by the supernumerary British officers, to whom I have referred. In this manner, a force of from 15 to 20 thousand native troops would be formed and led to action under the command of experienced officers, who would otherwise be idle and unemployed at home, and, as our allies by such a measure would be relieved from the necessity of maintaining so great a number of their own inefficient force, they could well afford to pay for the corps to be formed in the manner I have now mentioned. By such a measure our European officers would be honourably and lucratively employed in the service of India, at a moment when there could be no service for them at home, as a few of them only would be requisite here for the purpose of recruiting the regiments to which they respectively belong. If this suggestion shall receive the approbation of his Majesty, I need scarcely mention to your Lordship how absolutely essential it is that the utmost care and circumspection should be used so as to preserve the most accurate discipline and regular conduct on the part of the officers so employed, and that in disciplining and conducting the native troops they should be particularly attentive in no respect to hurt or outrage the feelings or prejudices of those whom they may be called upon to command. By a contrary conduct they would frustrate the whole measure, and, instead of conciliating the natives, prejudice them against our service; whereas by a conciliatory and kind mode of treatment in the conduct of this business, they would reconcile the native powers and their subjects more and more to desire a connection with us. And I am sanguine with hopes that the good effects of it once experienced would lead to the desirable end of our allies confiding in our strength, skill, and discipline, in place of collecting together and keeping up large bodies of undisciplined and expensive rabble such as in general compose their armies. In truth, by such an arrangement they would be

49

great gainers in point of strength, and equally so in respect of pecuniary saving.

From this letter and the papers accompanying it, your Lordship will be enabled to judge of the extent of ideas and measures which suggest themselves to me at the present moment. There are many points of detail and general policy, which, if there were leisure for it, I should be disposed to enter upon in consequence of the long dispatches I received from your Lordship during the short period you were at the Cape of Good Hope. You will perceive that on the subject which I have mentioned I have, to a certain extent, given you my opinion upon part of the subjects to which you desire in the aforesaid dispatches to call my attention, and to receive my opinion. Other matters of detail and of a less pressing nature must be reserved for some future conveyance. There is, however, one subject more which I wish to press upon the consideration of the governments of India, as it will add very considerably to our military strength in that part of the world.

Your Lordship will hear with much satisfaction, that in consequence of the menaces and arrogant language of our enemy, threatening by an invasion of our own island at once to strike at the whole vitals of our strength and power, a spirit of zeal, ardent loyalty, and national pride, has been excited to a degree unexampled at any period of our history, and the consequence of it is, that all ranks and degrees of men are coming forward to be trained in arms, determined to repel every attempt to insult our coasts, or to disturb the internal peace and prosperity of the country. We are, in truth, become an armed nation, and, in addition to all our other advantages, have formed a bulwark of internal security, founded upon the voluntary zeal, loyalty, and valour, of the country. I wish earnestly to urge your Lordship to take this statement under your consideration as applicable to the situation in India. If it be true that a successful invasion of this country would prove fatal to us, in every one interest worthy to bestow a thought upon, it is, if possible, still more peculiarly true with respect to his Majesty's subjects settled in India. A successful attack upon our possessions in India, and the overthrow of the British interest there, would be a death wound to every prospect which any civil servant of the Company can entertain. Why then, are not they, so far as consistent with their other avocations and duties, to devote some leisure hours in each week in order to learn the use of arms, and to form themselves into corps under the authority of government for the purpose of adding to our European strength in India, and preparing themselves, in case of the last extremity, to sacrifice their lives in defence of those interests upon which everything essential to them in life must depend? This is an advantage which, in the day of difficulty, no other European nation but ourselves have the means of resorting to. In former times, when we possessed mere factories in India, and when the interests we had to contend for were of a much more limited nature than those we now possess, I am well informed by some of the old civil servants of the Company, that that body of men formed and arranged themselves as a respectable militia, much to the benefit of our Indian interests. Surely now, when their numbers are multiplied fiftyfold, and when their interests are become even doubly more extensive, it would ill become them to lay by, slothful spectators, when so great a stake was contending for; a stake no less than the existence of the British power in India.

It does not occur to me that there is anything further material to be mentioned at present. I trust that your Lordship has established with your other friends in this country such channels of correspondence as may keep you informed of all other passing occurrences upon which you may desire to be informed. I am afraid the extensive nature of my correspondence must limit in a great degree my means of contributing to your amusement and information upon such general occurrences, being, however, resolved that on all extraordinary occasions, and on every point necessary for your information, comfort, or support, my correspondence shall not be defective by the channels either of public or private communication; and,

I remain, . . .

HENRY DUNDAS

PS. It is my intention to send copies of this letter and its relative papers to the governors of the Cape and of Ceylon, and of our other two presidencies of Madras and Bombay.

VII

The Earl of Mornington to the Rt Hon. Henry Dundas

23 June 1798, Fort William
Private: no. 5

My dear Sir

I arrived here on the 17th of May and took charge of the government on the 18th. My time has been occupied principally in considering the state of our finance, and of our general political system, on both of which subjects I hoped to have been enabled to send you ample details by this packet, which I detained with that view for a few days. But I find it impracticable to complete any satisfactory statement within any shorter period of time than the dispatch of the next packet on the 3rd of July. By that opportunity, it is my intention to give you a full view of the actual posture of affairs in India, more particularly with relation to the two great branches which I have mentioned.

You have probably received the inclosed proclamation from the Cape. Tipu neither has derived, nor can derive, any considerable assistance from the Mauritius. But the project, if not alarming, demands serious attention. I will use every effort to frustrate the intended blow, but I will hazard no attempt of which the success can be doubtful. In every other quarter all appearances of disturbance have ceased.

Upon the whole my health has stood this dreadful climate very well, although during the last week I suffered more than I should have expected from my sensations at my first arrival.

The absence of my family is most painful to me; if Lady Mornington[1] were here my mind would be quite at ease. The business is very extensive but by no means disagreeable, excepting some branches of it, I mean the judicial, which you will, I am persuaded, very soon separate from the council, and place in hands less embarrassed with other labour. If you can contrive to recall me to the remembrance of my friends you will render me a great service. I have not received a line from England since I left it.

Pray give my best compliments to Lady Jane. I have planned a dispatch for her, but never yet have had an half-hour to execute it.

Believe me, . . .

MORNINGTON

I was very glad to hear that you had prevailed on a person of Lord Clive's rank and character to accept the gov[ernmen]t of Madras. I have much to communicate to you on the state of that settlement.

VIII
The Earl of Mornington to the Rt Hon. Henry Dundas

6 July 1798, Fort William
Private: no. 6

My dear Sir

With my letter *no. 5* dispatched overland I transmitted to you a copy of the proclamation issued by the governor of the Isle of France so long ago as the month of February last.

[1] Hyacinthe Gabrielle Roland (d. 1816); married Mornington in 1793 after nine years as his mistress.

The first appearance of this proclamation at Calcutta was in a newspaper of the 8th of June, and the apparent imprudence and rashness of divulging to the world the matter which the proclamation contains induced me to doubt its authenticity, until within a few days of the date of my last dispatch to you, when I received authentic copies of the proclamation from Lord Macartney and from Sir Hugh Christian[1] at the Cape.

Even in the state of uncertainty which preceded the receipt of the dispatch from the Cape, I thought it advisable by a private letter to call the attention of the governor of Fort St George to the possibility of my being compelled to assemble the army upon the coast at an early period.

Since that time, I have received information, the correctness of which being corroborated from various quarters, enables me to state the nature and circumstances of Tipu's late conduct in a connected form.

Tipu dispatched two ambassadors to the Isle of France, who arrived at that island at the close of the month of January, hoisted Tipu's colours upon entering the harbour of Port Nord Ouest, were received publicly by the French government with every mark of distinction, and entertained at the public expense during their continuance in the island. Previously to their arrival, no idea existed in the island of the probability of a war between Tipu and the Company, nor the least rumour of an intended levy of men to be made for Tipu in that quarter.

The proclamation [was] issued two days after the arrival of the ambassadors, and was assiduously circulated through the town of Port Nord Ouest and publicly distributed at the house inhabited by the ambassadors. One of the ambassadors spoke the French language and they were accompanied by a person in the Turkish dress, who spoke French and English with uncommon correctness and fluency, and also appeared to be master of most of the country languages. This person had been at Basra under the name of Abdullah, at Surat under that of Dervish, and at the Mauritius passed under that of Talamas. He appears to answer the description of one of the agents of France mentioned by Mr Wickham.[2] The ambassadors spoke openly and on every public occasion avowed the propositions contained in the proclamation, and Talamas' conversation, though with more appearance of mystery and caution, corresponded in substance with theirs.

An universal belief prevailed in the Isle of France subsequent to the arrival of the ambassadors, that Tipu would make an immediate attack on the British possessions in India, but the temerity of his design was the subject of general ridicule.

[1] Rear-Adm. Sir Hugh Christian (1747–98); flag officer in command, Cape of Good Hope, 1798.
[2] William Wickham (1761–1840); minister to Switzerland, 1794–7, 1799–1802; under-secretary, home office, 1797–9.

You will observe in the proclamation a direct reference made to the powers of the ambassadors with respect to settling the pay and final discharge of the recruits to be raised. The ambassadors publicly acted under this reference, and concluded engagements with the recruits in the name of Tipu. Propositions were also made to a large body of the regular troops of France to enter into the service of Tipu. This was rejected and these troops sometime afterwards were embarked for France in consequence of the disturbances which prevailed in the island. But notwithstanding the rejection of the proposition made to the main body of the French force in the island, one hundred officers (few of much experience or skill) and fifty privates (the refuse of the lowest class of the democratic rabble of the island) were actually enlisted under the proclamation.

With this force the ambassadors embarked on the 7th of March, under every public honour from the French government, on board the French frigate *La Preneuse*, declaring an intention of proceeding to the island of Bourbon for the purpose of obtaining additional levies of men. The force so raised has since been landed at Mangalore about the middle of April; accounts vary with respect to their number, but the most probable intelligence is, that it does not exceed two hundred. Whatever may be its amount, the whole force has been received into Tipu's service with public marks of favour and honour.

The state of the Isle of France, of which more detailed accounts must probably have reached you from the Cape, may serve to explain the apparent absurdity of publishing the proclamation; for it appears probable that Monsieur Malartic took that step with the combined objects of exposing to the British government the desperate and treacherous designs of Tipu, and of relieving the island of some of its worst subjects. But whatever construction may be put upon the policy of Monsieur Malartic in this extraordinary measure, the intentions of Tipu Sultan admit of no question. He has entered into offensive and defensive engagements with the French, collected a force under those engagements, suffered that force to land in his country, admitted it into his service, and declared publicly through his ambassadors, that his preparations of war are complete, and that their object is the entire subversion of the British empire in India.

That he has not yet obtained a force equal to the magnitude of his design is a fortunate circumstance for our interests, but no justification of his aggression. The rashness, imbecility, and consequent ill success, of his councils can never be admitted to palliate the unqualified hostility of his actions. And on every principle of public faith and of the law of nations it cannot be denied that he has violated the subsisting treaties between him and the Company, and that his proceedings have been equivalent to a declaration of war.

Under such circumstances, it has become not only my right but my duty to take advantage of the moment of his actual weakness, and to strike an immediate blow against his possessions for the purpose of frustrating his preparations for war, before he could receive the succours, which it appears by the proclamation he had demanded from the Executive Directory as well as from the government of Mauritius.

The objects which appeared to me the most desirable, as well as the most practicable, were, first, to seize the whole maritime territory remaining in his possessions below the Ghats on the side of the coast of Malabar, in order to preclude him from all future communications by sea with his French allies.

Secondly, by marching an army from the coast directly upon his capital, to compel him to purchase peace by a formal cession of the territory seized on the coast of Malabar.

Thirdly, to compel him to defray our whole expense in the war, and thus to secure the double advantage of indemnifying us for the expense occasioned by his aggression, and of reducing his resources with a view to our future security.

Fourthly, to compel him to admit permanent residents at his court from us and our allies, a measure which would enable us at all times to check his operations, and to detect the intricacies of his treachery.

Fifthly, to make the expulsion of all the natives of France now in his service, and the perpetual exclusion of all Frenchmen both from his army and from his dominions, conditions of any treaty of peace with him.

Every motive of justice and policy appeared (and still appears) to me to demand the adoption of this or some other similar plan for reducing the power of Tipu to such a condition, as shall render him unable to avail himself of the solicited assistance of France, or of any other collateral aid which the course of future circumstances may offer to him for the prosecution of his declared design of expelling the British nation from India. The measure is not the less necessary for the purpose of applying a reasonable check to the rising influence of France in India.

The present state of our army in the opinion of all military men leaves no doubt of the ultimate success of the plan which I have stated; and if its speedy accomplishment had appeared to me as certain as its ultimate success, I should not have hesitated one moment in ordering the movement of the troops for that purpose. But upon consulting the persons most conversant with military details, I found that the actual state of the frontier fortifications of the Carnatic, of the train of artillery, and of the stores of grain and other provisions, was such, as not to admit of any sudden movement of a large force; although it appeared certain, that such a force might be collected within a very short space of time. I also found that the expense of making the necessary preparations would be very heavy, and that the result was likely to lead to a protracted and expensive, although according to every opinion, a successful war.

The present reduced state of the courts of Poona and Hyderabad admitted no hope of immediate assistance from either of those powers; and the embarrassment of our own finances, which had so lately engaged my most serious attention, now pressed with accumulated weight upon my mind. Under all these circumstances, I felt with the utmost degree of pain and regret, that the moment was unfavourable to the adoption of the only measure which promises effectual and permanent security to the territories committed to my charge, and that such a step was absolutely impracticable without a considerable reduction of the commercial investment, attended by all the destructive consequences which such a blow must produce upon the trade of the Company, upon their pecuniary affairs at home, upon the welfare of their subjects in India, and finally upon the general situation of the public revenue and credit of Great Britain. I was also aware of the evil effects which the mere fact of a war breaking out in this quarter might produce in England, under all the anxiety and pressure of the present moment.

These reflections led me to the determination of relinquishing the idea of making an immediate attack upon the possessions of Tipu; but I still felt that our reputation and honour as well as our future security demanded, that I should not suffer his late proceedings to pass without notice; and I am persuaded you will agree with me, that our tacit submission under an insult and injury of so offensive and aggravated a nature would greatly elevate the credit and hopes of Tipu and of France, and occasion a proportionate depression of our influence and consideration in the eyes of our allies and of all the native powers of India. On the other hand, the result of his embassy having only served to expose his treachery, and the weakness of the enemy in this part of the world, a remonstrance of a firm but temperate spirit will be sufficient to satisfy our honour, and to convince the native powers that our moderation alone induces us to abstain from that more vigorous course of which his conduct would furnish the ample justification, and of which our strength ensures the certain success. I have, therefore, called upon Tipu to make a public disavowal of the proceedings of his ambassadors, to declare distinctly the nature of his intentions towards us and our allies, and particularly to explain without disguise the destination of the force raised in the Isle of France and lately landed at Mangalore.[1]

I have communicated the proclamation in question, together with a statement of all the circumstances attending the transaction, to the courts of Poona and Hyderabad, and I have claimed their concurrence in the

[1] *Wellesley*, i, 59; this letter was not sent.

representation to be made to Tipu, and the co-operation of their respective forces in the event of Tipu's refusing to listen to the joint remonstrance of the allies, and of his compelling us to resort to arms.

The experience of Tipu's recent conduct evidently proves that we may be deceived if we found our calculation of his movements upon the ordinary principles of prudence and discretion. It is therefore possible that he may reject our moderate requisition, and suddenly involve us in a war. I have, therefore, thought it prudent to direct the army to be assembled upon the coast of Coromandel, and similar measures of preparation to be made at Bombay, but with no intention of applying any part of this force in active operations unless Tipu should either refuse to make the required explanation, or should at once commence war against our possessions. The nature of the present crisis appears, however, both to demand and to favour the execution of further measures of precaution, which will afford additional security to us in the event of war, and which may contribute to avert that calamity.

In my letters *no. 1* and *2* dispatched by Admiral Pringle from the Cape of Good Hope, I submitted to you my apprehensions with respect to the declining state of our alliance in India, and to the unfavourable change which had taken place in the relative situations of the several states of India with reference to our interests; and above all I warned you of the growing influence of France in the armies and councils of the native powers. I now feel the weight of the evil which I then anticipated. With a due confidence in the single strength of our own armies, we must acknowledge, that without the co-operation of the Marathas and the nizam, and particularly of the latter, at least to the extent of facilitating our convoys of provisions and stores, a protracted campaign in Mysore would be attended with great difficulty, if not with danger. The situation of the courts of Poona and Hyderabad is become much more alarming than I stated it to be in my letters from the Cape. If Tipu were to attack us in the present moment, we could derive no assistance whatever either from the nizam or from the peshwa; both those powers in their actual condition being utterly disqualified from fulfilling their defensive engagements with us. Sindhia, who with the greater part of his army has been for a long time in the neighbourhood of Poona, has imprisoned Nana Fadnavis, has usurped the whole authority of the peshwa (leaving however his person at liberty), and at the same time has threatened the dominions of the nizam. In the meanwhile, the French army at Hyderabad has been augmented to the number of 14,000 men; and although the death of Monsieur Raymond, and the resumption of the jaghir granted for the maintenance of the army, have to a certain degree reduced the political power of this faction, yet the command having been conferred on another Frenchman, and the numbers of the corps greatly increased, and its discipline considerably improved, the French party at Hyderabad cannot be said to be in any degree less formidable to the independence of the nizam or to our interests than I represented it to be in my letters from the Cape. And I learn by letters received this day from the resident at Hyderabad that since Monsieur Piron has taken the command, numbers of French officers have been added to it, and more are expected, although the routes by which they are introduced into the Deccan are yet unknown. The danger to be apprehended from this party is much aggravated by two circumstances which have recently happened. The one that Sindhia had placed the corps lately commanded by Monsieur de Boigne in the hands of a Frenchman; the other that Tipu Sultan (who was supposed to have been apprehensive of the growth of a French faction at Seringapatam) had manifested a disposition to admit French officers and privates to an unlimited extent into his service. It is probable that the expectation of crushing the nizam and the peshwa, by a co-operation with the French officers in the armies of the nizam and of Sindhia, as well as the hope of founding upon the ruins of the courts of Poona and Hyderabad an influence which might rival if not destroy the British power, may have reconciled Tipu to the perilous experiment of cultivating French principles in an Asiatic court. Azim ul Umra, the nizam's minister, is fully aware of the present danger of the nizam's dominions, exposed to the attack of Sindhia on the one side, and to the intrigues of the French faction on the other, and he has repeatedly applied for an increase of the British detachment serving with the nizam, promising that our agreement to that increase shall be immediately followed by the dismission of the whole of Piron's corps. A common apprehension of the designs of Sindhia has produced an union of interests between the courts of Poona and Hyderabad, and negotiations have been in agitation with a view to their mutual security against that danger which threatens equal destruction to both. On the other hand, the peshwa has expressed his desire to enter into new engagements with us; and the resident at Poona has declared, that if, under the circumstances of Tipu's preparations, it were thought advisable to send a British detachment to Poona, Sindhia could not on any just ground object to such a movement, and that the mere presence of a British force would effectually restore the power and authority of the peshwa. There can be no doubt that the inefficient state of our alliances has been one main ground of Tipu's late proceedings, and this circumstance may account in some degree for the audacious and confident spirit which marks the character of those measures. In the present posture of affairs, the position of Sindhia's army operates as an effectual check upon the motions of both our allies, and prevents either from affording us that assistance to which we are entitled by treaty. Thus Sindhia in reality renders the most useful service to Tipu, and frustrates the whole object of our defensive alliance. In the meanwhile, dissensions have broken out in the army of Sindhia, whose violence, impetuosity, and injustice, have disgusted all the ancient connections of his family. His dominions upon the north-western frontier of India are in a state approaching to general revolt; and although, in the present weakness of the internal governments of the nizam and of the peshwa, Sindhia is viewed with terror by both, there is no doubt that he is not in a condition to oppose any measures which we might think it necessary to take for restoring the consideration and strength of either; and it is more than probable that the result of such measures would be, to restrain his projects of aggrandizement and ambition, and to induce him to return peaceably into his own dominions. In this conjuncture, therefore, neither the nizam nor the peshwa are likely to view with any jealousy the assistance which we might choose to afford to either; while any opposition to such an arrangement on the part of Sindhia would be wholly unjustifiable and ineffectual. The enlargement of our subsidiary engagements with the nizam, and the conclusion of similar engagements with the peshwa under similar restrictions, confined to the case of defence against Tipu, would have been justifiable measures under any circumstances; but the aggression of Tipu places the arrangement on the most impregnable grounds of justice as with respect to Sindhia or any other power, while the accidental coincidence of the interests of the peshwa and of the nizam affords a reasonable expectation of success.

Under all these circumstances, I have thought it advisable to give to the residents at Poona and Hyderabad a power of requiring a body of troops from Bombay and Madras, directing that the dismission of the French army at Hyderabad should be a necessary condition of the increase of the British detachment at the nizam's court, and connecting the whole arrangement with various advantages which we may hope to secure by a new system of treaty, both with the nizam and with the peshwa; and I have further ordered, that no step towards a new arrangement should be taken at either court, without the previous consent and approbation of the other, and without their mutual acceptance of my arbitration for the final adjustment of all subsisting differences between them. It was necessary on this occasion to instruct the resident at Hyderabad with respect to the succession to the nizam's throne in the event of his Highness' death. As the nizam has lately admitted Secundar Jah, his eldest son, to the personal exercise of certain acts of sovereignty, which admission is deemed at that court a virtual nomination to the succession; as Secundar Jah is a friend to the British interests; and as none of the younger sons can reach the throne by any other means than by the assistance of the French and Tipu (with whom they are intimately connected), and by the total destruction of our influence at Hyderabad; I have directed the resident to support the right of Secundar

Jah. The detail of the principles of this decision will be forwarded to you by the next dispatch.

Overtures of the most friendly nature have been made to this government by the rajah of Berar, who has entered into engagements with the nizam for the purpose of restraining the ambitions of Sindhia. Without deciding at present how far it may be advisable to cultivate a closer connection with the rajah of Berar, it is my intention to send an ambassador to his court with the double view of ascertaining his precise objects, and of checking the motions of Sindhia; who will take alarm, whenever the news shall reach him of any intercourse being established between this government and the rajah of Berar.

I have lately received a letter from Zeman Shah containing a declaration of his intention to invade Hindustan, and a peremptory demand of the assistance of the nawab vizier and of mine for the purpose of delivering Shah Alam[1] from the hands of the Marathas, of restoring him to the throne of Delhi, and of expelling the Marathas from their possessions on the northwestern frontier of India. It is very difficult to form a conjecture with respect to the probability of Zeman Shah's being able to execute his romantic design. That he entertains such a design is unquestionable; and whatever may be the result, it is prudent to be on our guard, and in the meanwhile to derive every collateral advantage from his declaration.

I have, therefore, transmitted the shah's letter to Sindhia through the resident at Poona, with the view of suggesting to Sindhia the possible danger to his hereditary dominions; and I have expressed my entire disapprobation of the ambitious projects of Zeman Shah, and my disposition to enter into defensive engagements with Sindhia for the purpose of frustrating the threatened invasion; declaring to Sindhia, that, whenever he shall return into his own dominions, he will find the British resident at his durbar prepared to conclude such a defensive treaty, in which it is my wish to include all the allies of the British government. I have also signified to Sindhia in the most amicable terms my desire to witness his prosperity within the limits of his own dominions. As Sindhia must be perfectly aware of the disturbed state of his dominions, and must know that we hold his fate in our hands, I have every reason to hope that the accomplishment of my endeavours to restore our allies to the power of fulfilling their engagements with us will not be delayed by any opposition from him. But feeling the great importance of preventing the destruction of the power of the peshwa and of the nizam, whose dominions in the event of Sindhia's success would immediately be divided between Sindhia, Tipu, and the French, and whose ruin would furnish the most solid foundation for the

---

[1] Shah Alam II (1728–1806); mogul emperor, 1759–1806; since 1771, a pensioner of the Marathas.

power of the latter, I have directed the resident at Poona, if pacific representations should be rejected by Sindhia, to inform him, that the British force will be employed for the protection of the person and support of the authority of the peshwa; and if necessity should demand the employment of the force for those purposes, I have authorized that measure, provided in the opinion of the commanding officer of the detachment the force should be deemed adequate to the service required. I trust, however, that no such necessity will occur, and that Sindhia's sense of his perilous situation and real interest, added to the state of his army and of his dominions, will induce him to abandon his project of annihilating our allies. I therefore hope that, in the course of a few months, I shall have the satisfaction to find, that the result of these arrangements will have produced a considerable check to the growing influence of France in India; will have effected the re-establishment of our allies in some degree of credit and efficiency; and will have restored the general balance of power upon the foundations on which it stood at the conclusion of the treaty of Seringapatam.

In any view the effect of such a change in the face of affairs must be favourable to us; it may induce Tipu to postpone the execution of his comprehensive plans of vengeance; or if not, it will enable us to frustrate them with more facility and dispatch.

A full detail of my communications with Tipu, with Sindhia, and with the courts of Hyderabad and Poona, together with a more particular statement of the principles upon which the whole arrangement is founded, will be dispatched overland by express to the secret committee in the course of a few days. In the meanwhile, I thought it would afford you satisfaction to receive by the earliest opportunity the general outline of the system which I have deemed it my duty to pursue.

While Tipu shall possess the means of a ready intercourse with the French by sea, our possessions in the peninsula of India must for ever be exposed to alarm and danger, unless we are always careful to maintain our preparations for war in such an advanced state, as will at any moment afford us the facility of sudden and rapid movements of our military force. I have therefore directed the government of Fort St George to take immediate measures for placing in a respectable posture such of the frontier fortresses of the Carnatic as Lord Cornwallis directed to be maintained; and I have ordered that a provision of grain sufficient to maintain a large army in the field for three months be constantly stored in these fortresses; and that monthly returns of their state be forwarded to me. I have also ordered that a large train of artillery be immediately provided, and constantly kept in readiness for use in the field, either at Arnee or Vellore, and that periodical reports of the condition of this train of artillery be made to me.

I propose that these two regulations (although they must be the sources of considerable expense) should be permanent, until some material variation shall take place either in the appearance of affairs in Europe or in India.

Having thus submitted to you the general view of the steps which I have taken for providing against the event of a war with Tipu, I should think myself guilty of a breach both of public duty and of private friendship if I withheld my conscientious opinion, that the interests of the Company in India can never be secure, while Tipu Sultan shall retain the ready means of intercourse by sea with the French government.

His remaining territory on the coast of Malabar is his most powerful instrument of war; and in my decided judgement, it would be the most economical policy which could be adopted, to seize the first just occasion of depriving him of so formidable an engine of hostility, even at the sacrifice of a temporary suspension of the investment, and of a considerable present expense. Upon this important subject I wish to receive your instructions without delay: if the war should continue in Europe, there is little doubt that the impetuosity of Tipu will afford frequent justifiable opportunities to this government of reducing his power. My wish is to know distinctly, whether the Company be prepared to encounter the temporary inconvenience which must be endured before they can attain permanent security for their possessions in India. The orders of the court of directors and the opinions of this government have uniformly concurred in declaring, that 'the landing of any *considerable* French force in Tipu's country must be the signal for our attack upon him'.

I wish to know exactly whether the term *considerable* (which I observe constantly used) is to be construed as a limitation of my discretion. It appears to me that the landing of *any* French force in Tipu's country is a sufficient ground of war upon every principle both of justice and of policy; but more especially after the public declaration which he has made of his designs against our possessions. Any other construction will compel this government to remain an inactive spectator of his preparations for war in conjunction with France, provided only that those preparations be made gradually, and that the French force be introduced into his country in small detachments.

The systematic introduction of French officers into the service of all the native powers of India (which Mr Wickham describes as the fixed policy of France) has been pursued with unremitting assiduity and extensive success. If Tipu should at any time be enabled to derive succour from France, his movements might be seconded by the general co-operation of large bodies of French adventurers, who are known to maintain a correspondence and concert in all parts of India.

The destruction of the French army at Hyderabad would certainly operate as a considerable check to the growth of this formidable evil; the corps of Piron being the main spring of all the designs of the French party in India. But the only effectual barrier against the irruption of France into India, would be our possession of the whole of Tipu's maritime territory.

By this dispatch I have forwarded to the secret committee the detail of my proceedings with respect to Tanjore and to the state of our finances. I refer you to my minutes on both those subjects, and I request your early and most serious attention to the latter, particularly to the measures which I have recommended for increasing the export of British manufactures to India, and for furnishing a large annual supply in bullion to this presidency, leaving to us a proportionate part of the supply to China through the medium of the trade in opium.

Intelligence has reached me from various quarters which leaves no doubt that the government of the Isle of France has expelled the whole of the regular army, and all the partizans of the Executive Directory; that the squadron of frigates, which had also done so much mischief in these seas, had also been compelled to quit the ports of the island, and is gone partly to Europe, and partly to Batavia; and that the inhabitants of the Isle of France were resolved to oppose the landing of any force from France, an armanent being shortly expected from thence for the reduction of the island. My information further states, though not quite so positively, that there had been a friendly communication between our squadron from the Cape, lately cruising off the Mauritius, and the government of the island.

The annexed report of the colonial assembly of the island contradicts the idea of any favourable disposition towards us; but this may only be a disguise to cover the real design of the government until it shall be ripe for execution. You have probably received more accurate intelligence on this subject from the Cape. The whole island is now in arms, and (unless by a voluntary cession) I apprehend could not fall into our hands. The possibility of hostilities with Tipu renders it imprudent for me at present to give any assistance in the reduction of the Mauritius, but I deem that measure to be an object of the utmost importance to the security of India; and I know nothing that would tend so much to lessen the influence of France in this quarter, by abating the exalted notions now entertained of her invincible power. In the present state of the Mauritius, it seems certain that Tipu cannot expect any further assistance from that quarter, but I should not be surprised if the earnestness of his application to the Executive Directory, seconded by the effect of the proclamation issued by M. Malartic, were to produce an effort in his favour from France.

Believe me, . . .

M[ORNINGTON]

63

IX

The Rt Hon. Henry Dundas to the Earl of Mornington

13 August 1798, Whitehall
Private: no. 3

My dear Lord

I have been duly favoured with your Lordship's very important letters from the Cape of Good Hope of the following dates: (*no.1*) 23 February, (*no. 2*) 28 February, and (*no. 3*) 7 March 1798.

In my secret letter of the 16th of June last, I wrote your Lordship very fully on the subject of the hostile views of Tipu Sultan, as they had been stated to us by recent dispatches from the Cape, and also relative to the armament fitted out from Toulon, under the command of General Bonaparte. I at the same time enclosed a copy of a proclamation said to be issued by the governor of Mauritius, as well as the latest intelligence relative to the expedition above alluded to, by which it appeared that Egypt and India were the ultimate objects of the great preparations that had been made. Having in that letter fully detailed the measures proposed to be adopted at home, and pointed out such as appeared to be proper to be carried into execution by your Lordship in India, I shall not at present enter into any further detail on those subjects, but shall content myself with referring you to the dispatches you will receive by this conveyance through the secret committee, for a detail of the measures adopted by government for the better security of our Indian possessions.

In my letter of 16th June I observed that I had, to a certain extent, given your Lordship my opinion upon part of the subjects to which you had called my attention in your dispatches from the Cape, and stated my intention of reserving my sentiments on other matters of detail and of a less pressing nature for some future conveyance. This I intended doing by the present opportunity, but as the ships are to be dispatched immediately, and of which I was not informed till this morning, it is my intention to answer those letters, as well as any I may receive in the meantime, by the first ships of the ensuing season.

I am anxious to hear of your safe arrival in India, and of your having entered upon the very important functions committed to your charge, and in which I most cordially wish you success.

My dear Lord, yours, . . .

HENRY DUNDAS

X

The Earl of Mornington to the Rt Hon. Henry Dundas

24 August 1798, Fort William
Private: no. 7

My dear Sir

I have transmitted to the secret committee by this dispatch the several papers to which I referred you in my letter *no. 6*, dated 6th July.

I request that you will have the goodness to read them all in the order in which they are given in the list of the packet, being most anxious to meet your approbation in the discharge of the very arduous duties, which have demanded my attention at this early period of my government.

Intending to forward duplicates of those papers by the ship *Eurydice* now under dispatch, and at the same time to write fully to you on that subject, as well as on other topics, I shall add a very few lines to this letter.

You will observe that the only material variation between the ideas stated in my letter to you *no. 6*, and in my minute of the 12th of August, is the nature and time of the demand to be made by the allies from Tipu. This variation will be accounted for in my letter by the *Eurydice*.

My last accounts from Fort St George state that Tipu's army is gone into cantonment, and the sultan returns to Seringapatam. Since the failure of his embassy to the Isle of France his lofty tone is much abated; this evidently appears in his last letter to me on the subject of Wynaad. He will not interrupt the revival of our alliances. I refer you to my letter to the secret committee for the state of the negotiations at Poona and Hyderabad.[1]

The rumours of Zeman Shah's intended invasion gain additional credit. The return of Sindhia to his dominions (an event which I have now little doubt of being able to accomplish) will be the most effectual check to the shah's approach. I refer you to the printed papers forwarded by this dispatch, and to my letters to court of directors and to Mr Pitt, for an account of the voluntary contributions for the public service subscribed at this presidency.

It is impossible to speak in terms sufficiently strong of the unanimous spirit of loyalty and public zeal in these provinces. I am convinced that there is scarcely a man in the whole country who would not risk everything in the present contest.

Lord Clive was not arrived at Fort St George on the 9th of August, nor has any account of him reached India since the *Princess Charlotte* left him in latitude 10 South, of[f] the westward side of the Cape.

M[ORNINGTON]

[1] I.O.L/PS/5/23, p. 53.

XI

The Earl of Mornington to the Rt Hon. Henry Dundas

4 September 1798, Fort William
Private: no. 8

My dear Sir

Considerable difficulty and inconvenience are felt in the public service here from the want of early, regular, and authentic, information of the state of political affairs in Europe, and of the opinions entertained by his Majesty's ministers with regard to the designs of the enemy.

The want of such information appears to have been the cause of the relinquishment of the Manila expedition, under a false apprehension of the approach of a French squadron to these seas.

A similar defect of information leaves me in doubt whether a part, if not the whole, of the French fleet fitted out in the Mediterranean in the month of April last, may not be destined for India, not through Egypt, but by the ordinary passage of the Cape of Good Hope.

The sense of the embarrassments which must perpetually arise from such a state of uncertainty, induces me to suggest to you a plan for conveying intelligence to the British governments in India with such regularity and dispatch as shall keep them constantly apprized of the state of those circumstances, events, and opinions, by a timely knowledge of which the measures for the defence of these possessions may be regulated according to correct principles.

The system recently established for the overland dispatches to India now affords an opportunity of monthly communication between the government at home and those in this quarter. I submit to your consideration, whether it might not be advisable that your private secretary should transmit to me every month, by the overland dispatch, a short statement of all such events and movements, or preparations, of the enemy in Europe, as appear likely in your opinion to have any influence upon the safety of the British possessions in India.

This statement ought to be further extended to the desirable object of preventing any false apprehensions which might be formed in India with regard to preparations of the enemy, which you might know to have no connection with any design against this part of the world.

Your bulletin should therefore not only warn us of any intended attack, but explain the supposed object (according to your opinion) of any great naval preparations in the enemy's ports. To this should be added an intimation of any intended reinforcement either of the navy or army in India.

My wish is that your private secretary's communication should be made uniformly every month, although no important public event should have occurred in the preceding, or appear likely to occur in the ensuing month; it being often desirable to know that no material change is likely to take place in the state of political affairs.

Your private secretary could transmit copies or extracts from this information, according as you might think it expedient, to the governments of Fort St George and Bombay. The whole of this communication should be disguised in cypher.

A weekly newspaper is published in London, containing an abstract of all the intelligence of the preceeding week. It would be very useful to us here if the secretary to the court of directors, or to the board of commissioners for the affairs of India, were ordered to dispatch this newspaper to the three presidencies by every monthly packet.

I request your early and serious attention to these suggestions, as I am convinced that considerable public benefit would result from the immediate adoption of the plan which I have proposed.

The intercourse overland under the improved system of dispatch will become much more frequent than it has hitherto been, and will necessarily lead to the communication by that conveyance of some of those voluminous papers which have hitherto been reserved for the dispatches by the ships. In order to facilitate this intercourse, it would be desirable to introduce an abbreviated cypher into common use.

Our cypher no. 11, now commonly used, exactly doubles the size of every dispatch, and is besides so clumsily constructed as to be very liable to discovery.

I therefore wish that you would recommend it to the secret committee of the court of directors to furnish us as soon as possible with a new cypher, which shall be exempt from the defects of that now in use.

M[ORNINGTON]

XII

The Earl of Mornington to the Rt Hon. Henry Dundas

1 October 1798, Fort William
Secret and Confidential: no. 1

My dear Dundas
Having an opportunity of forwarding a letter to you by a conveyance on the security of which I can rely, I propose to lay before you some account

of the internal condition of this government as I found it at my arrival, and to add such suggestions as have occurred to me with relation to the present state of the council, and of other great branches of the administration. Sir John Shore is a man of great integrity, of considerable knowledge in the affairs of these provinces, and of very respectable talents; but the circumstance of his having been originally a Company's servant, and the facility of his temper and simplicity of his disposition, tended to weaken his authority, and to impair the vigour as well as the dignity of the government in his hands. It was not possible for him to maintain the consideration, which the station of governor-general requires, among persons with whom he had passed the greater part of his life on a footing of equality, and who were acquainted with all the little circumstances of his private character; which (however amiable and honourable) was not in every point calculated to restrain familiarity.[1]

The effect of these circumstances was to reduce the office of governor-general in the estimation of the settlement to a level little higher than that of the senior civil servant at this presidency. All the advantages which had been derived from the high authority and rank of Lord Cornwallis were entirely lost, and the efficiency and even the purity of the administration were considerably affected. Although I had learned something of the real state of this government during my passage, and during my continuance at the Cape and at Madras, I could not credit the extent of the mischief which it had produced here, if I had not felt those mischiefs severely in my own person, and if I did not every day trace them in every department of the public service.

One of the most singular, incredible, and dangerous, of these evil consequences is, that Mr Speke[2] has possessed an almost unlimited influence, not only in the distribution of the patronage, but in the formation of the most important measures of the government for the last three years. Mr Cowper[3] has so connected himself with Mr Speke, that they may be considered as one and the same person, acting entirely from the opinion of Mr Speke; to which Mr Cowper is so absolutely subservient, that it has happened to me more than once to have obtained Mr Cowper's decided opinion after full discussion on an important question, and to have seen that opinion completely changed by a slight intimation from Mr Speke. This strict union gave Mr Speke and Mr Cowper a decided advantage over the candid and artless character of Sir John Shore; and it is a certain fact that

[1] To Grenville, Mornington was more outspoken: 'His low birth, vulgar manners, and Eastern habits, as well as his education in the Company's service, . . . added to indolence, timidity, and bad health, contributed to relax every spring of this government from one extremity of the empire to the other.' *Dropmore*, iv, 381.
[2] Peter Speke; member of the supreme council, 1789–1801.
[3] William Cowper; member of the supreme council, 1790–1801.

they governed him, almost without his knowledge, but so notoriously in the eyes of the whole settlement, that no candidate for office thought himself likely to succeed, and few did succeed, without previously canvassing Mr Speke and Mr Cowper. That this was the case I obtain hourly proof; since scarcely a servant of the company applies to me for promotion without either boasting of the support of these gentlemen, or lamenting the want of it, or complaining of its exclusive and overbearing influence in all promotions under the late government.

You cannot be unacquainted with the character of Mr Speke. I am far from wishing to injure his reputation; and I understand that he is humane, generous, and honourable in private life. But of all the men I ever met (although not without a certain degree of parts), he is the most unfit to influence the government of any country, and above all governments of this, and above all parts of this government, that which relates to the distribution of patronage, and to the just selection of persons properly qualified for the public service. I refer you to Lord Cornwallis (indeed I believe I might even refer you to Sir John Shore) for the description of those strange defects in Mr Speke's character which entirely disqualify him for the conduct of any branch of this government. Mr Cowper is a man more fit for business; but I perceive nothing in his talents, knowledge, or industry, that would induce me to consider him in any superior light, if he were not so advantageously contrasted with his colleague. I have, however, already stated that Mr Cowper has submitted himself entirely to the guidance of Mr Speke. This coalition has filled all the offices in almost every department (but principally in the judicial) with the most improper and unqualified persons. The whole of the patronage has been distributed according to a regular system of interest and intrigue. Several instances have already occurred since my arrival, in which the nominees of these gentlemen have brought themselves and their patrons to disgrace. Two remarkable cases are those of Mr Hasilby, commercial resident at Comercolly (whom I have dismissed from his employment and suspended from the service for gross fraud and oppression), and of Mr Shakspeare, collector of the customs at Benares; both introduced into their offices by the influence of Messrs Speke and Cowper. This system has collected a sort of party about Messrs Speke and Cowper, consisting as well of expectants, as of the obliged and their friends.

The party is connected with another, from which it has derived no inconsiderable strength, that of Mr Pattle,[1] who possessed great influence with Sir John Shore, notwithstanding the violent contrast between the notorious profligacy of Mr Pattle's morals, and the real virtues of Sir John Shore. Mr Pattle, you will recollect, was sent out by the court of directors to

---

[1] James Pattle; register of the provincial court of circuit and appeal, Murshedebad, 1798–1802.

repair the losses of his gambling and debauchery in England at their expense in India. From his numerous family and connections established in India, and from his supposed favour at home, he has acted a distinguished part here during the last government, and (connected with Messrs Speke and Cowper) has had a large share in the distribution of office; insomuch that the 'interest of the Pattle family' (the term in familiar use) was deemed a powerful recommendation, and has been actually stated to me as such by more than one candidate for office. Mr Pattle has been most improperly placed in one of the most responsible stations in the province, paymaster of the nizamut stipends at Murshedabad. With this situation he also holds the office of chief judge of the provincial court of circuit and appeal for the same district, offices for which he is eminently disqualified by every possible defect of character, talents, and knowledge. This was one of the promotions of Sir John Shore.

Mr Pattle's passion for gaming continues unabated, and prevails to such a degree, that the other day one of his sons came from China to Calcutta, with a considerable sum of money in his pockets; the father induced the son to play, won all his money, and sent him back penniless to Canton. Of Mr Pattle's gratitude to his respectable patron I have ascertained the extent; having lately discovered, that he was deeply concerned in an intrigue with the ministers of the vizier for the purpose of overturning the credit of the resident at Lucknow, placed there by Sir John Shore. The final object of this intrigue was to force Mr Pattle upon Sir John Shore through the influence of the vizier and of his ministers; and to compel Sir John Shore to appoint Mr Pattle resident at Lucknow in the room of Mr Lumsden.[1] This machination was attended by circumstances, which, if they should be established by public proof, will compel me to proceed to measures of severity against Mr Pattle.

The faction created in this presidency by the combinations which I have described, was much discontented by my arrival. I am thoroughly convinced, that if I had arrived with a provisional appointment, they would have persuaded Sir John Shore to remain in the government for a long period; and thus would have accomplished the object, either of driving me out of the country, or of degrading my personal influence and authority in the commencement of my government. In the two or three first councils which I held, Mr Speke and Mr Cowper used some efforts to preserve the influence which they had exercised for so long a period. They were, however, soon convinced that my determination was to administer the government myself; and, without one harsh word on my part, the limits of our respective powers were established within the first ten days after my

[1] John Lumsden; resident at Lucknow, 1796–9; register of the court of sudder dewany and nizamut adaulat, 1799–1801.

landing. Since that period they have given me no trouble; and to all public appearance we are on the most cordial terms; but I cannot believe that they have parted willingly with so large a share of power, and convinced as I am of their being leagued together upon principles wholly unconnected with the good of the public service, I shall expect from them as much trouble as they may have strength to occasion, whenever any difficulty shall arise. However, I am so confident of my own intentions and of my personal authority, that I have not the slightest apprehension of mischief from any efforts of this faction whilst I can remain at the seat of government. My apprehensions are of a different nature, and I confess they keep me in a continual state of anxiety.

You may recollect with how much earnestness I pressed the provisional appointment of Sir Alured Clarke. I looked to that appointment as an effectual security against the dangerous influence of Mr Speke, in the event of my being called to any of the distant provinces or presidencies, or in any event which might suddenly remove me from the seat of government. You seemed to look with the same degree of confidence to this security. I am concerned to declare to you, that it will entirely fail, whenever necessity shall compel me to resort to it. I find Sir Alured Clarke a most worthy and honourable man, with a very amiable disposition, and a most sincere inclination to co-operate with me; I really feel great regard and esteem for him, and we have agreed most cordially on every occasion since my arrival in Bengal. But I must not disguise the truth; I have been entirely disappointed in my expectation of his fitness to hold this arduous government even provisionally. Some peculiarities of manner and trivial prejudices which he is apt to indulge have exposed him to ridicule and impaired his authority. He is not respected here to the degree that his intrinsic worth deserves.

In addition to this misfortune, he has not acquired such a knowledge of the business of this government as to enable him to act with any degree of confidence in it; and his ignorance in this respect is notorious to the whole settlement, and is avowed by himself. But his greatest misfortune is the decided influence which Mr Speke and Mr Cowper have acquired over him in the council; partly by the knowledge of some trifling details, not familiar to him, and partly by the advantage of always acting in concert. Sir Alured has no regard or esteem for either of those gentlemen, and has often complained to me of their mysterious and uncandid proceedings. Yet from want of local knowledge and of firmness, he is utterly unequal to contend any point with them, and therefore yields implicitly to their suggestions excepting in cases where I choose to interfere. On the other hand, I am sorry to observe, that they treat him with the most marked disrespect, and in a style wholly unsuited to his rank and gentlemanlike manners.

Under all these circumstances, I feel, that if the government were to devolve into Sir Alured's hands, the influence of which you, and the court of directors, and I, dread the effects, would be very likely to prevail; at all events, neither the talents, knowledge, nor authority, of Sir Alured Clarke are sufficient to enable him (without considerable assistance) to preserve this extensive and intricate government from confusion even for a short period of time.

With this scene before my eyes, I am afraid to stir from the presidency; and I dread the slightest symptoms of indisposition, lest the valuable interests committed to my charge should be exposed to hazard by my illness or death. The objections to giving the provisional appointment to any governor of Madras are in my mind insuperable; and Lord Clive is yet an untried man. The only expedient which occurs to me for securing the due administration of this government in all cases, is to substitute efficient and upright councillors, of respectable characters, and of correct views, in the place of Messrs Speke and Cowper. Until this measure shall be adopted, it will be utterly impossible to answer for the stability of the wise system of government established, under your direction, in the Company's possessions. With an efficient and upright council, the government would be safe in the hands of a person of less capacity than Sir Alured Clarke, and my mind would be at ease in any event which might happen to me.

I therefore recommend it to you in the most earnest manner to remove both the present councillors without delay. If you allow either of them to remain in the council, you will leave with him the seeds of faction, intrigue, and of incorrect principles of government, as well as of inefficiency and weakness in the administration of public business. The distressed circumstances of Mr Speke will require a pension; and I think it would be a very harsh measure to remove him without some effectual provision of that nature. Mr Cowper will also, I suppose, expect some such mark of favour; an annual charge of four thousand pounds would I imagine cover both pensions. The Company would be a considerable gainer by such an arrangement, even if an additional charge shall be incurred to that amount: but I am much mistaken, if I shall not be able to provide funds for this purpose without any increase of expense.

It is my duty now to mention to you the names of those who appear to me to be most fit to fill the places of Messrs Speke and Cowper, if these gentlemen should be removed.

On this part of the subject, I have no hesitation; and I am persuaded that there is not an impartial opinion in India, which would not at once point out Mr Barlow and Mr Bebb,[1] as the persons in this settlement best

---

[1] John Bebb; 3rd member, board of trade, Bengal, 1790–9; chairman, 1817.

qualified by talents, knowledge, reputation, and integrity, to fill the station of councillors of Bengal.

Mr Barlow is completely master of the political state of India, and of the whole system of the revenue of Bengal connected with the administration of justice. He drew the original regulations on which that system is founded. He is also thoroughly well acquainted with the affairs of the subordinate presidencies, and of all our dependencies; and upon the whole possesses a more comprehensive knowledge of the details of this government than any civil servant in the settlement. His judgement, discretion, temper, morals, and integrity, are universally acknowledged. Lord Cornwallis, I have no doubt, has repeatedly described his character to you. I feel myself bound by every sentiment of public duty, and by my regard for you, to declare, that Mr Barlow has even surpassed my expectations; and that I never met with a man of more worth in any part of the world.

To Mr Bebb the Company has owed for several years the success of their commercial investment from Bengal. He is a man of very general knowledge, and of the most unblemished integrity. No man in the commercial department can stand in competition with him on any ground. He has also the advantage, which Mr Barlow so eminently possesses, of being an object of respect to the whole settlement from the general tenor of his morals and conduct. With these gentlemen in the council, the two great branches of public business would be placed under the immediate superintendence of the persons best qualified to direct them.

Mr Barlow might take the department of the revenue, connected with the administration of justice, and might preside in the court of sudder dewany and nizamut adaulat.

Mr Bebb might take the commercial department.

Under such an arrangement, whoever might be governor-general would feel confident of his government, whenever his duty might call him to any distance from the presidency; and even his sudden death would not expose the interests of the Company to risk.

I am aware that Mr Graham[1] has a species of claim to succeed to the council in the event of any vacancy; but although I think Mr Graham would certainly be preferred to either of the present members of council (under all the circumstances to which I have adverted), I cannot be of opinion that he is by any means qualified for the station of councillor. His understanding is of a very inferior cast, his knowledge limited, and the application of it embarrassed by a want of perspecuity. He is not much respected, although I do not believe there is any sort of foundation for a suspicion of his integrity; but he is connected with some natives of bad

---

[1] Thomas Graham; senior member, board of revenue, Bengal, 1793–1807; member of the supreme council, 1801.

character. Compared with Mr Barlow or with Mr Bebb, no man who wishes for the prosperity of the public service would think of preferring Mr Graham for the council; and my sincere conviction is, that the public service would receive benefit by the revocation of Mr Graham's provisional appointment, if that appointment be still supposed to have any effect.

In a letter from the Cape I mentioned Mr Duncan of Bombay as a proper person for the council here; but from what I have seen of his correspondence and learned of his character at Fort St George and here, I must retreat that opinion. He is an honest man conversant with details of revenue; but the extreme confusion of his understanding (evident in his correspondence), his perpetual state of nervous anxiety in the most trifling subjects, and above all the facility with which persons of bad character obtain an ascendant over him, would render him an useless if not an irksome assessor in council.

Mr Bebb had made up his mind to return to England in the course of the next winter. Feeling the inestimable value of his services to the Company in the provision of the investment, and in the general management of the commercial concerns of the Company at this presidency, I have prevailed upon him to remain one year longer in Bengal, provided his health shall not require a voyage to Europe. If his health should admit of his continuance in this climate, I have little doubt that the offer of a seat in council would induce him to remain here for some time longer. In the event of Mr Bebb being called to Europe by the state of his health, I know no person in Bengal who possesses an equal degree of commercial information and character. Perhaps you could prevail on Mr Charles Grant[1] to take the commercial department in council here; if not, I would then recommend that Mr Harington,[2] now register of the supreme courts of appeal, should be brought into the council. Mr Harington is a man of excellent talents, and of the most unblemished integrity; he is very conversant with the general details of this government, having been sub-secretary for a considerable time; he stands next to Mr Barlow and Mr Bebb in general estimation, and is far superior in every respect to either of the present members of council, or to Mr Graham and Mr Duncan.

If the two civil members of council should be Mr Barlow and Mr Harington, my intention is to bring Mr Udny[3] (whose character you will learn from Mr Charles Grant) to the board of trade. Mr Bebb assures me that under Mr Udny's management the commercial concerns of the

---

[1] Charles Grant (1746–1823); director, Indian interest; chairman, 1805, 1809, 1815; noted philanthropist.
[2] John Herbert Harington; register of the court of sudder dewany and nizamut adaulat, 1796–9; 4th member, board of revenue, Bengal, 1799–1801.
[3] George Udny; commercial resident at Mauldah, 1787–99; 4th member, board of trade, Bengal, 1799–1801; member of the supreme council, 1801–7.

Company will be quite safe. Mr Udny has not yet been sufficiently distinguished in the service to be introduced into council. Under my first suggestion
the arrangement would be as follows.

Mr Barlow and Mr Bebb councillors.

Mr Harington to succeed Mr Barlow as secretary to the government.

Mr Udny to succeed Mr Bebb at the board of trade.

In the event of Mr Bebb's return to Europe—Mr Harington councillor,
Mr Lumsden, now resident at Lucknow (for which he is very unfit though
a good man of business), secretary to the government in the room of Mr
Harington. Mr Stuart (deputy register to Mr Harington, a young man of
great merit) would become principal register to the supreme courts of
appeal.

In this latter case, I must rely principally on Mr Udny, under my own
immediate direction, for the care of the commercial concerns of this
presidency.

Hitherto, I have urged the necessity of providing a more efficient council
merely with a view to the cases of my absence from the presidency, or of my
illness or death. I now wish to draw your attention to those considerations
which appear to me to demand the same measures even with a view to the
ordinary dispatch of public business during my presence at the presidency.

The ordinary business of the council is greatly increased since the
government of Lord Cornwallis, partly by the natural operation of the
regulations introduced by him, and partly by other circumstances. The
business in the military department has been greatly increased by the new
regulations, by the additional number of King's regiments, and by the
establishment of the board for improving the breed of cattle for the use of
the army. The business in this department cannot be expected to decrease.

In the public department, the business is considerably increased by the
transfer of the departments of salt, opium, and customs, to the board of
trade, who now bring all the details of these subjects before the governor-
general in council. But the principal increase of business in this department
arises from the great addition to the number of ships annually sent by the
Company to Bengal. From seven or eight that number is increased to from
forty to fifty. The establishment of the marine board has also added to the
extent and weight of the correspondence and business in this department.

The business of the revenue department has been diminished in a certain
degree, but not in any proportion to the increase of business in other
departments. The diminution has arisen from the conclusion of the
permanent settlement of the land revenue, and from the transfer of the
management of some branches of revenue, as well as from other arrangements.

In the secret, political, and foreign, departments the business has been much increased, principally by the addition to our territory on the coast of Malabar, and by the possession of the several French and Dutch settlements.

Nearly the whole of the business in the judicial department may be considered as an addition to the business of the council since 1793. In this department all new regulations for the internal government of the country are framed; all the correspondence with the civil and criminal courts, including those established in Benares in 1795, is conducted; and all the numerous references respecting the police are here considered.

The sudder dewany adaulat and nizamut adaulat form the most heavy addition to the business of the supreme council since the year 1793. The access of justice in the subordinate courts being greatly facilitated, the number of suits instituted has increased in proportion, and notwithstanding the regulation limiting the power of appealing to the sudder dewany adaulut to cases of contested property of the value of 5,000 rupees and upwards, the number of appeals has increased. The trials in the law courts being now more regularly conducted, and the evidence being taken more minutely, the proceedings upon the appeal necessarily become more voluminous. The duty of the courts of sudder dewany and nizamut adaulat *alone* would be sufficient to employ the whole time of the judges, especially if that duty were connected, as it ought to be, with the superintendence of the police, which still requires much regulation.

When you add to the mass of the ordinary details of business, the exclusive case of the whole system of the finance in Bengal and in all our possessions; the correspondence with the residents at the courts of the several native powers, including the whole scheme of our political relations in India; the management of Oudh, in which our stake is now become so considerable, as to require unremitting attention from the governor-general himself; and finally the general superintendence of all the concerns of this vast empire, with the charge of its protection and defence; I think you will admit that even in the ordinary administration of this government, supposing my health to continue uninjured, and no circumstance call me from the presidency, the public service must require the aid of an efficient council.

The fact is that Sir John Shore found himself obliged to leave the duties of the sudder dewany and nizamut adaulat entirely to the council; and accordingly they have been discharged during the greater part of his government by Mr Cowper, with the able assistance of Mr Harington, register to the courts. Upon my arrival I determined to preside in the courts regularly, and accordingly I sat for some days; but I found it utterly impracticable, without abandoning my other duties, to give that attention to the causes which could in any degree satisfy my judgement and conscience; and I have therefore been compelled by the pressure of indispensable hourly business to allow the courts of supreme appeal to revert to the management established by Sir John Shore.

I have indeed been further compelled for some time past to entrust much of the ordinary detail of the daily business to the council, constituted as it now is. The state of our finances and of our relations with the native powers, as well as the precautions which I have been obliged to take against the establishment of the French in India, have necessarily occupied too much of my time to admit of my entering as accurately as I could wish into all the details which come before the council. Although I hope that a residence of a few months more in this country may relieve me from much of that pressure which I have described, I cannot reasonably expect that I shall ever be able to give a due attention to the voluminous business of the courts of supreme appeal; and it is also probable that many future conjunctions of political affairs will demand my undivided attention, and will compel me occasionally to rely on the council for dispatch even of the current business of the several departments.

With these opinions I am therefore anxious to provide an efficient council without delay, and I cannot urge this point to you with more earnestness than I feel it. At the same time I think it necessary to apprise you, that I should prefer even the present councillors (whom I know I can prevent from doing mischief while my health shall continue and all circumstances shall allow me to remain on the spot) to any persons sent out from Europe, with whom I am unacquainted, and who, although of more talents and knowledge than my present assessors, might possibly give me more trouble.

In the persons whom I have named in Bengal, I am certain that I should find a cordial and zealous co-operation, while I should derive benefit from their abilities and information. With respect to the sudder dewany and nizamut adaulat it is become absolutely necessary to make some new arrangement. This necessity is evident from the inadequate manner in which the duty of the courts of appeal has been discharged. By referring to the papers annexed to this letter, you will perceive that of seventy appeals depending in 1797 only fourteen were determined within that year, and on the 1st January 1798 the number of appeals depending amounted to one hundred and thirty. By another paper you will find that on the 1st July 1798 the arrear of appeals was increased to one hundred and fifty-two; the number of appeals admitted from January to July having been thirty-four, and the number decided twelve.

I trust that much may be done for the correction of this evil, even as the courts are now constituted, by adopting the plan suggested by the register in the paper no. 2 annexed to this letter. I scarcely entertain a doubt that with a more efficient council the business of the appeals might be very creditably dispatched. If, however, I shall be mistaken, and the evil should become very pressing, it will be necessary to provide a remedy without delay. The first idea which occurred to me was to separate the courts of appeal entirely from the council, and to appoint a chief justice and two judges for the purpose, giving rank to the chief justice of the adaulat next to the King's chief justice, and to the two judges of the adaulat next to the junior judge of the supreme court of Calcutta.

But strong objections may be stated against this alteration. The courts entirely separated from the supreme government might lose a great portion of consideration and respect in the eyes of the natives. The state of the administration of justice in the provinces would no longer be brought under the observation of the government, and it might become difficult for the governor-general to estimate the character and merits of the several judges in the different districts. The judges being no longer under the immediate superintendence of government might become negligent, or the government might, from ignorance, neglect merit, and promote unqualified persons to high judicial stations. To unite, therefore, the objects of efficiency and consideration, it appeared to me that it might be advisable to increase the number of judges of sudder dewany and nizamut adaulat, by adding two assessors to the council when sitting as a court of appeal. With the aid of two assistant judges, I should hope, that any one of the members of council might with ease dispatch all the appeals on the file within the course of each year. An objection to either of these plans would be the additional expense of the salaries of the new judges: but I think that might be nearly met by limiting the number of members at the boards of revenue and trade to *three* instead of *four*, the former number being amply sufficient for any useful purpose. Even if this expedient should be delayed by the continuance in India of all the present members of the two boards, I have every reason to believe that a number of useless offices and abuses of establishments still exist in India, the reform of which will afford ample funds for the salaries of the new judges. A question will arise, whether the governor-general in council now possesses the right by law, either of increasing the number of the judges of the courts of sudder dewany and nizamut adaulat by adding assessors to the council, or of constituting courts distinct from the council vested with the same powers now exercised by the council in its capacity of supreme court of appeal.

The advocate-general is of the opinion that the governor-general in council possesses the right of adopting either plan. He founds his opinion on the act of 21 Geo. III, chapter 70, section 21, which recognizes courts of appeal appointed by the governor-general in council distinct from the council itself. Should the necessity appear for the increase of the number of judges of appeal, I shall not hesitate to appoint them under this law, trusting to you for indemnity if I should have exceeded my powers. In the meanwhile, I trust you will take the whole subject into immediate consideration, and perhaps you may think it expedient by way of precaution to insert in your first new law respecting India a clause for the purpose of removing all doubt with regard to the power of the governor-general in council to constitute courts of sudder dewany and nizamut adaulat by adding assistant judges to sit with the council, or by appointing judges entirely separate from it.

By the report annexed to this letter, and by the statement of civil suits decided and depending, you will be able to form a general idea of the state of the administration of justice here, and you will, I am persuaded, agree with me, that although much improved, it still requires further improvement. This is a subject which will occupy a large share of my attention as soon as I shall be a little more settled. It will be a most serious consideration to ascertain, how far it may be necessary to increase the number of courts in those districts where the accumulation of causes appears to be too heavy for the present judicial establishment.

Having thus opened to you without reserve my sentiments with regard to the existing defects in the council and to the mode of correcting them, I wish to call your attention in the next place to the command and state of the army. Sir Alured Clarke, with many excellent qualities, does not possess that activity and zeal which the present times require. The discipline of the army in Bengal has been much relaxed by the weakness and langour of the late governor-general. It requires a vigorous but at the same time a skilful hand to apply the necessary remedies to a body in such a state as the army of Bengal. The first and most essential improvement will be the establishment of regimental rank. This regulation I hold to be indispensable, and I anxiously expect your determination to carry it into effect. But even after the adoption of this improvement, much will remain to be corrected. An able, active, and firm, but discreet and temperate commander-in-chief is necessary to render this army in any degree an equivalent to the heavy expense which it has entailed on the Company. Sir James Craig[1] is (I believe) a man of ability, activity, and spirit, but I know him to be so deficient in temper and judgement that I should dread the moment when the army was entrusted to his command. Since I have been here I have witnessed such instances of indiscretion, caprice, and ill-temper, in his conduct (although not towards myself—Since I commenced this letter Sir James Craig, notwithstanding my having paid him the most marked and extraordinary attentions, has given vent to his intemperate spirit in a most improper letter addressed to me in council. I have treated his insolence

[1] Maj.-Gen. Sir James Craig (1748–1812); commander-in-chief, Cape of Good Hope, 1796–7; commanding in the Upper Provinces, 1798–1802.

with great moderation and good humour, but, if he should persist, I must be compelled to teach him his duty) as convince me that it would be impossible to carry on the public business with such a commander-in-chief, and that he would be an unfit instrument for the reform of the army. He is, however, respected by the troops under his command; and will always make an excellent second to any commander-in-chief.

In writing to you from Madras, I mentioned General Harris as a person who might be a proper candidate for this station. A more full knowledge of him has led me to doubt his capacity for so great a command. But he is a very honest man, of excellent temper, and of a degree of zeal and activity which cannot be too much commended. Of his conduct on the recent assembling the army on the coast, I shall have an opportunity of writing more fully in my letter to you of this date on the state of the government of Fort St George. I suspect from Sir Alured's conversation of late, that he begins to turn his thoughts homewards. This is the first rainy season which he has passed at Calcutta, and he has complained a good deal of indisposition, and appears to have suffered both in health and spirits. Perhaps the cold season may revive him. Personally, I have every reason to wish for his continuance; and having used every effort to render his situation pleasant to him, I flatter myself that he would willingly remain in India during the period of my government. You will advert, whenever an opportunity shall offer, to these suggestions relating to the chief command in India. If a war should happen in India, I leave it to you to consider whether you would think it advisable to entrust the conduct of it to Sir Alured Clarke. Whatever arrangement you may think it advisable to adopt, I must entreat that you will not afford Sir James Craig the opportunity of displaying his contentious talents in the supreme council.

Before I leave the subject of the army, I must assure you, that I expect no difficulty in carrying into effect any regulation which the government may deem advisable. I am told that some remains of a mutinous spirit are still to be found among the officers in certain corps. I am persuaded that if such a spirit exists at all, it is limited to a very narrow compass; the last voluntary contribution is a sufficient proof of the general temper of the officers.

Having judged it necessary to have a body of troops in readiness to reach the Northern Circars with all possible expedition, before the season would admit of moving by land, I have made the expedient of offering a bounty to such volunteers from the sepoy regiments as might be willing to go by sea to Masulipatam. At this presidency alone, two battalions amounting in the whole to 2,000 men have turned out 300 men. This is a spirit which deserves encouragement; and I am persuaded, that by due encouragement much might be done towards rendering this army more serviceable, in the event of any occasion which may require the embarkation of troops. I mean to reward the volunteers liberally, whether I shall find it necessary thereafter to embark them or not.

Now that I am upon the subject of the army, I may inform you that we are in great want of an efficient military auditor-general. I wish you could prevail on Lord Cornwallis' friend Capt[ain] Robinson[1] to return in the capacity of military auditor-general to Bengal.

I find that I have omitted one circumstance relating to the army which requires your early and serious attention. The Company's European army belonging to the establishment of Bengal has lately been recruited from the Cape of Good Hope. The recruits furnished from that place form about half of the whole European force of the Company at this presidency, and amount to about nine hundred men. These are all foreigners of different nations, but chiefly Dutch and German, and almost all were recruited from the prisoners taken on board the Dutch fleet which was captured in Saldanha Bay by Lord Keith.[2] I leave you to judge what reliance is to be placed on such a force. Sir A[lured] Clarke has told me plainly that he has no confidence in their fidelity. I have stopped the recruiting at the Cape, and I shall take early steps for getting rid of our foreign Europeans; but I fear it must be a work of long time unless you can aid us with a large supply of recruits from England, or abolish the Company's European army altogether; which would be of the greatest benefit to the whole service.

This army is very deficient in artillery. A considerable increase of that establishment is become essentially necessary.

I shall conclude this long letter by calling your attention to some points which appear to me defective in the constitution of the powers of the governor-general in council.

The governor-general in council ought to be the centre of all authority within the British possessions in India. Every other authority should be subject to him, with such limitations in the exercise of his power as may appear advisable. Without this authority it may become utterly impossible for him to preserve general order in time of peace, or to carry on either offensive or defensive war with vigour or effect.

In time of war his general plans for the public security may often require the immediate assistance of the fleet; but at present he possesses no power whatever of commanding its services. It is now mere matter of courtesy and favour in the admiral even to communicate his plans of operation to the governor-general. In Sir John Shore's government it has happened that the

[1] Capt. Sir George Robinson (1758–1832); military auditor-general, Bengal, 1798–1800.
[2] Vice-Adm. George Elphinstone, Lord Keith (1746–1823); flag officer in command, Cape of Good Hope and East Indies, 1795–6; flag officer in command, Mediterranean, 1799–1802.

admiral has entirely quitted these seas without giving any intimation of his intentions to the government of Bengal.[1] Admiral Rainier[2] has made the most full and timely communications to me of his views, and I have reason to believe that he will give a willing attention to my suggestions; but this personal attention is no security for the interests of the government. It is absolutely necessary to place the matter on some more solid foundation than that of mere courtesy.

The state of our alliances, and of Tipu's warlike preparations, added to the expectation of a French force at Mangalore, in my opinion demands the immediate presence of the admiral on the coast of Malabar. His own idea, however, was to have first visited the straits of Malacca; and the government of Fort St George interposed their advice for the purpose of inducing him to cruise off the Isle of France. I hope the admiral will follow my suggestion; but he may reject it, and if he should, I shall apprehend the most serious mischief.

The fleet in India in time of war can neither be directed with the utmost advantage to the protection of the trade, nor of the possessions of the Company, unless it shall be made the duty of the admiral at least to concert his operations with the governor-general. Cases might be stated in which the want of co-operation from the fleet in time of war might suspend all intercourse between Bengal and the other presidencies. The correspondence of the admiralty should be carried on through the supreme government, or at least communicated to it. On this subject it may be further observed, that the want of a controlling power over the officers of the King's navy, has often exposed the government here to the most disgraceful inconvenience, and impeded the Company's trade. A Captain Lindsey, who was here last year, actually from mere wantonness stopped the sailing of a valuable fleet for many months. It is difficult to convey an idea of all the mischief that arises from the uncontrolled power of the officers of the King's navy in this port. Some of them have threatened to fire upon the Company's ships under the most frivolous pretences, and they defy the Company's government on all occasions.

A notion prevails that the King's regiments are subject exclusively to the authority of the commander-in-chief, and that the Company's government has no concern with them. The patronage even of the Company's army (excepting the appointment of the general officers on the staff and of officers to command expeditions) ought, in my opinion, to be left by the governor-general almost absolutely to the disposal of the commander-in-

---

[1] Rear-Adm. Hon. William Cornwallis (1744–1819); flag officer in command, East Indies, 1788–93; brother to the governor-general; who sent his entire squadron home to England.
[2] Vice-Adm. Peter Rainier (1741 ?–1808); flag officer in command, East Indies, 1793–1805; famed for his love of mangoes.

chief. I have acted on this principle, and have carried it so far, as to allow Sir Alured Clarke to dispose of some branches of military patronage which have hitherto been most scrupulously reserved by my predecessors. But the commander-in-chief ought never to be viewed in the light of an equal and co-ordinate power with the governor-general in council. The commander-in-chief should appear to be no more than the instrument employed by the government for the command of the army; he should be a part, but not a rival, of the supreme power. The exclusive powers exercised by the commander-in-chief with respect to the King's troops tend to degrade the governor-general in council, and this evil effect will be increased in proportion to the increase of the King's forces in India.

The governor-general in council is now entirely passed by in the commissions, promotions, leave of absence, and in every branch of the establishment of the King's army. The whole correspondence respecting the King's army, either from the commander-in-chief, or secretary of state, or of war in England, is carried on exclusively with the commander-in-chief in India. Even the orders for some of the expeditions lately undertaken were not addressed to the government in India but to the commander-in-chief.

The patronage of the King's army ought, for the preservation of an unity of power, to be placed under the same species of control by the governor-general in council, which he now exercises over the Company's military establishments, with this difference, that no commission, *etc.*, *etc.*, should be granted otherwise than subject to the King's pleasure. The commander-in-chief's recommendation with regard to the patronage of the King's army [ought] to stand on the same ground as it does at present with regard to the Company's forces; and the correspondence with the secretary of war or other authorities in England [ought] to be carried on through the governor-general in council.

I am aware that this alteration cannot take place without a degree of change in the constitution of the office of governor-general. But I think that the change requisite for these purposes would be attended with many collateral advantages of great importance. My opinion is that the governor-general, in addition to his commission from the Company, ought to have a concurrent commission from the Crown, vesting him with such powers over his Majesty's naval and military force in India as might be deemed expedient. The same commission might subject any conquests made by the Crown in India to the control of the governor-general in council. It would also be desirable that the commission should be so framed as to render the governor-general the representative of the King in India, with the same rank and privileges (as far as circumstances will admit) which are annexed to the office of lord-lieutenant of Ireland.

Lord Macartney (whose knowledge and judgement on most questions appear to me admirable) expressed to me at the Cape his regret, that the governor-general did not hold a concurrent commission from the Crown. I confess that he attached more importance to such a commission than appeared to me (as I was then informed) to belong to it; but my experience of the state of this government, of the temper and disposition of its subjects, and of the nature of its component authorities, has convinced me, that it would be a most beneficial improvement of the constitution of the powers of the governor-general in council to vest him with a commission from the Crown, to be determined by the determination of the commission from the court of directors, according to the existing provisions of the law with respect to the resignation, absence, or recall, of the governor-general.

I cannot suppose that the Company can make any objection to their governor-general holding such a commission from the Crown; as it must tend to raise both the authority and dignity of their government in India, without in any degree affecting their power to control or change it.

I trust that you will reply to this letter by the earliest opportunity; so that your decision respecting the principal points stated for your consideration may reach me before the end of June 1799, when (if I am alive, and as well as I am at present) I mean to visit the Upper Provinces. Should you think it advisable to remove the present councillors in Bengal, the least harsh manner of doing it would be by some general regulation of a retrospective nature, limiting the time for which any councillor at any of the presidencies should hold his seat. The period of 5, 6, or 7, years would exclude both Mr Speke and Mr Cowper. But I must repeat my hope that Mr Speke (although I confess that his claims are applicable merely to the indulgence and humanity of the Company) will not be removed without an adequate provision. If you should limit the services of a councillor in future to the period of five years, no councillor retiring hereafter can have a claim to a pension merely from length of service. Mr Speke has now been nearly ten years in the council. Since I commenced this letter, I have happened to see a good deal more of Mr Graham, and I am convinced that no man (excepting Mr Speke) can be more unfit for a seat in the council.

It is my intention to forward to you by the next ships some observations with respect to the important questions of the legislative power of the governor-general in council, and of the extent of the jurisdiction of the King's supreme court at Calcutta.

This letter is written entirely for your private information. I therefore request that you will not suffer any third person to see it, unless you should think fit to show it to Mr Pitt or to Lord Cornwallis. When you have sufficiently considered the suggestions contained in it, I wish the letter to be destroyed, lest it should hereafter fall into indiscreet or improper hands.

Believe me, . . .

MORNINGTON

31 October 1798

Before I close this letter, I must inform you that it has been a matter of real satisfaction to me to find Sir Alured Clarke much more efficient under a pressure of difficulties than I had expected. His intentions are most honest, and he neither shrinks from responsibility, nor attempts to create embarrassments, nor is afraid to meet those which really exist. Still, with real regard and affection for him, I cannot conscientiously say that he is equal to this great command. Our last fortnight has been a trial of the fortitude of this government: the French in Egypt, and no certain accounts of their progress; Tipu eager for war; Zeman Shah supposed to have commenced his march towards Hindustan. In this crisis, Sir Alured was collected, firm, and calm; Sir James Craig was alarmed, nervous, and endeavouring to cast blame on others. Yet Sir J.C. is certainly a more able man than the commander-in-chief.

Capt[ain] Robinson is arrived.

The regulations for the army are also arrived. I am glad to see the regimental rank is to be established. The reductions of the allowances will operate very severely and generally; but you may be assured that I will carry the whole plan into effect; unless any part upon full consideration should appear to me really objectionable. Committees, and memorials, I am resolved to abolish.

I hear some strange reports of persons intended, or candidates, for the supreme council. One who was mentioned was the famous Lucknow or Fetter Johnstone, who married Courtney's daughter. I cannot believe it to be possible, that such a man should be sent to sit with me in council. Another person named was a Mr Johnstone, natural son to the commodore, who was lately recalled from Lucknow on account of his corrupt practices. These reports must be false.

I am very glad that the court of directors have formed a just estimate of Mr Pattle's merits. I trust they will be taught by this example, how injurious it must ever prove to their own interests and honour to obtrude such characters upon their governments in India. If the governor-general cannot be trusted with the administration of the Company's patronage in India, he ought to be recalled; but either to name persons in England to offices in India, or to send out such men as Mr Pattle with the full power of the interests and protection of the court of directors, is to weaken and degrade that authority in India, on the strength and credit of which the existence of this empire must depend.

85

The court of directors are entirely mistaken with respect to the increase of luxury and ostentation in Bengal. Never did so little of either (according to universal opinion, corroborated by incontestible facts) exist in this settlement. There is a very general spirit of order and economy. The spirit of gaming at cards or dice is by no means common at Calcutta, it is confined to a very few. The horse races are too many, and must be put down, so must the lotteries. The examples which I shall have to make of notorious gamesters will not be more than two or three; of whom, that child of the direction, Mr Pattle will be the first. The whole passage in the letter of the 25th May[1] is exaggerated, although it contains much good matter. I mean within the course of the year to take up the subject very seriously, and make a formal report upon it in council. It is not true that a disregard to religion prevails in this country; I chose my family from those whom I found on the spot, and they are all the reverse of irreligious. The only completely profligate character I have met is a Captain Calcraft, whom Lord Teignmouth most improperly, and towards me unhandsomely, placed in the situation of town major. I have not removed him partly from respect to Lord Teignmouth, and partly from motives of humanity.

I ought not to close this letter without mentioning that I think you have been remarkably fortunate in your choice of our chief justice.[2] He has been obliged to take some steps which required great firmness and temper, and he has manifested both. He is much respected, even by the bar, although he has curtailed their *refreshers*, which in this climate a man cannot well spare. I see a great deal of him, and derive great benefit from his friendly, able, and honest, advice.

XIII

The Earl of Mornington to the Rt Hon. Henry Dundas

6 October 1798, Fort William
Secret and Confidential: no. 2

My dear Dundas

The state of the government of Fort St George will form the subject of this letter. In the first instance, I wish you to read the inclosed copies of my correspondence with Gen[eral] Harris and of my letter to Lord Clive dated the 29th of July.[3] The former contains my ideas with regard to the defence

[1] *Wellesley*, ii, 738.
[2] Sir John Anstruther (1753–1811); chief justice, Bengal, 1798–1806.
[3] *Wellesley*, i, 223 fn.

of the Carnatic, and to the state of the military establishments on the coast of Coromandel: the latter contains nearly every observation which I made during my continuance at Madras. I have very little to add to the contents of those letters. You will perceive that I have found a spirit of counteraction at Fort St George to the measures which I have deemed it advisable to take for the defence of the Carnatic. For the proofs of the necessity of those measures, I refer you to my minute of the 12th of August.[1]

I am concerned to be obliged to inform you that the spirit of opposition to my orders at Madras has appeared exclusively among the confidential friends of L[or]d Hobart, and principally in the conduct of Mr Webbe,[2] the secretary to the government, and of L[ieutenan]t-Col[onel] Close,[3] the adjutant-general, both most intimately connected with Lord Hobart. All my intelligence from Fort St George concurs in stating, that the conduct of Mr Webbe particularly is to be ascribed to his gratitude for the unlimited confidence reposed in him by Lord Hobart, and to his resentment of Lord Hobart's removal. The information which I received during my residence at Madras, as well as my personal intercourse with Mr Webbe, convinced me that he had possessed during L[or]d Hobart's administration an influence in the government far above the level of his situation, and that he arrogated to himself a degree of power incompatible with his subordinate duties. He is a man of a certain degree of talents, and sufficiently informed in the details of the government of Fort St George, but his general knowledge is superficial, his understanding incorrect, and perpetually disturbed by the most violent and ungovernable temper I ever encountered in the whole course of my public life.

His unbounded influence over Lord Hobart will account for those repeated sallies of violence so repugnant to Lord Hobart's temper and character, and I am convinced that the indecency and insolence (for those terms alone can express the truth) of the letters from Fort St George to Sir John Shore are principally to be ascribed to Mr Webbe. This gentleman has acquired such an ascendancy, that even under Gen[eral] Harris (who placed no confidence in him) he was able to carry through the council at Fort St George several letters to this government of the most disrespectful tendency. I have severely reproved their impropriety without entering into any controversy; a system which I shall steadily pursue in whatever hands the gov[ernmen]t of Fort St George may be placed.

It is impossible to speak in terms of sufficient commendation of the zeal and alacrity with which Gen[eral] Harris has executed my measures

---

[1] *Ibid.*, p. 159.
[2] Josiah Webbe; secretary to government, Madras, 1797–1800; chief secretary, 1800–1; resident at Mysore, 1801–3.
[3] Lt-Col. Barry Close; adjutant-general, Madras, 1796–9; resident at Mysore, 1799–1801; resident at Poona, 1801–11.

for the defence of the Carnatic, and for the revival of our alliances, in opposition to the bold counteraction of Mr Webbe, who has thrown every possible difficulty in the way. If it had not been for Gen[eral] Harris' firmness, the army on the coast of Coromandel never could have been assembled; nor could I possibly have overturned the French party at Hyderabad, or revived our defensive alliances. I feel so much gratitude to Gen[eral] Harris, both on public and private grounds, for his useful assistance in this arduous crisis, that, if you should approve the general system of measures which I have pursued for frustrating the designs of Tipu and of the French, I must request you in the most earnest manner to urge the necessity of conferring upon Gen[eral] Harris some immediate mark of the King's favour. If you should not think it unadvisable, I should wish you to lay before his Majesty my humble opinion, that nothing would contribute more to the vigour, efficiency, and honour, of the British gov[ernmen]t in India, than an early mark of favour conferred upon a person who has been principally instrumental in carrying into effect measures, with the success of which the safety of our empire in India is intimately connected. General Harris has a large family, I therefore suppose (but I do not know it, having had no communication with him on the subject) that a regiment would be the most acceptable favour to him. I imagine that he must already be entitled to a regiment, and I wish that a red ribband should be added to it.

Your would greatly strengthen my hands by a public declaration that Gen[eral] Harris was distinguished in consequence of his zealous and speedy execution of the orders of the governor-general in council. You will observe by a comparison of the dates, that the Guntur detachment was ready to march to Hyderabad before the subsidiary treaty was signed by the nizam; and Gen[eral] Harris' letters, as well as a most improper letter from the government of Fort St George drawn by Mr Webbe and dated on the 3rd of August,[1] will manifest to you as well the nature of General Harris' difficulties as of Mr Webbe's opposition.

My letters to Lord Clive will show you the manner in which I have opened my correspondence with him. He (who arrived at Madras on the 21st of August) has answered me with the utmost degree of cordiality in a very sensible letter, which conveyed to me a most favourable impression both of his understanding and temper.[2] He appears, however, to be more alarmed than becomes a man of good sense at the present situation of affairs in India; and it is too evident that Mr Webbe has already impressed him with some erroneous and dangerous notions. For Lord Clive's sake I trust the delusion will not last; but I am grieved to say that my intelligence from Madras leads me to apprehend that Mr Webbe has obtained great

[1] *Wellesley*, i, 236 fn.   [2] *Ibid.*, p. 222.

ascendancy over his mind; that Mr Petrie[1] (on whom, I suppose, you relied for guiding Lord Clive's first steps) has apparently lost ground in an equal proportion; and that Lord Clive's want of habits of business, and ignorance of Indian affairs, will probably expose him to great danger at Madras. But I trust my earliest impressions of his character, founded on his first letter to me, will prove more just than my subsequent intelligence. From me he will always meet with the utmost degree of personal respect and attention; and I hope, after the timely caution I have given to him, that he will not suffer Mr Webbe to introduce any indecorous language into the public correspondence with this gov[ernmen]t. At all events I have little doubt that he will give a ready obedience to my instructions; but even if I should be disappointed in all my expectations, I shall not be embarrassed; being resolved, while I hold this arduous gov[ernmen]t, to carry into effect with a vigorous hand, in the face of all counteraction, and without regard to any personal considerations, whatever measures shall appear to my judgement and conscience to be necessary for the safety and prosperity of the interests committed to my charge.

I have not received any letter from Lord Hobart of a later date than the 16th Sept[ember] 1797; he then writes to me in such intemperate language, that I am resolved never to answer his letter. I understand that his suite at the Cape spoke of me in the same terms; and that his Lordship is returned to England with very unfavourable sentiments respecting me. Recollecting all the circumstances of my friendship for Lord Hobart, as well as of my appointment to this charge, I cannot feel any other anxiety with regard to his language and conduct towards me, than that they should not expose himself to the imputation of injustice and ingratitude.

My dispatches to the secret committee will furnish you with the account of my negotiations with the nabob of Arcot. I have added to this letter two notes of conversations between the nabob and Mr Lushington[2] which passed previously to my arrival at Fort St George. These notes contain a most striking picture of the nabob's character and of the state of his mind. They are so entertaining that I am afraid you will be tempted to put them in circulation for the public benefit; but I trust you will see, that your good humour must be restrained, as they contain matter which might be injurious to L[or]d Hobart, in the opinion of those who are not as well acquainted with the nabob's character as you are. Although I cannot think that Lord Hobart's treatment of the nabob was entirely proper, I know that his Highness exaggerates to a very high degree the injuries of which he complains, and I have reason to know by experience that his Highness is

---

[1] William Petrie; member of council, Madras, 1790–3; 1799–1809.
[2] Stephen Rumbold Lushington; secretary, board of revenue, Madras, 1798–9; collector, Southern Polygar peishcush, Ramnad, 1799–1801.

endowed to the utmost extent of perfection with the Asiatic qualification of a most noble contempt for the truth.

You will learn the state of the question of the Tanjore succession by the dispatches from Fort St George. Serfoji being in quiet possession of the musnud, and the committee of inquiry appointed, I shall have full leisure to examine the state of the country of Tanjore, and you shall receive my opinion soon on that subject.

While I am closing this letter, I have received a letter from my brother Colonel Wellesley,[1] who had just arrived at Madras with the 33rd Reg[imen]t. I enclose an extract of it, which will give you an idea of the state of Lord Clive's situation and character at Madras. I hear from all quarters very unpleasant accounts of the want of confidence in L[or]d Clive's talents and knowledge of business; but comparing his letters to me with my brother's reports (who had conversed with him for several hours on the state of public affairs), I still entertain a hope that he may become an useful assistant in this important juncture.

29 October 1798

I am happy to inform you that my recent intelligence from my brother at Madras, and a letter from Mr Petrie (who has desired to open a private correspondence with me), bring me very favourable reports concerning Lord Clive. I trust he has shaken off all undue influence, and recovered the tone of his spirits, and I have every reason to hope that the military preparations are now proceeding according to my wishes.

Ever yours sincerely,

MORNINGTON

XIV

The Earl of Mornington to the Rt Hon. Henry Dundas

11 October 1798, Fort William
Private: no. 9

My dear Sir

I now resume the subject of my letters *no.* 6 and 7 of the 6th of July and 24th of August, dispatched in duplicate overland and which I send in triplicate by this dispatch.

A triplicate of the overland packet addressed from me in council to the

---

[1] Lt-Col. Hon. Arthur Wellesley (duke of Wellington); arrived in India, 1797; commander at Seringapatam, 1799–1800; 4th son.

secret committee under date the 23rd August is forwarded to the secret committee by this dispatch, together with a triplicate of a letter under date the 3rd of October from me in council to the secret committee, of which the original and duplicate were dispatched overland. Several papers too voluminous to be sent overland now accompany the letter of the 3rd October. They will furnish a view of our political situation down to the latest date. I request that you will read the contents of both packets in the order in which they are numbered.

To this information, I have added a *secret and confidential* letter *no. 2* addressed to you on the state of the government of Fort St George, and I beg leave to call your particular attention to the private correspondence between me and General Harris, which forms an inclosure in that letter.

I now proceed to submit to you the progress which I have been able to make in my proposed measures for frustrating the designs of Tipu and of France. My objects, as already detailed to you, have been to assemble the army on the coasts of Coromandel and Malabar; to revive our defensive alliances against Tipu, and to check the growth of the French influence in the Deccan; to secure the presence of the fleet on the coast of Malabar at the earliest possible period; and to lay the foundations of a permanent improvement of the military establishments of Fort St George, and of the defences of the Carnatic.

From my private correspondence with General Harris, and from the letter of the government of Fort St George addressed to me in council, under the date of the 10th of July,[1] you will learn the counteraction which I have met in my endeavours to place our possessions upon the coast of Coromandel in a respectable posture of defence.

From the whole tenor of my correspondence, public and private, as well as from every document contained in my dispatches since my arrival in Bengal, you will perceive that so far from imagining that I can ever be called upon to justify my orders for assembling our armies in the peninsula of India, my only doubt has been, whether I ought not to have attempted a bolder effort, with a view of anticipating the meditated attack of Tipu, and of his French allies. The measures of preparation and defence which I have ordered, are so evidently essential to the preservation of the British empire in India, that I should have deemed myself absolutely unpardonable, if I had either neglected them, or had been deterred from carrying them into effect by such arguments as those which you will find in the letter of the 10th July from the government of Fort St George. My *secret and confidential* letter *no. 2* will disclose to you the quarter from which the opposition at Fort St George has proceeded.

The army, however, is assembled on the coast of Coromandel, and

[1] *Wellesley*, i, 214 fn.

although wholly inadequate at present to purposes of offence, it at least affords a better protection to the Carnatic than when dispersed, and when utterly unable to offer any sort of resistance on any part of our frontier.

I shall be able to reinforce the army in the Carnatic by an addition of about 3,000 volunteers from the native regiments on this establishment, as soon as the state of the season will admit of landing them at Madras. The volunteers have offered themselves for embarkation under the proposed bounty with very great alacrity, and I am persuaded that, if the number had not been limited by my orders, it would have been much more considerable. The men who have turned out for service are chiefly those who have already been on the coast and have obtained medals for their services. They are, in fact, the flower of this army.

At Bombay I have found no obstacle whatever in carrying into effect the assembling of the army and I have every reason to be satisfied with the zeal and diligence of Mr Duncan and General Stuart,[1] and with the excellent abilities of the latter I trust that the army at Bombay and in the Malabar is now in a forward state of preparation.

The government of Fort St George, previously to the arrival of Lord Clive (having in their letter of the 10th July deprecated every measure of precaution for the protection of the Carnatic against the threatened invasion of Tipu), expressed in their letter of the 3rd of August an equal disinclination to the orders which I had given for assembling a detachment in the Guntar Circar, with a view to the revival of our defensive alliance with the nizam, and to the destruction of the French party at Hyderabad. The opposition proceeded in both instances from the same quarter, and was met by me with the same determination to pursue the line of my duty to the best of my judgement, and to reprove the factious spirit which had attempted to obstruct them.

In pursuing this course, I have concluded a subsidiary treaty with the nizam on the principles stated to you in my *private* letter *no. 6*, in my instructions of the 8th of July to the residents at Poona and Hyderabad,[2] and in my minute of the 12th of August. A copy of that minute, and a translation of the treaty for your private use accompany this letter. You will find some parts of the translation rather awkwardly expressed, but as the substance of the stipulations appeared to me highly favourable to our interests, and as any delay might have hazarded the success of the whole plan, I ratified the treaty without alteration. Being satisfied with the manner in which Captain Kirkpatrick,[3] acting resident at Hyderabad, had executed

---

[1] Lt-Gen. James Stuart; commander-in-chief, Bombay, 1797–9; commander-in-chief, Madras, 1801–4.

[2] *Wellesley*, i, 94, 113.

[3] Capt. James Achilles Kirkpatrick (1764–1805); resident at Hyderabad, 1798–1805.

my instructions, I have appointed him resident at that court in the room of his brother, Colonel Kirkpatrick, who has resigned. I refer you to Captain Kirkpatrick's correspondence and to the letters which I have received from the nizam, from Azim-ul-Umra, and from Mir Allum, since the signature of the treaty, for a view of the actual posture of our alliance with the nizam.

I am endebted to the firmness and spirit of General Harris for having assembled the Guntur detachment with every possible degree of expedition. But you will observe by the letters from the resident at Hyderabad, that, whether from neglect, or wilful omission in some of the subordinate departments of office at Fort St George, the troops had not been furnished with money sufficient to enable them to quit the Company's territories. This circumstance must retard their advance to Hyderabad. I still, however, entertain little doubt that I shall soon be enabled to forward you intelligence of the complete dismission of the French party. I look upon that event to be, not only highly desirable, but indispensable to the possibility of maintaining a contest with Tipu, if he should think fit to attack us, especially if he should receive any succour from France. I refer you on this point to my minute of the 12th August.

The success of the negotiation at Poona has been impeded by the error of the resident.[1] The peshwa had for months past earnestly solicited from us all the substantial parts of the arrangement proposed to him under my instructions of the 8th July; and at the moment when the abstract of my instructions reached Poona, the distress of the peshwa was at its extreme point of exigency. For although Sindhia had fallen into the hands of his own tributary chieftains; and they then possessed the whole power over his army; yet as they were at that time adverse to the peshwa's authority, their ability and character rendered them much more formidable to the peshwa than even Sindhia himself had ever been. In this state of things there can be no doubt that nothing but mismanagement could have checked the success of my propositions. Colonel Palmer (as you will observe by reading his letters) opened the negotiation by resorting in the first instance to Nana, without having obtained the previous concurrence of the peshwa. This ill-advised step necessarily excited the jealousy of the peshwa, and afforded a favourable opportunity for the intrigues of Govind Kishen,[2] and of the other enemies to our interests. The restoration of Nana is certainly a most desirable object for our interests in the present crisis; but it is an object which could not be urged without an undue interference in the peshwa's government. Nana's restoration would have been the natural

---

[1] Col. William Palmer; resident with Sindhia, 1787–97; resident at Poona, 1798–1801.
[2] Govind Kishen was Tipu Sultan's vakil at Poona.

consequence of the success of my propositions, and his continuance in power would have been secured by the same event.

Colonel Palmer appears to have seen nothing but the necessity of restoring Nana, and not to have reflected that the measure, however desirable, could only be attempted through the peshwa's consent.

You will, however, observe from the correspondence, that Colonel Palmer soon recovered himself, and has conducted the subsequent stages of the negotiation directly through the peshwa. The transactions at Poona will show how active Tipu has been at that court, and how dangerous an influence he maintains there through the intrigues of Govind Kishen. Although it is difficult yet to form any certain judgement of the issue of the negotiation at Poona, I am disposed to believe that the conclusion of the treaty of Hyderabad, under the circumstance of an opening being left for the accession of the peshwa, will induce him to enter speedily into our views. He stated no objection when Colonel Palmer first apprised him of our intended arrangements in favour of the nizam; and he has hitherto declared his intention to fulfil his defensive engagements with us in the event of hostilities with Mysore. If, however, he should prove unfaithful, the affairs of the Maratha empire are still so disordered that the utmost we can now apprehend is the neutrality of the court of Poona. Under such circumstances, it will certainly be a most important advantage to have secured the cordial co-operation of the nizam, and to have removed all French influence from the Deccan.

Since I have begun this letter, I have received a dispatch from Colonel Palmer giving an account of his having announced to the peshwa the conclusion of the treaty of Hyderabad. The peshwa received the communication without the least symptom of jealousy or alarm, expressed his own wish to enter into similar engagements with the Company, and signified his intention of opening an immediate negotiation with Colonel Palmer for that purpose. Colonel Palmer, however, does not believe that the peshwa will enter cordially into our views unless Nana shall be restored to the administration, an event which is expected to happen within a short period of time.

If the peshwa shall ultimately accept my propositions, it is my intention to cement the whole of my plan by a new treaty of defensive alliance between the Company, the nizam, and the peshwa; the stipulations of which shall remedy every defect in the subsisting treaties, by defining whatever is vague, and by explaining whatever is obscure in our present reciprocal arrangements. This was an object which Lord Cornwallis endeavoured to accomplish during the last months of his continuance in India. It is unquestionably not only a desirable, but a necessary improvement of our security in the present crisis; the subsisting defensive treaties with the nizam and the peshwa being very ambiguous and loose as well as defective in many essential articles.

The circumstances of the moment will probably enable me to extend our system of defensive alliance to the case of a French invasion in India, whether connected or not with the cause of Tipu. As our treaties now stand, if a French army were to land in any part of our territory, we could not claim assistance either from the nizam or the peshwa, unless Tipu had previously avowed a connection with the French, or had manifested the existence of it by some overt act.

Sindhia has received my propositions very favourably, and I have every reason to believe that he will endeavour to return to Hindustan, where the internal commotions in his dominions, and the increasing rumours of the approach of Zeman Shah, render his presence absolutely necessary to his own preservation. Sindhia's letter to me in answer to my propositions, and to my letter communicated through Colonel Palmer, forms a number in the packet to the secret committee of the 3rd October. The situation of Sindhia is at present such, that we have a good deal to hope, and nothing to fear from him. He will be useful to us if he should return to his own dominions, and if he should not, his power must fall to ruin.

In my letter *no. 6*, I informed you that I had actually forwarded a representation to Tipu, and had called on the allies to concur in it. The fact was that I had drawn a paper for that purpose, and had prepared it for dispatch to both the allied courts; but a more full consideration of the whole political state of India induced me to think that it would be advisable to postpone any remonstrance to Tipu, until our preparations should be further advanced, and until I had been able to ascertain the disposition of our allies, as well as their means of assisting us in the event of a contest with Mysore. It appeared also to me that the presence of a British fleet upon the coast of Malabar might incline the sultan to give a more serious consideration to our representations. A further advantage which recommended this delay was, that it would afford me the opportunity of accommodating the nature and extent of my propositions to my means of enforcing them. My minute of the 12th of August will furnish you with the outline of the remonstrance which I should hope we may be enabled to make to Tipu without the hazard of immediate war, and with the prospect of obtaining from him some degree of security against his future machinations.

The drafts of a letter which I have received from the nizam and the peshwa (and which form a number in the packet of the 3rd October addressed to the secret committee) will serve to prove the sense which our allies entertain of Tipu's aggression, as well as their concurrence in my principles with regard to the general nature of the satisfaction to be required from him. You will observe, however, that I have still reserved to myself the power of framing the remonstrance to Tipu according to the circumstances of the conjuncture in which it may be expedient to apply to him. The moment, I trust, is not far distant when the French party shall have been expelled from the Deccan, when the fleet shall be on the coast of Malabar, and when our military preparations shall be sufficiently advanced to enable me to bring every point of difference with Tipu to a distinct issue.

By my correspondence with Admiral Rainier, which forms a number in the packet to the secret committee of 3rd October, you will perceive that I have induced him to proceed immediately to the coast of Malabar. I trust this disposition of the fleet will prove an efficient check upon Tipu's intercourse with the French.

My instructions to the government of Fort St George on the subject of the defects in their military establishments were dispatched on the 20th July. I have not yet received the report which I desired; and I have reason to apprehend that the necessary preparations for the defence of the Carnatic are carried on with less zeal and energy than the occasion requires. Even now, that government appears unwilling to push our preparations with the requisite alacrity, lest the forwardness of our defence should invite an attack from Tipu at an earlier period than he would otherwise be disposed to move. I know that Tipu will attack us, whenever he shall imagine that he can do so with advantage; but I never can believe that his inclination to make the attack will increase in proportion to the augmentation of our means of repelling it. In the defenceless state in which I found our possessions on the coast of Coromandel, at a time when a large proportion of Tipu's army was actually in the field, the Carnatic lay completely at his mercy. It was, however, probable at that time, as it is now, that Tipu would not be disposed to move previously to the arrival of an additional force from France; an event which was not to be expected until after the close of the monsoon on the coast of Malabar. Under these circumstances, it was apprehended by the government of Fort St George, that any attempt to collect our forces might induce Tipu to make an immediate attack upon the Carnatic.

I felt at that early period, that a moment of hazard must be passed during the necessary interval between the commencement of our preparations, and the time when they could be so far advanced as to secure us against the effects of a sudden blow. The degree of this hazard appeared to me to be inconsiderable; but if it had been greater, I should have incurred it, rather than have relied on the other alternative of remaining in a defenceless state, and trusting to the forbearance of Tipu.

General Harris' private letters will show the duration of the period of danger according to his opinion.

It will not escape your observation, that the argument of the government of Fort St George against the prudence of arming, would have been stronger every day in exact proportion to the progress of Tipu's preparations. The danger, therefore, of taking any steps for our defence would have increased with the probability of the attack; and the moment must ultimately have arrived in which we should have been compelled, either to assemble our army under circumstances of augmented danger, or to abandon all hopes of resistance.

My judgement clearly was, and is, that the earliest possible effort to recover our means of repelling the enemy must at all times be the safest step which could be taken. Having held this opinion even before the commencements of our preparations, I now feel still more strongly the absolute necessity of urging them on with every practicable degree of dispatch, until we shall be in a state to meet Tipu in the field either for the purposes of offence or defence.

Notwithstanding all that has already been stated in the course of this and my former dispatches, as I am aware that the necessary consequence of our present military preparations must be an increase of expense, and a suspension of part of the advantages now derived from India to the affairs of the Company at home; I am desirous in this place to bring under one point of view the considerations which induce me to think, that our safety in India, for some time to come, cannot be secured otherwise than by maintaining our several military establishments in a state of readiness for the field, and by some augmentation of our force.

The engagements which Tipu has contracted with the French, and the public proofs which he has given of his readiness to receive in Mysore as large a force as they can furnish, are circumstances which form a new feature in our political situation in India. The intercepted correspondence between M. du Buc[1] and Tipu, which forms a number in the packet of the 3rd of October, contains an additional proof of the nature of Tipu's connection with the French, as well as of his present views. On their part, the French have manifested not only every intention to co-operate with Tipu, but I am bound to conclude, from all the intelligence which I have been enabled to obtain, that they have actually fitted out considerable armanents with a view of reaching India, either by the Cape of Good Hope, or through the Red Sea, or by a combined attempt through both passages. If they should attempt the passage by the Cape, and should succeed in eluding the vigilance of our fleets (an event at least possible), they might land upon the coast of Malabar a force which would become formidable to us in an unprepared condition. On the other hand, it is hardly to be supposed that,

[1] Du Buc was sent to France early in 1799. He was captured in the Seychelles in September while on his way to the Red Sea.

with our army in the field on the coast of Malabar, it would be practicable for the French to convey by the Cape of Good Hope, without interruption from our fleets, any force so considerable as to be a subject of alarm to us.

I have just now learned, though from doubtful authority, that the French obtained possession of Alexandria in the month of June. Combining this report with the news received from Europe of the sailing of the fleet from Toulon towards the middle of May, the event, however extraordinary, is not improbable. If the French really have taken Alexandria, difficult as the attempt may be, I conclude that they will omit no exertion to assist Tipu, and, at least, will use every means to instigate him to war. The terror of their victory in Egypt (where I hear they have made an immense slaughter) will greatly serve their cause in India, and perhaps elate Tipu so highly as to induce him to commence hostilities.

My information, however, leads me to believe, that even without meeting any opposition in Egypt, the French could not reach India from thence in any numbers for a considerable time, and that if a vigilant cruise of three or four ships could be established off the straits of Bab-al-Mandab, it would be nearly impracticable for any vessels which the French could collect in the Red Sea to force a passage through the straits. But I am not yet apprised whether the admiral will be able to provide for this object without abandoning the protection of the trade of Bombay and of the coast of Malabar. It appears possible that a part of the armament from Toulon may be destined for India direct, while the remainder shall operate in Egypt. A squadron leaving the Mediterranean with this view before the end of May might have entered the Red Sea before the admiral can have occupied the straits of Bab-al-Mandab. This is not, I trust, a probable, but it is far from an impossible event, and its consequences would be to remove a main obstacle to the operations of the French against India from Egypt. Whether, therefore, the operations of the French against India be directed through the ordinary passage by the Cape of Good Hope, or through the Red Sea, or through both, it is equally incumbent on us to maintain Bombay and Malabar in a respectable posture of defence. I have already suggested the possibility of Tipu's mind being so elevated by the first account of the French successes in Egypt as to break out into immediate hostilities. These considerations apply not only to the necessity of keeping the field in Malabar, but to that of continuing the army in the Carnatic in a state of forward preparation.

On the north-west frontier of India a greater probability appears, than has yet existed, of the approach of Zeman Shah. Gholam Mohammed, the Rohilla chief, who was the leader of the rebellion in 1794, is returned into Rohilkhand with a mission from the shah, and is endeavouring to excite the Rohilla chiefs to commotion. This premature step, although a strong indication of the serious intentions of the shah, will, I trust, enable me to give an immediate check to the spirit of revolt in that quarter, from which he would have derived great assistance in any attempt upon the frontier of Oudh. With this view, I have invested Sir James Craig with the command of the troops in the vizier's dominions, and I have directed the corps stationed at Fathigur to advance into Rohilkhand for the purpose of securing the persons of the leaders of the projected revolt, and of crushing the seeds of commotion before they shall have gained any height. Even after this object shall have been accomplished, it will still be necessary to maintain a large force on the frontier of Oudh, as long as any danger of Zeman Shah's approach shall exist.

The necessity of protecting Ceylon, and also our various acquisitions in the Eastern Seas, has diminished our disposable force at Madras, and in some degree at this presidency.

If the French should be enabled to reach the coast of Malabar with any considerable force, I am persuaded that one of their first objects would be to seize Goa, as being the strongest place and the best harbour in which they could readily establish themselves in that part of India. From Goa they would have the power, with great advantage, of affording assistance to Tipu, as well as of receiving, from time to time, whatever succour might be furnished from their newly acquired dominion in Egypt.

Having at a very early period foreseen the importance of Goa, I have already obtained much information on the subject from Mr Duncan and General Stuart, and I mean to direct them to endeavour to take effectual means for protecting it against any attempt of the French. This operation may possibly require a considerable force. If the peshwa should revert (as I trust he will) to his former wish for the aid of a subsidiary force from the Company, this service will also become an additional call upon our army at Bombay. The combination of all these circumstances, on every side of India, will probably require an increase of our force at all the presidencies. You will observe, however, that the greater part of the expense of this augmentation at Fort St George and Bombay will be defrayed by the nizam and by the peshwa; and by referring to my letter to the secret committee, under date the 3rd October, you will perceive that it is my intention to provide for the expense of the augmentation of our army in the province of Oudh by a proportionate reduction of the vizier's present military establishment, and by charging him with the pay of our increased force.

It is my intention, by the ship which carries this dispatch, to represent to Lord Macartney and to Sir Hugh Christian the necessity of their contributing to the defence of the coast of Malabar, provided they shall be satisfied that the efforts of the French are directed solely to India, and that no attack is to be apprehended against the Cape. I should hope that, under such circumstances, we might expect to receive from the Cape the assistance of several ships of war, and of at least one regiment of European infantry, before the end of the month of February. I also place great reliance on your vigilance and alacrity, being persuaded that my letters from the Cape, M. Malartic's proclamation (which I conclude you must have received in the beginning of the month of June), and the movements of the French towards India, will have concurred to induce you to reinforce the army and navy in this quarter. My endeavours shall be directed to keep our expenses on the lowest possible scale consistent with the permanent security of our possessions. You will perceive by the estimates dated the 20th September, and transmitted with the packet of the 3rd October, that our resources have proved more favourable than we expected on the 18th May. Still, however, it will not be possible for us to meet our difficulties without assistance from home in the manner suggested in my letter to the secret committee of the 3rd of July.[1]

Whatever may be the result of this crisis, I trust that your opinion and that of my friends at home will be, that I have not been deficient either in diligence or zeal for the public service. My health is now, and has been throughout the whole of the rainy season, much more favourable than I have remembered it for some years past in England; circumstance remarkably fortunate under so great a pressure of business. I am confident that the ultimate issue of this alarm will be prosperous to our affairs; but I do not apprehend that I shall find myself oppressed by the labour to which any turn of our fortune may subject me. My mind would be perfectly composed, if I could expect to meet a correspondent disposition in those who must be charged with the execution of my orders. I refer you to my *secret and confidential* letters for an explanation of my apprehensions on this point, the sole object of my anxiety, and the only real peril in the present situation of India.

Believe me, . . .

MORNINGTON

PS. I have annexed to this letter two papers drawn up by Captain Malcolm, late town major of Fort St George, one on the state of Tipu's army and resources, the other a general view of our present political situation. The latter is curious, as Captain Malcolm had not seen any of my letters or minutes on the same subject, and only knew that a detachment was ordered to Hyderabad. I had no knowledge of Captain Malcolm, nor was he recommended to me before I met him at Fort St George. He is a very promising young man. I have appointed him assistant to the resident at Hyderabad.

I also enclose copies of several papers received from Bombay on the subject of Goa.

[1] *Wellesley*, i, 244.

XV

The Earl of Mornington to the Rt Hon. Henry Dundas

4 November 1798, Fort William
Private: [*Separate*]

My dear Dundas

If my several overland dispatches have been received, you will have seen that I had anticipated on the 20th of June the orders which you issued in your letters of the 18th and 19th of the month, and which I received on the 18th October. I cannot describe the satisfaction I feel in having so happily conformed to your opinions. If I am not mistaken, the ultimate result will be prosperous and honourable to the British name.

On the 11th of October I learned [of] the descent in Egypt, and on the 31st [of] Nelson's glorious victory.

This day I received official accounts that the nizam had disarmed the whole French corps in his service, and delivered over the officers to the British resident on the 22nd October.

Our army is in the field everywhere, and our spirits are high. We neither court, nor fear war. I refer you to our dispatch of this date.

My health is miraculously good, but I am miserable without Lady Mornington, whose arrival here at present would produce no sort of inconvenience. For God's sake provide a good ship for her in May or June, and send her to me.

You have behaved very ill, so have Pitt and Grenville, with regard to your pictures. I have received the speaker's done by Copley, and I cannot express how great a comfort it is to me. It is an admirable likeness. Pray remember me to Lady Jane.

Ever, . . .

M[ORNINGTON]

The *Eurydice* will sail in a few days with full dispatches on all points.

I entreat you not to name any supreme councillors until you receive my dispatches by the *Eurydice*.

XVI

The Earl of Mornington to the Rt Hon. Henry Dundas

12 November 1798, Fort William

Private: no. 10

My dear Sir

My last *private* letter to you was closed on the 11th of October. On the 18th I received the dispatch of the secret committee dated the 18th of June, and forwarded overland; and on the same day a confirmation of the report of the progress of the French arms in Egypt.

It is difficult to express the satisfaction which I derived from finding, that the measures which I had taken in consequence of the alliance formed between Tipu and the French, corresponded so happily with your principles and views on the same occasion. You will observe by a reference to my several dispatches, that I had not only anticipated all your orders before the overland dispatch had left England, but that the whole course of the ideas which passed through my mind during the late critical conjuncture of our affairs in this quarter, coincided entirely with the tenor of your opinions.

On the only point which you have thought too delicate to decide at home, I am happy to be able to remove your apprehensions. My former letters will have apprised you of the signature of the treaty of Hyderabad, and of the approach of the British detachment to that city. The detachment, under the command of Lieutenant-Colonel Roberts, arrived at Hyderabad on the 10th of October; and on the 22nd of October the British troops, under the orders of the nizam, and with the co-operation of a body of 2,000 of his cavalry, surrounded the camp of the French army, disarmed all the sepoys, and secured the persons of the French officers then in the camp. This operation was happily effected without bloodshed, and without contest. A mutiny having broken out in the French camp on the preceding day, and the sepoys having imprisoned their officers, the resident at Hyderabad and Lieutenant-Colonel Roberts, with the consent of the nizam, judiciously availed themselves of the favourable opportunity to execute this important measure without difficulty or danger.

The amount of the French force disarmed on this occasion was about eleven thousand men, from which circumstance you will observe that a part of the corps was absent, on detachment, as will appear by reference to the return no. 2 of the French officers arrested on the 22nd of October. Measures have been taken for the arrest of those who commanded the detached force. The French officers, by my particular orders, were treated with every practicable degree of attention and humanity. At the period of their arrest by our troops, their persons were in confinement and their lives in danger from the mutiny prevailing in their camp, and the greatest difficulty which Colonel Roberts encountered was that of rescuing the imprisoned officers from the violence of their own sepoys. Particular care was taken to save the property of the officers for their use, as well as to obtain for them such arrears of pay and allowances as were due to them from his Highness. Captain Kirkpatrick informs me that he has been completely successful in effecting both these desirable objects. The French officers are now on their passage to this presidency on board the *Bombay* frigate, which I had previously stationed at Masulipatam for their accommodation. On their arrival at Calcutta, it is my intention to receive them with the consideration due to their respective ranks and to allow them every indulgence compatible with the security of their persons. I propose to send them to Europe by the earliest opportunity, using the precaution of dispersing them in different ships. On their arrival in England, I have engaged that they shall not be treated as prisoners of war, but shall be immediately transported to France, without suffering any detention for an exchange of prisoners.

I am persuaded that you will consider this event as a circumstance of peculiar good fortune in the present moment. The effects of it must be to secure to us whatever benefits can be derived from the cordial co-operation of the nizam in the event of a war with Tipu. And in the meanwhile, so considerable a reduction of the French influence in India must be viewed as an important benefit, at a moment when the adventurous and enter-prising spirit of that nation is directed to the object of erecting an empire in India on the ruins of ours.

With respect to the court of Poona, our affairs in that quarter also have taken a favourable turn. Nana Fadnavis has been restored to the ministry and has publicly taken charge of the affairs of the government. I have already informed you that the peshwa had concurred without hesitation in all my arrangements at Hyderabad, and had uniformly professed his determination to abide by his defensive engagements with us in the event of hostilities with Tipu. The restoration of Nana secures the peshwa's faithful execution of those engagements, and affords a strong ground of expectation of further improvements in the nature of our connection with that state. Neither Tipu nor the French will ever acquire any influence at Poona while Nana shall hold the reins of power. Nana has too much wisdom to involve the Maratha empire in such desperate connections.

On the 31st of October we learned the satisfactory intelligence of the glorious victory at Aboukir, which I immediately announced by a circular letter to all the princes of India, not omitting Tipu Sultan. Being still uncertain of the fate of the French army, I have not relaxed any part of our military or naval preparations, for the nature of which I refer you to my letters to the secret committee. But I have deemed this a favourable opportunity for opening a negotiation with Tipu Sultan, which you will observe the state of affairs at Hyderabad and Poona now admits of my commencing in conformity to my original view of the subject. A copy of my letter to Tipu forms a number of the secret packet.[1]

I wish it were in my power to express my satisfaction in the alacrity with which the government of Fort St George have executed my orders for the defence of the Carnatic. But I am concerned to state that, notwithstanding the cordial disposition of Lord Clive to second my exertions in the public service, unnecessary and unwarranted delays have prevailed in the military equipments in that quarter; and the movement of the battering train towards the frontier (a measure absolutely necessary for the purpose of giving effect to our negotiations with Tipu) has been delayed several weeks, until at length no alternative was left but that of deferring the movement altogether until after the monsoon, or of attempting it during the monsoon at the hazard of interruption from bad weather. The latter alternative, after much hesitation, was adopted.

You will perceive by the secret dispatches, that I have taken measures for embodying the Calcutta European militia. I expect that their number will not fall short of fifteen hundred men. This useful institution had grown obsolete. As I conceive that great advantage might be derived from it in any case of sudden emergency, I have availed myself of this opportunity to revive it, intending to place it on a permanent foundation.

Our accounts of Zeman Shah are still extremely vague and contradictory. I have, however, thought it prudent to continue our preparations on the north-western frontier, where I trust our defences are perfectly secure.

The present cordial intercourse between England and Russia ought to afford you the means of relieving us from that perpetual alarm of an invasion from Kabul. If the emperor of Russia could be induced to countenance, even in a slight degree, the power of Baba Khan,[2] the present sovereign of Persia, a cause of apprehension might be excited on the confines of the shah's dominions, which would effectually check his ambitious designs against the tranquillity of Hindustan.

My letters to the secret committee contain so full a detail of all the circumstances of our present situation, and of the steps which I have taken for the purpose of meeting the exigencies of the moment as they have arisen,

---

[1] *Wellesley*, i, 326.
[2] Fath Ali Qajar, shah of Persia, 1797–1834; until his accession known as Baba Khan.

that I do not feel it necessary to trouble you with any further particulars in this letter.

I have received the military regulations, and I have already given the necessary orders for carrying into execution that part of them which relates to the promotion of regimental rank. With respect to the reduction of the allowances, it is a question which I have not yet decided, whether it might not be advisable to postpone for a time a measure which would necessarily tend to slacken the zeal of the officers who may be called into the field in the present crisis. But this is a consideration merely of time, and of prudence; for the temper of the army is such, and, I trust, my authority is so firmly established, that I have no expectation of meeting with any difficulty or danger in carrying the orders of the court into effect. I may hereafter suggest some observations on some parts of those orders.

The dispatches to the secret committee, and to the court of directors, will show you the amount of the voluntary contributions within these provinces. When you will recollect that the greater part of it is furnished from the annual income of the subscribers, I think it will appear sufficient testimony of their zeal and public spirit. The same spirit has appeared on the occasion of the calling out of the militia. All descriptions of the European and Armenian inhabitants of Calcutta have manifested the utmost degree of alacrity in offering their personal services.

21 November 1798

I have received your *private* letter of the 16th June. You will observe, from the whole of my dispatches, that my opinions entirely agree with yours with regard to the possibility of the success of the late attempt of the French to penetrate to India through Egypt. The French might have reached Suez early enough for the passage to the coast of Malabar, and might have found in the ports of the Red Sea conveyance for a very considerable body of troops, had not the whole project been frustrated by the vigilance of his Majesty's ministers in England, and by the skill and valour of his naval commanders in the Mediterranean.

The secret and sudden reinforcement of Lord St Vincent's[1] fleet, under the alarm of an existing rebellion in Ireland, and of a menaced invasion both of that kingdom and of Great Britain, was the conception of a masterly spirit, combining all the advantages of wisdom, boldness, and dispatch. If, however, the success of this most ably conceived and happily executed enterprise had been disappointed, I trust that the early precautions of preparation and defence which had been taken in India, would have

---

[1] Adm. John Jervis, earl of St Vincent; flag officer in command, Cadiz and Mediterranean, 1795–9; first lord of the admiralty, 1801–4.

opposed an unexpected and effectual check to the progress of the French arms.

The necessity of executing your plan for distributing the supernumerary King's officers among the armies of the native powers is greatly diminished by the successful blow which I have been enabled to strike against the French party at Hyderabad. But I will turn my attention immediately to your suggestion, and will give you my ideas in detail on the subject by the ships; premising nothing more, than that my present opinion inclines me to prefer the extension of the system of a regular subsidy from the native powers (the officers bearing their commissions from the British government) to any other mode of correcting the evil, on which I furnished you with so many details in my dispatches from the Cape.

This opinion will admit of a provision for the supernumerary King's officers, in a manner perhaps more satisfactory to them, than by placing them under the direct authority of the native princes; but both plans may be combined, and the operation of one will correct the defects of the other.

The principle, which dictated your wish of distributing the supernumerary King's officers in the service of the native powers, leads me to hope, that you will approve my late measures at Hyderabad, and to flatter myself, that in this instance also I have anticipated your wishes.

The same observation may, I trust, be applied to the measure of calling out the militia; by which I expect to accomplish all the important objects so forcibly recommended towards the conclusion of your dispatch of the 16th of June. Although the dispatch was of a private nature, your sentiments and expressions appear to me so well calculated to animate the zeal which you desire to encourage, that I mean to publish the concluding passage of your letter in the orderly book of the militia.

Believe me, . . .

MORNINGTON

XVII
The Earl of Mornington to the Rt Hon. Henry Dundas

12 November 1798, Fort William
Secret and Confidential: no. 3

My dear Dundas

Although the appearance of affairs at Fort St George is much improved, I ought not to conceal from you any information which can throw light on the late transactions in that quarter. All my private intelligence from Madras concurs in stating the efforts of the faction in that settlement to have been unremitting from the moment of my first orders for assembling the army.

I now know that on receiving my letter of the 10th August, Mr Webbe drew an answer of the most refractory kind, and endeavoured to prevail on General Harris and the council to sign it. General Harris prevented this measure by declaring that he was convinced I should suspend the council the moment I received such a letter. In this opinion General Harris was perfectly correct. I certainly would have suspended the council without hesitation, if they had shown any further symptoms of a disposition to impede the progress of measures absolutely necessary for the public safety. You will remark, in the letter of the 3rd of August from Fort St George, a striking contrast between the spirit in which the letter is drawn, and the minute of General Harris on which it is founded; and it will not escape your attention that the object of Mr Webbe in that letter (expressed in most disrespectful terms) is to fix a charge of inconsistency upon me in my orders for assembling an army in the Carnatic, and a detachment in the Guntur Circar. The result of those combined operations proves their consistency; the one having deterred Tipu from moving into the Carnatic, while the other has effected the total subversion of the French party at Hyderabad, and revived our alliance with the nizam.

You will not be deceived by the professions of cordial co-operation contained in the correspondence of the government of Fort St George. The fact is that every art has been employed to thwart and calumniate my orders; a general feeling of despondency and discontent has been excited in the settlement; the advance of the preparations of defence has been delayed on the most frivolous pretexts; the conduct of the government has approached as nearly as was safe to positive disobedience; and the spirit of my orders has been counteracted in every instance. You will find a sufficient proof of this fact by referring to the account of the delay in supplying the Guntur detachment with money, and to the scandalously defective equipment of that detachment; which L[ieutenan]t-Col[onel] Roberts writes 'was worse provided in every respect than any army he ever saw'. To these circumstances must be added the delay of the battering-train.

These embarrassments are the more to be lamented as they have arisen when both Gen[eral] Harris and Lord Clive have sincerely intended to pay a prompt and zealous obedience to my orders. But neither of them are equal to cope with the arts of the faction which conducts the government. Orders have been retarded in their passage from office to office, or frustrated in the mode of executing them; and every contrivance has been employed to embarrass and to delay.

On all these points, I believe many details will be furnished you by

Mr Petrie, whom the same faction has contrived to exclude from the council by persuading Mr Saunders to retain his seat. Of Mr Petrie I know nothing, but what appears in his letters to me, which are most able as well as zealous. He seems to me to be a man well fitted for business in critical times.

You will perceive in the political and secret letters of the 15th October dispatched from Fort St George (in the political letter), an attempt to cast doubts on the nature of the connection between Tipu and France; to suggest that Tipu is a moderate and inoffensive neighbour, and to question the whole policy of my later measures; and this, in expressions as disrespectful as could be used with safety. You will observe in the secret letter, an attempt to deny any intention of disputing the policy of assembling the army, but I refer you to a comparison of paragraph 10 with paragraph 48 of the secret letter, and with the political letter, for an exposition of the real views of the writer. The object of the letter of the 10th of July[1] must have been, either to prevent the assembling of the army by suggesting that our preparations would provoke Tipu to war, or to detail possible difficulties and embarrassments without any tendency to a practical conclusion. The first part of this alternative I have already discussed in my former letters and minutes; the second (on which Mr Webbe is now disposed to rest) is little short of a plain admission of factious views. I cannot comprehend to what other motive than faction, are to be ascribed statements of difficulty leading to no practical conclusion in a moment of public danger.

I must also request you to notice that the political letter of the 15th October is evidently calculated to impress the court of directors with an idea that my system of policy transgresses the line of security and self-defence; and you will remark, that with this view, many matters are inserted in the political letter which ought to have been reserved for the secret department. This is done for the purpose of giving the faction at Madras the advantage over me of pre-audience in the court; for Mr Webbe is too well acquainted with the rules of business not to know, that the grounds and objects of my system of policy, would *by me* be communicated to *the secret committee only*. Lord Clive has been induced to sign these letters, although the greater parts of the events detailed in them passed previously to his arrival in India. This is entirely contrary to established usage. The matter of the letters should have been separated, and the relation of those transactions which passed previously to the arrival of Lord Clive should have been attested by General Harris and the council. The object of this manoeuvre on the part of Mr Webbe is to involve L[or]d Clive in the dispute, and to commit him against me. This, however, has not succeeded. I impute nothing to L[or]d Clive, but ignorance of official forms.

[1] *Wellesley*, i, 214 fn.

It is with the most real concern that, after a full and impartial inquiry, I am compelled to declare to you, that I believe Lord Clive is not equal to his situation, either in point of talents, or of knowledge. His intentions are, however, so indisputably pure and honourable, and he has shown so much desire to act cordially with me, that I should be quite certain of his becoming an useful support, if he were not so much in the hands of Mr Webbe. With a full knowledge of my opinion of that gentleman, Lord Clive has been so deceived as to request from me a discretionary power of imparting to Mr Webbe my private and confidential communications to his Lordship. If Mr Petrie were in council, I entertain a hope that Mr Webbe would lose his ascendancy in some degree; but as the matter now stands, I am seriously apprehensive for the safety of our possessions in the Carnatic, the care of which requires a considerable degree both of ability and vigour.

13 November 1798

However, my accounts of this day from Madras give me more hopes. They had just received the news of my bloodless victory at Hyderabad, which has considerably raised the spirits of Lord Clive and General Harris, and I hope depressed those of the faction in an equal proportion. I have endeavoured on this occasion to apply a *tonic* to Lord Clive's constitution. I enclose a copy of it, and I entertain a sanguine hope that it may prove useful.

My earnest request to you is, that you will, by the earliest possible opportunity overland and by sea, convey to India through the secret committee, a most pointed censure of the letters of the 10th of July, and of the 3rd of August from Fort St George. From this censure you will except General Harris, and direct your thunder against the subordinate officers of government. That you will also censure the political and secret letters of the 15th of October, and remark the gross misrepresentation of my measures, as well as the inconsistencies which those letters contain. From this censure, you will except Lord Clive, and refer to my secret letter in council, and to my separate letter to the court of directors, to show the cordial union which subsists between us; expressing a confidence, that Lord Clive will not suffer the arts of any faction to interrupt our mutual harmony.

If you will immediately send out censures to this effect, I trust my authority will stand on a firm basis, but if any disposition to balance or compromise between me and the authors of the letters in question should appear in your dispatches, it will become quite impossible for me to hold the charge of the government general with any hope of enforcing due respect or prompt obedience to my orders in any part of India. I think you ought also to direct me (through the government of Fort St George) to remove from their offices any persons whom I believe to have been concerned in the late factious proceedings at Madras. No government can proceed with safety against such a new and dangerous species of secret influence; by which those who ought to obey now govern, without responsibility and without the possibility of control. If Mr Webbe's libels of the 15th of October, or any other from the same manufactory, should make any unfavourable impression of my conduct, I trust to my friends for my defence in the publication of my several minutes and letters.

You will decide upon the reports which you will receive from this country, and upon your own judgement and knowledge of the interests of India, whether my conduct has corresponded with the exigencies of my duty. That the crisis has been most arduous and difficult, cannot be denied, and it is equally unquestionable that the part which I have acted has been strong and decided. It is therefore evident that my measures have been either very proper or very much otherwise.

In assembling the army, I encountered the clamour of the whole settlement of Madras, exasperated by the arts of a faction into a belief, that I meant to precipitate a war with Tipu, and that he would be at their gates before two regiments could be assembled.

In the fiercest moment of this infatuation, and with all Mr Webbe's artillery pointed against me, I detached a large force to Hyderabad, knowing well that although this measure would augment the alarm at Madras, its success was indispensable to the possibility of either resisting or of attacking Tipu, under the circumstance of his recent alliance with the French. My most authentic accounts have convinced me that the effect of my orders for assembling the army has been to keep Tipu out of the Carnatic; and the blow struck against the French power in the Deccan is now the very ground of confidence and exertion at Madras, among the same persons who were loudest in condemning the detachment of so large a part of the centre army to this object. After General Harris' declaration, 'that his force was still equal to cope with Tipu', I think I need not jusify this measure to you; who, in the face of the most formidable preparations for the invasion of Great Britain and Ireland, and of a rebellion in the latter, detached a large naval reinforcement to strike a blow in a distant quarter, the effect of which, you knew, would be felt at home.

If I should be so fortunate as to meet your approbation, I am persuaded you will declare it in such a manner as to strengthen in my hands the government which is under your political superintendence.

I am desirous that Captain Kirkpatrick, the resident at Hyderabad, should be made a baronet. He deserves it at least as well as Sir Charles Malet,[1] or Sir John Kennaway.[2]

[1] Sir Charles Warre Malet, Bart. (1753–1815); resident at Poona, 1786–97; member of council, Bombay, 1797–8.
[2] Sir John Kennaway, Bart. (1758–1838); resident at Hyderabad, 1788–94.

I like Sir Alured Clarke better every day, and dislike Sir James Craig in the very same ratio. Clarke is no maker of difficulties, and always ready to encounter them in his own person; Craig has established the most prolific forge of difficulties and embarrassments which I ever beheld. How he disposes of his own manufacture remains to be seen.

I entreat you to consider, and reply to my suggestions respecting the supreme council of Bengal without a moment's delay. Everything may depend on your arrangement of that business.

Ever, . . .

MORNINGTON

Our respectable friend Lord Cornwallis is misinformed with regard to the French influence in India.

XVIII

The Earl of Mornington to the Rt Hon. Henry Dundas

24 November 1798, Fort William
Secret and Confidential: [*Unnumbered*]

My dear Dundas

I have sent you an ample budget by this dispatch. I write this note principally to request, that you will send Lady Mornington out to me, if you can prevail on her to encounter the voyage, and to quit her children. I am now so firmly established here, that no possible inconvenience can arise from her arrival; and I really suffer much in my spirits from the want of her society.

If you see no objection, I beg that you will allow my brother Mr Pole[1] to see my private and secret correspondence with you. It is possible that Grenville and the speaker may be anxious to know more particulars of my conduct, and of the state of affairs here, than be collected from the public accounts. I am persuaded you will indulge their regard for me as far as may be consistent with propriety.

I send you a paper of suggestions respecting the manning of the navy in India, to which I entreat your serious attention. This disorder and distress to which we are every day subject for want of authority over the naval officers threaten the worst consequences. I must also call your attention to

[1] Hon. William Wellesley-Pole (Lord Maryborough, 3rd earl of Mornington) (1763–1845); 2nd son.

the question stated in my letter (*Secret and Confidential no. 1*) relating to the powers of the gov[erno]r-gen[era]l in council as applicable to the King's troops. The King's officers now openly deny the power of the Company's gov[ernmen]ts, or of the court of directors, to lay down rules for their conduct towards the native princes, or on any other subject. Read the trial of Colonel Oliver at Fort St George, and the case of Colonel Lindsay at the same presidency. There is no effectual cure for this evil but a King's commission to the governor-general.

Every hour confirms to me the importance of our late success at Hyderabad. I enclose extracts of some letters from Madras on the subject, and I request you to read Captain Kirkpatrick's letters attentively, particularly the latter ones. We shall be able to procure many fine recruits for the army in the Carnatic from Hyderabad. The arsenals, foundries, and magazines, attached to Piron's corps form a new feature in the case. I forget whether I have told you, that the standard of the corps was, not the nizam's flag, but the *drapeau tricolore*, with various other republican emblems. These I shall send to you by the regular ships.

Pray make Kirkpatrick (James *Achilles*) a baronet. You know his father is a respectable man; so is his brother, who arrived in India from the Cape in the middle of Sept[ember], and is now my military secretary.

Ever yours,

M[ORNINGTON]

XIX

The Earl of Mornington to the Rt Hon. Henry Dundas

26 November 1798, Fort William
Secret and Confidential: [Unnumbered]

My dear Dundas

As my brother Colonel Wellesley will certainly be included in the next promotion of major-generals, he will be obliged to return to Europe unless he is appointed to the staff in this country. He has been of the most essential service to me, both at this presidency and at that of Fort St George, where indeed he has done more towards keeping things in a right course, and promoting my views for the public service, than any other person. For these reasons, I am very desirous that he should remain in this country as long as I am likely to continue in the government, and I earnestly request that, upon the next promotion of major-generals, you will use your endeavours to get my brother appointed to the staff either in Bengal or upon the coast. My letters from Madras received just now render me anxious to secure my brother's continuance in India; I can assure you that he will honourably and ably answer any call of duty either civil or military.

I am most happy to be enabled to tell you, that my letters from Madras of this day contain the most satisfactory accounts of vigorous and active preparation for war. Petrie and my brother have done infinite service, and my Hyderabad victory has raised the spirits of all at Madras.

A report has just reached me (which however upon every calculation appears impossible) that Bonaparte had passed Basra on his march to Moultan with 35,000 men; and would join the shah at Delhi in the month of December. The accounts of the shah are still vague and contradictory. However, I think he will penetrate at least as far as Lahore this season.

Ever yours sincerely,

MORNINGTON

XX

The Rt Hon. Henry Dundas to the Earl of Mornington

27 November 1798, Whitehall
Private: no. 4

My dear Lord

I have been duly honoured with the receipt of your Lordship's letters from Madras, dated the 8th of May, and of another from Calcutta, dated the 23rd of June last.

I most sincerely congratulate your Lordship on your arrival at Fort William, and upon your assumption of the government of that presidency; and trust you will soon find little or no inconvenience from the climate, tho[ugh] it may appear dreadful at present.

By the present overland dispatch, I can do little more than advert to the contents of the letters from your Lordship, the receipt of which I have above acknowledged. One point, however, in your letter from Madras affords me the highest satisfaction; I mean where you state the Coast army to be in the finest condition, and to be one of the noblest bodies of men in the world.

I trust your Lordship will find the Bengal army far more respectable as to order and discipline than has been generally supposed. Lord Teignmouth has spoke very favourably to me of it, and especially to the troops in the Upper Provinces, and has done ample justice to the abilities and exertions of General Craig.

His Lordship has left with me the draft of the confidential letter he wrote to your Lordship, to be delivered to you on your arrival at Calcutta. I have not had time as yet to attend to it, but from the conversations I have had with Lord T[eignmouth], I have no doubt but he has stated his sentiments in the most friendly and unreserved manner.

I have carefully perused your orders to Madras and Bombay (received from the latter presidency) in consequence of the proclamation issued at the Mauritius; and it is a pleasing circumstance to find, that at the exact period we were framing our order here on that subject, you were anticipating them by the orders issued by your government. As your Lordship must 'ere now be in possession of the orders of the secret committee of June last, I shall not here add anything further.

I shall anxiously expect the details your Lordship has promised relative to Arcot and Tanjore, the finances of the Company, and the general politics of India. On the latter subject I intended to have written to your Lordship by an early opportunity, but shall defer it till I am favoured with your promised detail. Indeed, the pleasing change that has taken place in public affairs by the glorious victory of Admiral Nelson, as well as the uncertainty of Tipu's designs, render it unnecessary at present to enter particularly on the subject. I am confident your Lordship is feelingly alive as to the necessity of vigilantly watching and guarding against the designs both of Tipu and the French; as well as of such of the native powers who may be suspected of being inimical to the interests of the British nation in India.

I am happy your Lordship is pleased with the appointment of Lord Clive to the government of Madras. I trust he will do honour to our choice. In this opinion I am much confirmed by Lord Teignmouth, who has stated to me that his Lordship constantly grew upon him in the several conversations he had with Lord C[live] at the Cape.

As your Lordship will receive by this conveyance several letters which we have directed the secret committee to transmit, it will be unnecessary for me to enter into any details of their contents.

I am, . . .

HENRY DUNDAS

XXI

The Earl of Mornington to the Rt Hon. Henry Dundas

3 December 1798, Calcutta
Private: no. 11

My dear Dundas

By the *Eurydice*, which ship sailed on the 28th of November, I have dispatched to you *secret and confidential* letters *nos. 1, 2,* and *3*. As some passages of them are necessary for the purpose of explaining my *private* letters dispatched overland, I have directed those passages to be extracted and sent in cypher by this conveyance. The *secret and confidential* letter *no. 1* contains my opinions with respect to the supreme council; of the chief command of the army; and of my own powers in several essential points. I have only to request, in relation to the subjects contained in that letter, that you will take no steps with respect to any change in the council, or in the command of the army, before you shall have received my *secret and confidential* letter *no. 1*. On this point, I am extremely anxious, and I request that you will not name even a provisional successor either to the chief command, or to the supreme council, until you shall have been able to consider that letter.

[Not signed]

XXII

The Earl of Mornington to the Rt Hon. Henry Dundas

26 December 1798, On Board the Yacht
Private: [*Separate*]

My dear Sir

You will receive with this letter a box containing the standards of the late French party at Hyderabad. I beg you particularly to remark the emblems upon the top of the standards; the sword bearing the cap of liberty over the crescent, the meaning of which is too obvious to need any explanation.

I have also sent you another box containing a fusee manufactured at one one of M. Piron's arsenals, which, however, I would recommend to you to have proved, before you attempt to kill a pheasant with it. You will observe the cap of liberty upon the stock of the fusee.

The standards you will present to the court of directors, or not, as you think proper.

This is dated from on board the yacht on my way to Madras, whither I am going for the purpose of endeavouring to bring matters to an issue with Tipu Sultan.

Yours sincerely,

MORNINGTON

You shall hear from me upon my arrival at Madras.

XXIII

The Rt Hon. Henry Dundas to the Earl of Mornington

29 December 1798, London
Private: no. 5

My dear Lord

I have wrote to you many occasional letters since the one I wrote to you in the month of June last; but few of them were sent, because from the total want of information for a long time of what was passing in Egypt and the Levant, and afterwards from the rapid change which was produced in those quarters by Nelson's splendid victory, I was literally not in a situation to give you any new idea beyond what I have detailed in my letter in the month of June. I have contented myself at present with barely alluding to Nelson's victory, and the state of affairs in the Mediterranean and Egypt, because I know from the steps that have been taken to convey information of those transactions directly to India, your Lordship and the governments in India are informed of them as soon as we are here. I have left myself perfectly at ease with regard to what was going on in India, amidst the arduous points on which I had every reason to believe you would be called upon to act, because from your letters, particularly the one recently received of date 6th July, compared with what I had wrote to you in the month of June, when the scene first opened, I had the satisfaction to perceive that our ideas were so much in unison, as to leave me no doubt that your conduct would be precisely what I could wish.

I know not yet whether anything decisive has happened to Bonaparte and his army in Egypt. If there has, you have heard it long before you can receive this. Our last authentic accounts were that he and his army were labouring under every species of difficulty, and recent reports, not however sufficiently authenticated, have reached us, that he himself had been murdered at Cairo, and the remains of his army, of course, put into great dismay and confusion. This is all that at present I am in a situation to state to you with any authenticity; at the same time, from every collateral circumstance, entertaining the most sanguine hopes that he and his whole army must go to destruction. This feeling, however, has not and shall not relax my intention to give to you in India every aid of men and money that I possibly can, keeping always in view that you are or may be involved in hostilities and consequently in expense. If no French assistance arrives, which is not likely to arrive, I take it for granted, that you will be enabled to shape your conduct with regard to Tipu exactly as circumstances may dictate to your own judgement and discretion.

The pressure of other business, and the uncertainty whether this letter may go to you by sea or overland, in the first instance, prevents me at this moment writing to you more at length. But it is my intention to take the first days of the holidays to write to you at full length in answer to your letter of the 6th July; and I shall, at the same time, detail to you without reserve, every idea that occurs to me respecting India. Being possessed of these sentiments, it must be left entirely to your own judgement to apply them as circumstances may suggest.

As for our situation at home, it is everything we could wish. We have followed the blow given in the Mediterranean by Lord Nelson in the capture of Minorca, of which the accounts are received within these few days. The authentic accounts are not yet arrived, but we are in daily expectation of hearing [of] the recapture of Malta; and our success in the Mediterranean has emboldened Naples to take up arms against France in Italy. Whether this circumstance, or indeed any other, will induce Austria and Prussia to act upon their true interests, by returning to a confederacy against France, remains to be proved. Russia has shown them a noble example. Laying aside all former jealousies and animosities, she proffered her aid to the Ottoman Porte, when the French directed their attacks against Egypt; and amidst all the extraordinary events which the present times have exhibited to the world, it is not the least extraordinary to see a Russian fleet in the Levant. So, however, stands the fact.

As to our civil and domestic situation, it is equal to the proudest wish of our hearts. Founded chiefly on the voluntary zeal and exertions of the country, we have not less then 240,000 men in arms within the island, and we may carry that principle as far as we please. No democrat dare show his face: government popular in every ale-house: our commerce and revenue flourishing beyond all former example: public credit thoroughly restored, and in order to render it beyond all future peril, the idea of raising a great part of the supply within the year has become so universally recognized and approved, as to enable Mr Pitt to bring forward the measure of raising ten millions annually by a direct tax upon income, and against the measure not a murmur without doors, but the reverse, and in Parliament the opposition has been so feeble as not to be worth mentioning. As long, therefore, as our enemies shall choose to be distracted, so long are we in a condition to carry on the war, and the wealth of the country is so great as to make the burden of it to be little felt. The most pressing subject now remaining is the situation of Ireland. All the attempts of France to invade it have been discomfited, either by the surrender of their troops when landed, or by the capture of their fleets and troops by the navy, without permitting them to land. Notwithstanding all our exertions at home for our own security, and notwithstanding the appropriation of considerable force to our distant possessions and the Mediterranean, we have been enabled to send to the assistance of Ireland within the year not less than 25,000 troops, consisting partly of regular force, but chiefly of fencible and militia regiments who have volunteered the service. It is now decided that the plan of union is to be immediately brought forward, and the whole strength of government applied to carry it through.

For the reason I have given to you, I cannot write to you today more in detail, but I flatter myself the short sketch I have given you of the leading points worthy of being communicated to you, will afford you not an unpleasant morsel.

Lady Jane is well and desires to be kindly remembered to you, and I remain,

My dear Lord, . . .

HENRY DUNDAS

XXIV

The Earl of Mornington to the Rt Hon. Henry Dundas

12 January 1799, Fort St George
Private: no. 11

My dear Sir

I refer you to my public and secret dispatches of this date to the court of directors and to the secret committee[1] for the motives which induced me to proceed to this presidency, as well as for the general state of public affairs in India.

[1] *Wellesley*, i, 406.

My principal object in this letter is to inform you that the evils of which I complained in my *secret and confidential* letters *nos. 2* and *3* are entirely at an end.

They began to subside at the first news of the success at Hyderabad, and they have entirely vanished since my arrival here.

I find that my brother's report (to which I alluded at the close of that part of my *secret and confidential* letter *no. 2* dated October the 12th) is much more true than the opinion of the public on the same subject.

The person,[1] of whom I have made such frequent mention in my *secret and confidential* letters *nos. 2* and *3*, as having taken advantage of his situation to counteract the execution of my orders, has entirely changed his conduct, and is now become a very useful servant to me. Notwithstanding this circumstance, I think it necessary to repeat my requests contained in my *secret and confidential* letter *no. 3* under that part of it dated the 13th of Nov[embe]r.

I cannot too strongly press the necessity of your giving the earliest attention to the latter part of my dispatch of this date to the secret committee.

You will be glad to hear, that I not only continue to enjoy very good health, but that I feel myself much the better for my voyage from Bengal to this place.

My letter to the secret committee contains the exact state of my sentiments with regard to the issue of the present crisis. I have no doubt that it will be prosperous, and I now apprehend no other difficulty than that stated at the close of my dispatch of this date to the secret committee.

Believe me, . . .

MORNINGTON

XXV

The Earl of Mornington to the Rt Hon. Henry Dundas

12 January 1799, Fort St George
Secret and Confidential: no. 4

My dear Dundas

You will be glad to hear that I find Lord Clive (although the most reserved and therefore awkward of men) a very sensible and discreet person. He has

[1] Mr Webbe.

much more efficiency in him than is supposed by the world, and even by those in this settlement who see him every day. With me he is now quite at his ease; and if we were brothers, we could not act more cordially together. I have used every endeavour to render my presence here rather an accession, than a diminution of power and influence to him. He knows and feels this very properly. His temper is excellent, and his intentions pure and upright.

All faction is dispelled, and Webbe is become an useful and valuable servant. But affairs here were in a lamentable state before the success at Hyderabad; and a lecture from home (according to the suggestion contained in my letter of the 12th and 21st November, s[ecret and] c[onfidential]) is necessary for the prevention of such mischief in future times.

The improvement of affairs here, the state of Lord Clive's mind, and the advancement of the preparations, are to be attributed principally to my brother, Colonel Wellesley. I must repeat my earnest request, that you will, as soon as possible, make him a major-general on the staff of India. He has been most useful to me. He is intimately acquainted with the affairs of this country, and universally beloved.

I trust you will not delay the execution of my suggestions respecting *Barlow* and *Bebb* in Bengal. Everything may depend on your arrangements in that quarter. For God's sake do not send me a troublesome or an inefficient assessor from home. Rely on it, the best arrangement is that which I have suggested.

Remember my ideas respecting a royal commission; and, above all, a power of superintending the *fleet* in India. Without the latter, I cannot answer for anything in times of war.

This note refers to 3 s[ecret and] c[onfidential] letters dispatched by the *Eurydice*.

I am concerned to hear that you have been unwell. We cannot spare you in these times. I never was so well in my life; and if it were not wrong, I could lead the army myself. I have no doubt of speedy tranquillity and lasting security in India; but you must not forget the last paragraphs of my letter of this date to the secret committee.

My love to Lady Jane. This country is at present delightful. I prefer it to Bengal.

Yours ever affectionately,

M[ORNINGTON]

Petrie is in council, by my interference, and very useful, able, and well meaning. You ought to bring Mr Thomas Cockburn[1] into council here. He is the best and ablest man in India after Barlow.

---

[1] Thomas Cockburn; member, board of revenue, Madras, 1795–1800; 2nd member, 1800–1; senior member, 1801–3.

The nabob has behaved very ill since my arrival. You shall soon here more on that subject. I mean to take this opportunity to urge a complete arrangement.

XXVI

The Earl of Mornington to the Rt Hon. Henry Dundas

21 February 1799, Fort St George
Secret and Confidential: no. 5

My dear Sir

I refer you to the dispatches of the 12th and 13th Feb[ruar]y to the court and secret committee[1] for the state of political affairs here. I mean soon to give you full details of our present situation and probable prospects. In the meanwhile, I can assure you that I am now perfectly at ease with respect to the former, and very sanguine in my expectations of the latter. I am highly satisfied with the conduct of this government. All faction is fled; and those of whom I complained most justly in the summer have now seen their error, and are become useful servants to the public. I am quite surprised that we should have had no intelligence from the Red Sea since the 26th of August, nor any account of the state of the French army on which we can rely. But come what will, we are ready, and I believe a more gallant, well-disciplined, and well-appointed, army never took the field. The nizam was so alert, that General Harris was obliged to issue an order to Mir Allum to halt, lest the army under the command of the latter should join ours before we were prepared to receive it. The late French sepoys are now under the command of Capt[ain] Malcolm, and of several British officers, and although they have been a little refractory, there seems great reason to hope that Malcolm will form them into a serviceable corps. They are the finest men in the army, as my brother Henry[2] informs me, who has pased some days in camp.

You will judge of my affliction at the unfortunate affair of Benares. I refer you to my dispatches, and to my private letter to the chairman, for such details as I have received of that atrocious transaction. Cherry[3] was the victim of his own credulity. He never would believe that Vizier Ali was capable of guile or mischief. In fact, the character of Vizier Ali had become a

[1] *Wellesley*, i, 429, 434.
[2] Hon. Henry Wellesley (Lord Cowley) (1773–1847); private secretary to the governor-general, 1798–1801; 5th son.
[3] George Frederick Cherry; senior judge, court of circuit and appeal, and agent of the governor-general, at Benares, 1796–9. Murdered.

party question between Cherry and Lumsden, and the former actually dis-
regarded the repeated warnings of the letter. The latest advices render it
probable that Vizier Ali will be taken. In that event, a question of great
delicacy will arise with regard to his punishment. I fear I cannot receive
your opinion on it, before I shall be called on to act; but at all events I
wish to learn your ideas. Accident may keep Vizier Ali out of our hands for
six or seven months. There is no apprehension of any commotion in Oudh
or Benares.

Believe me, . . .

MORNINGTON

XXVII

The Earl of Mornington to the Rt Hon. Henry Dundas

16 March 1799, Fort St George
Secret and Confidential: no. 6

My dear Sir

Since the date of my *secret and confidential* letter *no. 5* (the 21st February),
no material variation has taken place in the state of affairs in India.
Dispatches have been received as late as the 19th of November from Capt-
[ain] Wilson,[1] who has been sent by the government of Bombay to the Red
Sea, containing satisfactory accounts of the state of the French forces in
Egypt. But the tenor of these dispatches has been since contradicted by
advices from Constantinople of the 8th December. We have received no
account of the arrival of Commodore Blankett[2] at this station.

I refer you to my dispatches to Lord Grenville for an account of the
embassy which Tipu Sahib has sent to France. I addressed these documents
to Lord Grenville as the substance of them is intimately connected with the
conduct of the Danish government in India. I have desired him to lay the
whole before you without delay.

My letter to the secret committee of this date will give you the outline of
the movements of the army. Before the period of the next overland dispatch,
I trust that I shall be able to send you a satisfactory account of the state of
affairs in Mysore.

---

[1] Capt. Samuel Wilson; military secretary to the governor of Bombay;
political agent in the Red Sea, 1798–9.
[2] Rear-Adm. John Blankett (d. 1801); flag officer in command, detached
squadron, Red Sea, 1798–1801.

In my letter to the secret committee, I have not mentioned, that a number of papers were taken in the house of Vizier Ali at the time of his flight from Benares. These papers contain matter of very great importance. They prove the existence of a connection between Vizier Ali and Sindhia, which must have commenced a very few weeks after the settlement of Vizier Ali at Benares in February 1798. They also prove that Vizier Ali had dispatched a vakil to Zeman Shah, and had made himself the channel of communication between that prince and the leading disaffected mahomedans in the Company's provinces. They further prove that Vizier Ali entertained a spy at Calcutta, who professed to have opened a negotiation with several natives of distinction at that place. It appears also from these papers, that some persons of consequence at Benares were accomplices in the plan of the late outrage committed in that city. I state to you merely the general outline of these very extraordinary papers, which I have received from Calcutta within these few days. Every precaution has been taken to prevent the consequences of any movement on the part of Sindhia's generals in Hindustan in favour of Vizier Ali, and in the present distracted state of Sindhia's councils and armies, and in the exhausted condition of his treasury, no danger seems likely to proceed from that quarter.

I shall forward to you a more particular statement of my opinion upon these papers at the earliest possible period. On some of them I shall hardly be able to form a competent judgement previous to my return to Calcutta. The reports of the spy appear to me to be exaggerated, if not entirely false. Upon the whole, I apprehend no mischief of any consequence from the late events at Benares. Duncan has expressed a strong wish to return to his old situation at that place; but requires to be reinstated exactly in the same authority which he possessed before. This arrangement would not be effected without an alteration of the whole system of judicature and revenue now established at Benares. On my return to Calcutta, I shall be able to form a judgement whether any public benefit might be expected from the restoration of Duncan under such circumstances.

I take this opportunity of entreating you, in the event of peace with France, to consider most seriously the danger of returning any of her possessions on the continent of India. The same observation applies with equal force to the Dutch possessions, as long as Holland shall remain a vassal of France. Above all, I trust you will not give back any part either of the French or Dutch possessions on the coast of Malabar, from whence the intercourse with Tipu is a matter of so much facility. Pondicherry, Chandangore, and Chinsurah, will become the sources of the most serious mischief to India, if they should return into democratic hands at the peace.

In none of my dispatches to the secret committee have I yet stated the principles of the adjustment with Tipu Sahib, which I conceive to be necessary to the security of the Company's possessions under the circumstances of the present moment. My mind is, however, completely made up upon the subject; and I have furnished General Harris with drafts of preliminary articles of a treaty to be concluded, whenever circumstances shall admit. The details of these articles would be too bulky for an overland conveyance, and in the present moment it would be premature to trouble you with them. The general outline of some of the articles you will find at the conclusion of my minute of the 12th of August last (enclosed in *private* letter *no. 9*).[1] Since that period a material variation of circumstance has taken place; not only by the disclosure of the French designs in Egypt, and by the establishment of their army in that favourable position for assisting the sultan, but also by the accession of strength which we have received at Hyderabad, and by the rapid progress of our military preparations. Every consideration of justice and policy demanded the reduction of the sultan's power, from the moment that he was proved to have been a party to M. Malartic's proclamation. The defect of means prevented my attempting any such reduction in the summer. At present, the necessity of reducing his power is considerably increased; and fortunately our means of effecting that indispensable object have received a proportionate augmentation. With this view of the subject, it is my intention to compel the sultan to pay a large proportion of the expenses, which he has forced us to incur, and also to cede to the Company the whole of his remaining territories on the coast of Malabar below the Ghats, with a small tract of territory which shall connect our possessions in Dindigul with Palghautcherry. To the Marathas and to the nizam, I propose that the sultan shall cede a territory equal in value to that ceded by him to the Company. The allies will, of course, divide equally whatever sum of money may be paid by Tipu on account of the expenses of the war. This is the outline of the proposed adjustment, if Tipu should think fit to treat for peace previous to the siege of his capital. If he should compel us to open our batteries against the place, I have directed General Harris to require the cession of half his country, and the payment of two crores of rupees; and if he should compel us to take Seringapatam, I have reserved to myself the power of making such arrangements as may appear advisable in that extreme case.

I think it proper to inform you that, early in December last, the sultan's principal manager on the coast of Malabar (who was employed as a deputy on his part in the late conferences with respect to the boundaries of Coorga) made overtures of a confidential nature, through a secret agent, to our commissioners employed on the same occasion. The amount of his communication was that Tipu had positively entered into a strict alliance with the French nation, and that the port of Onore, on the coast of Malabar, was to

[1] *Wellesley*, i, 159.

be ceded to the French as the price of their assistance in supporting the interests and views of the sultan. This circumstance is a sufficient proof of the danger of leaving any part of the coast of Malabar in the hands of Tipu.

Believe me, . . .

MORNINGTON

XXVIII

The Rt Hon. Henry Dundas to the Earl of Mornington

18 March 1799, Wimbledon
Private: no. 6

My dear Lord

As the ships at present dispatched are under orders to sail, it deprives me of the opportunity of writing to you upon the important subjects treated of in your letters, lately arrived overland. These letters are so voluminous that they are not yet deciphered; and from what is reported to me as to the progress made in deciphering, I have great doubts if these dispatches will be ready to be brought under my view before the ships actually sail. From your general letter to the secret committee, and your letter to myself of the 24th of August last, I perceive that the subjects of those undeciphered papers are of a very interesting nature, and your Lordship may be assured of hearing from me by the first opportunity after I have considered them.

It is my intention, in my present letter, to advert to some of the general topics to which you have referred in your letter of an earlier date, and the subject of which I may not have exhausted in any former communication.

It is impossible for me not to begin with noticing the letter recently received, enclosing the treaty you have made with the nizam. Your Lordship has long before this time anticipated the satisfaction I have derived from that transaction, which has been completed in so masterly and effectual a manner. Long before this, I trust, it has been carried into final execution. I have long felt uneasy from the circumstance of the French force in the service of the nizam; and it was, perhaps, the circumstance of all others which gave me the most uneasiness, when I became satisfied that the powerful armaments under Bonaparte were destined for Egypt, as his best road for the annoyance of our Indian possessions. Your treaty with the nizam effectually puts an end to every alarm upon that part of the business, and whether you consider it negatively as removing the French force from

125

our neighbourhood, or positively in respect of the additional strength it affords to ourselves and the aid it gives to our finances, it is a transaction which tells in our favour in a variety of ways, and was well worth accomplishing at any risk, even if the Maratha powers had been dissatisfied with it. I do not, however, see any real foundation for their being so, and I trust it will not be long before I shall hear that your Lordship has been able, by proper exertions with the Marathas, to connect them with the nizam and us still more closely, upon the principles of a common interest of defensive alliance against Tipu, and every power in alliance with France.

Upon the subject of the rajah of Berar, it is only necessary for me to say, that in so far as my general knowledge and recollection of Indian affairs enable me at present to decide, it appears to me that he has always been friendly to the British interests in India; and I should conceive that in no respect a close connection with him can be prejudicial to our defensive system, and the desire of preserving the general peace of India, which, if it can be observed with honour, is certainly our wisest system; and as it is most likely to be disturbed by the hostility of Tipu, it of course follows that every connection, which strengthens our power against him, must be ultimately beneficial to the Indian interests of Great Britain. This, naturally, leads me to advert to the views of Zeman Shah, and the situation of Sindhia as connected with that subject.

It was some time ago the fashion, in my opinion too much, to undervalue the menaces of Zeman Shah respecting India, but I think that opinion is gradually wearing away as it ought to do. You are more in the way of collecting accurate information than I am; but if the French were ever to obtain such a footing as to enable them seriously to distress us, I have long thought that it would be a material point of the plan to obtain the co-operation of Zeman Shah. And even if Tipu himself, from any misguided ambition, should be induced to undertake any extensive project against us, I must always believe that his best endeavours would be used to obtain the assistance of Zeman Shah. I take it for granted Mr Jones,[1] at Baghdad, transmits regularly to India the information his situation there enables him to collect; but in case, by any accident, it should not have reached you, I herewith send you a copy of the information recently received from him on the subject of Zeman Shah, and comparing it with others, it strongly confirms me in the belief of his hostile designs, and that we ought to keep a very watchful eye upon the motions of that prince, whose talents, military force, and pecuniary resources, afford to him the means of being a formidable opponent. It would be too strong for me to state, that under no circumstances our own forces were to go beyond our own provinces and the territories of the vizier; but the temptation must be very

[1] Harford Jones (Brydges) (1764–1847); resident at Baghdad, 1798–1806.

great, and the advantage very evident, to induce us to do so. The means of resisting any intended aggression on the part of Zeman Shah appear to be the following. First, to encourage and keep up those distractions and animosities within his own territories, the apprehensions of which must always, to a certain degree, keep him in a state of alarm, and which obliged him to return rapidly from his last attempt to invade Hindustan. Secondly, every encouragement should be given to the Sikhs and Rajput tribes to harrass and distress him in his progress. But lastly, what of all others appears most material is, upon the ground of his own danger, to engage Sindhia cordially in that defensive system of alliance, which it is our interest, by every means, to strengthen and confirm, with a view to the security of our Indian empire. It is perfectly obvious, that if ever Zeman Shah gains a material footing in Hindustan, Sindhia and his power must fall the first sacrifice to his ambition.

Under these circumstances, I do not think your Lordship can do a more essential service to the interests of your country in India, than by using your best endeavours to soothe and heal those jarring animosities which annihilate the force of the government of Poona, and render them an easy prey to the restless ambition either of Tipu Sultan or of Zeman Shah. Nothing can more effectively tend to secure this object, than persuading Sindhia to abandon that system of wickedness, perfidy, and intrigue, which he is now pursuing at Poona, and engaging him to return to the care and protection of his own territories, which require his best attention, and must ultimately tend to gratify his ambition, and consolidate his power, more than any advantages he can hope to attain by aiming at more remote or distant objects of ambition. I cannot more strongly convey to your Lordship the importance I attach to the suggestions I have laid before you, than by stating it as my opinion, that if you are able to consolidate in one defensive system, the nizam's power, the Maratha power, and the power of Great Britain in India, we have nothing to fear in that quarter from any combinations that can be formed against us. I think in some letter you ask me whether the influence of Russia in Persia might not be used with effect to check the views of Zeman Shah. It will be the business of Mr Jones at Baghdad, and the other residents in that part of the world, to convey to us such information as they can collect, relative to the state of Persia, and we may act accordingly; and in the case of extremity, we might be obliged to act differently from what theory and a well-digested policy may suggest. But however well we at present are with the court of Russia, and however happy I am in the prospect that we may long be so, it must be some such extremity as that I have suggested, which should induce me to think it wise, at all to involve Russia in any of our Indian affairs and alliances.

Upon the subject of Tipu Sultan, I have little to say in this letter, further than to express my approbation of the line of conduct you have pursued relative to that restless prince. You will have seen long before this, from the letter I wrote to you in the month of June last, how much the principles upon which you acted correspond with the suggestions I laid before you at that time, when the object of Bonaparte's expedition was not ascertained, but which for the reasons I then gave, I was satisfied was intended for the prosecution of those objects which afterwards proved to be the case. The first thought which you seem to have entertained, *viz.* that of attacking Tipu in consequence of his conduct at Mauritius, was a very natural feeling, and there can be no doubt that the ambassadors he sent there, and the alliance he appears to have formed upon principles hostile to us, would have fully justified you in any measures you might have thought proper to adopt. His conduct was tantamount to a declaration of war against us, but still I think you judged well in not bringing it to that extremity. By the line of conduct you have pursued towards him, you have asserted the pride and honour of the British name, which must never for a moment be let down; but you have done it in a manner to enable you to review, deliberately, your resources, and to arrange your force in such a manner as will enable you to act with effect, if the humility of acknowledgements is not adequate to what our power, and the justice of our cause, entitle us to demand. By this delay, likewise, you have accomplished the important point of strengthening the connection with the nizam, and of disbanding that pernicious French force which had grown up within his territory. Besides this, you have received the additional confidence naturally resulting from the military force which has been sent to you from this country and from the Cape, and I likewise trust that the bullion which has been sent from this country has reached you before this time, and has tended to enliven your circulation and resources. It shall not be my fault if much more is not done in the same line in the course of the present season, but I do not enlarge upon that subject at present, as I will have occasion to advert to it in a letter upon the trade and finances of India, which I intend to write to you [in] time enough I hope to go by the present conveyance. Neither has the delay been attended with any detriment to your affairs.

It is unnecessary to trouble you with any details with regard to the situation of the French army in Egypt. Our information of what passes there is so slow and tedious; I trust that the means which have been taken to supply you with intelligence from thence, have kept you as well and early informed in India, if not more so than we are at home. But from what we have learned from various quarters, I flatter myself Lord Nelson's splendid victory, and the exertions of our fleet in the Mediterranean, leave us little reason to apprehend any danger at present to India from the French force which has landed in Egypt. I trust that army will find its grave in

Egypt, and consequently, as Tipu must be well informed of those circumstances, you will not find, that his expectation of a French succour will add much pride or vigour to his communications with you.

As your Lordship is perfectly familiar with the different points of which I have treated in this letter, I have not thought it necessary to trouble you with minute details on each topic; but I flatter myself I have said enough to make you perfectly acquainted with my sentiments on those leading points of Indian policy. The result of the whole is, that our security rests, primarily, on our own reputation and power; but that in order to render our exertions efficient and permanent, it ought to be our unceasing care to keep the power of the nizam, and of the whole branches of the Maratha confederacy, in a strict amity with us, for the purpose of establishing an impregnable barrier against all Asiatic ambition, whether acting separately or in co-operation with European allies. As an essential ingredient of this system, I have no hesitation in stating that your Lordship is warranted to consider the nourishing and maintaining any French force or Frenchmen, within any of their territories, as an insurmountable bar against any close connection with us.

It still remains for me to state to you my opinion upon one or two separate points on which you desire to be advised.

You desire to know what is meant by a *considerable French force*, which is the expression generally used in the instructions from home on the subject of Tipu Sultan receiving [a] French force into his country. The application of the principle to the particular occasion must be left to the exercise of sound discretion, but as a general principle, I have no hesitation in stating that, we are entitled under the circumstances of the present times, to consider the admission of any French force into his army, be it greater or smaller, as direct hostility to us.

In some of your letters, I perceive your Lordship is strongly impressed with the necessity of depriving Tipu of his maritime possessions, with a view of our security and the means of preventing his communications with the armaments of France. I doubt if your ideas do not go too far on the subject. The expense of fortifying and garrisoning them would be very considerable, and the end in view would not be answered without a large force constantly stationed on that coast, to prevent the invasion of a French fleet if they were in a condition to attempt it. I take it Mangalore is the only harbour he possesses, and it is not adequate to the reception of ships of large force. It behoves them to keep out at sea, beyond the protection of any guns from the shore. If I am right in my information on that subject, it does not occur to me that it is more favourable to an aggression against us than any other part of the open beach along the whole of that extensive coast. I am so much impressed with that idea, as to have conceived a strong opinion that, if the

French were successful in sending an armament to Tipu, Goa is the point they would most likely first aim at. Some very intelligent persons have mentioned to me that Diu would be an useful acquisition to France, with a view to co-operating with any hostile attempts against us from that quarter of India. These are points which are essential to be attended to in our transactions with Portugal, so as in some way to put them in our possession. They are of no use whatever to Portugal, and may be made the instruments of incalculable mischief to us.

I shall be glad, however, to have your sentiments again on these points, in consequence of what further information you may be able to collect upon them.

I remain, . . .

HENRY DUNDAS

XXIX

The Rt Hon. Henry Dundas to the Earl of Mornington

18 March 1799, Wimbledon
Private: no. 7

My dear Lord

I have now before me your minute of the 19th of June last respecting the finances of India, and also your recent letter upon the same subject, dated the 23rd of August last and addressed to the secret committee of the court of directors. The financial state of our affairs in India, and the arrangement of them in future, will be the subject of official correspondence from the court of directors by some early conveyance; but the present situation of the commerce and finances of India have suggested to my mind many important considerations, which I would think it wrong to withhold from you in the form of a private communication, as the opinions I shall lay before you may probably operate upon your conduct, previous to the period when the same opinions may reach you in the more tedious form of dispatches through the medium of the court of directors. This mode of earlier communication with you is the more necessary, as I am aware some of the opinions which I hold will be the cause of a difference of opinion among the directors, and must, ultimately, be settled by the authority of the board of control, a form of proceeding necessarily productive of delay.

If there had been the prospect of the war coming to any speedy conclusion, I should not have been [made] uneasy by the circumstance of a very considerable addition to the debt in India, for the purpose of continuing a large investment from an Indian capital; because from the experience I have already had in extricating their affairs, under very unpromising circumstances, I should have felt perfectly satisfied, that a few years after the return of peace would have sufficed speedily to wipe off the debt which the mixed exigencies of war and commerce had created. This, however, has its bounds; for if the debt in India is allowed to increase so much as to become unwieldly and unmanageable, we are cut off from the means of extricating our affairs when peace shall have returned. The loans, from being made in times of difficulty, are accomplished at an exorbitant rate of interest, and thereby exhaust the whole of the surplus revenue, which is to operate as the sinking fund for the redemption of the debt after the return of peace. It is the more necessary I should give a particular attention to these considerations, because it is very natural for the court of directors to turn their eyes chiefly to the state of their affairs in Leadenhall Street, and both they and the proprietors are flattered by the view of sales at home uncommonly large, and a swelling balance in their coffers at home, while at the same time it is obvious to every person who will take a comprehensive view of their affairs, that this flattering delusion, permitted to go on for a very few years, would bring irretrievable ruin upon the finances of India, and totally disable us from maintaining that pre-eminence of wealth and power, which has proved so important to the general interests of the British empire.

Viewing this subject in all its bearings, I am well aware of the importance of keeping up the means of a large investment from India. This principle is important, not only from the encouragement it affords to the navigation and shipping of the kingdom, from the addition it makes annually to the wealth and capital of the country, and from its being a fruitful source of revenue; but in addition to all these and similar considerations, I must add the necessity of such an investment, as immediately connected with the prosperity of our Indian provinces. It is to the increased exports from India to Europe that we are to attribute the increase of Indian prosperity, industry, population, and revenue; and the manufacturers of that country would be reduced to very deplorable circumstances, if any severe check was to be given to the usual investment and exports from India. These considerations necessarily lead to the conclusion of bringing home as large an investment as our means will enable us to do. I see no difficulty in accomplishing this; but it must be done by means which do not lead to the ruin of our finances in India. The same circumstances which have led to put the whole commerce of the world into the hands of this country, do operate in a proportionable degree to extend, beyond the example of all former times, the trade of the East India Company, and the produce of their sales in

Leadenhall Street. This ought to be encouraged by every means; but the overflowing balance from thence arising, after defraying their necessary burdens at home, ought to be employed in the purchase of bullion to be conveyed to India and China, for the purchase of a large and profitable investment. The times, from the influx of wealth into this country, are highly favourable to such an operation, the beneficial effects of which are obvious in a variety of ways. Your Lordship states, and all the other settlements concur in the same statement, that our Indian possessions are greatly distressed from the want of specie. The measure I have mentioned effectually removes that distress, and is likewise productive of another essential benefit. It is stated that the increase in loans at so high a rate of interest checks all private credit, and obstructs all other pecuniary transactions; but this inconvenience would not be found if the system I have alluded to was carried into execution.

It is with much satisfaction I observe in some of your Lordship's recent dispatches, that you find yourself warranted, by the opinions of some of the most intelligent persons upon the spot, that the export of manufactures from this country may be considerably increased. This is certainly the most desirable of all resources for the supply of a commercial investment from India, and it ought to have no limits, except what are prescribed by the power of selling them in India or China.

Another commercial resource is what can be got in India upon the foundation of the remittance plan. This, I understand, has likewise received a check in consequence of the high rate of interest paid for the government loans in India; but if these loans are stopped, and the capital of the debt itself considerably diminished each year by the remittance plan, an effectual cure is administered to this inconvenience, and the commercial resources of the Company materially aided without the necessity of extravagant loans for that purpose.

These are the outlines of the system, which, in my opinion, ought to be pursued during the remainder of the war; and as, during its continuance, our commerce will remain unbounded and the wealth of the world continue to be collected here, no inconvenience whatever can arise from the export of bullion to India and China. On the contrary, I understand it would rather be, in this point of view, materially convenient. The result, therefore, of what I have stated is, that the investment ought not to be diminished, but kept up to its present standard, and the revenues for doing so are, first, the surplus revenues in India, after defraying the expense of establishment and the interest of debt. This fund will increase in proportion as the debt is diminished by the plan of remittance. Secondly, by bills upon the East India Company, to the amount of what can be got there applicable to the reduction of the capital of the debt in India. Thirdly, an increased amount of the export of manufactures from this country, which, generally upon an average, has been reckoned for some years past for India, exclusive of China, to amount to about £500,000. And lastly, a remittance of bullion to whatever amount may be necessary, joined to the above-mentioned resources, to keep up the usual investments from India.

If this system is adopted and invariably adhered to, we will be enabled, without any material inconvenience, to continue the war so long as our inveterate enemy shall be disposed, or in a condition to carry on the contest. The many other collateral advantages resulting from such a system, and connected with the safety and prosperity of India, are so obvious, it is unnecessary to trouble your Lordship with detailing them.

Having stated all that appears to be necessary, so far as concerns the finances of India, and the commercial resources of the East India Company as connected with their finances, I wish now to direct your Lordship's attention to the trade of India in a more extended point of view.

It is notorious that, at no period, the capital or commercial powers of the East India Company have been able to embrace the whole, or near the whole, of the wealth of India exported from thence by trade to Europe. This is placed beyond a doubt by the great share of the India trade now in possession of neutral nations, a great part of which rests upon the capital and fortune of the servants of the East India Company. I endeavoured to remedy this obvious absurdity by obliging the East India Company to allot a certain proportion of tonnage to the purposes of private trade. They agreed to it with reluctance, and it is so managed as to render the provision almost illusory. I need not enumerate to your Lordship the causes which have rendered it of no avail: they appear in the applications made to the government of India by the resident traders in India, and are recorded in the correspondence between the board of trade and supreme council in India, so that they must be perfectly familiar to your Lordship. In truth, there is no remedy for this evil but two. First, alluring the trade of India to resort to the port of London, by diminishing the expenses of doing so. The second is, by authorizing the governments of India to license the appropriation of India-built shipping to the purpose of bringing home that Indian trade which the means and capital of the East India Company is unable to bring home. The first of those ways will, I trust, be effectuated by the bill which Mr Pitt has agreed to introduce for the reduction of the duties upon imports from India, and the second must be accomplished by giving to the government in India that authority to license India-built shipping, to which I have already alluded.

This last measure will, I take it for granted, undergo much discussion before it can be carried into execution, but it must be carried. The whole weight of the shipping interest will be opposed to such a proposition, under a most false and erroneous idea that it is prejudicial to their interests: nothing but ignorance of the subject could lead them to entertain such an idea. They made an attempt to accomplish it by inflaming the interests of the ship carpenters in the River Thames, at the time of the general mutiny in the navy. It was unhandsome proceeding upon their part, and was resisted by me in a letter I then addressed to the principal ship-builders in the river. I do not know whether they did not choose to answer it, or whether they found it to be answerable, but I never received any reply to it. I have often thought upon the subject since, and the more I have thought upon it, the more I am convinced of the truth of every proposition which the letter contains. I send you a copy of it, and you may rest assured that no exertion shall be wanting on my part speedily to introduce into practice the system detailed in that letter.

It has not reached me in any authentic form, but I am credibly informed that your Lordship, upon the application of the resident traders in India, has authorized a number of India-built ships to be taken up, for the purpose of bringing home the surplus trade of India. I hope the information is true, both because it is a measure of much wisdom, and because it will bring the point directly to issue, and you need not be under any apprehension as to the result to it.

Although, from the influence I have stated, there may be a contest in the court of directors with regard to the subject last mentioned, I do not believe there will be any material objection offered against any of the other measures I have had occasion to treat of in this letter. Indeed, one leading principle has already been acted upon to a considerable extent, for the court of directors have already sent out to India bullion to the amount of £159,226, and they have it in contemplation to send more. In short, I make no doubt of their being induced to send out what is requisite for the accomplishment of the commercial plan I have detailed in the course of this letter.

I have nothing further to trouble you with at present. It is only necessary for me to remind you, that although the opinions I have laid before you rest for the present merely upon the footing of a private unofficial communication, I trust they, or the substance of them, will speedily be conveyed to you in due official form.

I remain, . . .

HENRY DUNDAS

XXX

The Rt Hon. Henry Dundas to the Earl of Mornington

19 March 1799, Wimbledon
Private: no. 8

My dear Lord

The progress of the Indian business has been unusually retarded this winter by the animosities and divisions we have got into among the directors, and I am sorry to say that the conduct of the chairman has not been what I could have expected from him. I send you the paper which Mr Scott has circulated among his friends, and when it appears that Mr Bosanquet[1] was in possession of the judicial proceedings which passed at Manila, Mr Pitt and I can scarcely find grounds to exculpate the chairman from malicious motives in making the charge, founded upon materials which the judge at Manila had so properly reprobated with great accuracy and ability. This has the worse appearance as the chairman and Mr Scott had differed much for some months before on questions of extravagant freight, in which the great body of the directors had joined Scott and left the chairman; and it is imputed to him that he brought forward this calumnious charge on the ground of pique and spleen, and has allowed himself to be made the dupe of the shipping interests in Leadenhall Street. In the question of acquitting Scott, he was supported by only two other directors, and they are supposed to be Mr Elphinstone and Mr Cotton.[2] How deeply this last is in that faction, you will judge from a pamphlet he has lately published, of which I will desire Cabell[3] to send you a copy. It is a piece of very flimsy nonsense, at least the latter parts of it, but it shows you the spirit of monopoly which activates them, but which we shall very soon crush.

Yours very sincerely,

HENRY DUNDAS

PS. Mr Cabell has the pleasure of enclosing a masterly reply to Mr Cotton's pamphlet, which he hopes will be acceptable to Lord Mornington.
19 April 1799.

---

[1] Jacob Bosanquet; director, City interest; chairman, 1798, 1803, 1811.
[2] Hon. William Fullarton Elphinstone; director, Shipping Interest; chairman, 1804, 1806, 1814. Joseph Cotton, director, Shipping Interest.
[3] William Cabell; assistant-secretary (permanent), board of control, 1795–1800; died, 23 May 1800.

XXXI

The Rt Hon. Henry Dundas to the Earl of Mornington

21 March 1799, Whitehall
Private: no. 9

My dear Lord

I think it better to send you in a private communication, than by a public letter, the accompanying papers, which have been sent to me by Lord Grenville.[1] I take it for granted you will not have much difficulty in finding out the author and dealing with him as he deserves.

Yours sincerely,

HENRY DUNDAS

XXXII

The Rt Hon. Henry Dundas to the Earl of Mornington

21 March 1799, Whitehall
Private: no. 10

My dear Lord

By this conveyance, I have troubled your Lordship with a dispatch on the general system of alliance which we ought to pursue with a view to the security of our Indian possessions, and likewise with a dispatch on the subject of our Indian finance and commerce. In the present letter, I wish to bring under your view a few observations on the interior administration of our different settlements.

On the subject of Bengal, I have much satisfaction in feeling that I have occasion to say very little. The wise system adopted during Lord Cornwallis' administration, and to which I make no doubt you adhere, leaves no reason to apprehend any real danger to the wealth and resources of the valuable provinces under your immediate administration. I think for the last two years I have observed that the arrears of land revenue were somewhat larger than they used to be. I trust this has been owing to some accident, and not to any defect in the system of permanent security given to the landholders of

---

[1] Robert Liston, the minister in Washington, reported that articles from Calcutta, critical of British rule, were appearing in the Philadelphia newspapers. Add. MSS. 37274, f. 122.

India. Among the many other important benefits expected to arise from that beneficent plan, a prominent one was the regularity in payment of the stipulated jumma, and nothing has ever occurred to me, or been stated to me, which had the tendency to lessen the prospect of that benefit resulting from it. I could not, however, refrain from bringing the circumstance to which I have referred immediately under your view.

As we have limited the extent of land revenue in India, by the measure of permanent settlement, it has sometimes occurred to me to reflect, that the principles, which led to the adoption of that system, naturally opened a prospect of other sources of revenue, in so far as it entitled us to expect an increase of the wealth, industry, and population, of the country. Every circumstance which has since happened, has led to the conviction that these effects have been produced by it. The increasing produce of the revenue on salt, opium, and spirituous liquors, all tend to corroborate this observation. I wish, therefore, to direct your attention to consider and report to me, how far, in your opinion, there is, either in the articles I have mentioned, or in any others of a similar nature, any prospect of raising more revenue on articles of general consumption among the natives of India. This can never be attempted but with a perfect consideration of their happiness and content, and I am likewise aware that a people, whose wants are very limited and simple, do not present to their government the same various objects of taxation which exist in other countries differently circumstanced. It appears, however, to be a point worthy of your consideration, if possible at all times to ensure a revenue in India equal to all the exigencies, not only of our expensive establishments, but for the payment of a tribute to this country through the medium of a beneficial and increasing commerce.

The circumstance, connected with the government of Bengal, to which I can look with the least confidence, is the situation of Oudh. I trust the late arrangements made by Lord Teignmouth may enable your Lordship to give further improvement to this essential part of our system. I have nothing very minute to suggest; all I have to say is comprehended under two general heads. The first is a just and pure administration by the vizier of his own country, in which is comprehended an accurate collection of his real revenues, and an economical expenditure of them. The second is that he could be induced to keep an efficient military establishment for the security of his own and our frontier. This object can be accomplished best by dispersing his useless rabble, and forming an army to be kept up and disciplined under our immediate superintendence.

Respecting the affairs of the Coromandel Coast, I had so full a communication with you before your departure, it is not necessary to add much more at present. I think, for some time past, the interior administration of affairs there have considerably improved. Their revenues are increasing, their estimates are made with more accuracy, and their accounts are kept much more regularly than they used to be; and I have a perfect reliance on the assiduity, talents, and integrity, of Lord Clive, that the improvement will be progressive. Our chief difficulties in the administration of the Carnatic are—first, the anomalous connection in which we stand with the nabob of Arcot—secondly, a similar inconvenience attending the government of Tanjore—thirdly, the insubordination and distractions so frequently prevalent in the Northern Circars.

The double government existing in the Carnatic has long been felt as a serious calamity to that country. It enfeebles the natural resources of the country, and above all, tends to continue that system of intrigue and consequent corruption, which has been imputed to the Madras government so much more than to our other settlements. It is singular to remark that the country of Oudh is the other part of India where the purity of the Company's servants has been most suspected, and that the same circumstance of a double government has always been assigned as the cause. Consistently with our treaties with the nabob of Arcot, we cannot at present materially meliorate his government, but must wait favourable opportunities, and embrace such means of conciliation and attention to him as are most likely to accomplish this desirable object. We must lay our account with being at all times obstructed in those views by that corruption and intrigue to which I have referred. Nothing will counteract it but a pure and steady government, acting instantaneously against any of the Company's servants, who may be detected in those practices. Lord Hobart's administration was characterized by a very laudable spirit in this respect, and you cannot doubt that the same purity and spirit will actuate the conduct of Lord Clive, who will have the additional advantage of the newly established judicature to aid him in the punishment of those offenders. I have always thought, however much it has been the fashion to clamour against it, that the supreme judicature at Calcutta has had very beneficial effects in preserving the purity of the servants under that presidency.

The affairs of Tanjore are more simple in their nature, and less complicated in their administration. It is exposed, in a certain degree, to the same inconveniences which have been injurious to the government of the Carnatic. But from the recent transactions which have taken place there, and from the feelings of gratitude which appear on the mind of the rajah, I flatter myself he will be inclined more and more to listen to the admonitions of our government, to whose power and justice he is indebted for his situation. If those sentiments regulate his conduct, our part is simple and easy. We have nothing to ask of him but a pure and virtuous administration of the affairs of his country; the effects of which will be equally felt by him and us, in the respective interests we have in the prosperity of Tanjore.

The Northern Circars have certainly never produced to us those advantages which the extent of the country, and the fertility of its soil in many parts, entitles us to expect. I know not to what cause to attribute it, but the inhabitants of some of its higher parts seem to be in a state of very uncivilized society, and this can only be gradually removed, by a steady, just, and vigorous government. We must not too rapidly apply to that part of our possessions the same principles of government which have been wisely applied to the more civilized provinces of Bengal. I believe the same observations may, to a considerable degree, be made with regard to some parts of the Circars, that I shall immediately bring under your view with regard to the Malabar provinces. From the situation of the countries in our possession on the coast of Malabar, they are calculated to be either a great security, or a great annoyance, to our power in India, and whether they shall be the one or the other depends much on the manner in which they are managed. I was much struck with a letter I received from General Stuart on this subject. He is an intelligent man, and being the result of his own observation on the spot, I am the more disposed to rely on the solidity of his observations, and I recommend them to your serious attention. I send you an extract of the letter to which I refer, and your Lordship will observe that I have made considerable use of it in the public dispatches, which go by this conveyance to the Bombay government. Among other particulars in this letter, the concluding part attracted my attention, and, as coming from so excellent a military authority, they tended to confirm an opinion I have long been inclined to entertain, I mean the impropriety of too much dividing and distracting our force on the Malabar coast. We ought undoubtedly, at all times, to maintain an efficient government at Bombay, for the safety of the island and the many valuable interests established there; but having done this, the great body of our army under that presidency ought, in my opinion, to be concentrated in some position on the Malabar coast, best calculated to make an impression on Tipu's country, if, at any time, we are compelled to engage in hostilities with him. I wish this part of the subject to be duly examined, and if the idea is a right one, it ought certainly to be acted upon systematically. It is impossible we can allow our troops to be expended in hunting through the jungles in the Malabar country after every refractory rajah, who may be disposed to be troublesome. The late transactions with the Cotiote Rajah ought to afford us a satisfactory admonition.

I remain, . . .

HENRY DUNDAS

XXXIII

The Rt Hon. Henry Dundas to the Earl of Mornington

23 March 1799, Whitehall
Private: no. 11

My dear Lord

I have received your overland dispatch of the 8th September, on the subject of monthly intelligence being conveyed to you by bulletin by my private secretary. There can be no difficulty in arranging such a mode of communication. Mr Huskisson, as being in my confidence in many particulars entrusted to no other, is the person proper to be employed, and I have given him directions accordingly; and likewise as to sending you a proper cypher for the purpose of corresponding with me. At present the cypher you use in corresponding with me is the India House cypher, which I understand is a bad one; and besides, I may not choose that the gentlemen in Leadenhall Street should know the contents of my private correspondence with you.

From a desire to save my eyes as much as possible, and not to give more trouble than necessary to you in reading my letters, they, with very few exceptions, will be wrote by the hand of my private secretary.[1] As I have now got both Canning and William Dundas[2] to be members of my board, I probably may introduce them into the train of conveying some of my confidential sentiments to you. In short, in some way or other, you may rest assured of being kept duly informed of everything material for you to know. But don't be surprised if you do not receive pointed intelligence from home at times when you may naturally expect it. A very strong illustration of this occurs in the very important transactions connected with Bonaparte's expedition. From the time I wrote to you my conjectures and ideas on that subject in June last, I was in a state of perfect uncertainty for many months, till we at last heard of the capture of Malta and then of the landing at Alexandria. This intelligence came under very alarming circumstances, being attended with information that Admiral Nelson, having reached Alexandria before the French armament, and not finding them there, had returned to Sicily in quest of them. This state of miserable anxiety continued down to the time of the accounts arriving of his glorious victory. This set us at ease, the more so as the letter I received from Lord Nelson announced to me, that he has used the wise precaution of sending the same accounts to India that he sent home to us, so that you would be informed at

---

[1] Robert Saunders Dundas (2nd Viscount Melville) (1771–1851); until 1800 private secretary to his father; president of the board of control, 1807–12.
[2] Dundas' nephew.

the same time we were. Indeed, my opinion is, that the measure which has been taken of placing Mr Jones at Baghdad, as a centre of negotiation and intelligence with India, will have the effect of informing you of every trans-action in the Mediterranean and the Levant fully as soon as we learn them at home. If it was not for this circumstance, I should have been often very uneasy indeed in the course of these ten months past. At this moment, we know nothing with certainty of the state of Bonaparte's army. We in general hear that he had reached Cairo, and that his army was mouldering away under many hardships, so as to leave no apprehension of his reaching India in the manner it is supposed he intended; and the precautions, which these retardments of his progress, have enabled both you in India and us at home to use, have greatly removed the cloud which, for some time, darkened the eastern hemisphere. We have got Minorca, and are in daily hopes of the surrender of Malta, so that with these various aids and the continuance of a powerful navy in the Mediterranean, it seems scarcely possible that any reinforcements can be sent to the French army in Egypt; and if it is not reinforced, I should hope the Russians, the Turks, and the Arabs, will dispose of the land force as completely as Lord Nelson has of the naval part of the armament. But although we have got this vantage-ground respecting India, it is still necessary not to relax our vigilance a single moment.

I am, . . .

HENRY DUNDAS

XXXIV

The Rt Hon. Henry Dundas to the Earl of Mornington

25 March 1799, Wimbledon
Private: no. 12

My dear Lord

In the letter I wrote you a few days ago, I mentioned Mr Pitt's intending immediately to introduce a bill for reducing the Indian duties. The bill is introduced,[1] and I send you the rough draft of it, not having time to order a copy of it, in case I should miss the ships under orders to sail.

Yours sincerely,

HENRY DUNDAS

[1] *Parlt. Hist.*, xxxiv, 1.

XXXV

The Rt Hon. Henry Dundas to the Earl of Mornington

17 April 1799, Wimbledon
Private: [*Separate*]

My dear Lord

I received your letter respecting your brother, Colonel Wellesley. So many colonels must be included in the next promotion of major-generals, it will of course be kept off as long as possible; but when ever it does happen, I shall take care that he shall be upon the staff in India.

I remain, . . .

HENRY DUNDAS

XXXVI

The Earl of Mornington to the Rt Hon. Henry Dundas

21 April 1799, Fort St George
Secret and Confidential: no. 7

My dear Dundas

I have been fortunately able to appoint Capt[ain] Salmond[1] one of my aides de camp a few days after his landing here. I have written to Mr Scott on the subject. Mrs Salmond is very well, and better looking than any of our Bengal ladies.

I enclose two very curious papers respecting a treaty concluded between Tipu Sultan and the French in 1797. Lord Hobart is in possession of further information on this subject, which he received from Mr Webbe. My firm belief is that the outline of the treaty is correct. It reached Webbe through a very credible channel.

I am under great uneasiness respecting the chief command of the army in Bengal, which I hear is to be given to Sir James Craig the moment Clarke shall retire; an event not distant. If this event should happen, I am convinced from the universal report of Sir J[ames] Craig's temper, and from

---

[1] Capt. James Salmond (1766–1837); military secretary to the governor-general, 1799–1800; military auditor-general, Bengal, 1800–3; married, 2 July 1798, Louisa, daughter of David Scott.

what I have seen of his letters, that it will be impossible for me to remain in India. I am at present on good terms with Craig, but I was obliged, as I hinted to you by the *Eurydice*, to take him down from his exalted station. In council, and in all discussions, I know he will be intolerable. He has rendered some service to the army, but he is very ignorant still of the real nature of our native troops, and of their comparative value with those of the country powers. The proper arrangement would be *Harris* to Bengal, *Stuart* to Madras, *Craig* to Bombay. If Harris should choose to return to Europe with his Mysorean laurels (for laurels he will gain), then Stuart to Bengal, Craig to Madras, and who you will to Bombay. Harris is far from an able man, but he is active, zealous, and honest, and warmly attached to me. Stuart would be extremely useful on this coast, where much improvement in the military establishment of an economical, as well as of every other, description, must be introduced at the conclusion of the peace. Stuart is unquestionably the best officer in India, and Bengal (notwithstanding Lord Teignmouth's opinion), believe me, requires much correction. In any event, for God's sake spare me from Craig's pugnacious spirit of wrangling. I have heard from other quarters that Gen[eral] Stuart[1] who was in Portugal (Lord Bute's brother) is to succeed Clarke. I am persuaded you will never permit such a madman to enter India. Let me have a sober, well-tempered, tractable man, and I am content. I trust you will give serious attention to my suggestion relative to the independence of the King's army in the government. The King's army now in India forms an immense force. Is it wise to rest such an instrument in the hands of any but the supreme power? A refractory commander-in-chief might now soon become a much more powerful man than the governor-general.

I wrote to express my wish that Lady Mornington should come out to me. She has written to me expressing such fears of the voyage and climate, and stating such reasons against quitting my children, that I have relinquished the idea of urging her to come. I beg you will not allow her to be teased into embarking; as I should ever afterwards be miserable if anything untoward should happen to her.

I trust you will suggest to the directors the propriety of conferring some mark of distinction on our gallant, beloved, but still suffering friend, Capt[ain] Cooke of the *Sybille*, who took the *La Forte* at the mouth of the Ganges. Urge Lord Spencer[2] to show him honour, and urge his Lordship to put his admirals under my orders. They should be directed in time of war never to keep fewer than three frigates at all seasons in the bay of Bengal, and a large force at Bombay. These points have both been entirely

---

[1] Lt-Gen. Sir Charles Stuart (1753–1801); 4th son of the 3rd earl of Bute.
[2] George John, 2nd Earl Spencer (1758–1834); first lord of the admiralty, 1794–1801.

neglected, hence our disgraces at the mouths of the Ganges, and the capture of the *Raymond* and *Woodcot* etc.

I cannot speak in too high terms of L[or]d Clive's temper and honour; but by the next dispatch I shall send you some hints respecting his fitness for this gov[ernmen]t and eventually for the gov[ernmen]t-gen[eral]. I really love him, but I know you expect me to speak without favour or affection on all public subjects, and above all on the characters of men. Webbe has obliterated all his offences, by the most diligent, active, and zealous, service; and to the astonishment of everybody (particularly of Petrie), I have never uttered a harsh phrase, or shown a symptom of coldness or dislike to him, who certainly was engaged in a very dangerous and unwarrantable faction against me. But he is a convert, and I not being a Hindu have admitted him into the pale of my good graces. *Mihi cum republica in gratiam rediit.*

I mean tomorrow to open my batteries against the nabob. I have advanced my parallels very near Chepank, and if I do not succeed in taking the place, I think I shall be able to make a lodgement, from whence successful operations may be carried on in another campaign. The affairs of Tanjore will still prove a knotty point. The question is made an object of party, and the difficulty of reaching the truth is almost incredible.

Fred[erick] North[1] is here. He does business very well, and maintains himself gravely as a governor should. He is respected and thought efficient. You ought to confirm his appointment of Mr Carrington,[2] a valuable man, especially at Ceylon in its present state. It is said that L[or]d Clive will not remain here more than a year. It that case, North will make an excellent governor of Madras, and I would then strongly recommend that Ceylon should be made a dependency of Fort St Geo[rge], and the expense of the separate gov[ernment] saved.

Petrie is a useful man, and very cordial with me, but he is not respected here, and the government ought not to be left for any time in his hands, although I am persuaded his intentions are pure and public spirited. There is a species of repugnance to his society among all the best people here, which looks as if all had not beeen right formerly.

How I lamented my poor friend Christian! I hope you will assist his family. I know they must be in distress. Pray remember me kindly to Lady Jane.

Ever yours, . . .

MORNINGTON

[1] Hon. Frederick North (5th earl of Guilford) (1760–1827); governor of Ceylon, 1798–1805.
[2] Carrington had practised as a barrister at Calcutta, 1794–8; appointed chief justice, supreme court of appeal, Ceylon, 1799; had to resign immediately through ill health.

15 May 1799

The nabob will do nothing right. It is perfectly desperate to attempt any negotiation with him while Mr Johnstone (the Plugger's protégé), and a whole tribe of Europeans of the same class, surround him and declare that I have no power to enforce my propositions.

XXXVII

The Earl of Mornington to the Rt Hon. Henry Dundas

22 April 1799, Fort St George
Private: no. 12

My dear Sir

My last *private* letter to you was dated the 12th of January, and my last *secret and confidential* letter 21st of April. Since the latter date, I have received your letters of 13th of August and 27th of November 1798. The latter is numbered, but your previous letters are without any number. My dispatches to the court of directors and to the secret committee will advise you fully of the state of affairs in the peninsula of India and in Bengal. Although we have discovered a most extensive conspiracy in the one quarter, and are engaged in a war in the other, I have little doubt that the general result of both events will very speedily prove favourable to the British interests in India. With regard to the conspiracy (of which you will find the outline stated in my dispatch to the secret committee),[1] its season-able discovery will, I trust, not only frustrate the views of those concerned in it, but enable me to introduce such an ameliorated system of police in the provinces, as shall effectually preclude any future mischief either from this or any similar plot. My powers under the existing laws are amply sufficient for this purpose as far as regard the provinces. But some doubts have arisen with regard to the legislative power of the governor-general in council as applicable to the town of Calcutta. These doubts cannot be solved too soon by act of Parliament, and I am clearly of opinion that the public safety absolutely requires, that the legislative powers of the governor-general in council shall be extended over the town of Calcutta precisely in the same manner as they are over every other part of the provinces. Until this can be done by a special act of Parliament, I shall not scruple to enforce such regulations as shall appear to me to be necessary for the public security,

[1] *Wellesley*, i, 535.

relying on the justice of Parliament for an indemnity, if I should find myself compelled to transgress the law.

With regard to the war, I enclose copies of private letters from my aide de camp Major Beatson, and Colonel Wellesley, which, together with the public dispatches, will I trust convince you that every prospect exists of a favourable and speedy issue to the great enterprise which I deemed it my duty to undertake. The general tenor of these letters is confirmed by every advice from the army, and I entertain little doubt that the next dispatch overland will carry to you the intelligence, either of the capture of Seringapatam, or of a conclusion of peace on such terms as shall render any future invasion of this part of India by the French a matter of almost insurmountable difficulty to them, and of little or no danger to us.

To these letters, I have added some drawings which will throw further light on the distribution of General Harris' army; the nature of his position before Seringapatam; and the operations of the forces of General Stuart and Tipu Sultan on the 6th of March, when General Stuart obtained a victory, which, considering all circumstances, I do not hesitate to pronounce equal to the most brilliant achievement recorded in the annals of our military glory in India. I have also enclosed returns of the force now in the field under Generals Harris and Stuart, and the last authentic accounts which I have been able to procure of Tipu Sultan's military establishment.

By an extraordinary effort, I have been enabled to overcome all financial difficulties, which for some time threatened to delay the movement of the army. The effect of our detected conspiracy and hitherto prosperous war, has been to lower the discount upon Company's paper both here and in Bengal. In the latter place, the 12 *per cent* paper is at a premium. If the war should terminate (as I think it must) in this campaign, I shall be enabled immediately to make a large addition to the commercial investment. We are still utterly ignorant of the condition of the French army in Egypt, and no advice has reached us of the arrival of Commodore Blankett in the Red Sea. The distractions in the Maratha empire increase every hour, and the policy of the several actors in the intricate scene of reciprocal distrust and irreconcilable interests, appears to be so little guided by any of the common motives of human action, as to confound all speculation and to frustrate every rational system. One circumstance, however, appears evident, that the weakness and poverty of all parties, as well as their mutual jealousies and incurable treachery, will prevent any movement which can prove injurious to our interests. I shall hereafter transmit to you a more detailed account of the state of the court of Poona, and of the course of the recent intrigues of Sindhia and the peshwa, which form a perfect anomaly in diplomatic history.

I was very happy to learn that you approved my orders of the 20th of

June, issued in consequence of the proclamation at the Mauritius. I have the satisfaction to know that to those orders, the safety of the Carnatic is now attributed by every intelligent man in this settlement.

I continue to receive the most unqualified, generous, and cordial, support from Lord Clive, and from all the members of this government, as well as from the whole body of the civil and military establishment at this presidency. I have endeavoured in my conduct towards Lord Clive to prove that the governor-general may visit Fort St George without diminishing the influence, authority, or patronage, of the governor of this presidency; and by delegating to Gen[era]l Harris the most extensive and active powers which it was possible for me to frame, I trust I shall succeed in manifesting to the native states of India, that a provincial commander-in-chief may carry into the field the full energy, weight, and vigour, of the government-general, whenever the occasion may demand such an effort.

I have added to the enclosures of this dispatch, the Coorga Rajah's account of Gen[era]l Stuart's victory: it is a curious and interesting paper. I trust you will urge the establishment of the regular monthly overland packet from London to Bombay. It is an object of the utmost commercial and political importance, and not to be sacrificed to any inferior consideration of minute economy.

Believe me, . . .

MORNINGTON

XXXVIII
The Earl of Mornington to the Rt Hon. Henry Dundas

12 May 1799, Fort St George
Private: no. 12A [recte 13]

My dear Sir

I have the satisfaction to enclose you a copy of the dispatch from General Harris received this day,[1] and also a copy of a letter from Major Beatson, and extract of a letter from Captain Macaulay. The papers require no comment; and I do not wish to delay, for a moment, the transmission of the important and glorious intelligence which they contain. I refer you to my separate dispatch to the court of directors[2] for such further information as the shortness of the time has admitted me to communicate by this op-

[1] *Ibid.*, p. 577.   [2] *Ibid.*, p. 568.

portunity. I also add a copy of a letter just received from Major Doveton, which I trust will prove satisfactory to you.

I flatter myself you will *now* be of opinion that I have fulfilled my promise contained in my *private* letter *no.* 5, 23rd June 1798, that 'I would use every effort to frustrate the blow meditated by Tipu Sultan in concert with France, but that I would hazard no attempt of which the success could be doubtful'.

Our last authentic accounts from the Red Sea are as late as the month of March. General Bonaparte was then in considerable force in Egypt, had fortified Suez, and was collecting craft at the head of the gulf. Commodore Blankett had not arrived at his station, and accounts from the Cape state that in the month of January he had advanced but a few degrees to the northward of the line, was struggling with adverse winds off the coast of Africa, was distressed for provisions, and would probably be compelled to return to the Cape. The *Centurion* and *Albatross*, with two small cruisers, were gone up the Red Sea, for the purpose of destroying the craft collected by the French.

In this state of affairs, I trust you will view with satisfaction the seasonable reduction of Tipu Sultan's power.

The conduct of the army in Mysore exceeds all praise. You will, I doubt not, remember my former suggestions respecting Lieut[enant]-General Harris.

The 86th regiment, the last of the expected reinforcements from the Cape, arrived here on the 9th inst[ant]. We have received from the same quarter an effective force of 3,000 Europeans within an incredibly short space of time, as sufficient testimony (if any were wanting) to prove the solid advantages of that useful possession. All our European reinforcements are arrived in perfect health.

Yours most faithfully . . .

MORNINGTON

XXXIX

The Earl of Mornington to the Rt Hon. Henry Dundas

13 May 1799, Fort St George
Private: no. 13 [*recte 14*]

My dear Sir
To my dispatch of yesterday, I have thought it might be satisfactory to you to add the enclosed letter just received from Captain Macaulay, by which

it appears, that Futteh Hyder, the son of the late Tipu Sultan who still kept the field, has offered to surrender. This circumstance may be considered as the close of the war. By another letter from Captain Macaulay, it appears that my presence is now expected and desired by General Harris at Seringapatam, and that the communication between Madras and that city is likely to be opened immediately. I shall accordingly proceed forthwith to Seringapatam, from which place I shall regularly advise you of the progress of my endeavours to draw from our present proud and commanding situation the substantial benefits of durable security.

Ever yours . . .

MORNINGTON

XL

The Earl of Mornington to the Rt Hon. Henry Dundas

16 May 1799, Fort St George
Private: no. 14 [recte 15]

My dear Sir

Yesterday I received the enclosed dispatch from Lieutenant-General Harris,[1] containing the details of the capture of Seringapatam. They require no comment; and I am persuaded that no solicitation is necessary on my part to induce you to recommend the incomparable army, which has gained this glorious triumph to the particular notice of his Majesty, and to the applause and gratitude of their country. The unconditional submission of Kummur-ud-Din, accompanied by that of Futteh Hyder, will, I trust, much facilitate the means of making a new settlement. I am on the point of setting out for Seringapatam, and I have no doubt that, in any possible case, I shall be able to add to the annual revenues of the Company in the peninsula of India, a sum not less than 12 lakhs of pagodas, with the additional advantage of contracting and strengthening our frontier, and of establishing a continuity of our territory from the coast of Coromandel to that of Malabar.

In our present situation, the arrival of a French force in India would be rather a desirable event than otherwise;[2] and I am confident that the result

[1] *Ibid.*, p. 569.
[2] 'If Bonaparte should now choose to visit Malabar,' he told Pitt, 'I trust he will find supper prepared for him before he has reached Calcutta.' P.R.O. 30/8/188, f. 91.

must be accession of reputation and honour to our troops, and the disappointment and ruin of the enemy. If the French should be established in Egypt, it might be advisable to consider, whether an expedition might not be fitted out from India to co-operate by way of the Red Sea with any attempt which might be undertaken from the Mediterranean. I cannot venture to prepare any such expedition without orders from England; but if I should receive them, you may be assured that they will be executed with alacrity and diligence, not only by me, but by the whole army in India.

I enclose a statement of the discount on public securities in Bengal, since the commencement of the war, but not brought down to the period of time when the effect of the conquest of Mysore could be known.

Believe me, . . .

MORNINGTON

P.S. 17 May 1799

I enclose an extract from a dispatch of L[ieutenan]t-Gen[era]l Harris just now received, by which you will perceive that Futteh Hyder, Purneah, and Mir Kummur-ud-Din have all submitted, and that the latter is actually arrived at the headquarters of the British army.

18 May 1799

I enclose an extract just now received, by which you will learn that we have been fortunate enough to find Tipu's correspondence with France. The colours of the fort of Seringapatam, borne by General Harris' son, together with a duplicate of this dispatch and several details, will be sent to England in a frigate within a few days. Mir Allum is to meet me at Rykottah. The nizam has given me full powers to conduct his interests on this occasion. The peshwa will do no mischief: on the 9th day of May (5 days after the death of Tipu) his Highness the peshwa in full durbar announced his intention to take the field against the sultan; but he cannot move; and I shall easily make it his interest to remain quiet. Sindhia's affairs are more embarrassed than ever, his disposition is universal rapine and plunder, and although his professions are amicable, he would plunder us or the nizam or anybody, if he possessed the power. But our superiority and his own distress will be sufficient securities for his conduct.

XLI

The Earl of Mornington to the Rt Hon. Henry Dundas

16 May 1799, Fort St George
Secret and Confidential: Unnumbered

My dear Dundas

The subject of this letter is of the most delicate nature, nor should I ever have touched upon it, if I did not feel myself bound to such an unreserved communication by the strongest motives of private friendship for you, as well as by those of public duty.

My long residence here has enabled me to form a deliberate judgement on the character of Lord Clive, which his unexampled reserve renders very difficult to discover. This peculiar part of his character may account for the apparently inconsistent opinions which I have already written to you on the subject.

He is a man of the most strict private honour, of a generous, manly, and artless, disposition; without a trace of jealousy or of any low passion in his mind; his temper is admirable; and he is extremely susceptible of feelings of private gratitude, friendship, and attachment. He has also a strong sense of military and political glory and fame, as connected with vigorous and decisive councils. His understanding is not deficient, where he has full leisure for consideration, and he is remarkably discreet and secret in the conduct of affairs entrusted to him confidentially.

On the other hand, he is so totally ignorant in business, and so entirely unused to public subjects, that it is painful to himself and to others to discuss any such topics together. His comprehension is nearly the slowest and the most perplexed I ever met, and his memory is remarkably weak; so that after having taken great pains to reach his understanding, when you have arrived at that point, it is difficult to make any lasting impression. His ignorance and want of habit in public affairs produce an effect similar to a relaxation of public principle. He has no fixed notions of the faith of treaties, of the obligations of public justice, or of the duties of moderation; still less does he feel a sense of the necessity of administering an extensive patronage by the rules of impartiality without favour, affection, or prejudice, and without regard to the importunity of solicitation, or to the calls of private friendship. With much private worth, he is, therefore, deficient in public and political morality, merely because the whole current of his thoughts has been accustomed to the confined channel of retired and private life. From the same cause, he is apt to take partial and imperfect views of affairs and events, and to conceive false hopes and fears, and to frame visionary and impracticable plans for the regulation of interests, of which he does not comprehend the magnitude, intricacy, or relation. He is apt, from the same cause also, to bestow much pains on trivial points. I wish I could flatter myself that his defects were likely to be corrected by a longer experience in public office; but his habits are now too inveterate to be changed. His mind never can be extended to embrace political subjects, or indeed any branch of public affairs. He does not possess any fund of materials for the improvement of his judgement, and so little is he disposed to seek for knowledge, that he does not even converse on topics of business with any one of the men of experience, ability, and character, here, but seems to avoid all such discussions with the utmost degree of study and care. He has no idea of the distribution and value of time; and I have known him sit four hours in my room in a morning, having nothing to communicate, and in perfect silence, while I have remained in the same awkward and ludicrous state, and lost (what in this government it is difficult to spare) the best hours of the morning. On the whole he is the most inefficient and unqualified man, whom I ever saw in a high public station.

Next to the importance of real talents in a great government is the estimation in which the character of the governor is held by his subjects. In this respect Lord Clive is peculiarly unfortunate. The public opinion places his talents, knowledge, and fitness for business, on a scale even below their real standard. He possesses no weight or authority whatever, and the universal sentiment here is that of astonishment, how such a man should ever have been chosen to such a situation, or should ever have accepted it. I am now intimately acquainted with every valuable servant in this settlement, and I assure you that what I state is the opinion of them all without one exception, and that they feel it the most strongly.

Personally, I cannot desire a governor of Fort St George more satisfactory and pleasant to me in every respect. I sincerely regard Lord Clive; and I never met a person for whom I conceived more private goodwill on so short an acquaintance. But he never will correct the numerous defects of this [governmen]t, which require a vigorous and skilful hand, and above all great personal authority. What may be my fate is uncertain; but I trust in God you will never, under any circumstances, send Lord Clive to Bengal. If you do, the whole system will fall to ruin.

The general opinion seems to be that Lord Clive will not remain long in India. His health has suffered, and Lady Clive detests the country. If Lord C[live] should return to England, you ought not to leave Petrie in the government. He is not respected, and I fear does not deserve to be respected, although his present views appear to be pure. He has no authority whatever here. To me he behaves irreproachably; and you probably know that I persuaded Saunders to resign for him. He has been very grateful for this interference; but I am not on that account to conceal the truth from you. I believe that Frederick North would succeed here, if anybody can, and you might then save the charge of the separate government at Ceylon.

Believe me, . . .

M[ORNINGTON]

I have omitted to observe that Lord Clive's private letters are written in a style far surpassing his real talents. I have known similar instances.

Burn this letter when read.

I mean to take Lord Clive to Seringapatam with me, although so far from being useful, I know he will be burdensome to me. But he would be miserable, if he did not accompany me. His ruling passion is frequent change of place and a sort of puerile curiosity of seeing the world. Added to this, he is anxious to share the triumph of measures in which he has borne no other share than goodwill and honourable obedience. He certainly ought to remain at Madras; but I cannot bring myself to insist on anything disagreeable to so good a creature; and I shall feel a real pleasure in making him happy, although at the expense of my own convenience, and possibly to the interruption of public business, in which he is utterly incapable of affording any kind of assistance. Notwithstanding the freedom of this disclosure to you, I always treat him with every mark of respect, and when complaints are made to me of his ignorance, incapacity, and weakness, I always impute these appearances to his natural reserve.

In my public dispatches I give credit to him for his exertions, because he meant well; but if I had not arrived here, and taken the whole conduct of the army into my own hands, not a man nor a gun would even have been in Mysore. The council were all engaged in private quarrels and petty intrigues; Lord Clive and Petrie detesting Harris; Harris (who himself is the most stupid and inefficient of human beings) despising Lord Clive and hating Petrie. The habitual interference of this government in all military patronage (a most fatal system established by Lord Hobart) rendering Harris even more contemptible than his natural character necessarily had made him in the eyes of the army. I immediately encouraged the best officers in the army to form Harris' staff, I prevailed on him to listen to their advice, and I then delegated to him such ample and extraordinary powers, as rendered his influence with the army decisive; and manifested my firm resolution to support him at all hazards. By these measures, the natural irresolution of Harris was animated to firmness and exertion, and the confidence and active service of all the best officers of the army was secured. Among these, L[ieutenan]t-Col[onel] Close stands first. I know no man to whose single exertions our success is so much to be attributed. He is one of the ablest officers in any service. You will not suspect me of partiality to him, as you know the part he acted in endeavouring to check the preparations in July 1798.

I can only repeat here, what I have I believe already stated in a former letter. If the war has been rashly undertaken, without sufficient grounds of justice or policy, if it has been ill planned, and ill executed, and if its consequences appear to menace the stability of our power in India, to degrade our character, impair our resources, animate our enemies, and depress our friends and allies, I am the *sole* criminal. To me *alone* all the blame is imputable; and let the punishment fall on my head. But if the picture be reversed, I must claim the *sole and exclusive* merit of whatever is honourable, proud, and commanding, in our present situation in India. I rely on your justice and honour to judge my conduct not partially, but equitably and fairly, and to secure for me that place in the opinion of the King and of the nation, which I shall appear to you really to deserve.

XLII

The Earl of Mornington to the Rt Hon. Henry Dundas

19 May 1799, Fort St George
Secret and Confidential: no. 8

My dear Dundas

The detention of the *Sarah Christian* enables me to acknowledge the duplicate of your *private* letter *no. 5*, 29th December 1798. The original has not yet reached me. It has been an inexpressible satisfaction to me to find that to that date my measures and principles had so exactly accorded with your opinions, and I trust that the intelligence which you will receive by this conveyance will equally meet with your approbation. At this distance, however, and with an anxiety which I cannot deem blameable, it would have gratified me if the secret committee or the court of directors had expressed some acknowledgement of my services, in having anticipated their orders of the 18th of June, and in having placed all their possessions in a respectable state of defence. Instead of this, in the very same packet, I receive from Mr Bosanquet a very familiar and absurd epistle, deprecating hostility in India in a tone the more remarkable because it is diametrically opposite to the orders from the secret committee and to the spirit of all your letters. Mr Bosanquet has also favoured me with two letters,[1] one dated in June the other in August last, written (as their author modestly expresses it) for the purpose of assisting my judgement in deciding the arduous questions then before me. In the first of these letters, he advises me to compromise matters with Tipu Sultan, even if I should discover that that implacable enemy had formed a connection with France; and in the second letter, this notable statesmen advises me to retrocede Tipu's possessions on the coast of Malabar to that prince, as an expedient which might probably conciliate him and avert the danger of a French invasion. Mr Bosanquet was so completely satisfied with the wisdom of these spirited counsels, that he sent copies of both letters to Lord Clive, who read them with a degree of admiration precisely similar to that which they raised in my mind, and will, I doubt not, raise in yours. I trust you will be of opinion that I have taken a more effectual course for averting the dangers of a French invasion than that suggested by Mr Bosanquet. I received with infinite pleasure your communications respecting the present state of affairs in England. You may perhaps recollect, that in discussions with you and Mr Pitt I have always suggested the necessity of an union with Ireland. I think you will act wisely in applying the whole strength of government to accomplish that most desirable object in a crisis so favourable to its success. We have learned the sad fate of the king of Naples, but still entertain a hope that the Emperor will attack the French in Italy. The last accounts from Egypt are very unsatisfactory. It appears that the French had made a considerable progress in Syria, and also had fortified Suez and were collecting craft at the head of the Arabian Gulf. The *Centurion*, *Albatross*, and two of the Company's cruisers, were gone up the gulf, and the *Princess Charlotte* armed Indiaman, and *Fox* frigate, were cruising off the straits of Bab-al-Mandab. Admiral Rainier was at Cannanore on the 8th of May. At my advice he has blockaded Tipu's ports during the whole of this last monsoon. This station, I am persuaded, has been very useful, altho[ugh] not conformable to the polite policy of Mr Bosanquet. We have no news of Blankett since the month of January, when he was struggling with contrary winds a little to the northward of the line in the Mozambique Channel, and was likely to be obliged to put back to the Cape. By advices this day received from Seringapatam, I think it possible that I may be able to effect a settlement there without quitting this presidency. My brother [Henry] and Col[onel] Kirkpatrick are now far advanced on their way to Mysore, and I shall wait for their report before I move. In the meanwhile, all is quiet in that quarter and you may consider peace as concluded. I shall proceed forthwith to enlarge the investment. I find that my estimate trans-

[1] Bosanquet considered that the French expedition to Egypt was the greater threat to British India. W.O. 1/893, p. 259.

mitted on the 3rd of July 1798 gave great alarm to the court of directors; and Mr Bosanquet, with his usual pertness and flippancy, has been pleased to inform me that it must have been formed in a gloomy moment. The minute which accompanies the estimate distinctly states an expectation that the result would prove more favourable than my calculation; but adds that it is a necessary caution in all estimates from India to state the receipts lower, and the charges higher, than either are likely to prove. In September, the state of the finances justified a more favourable representation on secure grounds, and accordingly I then forwarded an amended estimate. Bosanquet has sent me some observations on the first estimate, which prove that he is entirely ignorant of the finances of India. I think it extremely probable that I may be able from the public treasure of Mysore to pay the whole expense of the campaign; and I am resolved that Seringapatam, in whatever hands it may nominally be placed, shall be a British garrison. It would be premature to enter any further into my views with respect to the distribution of the conquered kingdom; but I have little doubt that we may be able to conciliate the Marathas without any injury either to ourselves or to the nizam.

Believe me, . . .

MORNINGTON

XLIII

The Earl of Mornington to the Rt Hon. Henry Dundas

7 June 1799, Fort St George
Private: no. 15 [recte 16]

My dear Sir

My separate dispatch of this date to the court of directors will apprise you of the events which have happened in Mysore since the date of my last *private* letter (*no. 14*), the postscript of which was closed on the 18th of May. Nothing can be more favourable than the state of affairs in that quarter. The accounts which I have received from Mr Henry Wellesley and from Colonel Kirkpatrick induce me to believe that I shall effect the settlement of the country with more advantage from this place than if I were to proceed to Seringapatam; and I shall therefore remain here unless they should be of opinion that my presence upon the spot may be useful. In the meanwhile, the information which I have collected has enabled me to determine the basis and outline of the new settlement of the extensive empire, which the glorious success of the war has subjected to our power. I enclose two papers, no. 1 an account of the revenues of the late Tipu Sultan for the year 1797/8, taken from authentic records found in the palace at Seringapatam, and explained by Purneah Dewan to the late Sultan. No. 2 is a memorandum containing the general heads of the settlement which I propose to carry into effect without delay. I do not transmit this paper to you as perfectly accurate in all its details, but merely as being sufficient to furnish you with a general view of my plan. I can, however, venture to promise, that whatever variation may be made from this paper will be in favour of the revenue and power of the Company, and of those allies who have proved faithful to their engagements.

I shall transmit to you by a more convenient opportunity an accurate view of the motives which have induced me to adopt the settlement now carrying into effect in preference to any other. For the present it may be sufficient to observe, that to have divided the whole territory between the Company and the nizam, while it would have afforded strong grounds for jealousy to the Marathas, would have aggrandized the nizam's power beyond the bounds of discretion, and would have left in our hands a territory so extensive as it might have been difficult to manage, especially in the present state of the Company's service at this presidency. To have divided the territory into three equal portions, allowing the Marathas, who had taken no part in the expense or hazard of the war, an equal share in the advantages of the peace, would neither have been just towards the nizam, politic in the way of example to our other allies, nor prudent in respect to the aggrandizement of the Maratha empire. To have given to the Marathas no larger a territory than is now proposed, while the Company and the nizam divided the whole of the remainder to the exclusion of any central power, would have been liable nearly to the same objection as that stated against a total exclusion of the Marathas from all participation. The establishment, therefore, of a central and separate power in the ancient territories of Mysore appeared to be the best expedient for reconciling the interests of all parties. It would certainly have been desirable, that that power should have been placed in the hands of one of Tipu's sons, but the hereditary and intimate connection established between Tipu and the French, the probability that the French may be enabled to maintain themselves in Egypt, the perpetual interests which Tipu's family must feel to undermine and subvert a system which had so much reduced their patrimony and power, added to their natural hatred of the English name and to the aspiring ambition, indignant pride, and deadly revenge, congenial to the mohammedan character, precluded the possibility of restoring any branch of the family of the late sultan to the throne, without exposing us to the constant hazard of internal commotion and even of foreign war. Such a settlement would have cherished in its bosom a restless and powerful principle of its own dissolution. We could never have expected harmony or concord, or a spirit of friendship and alliance, where no true reconcilement could grow. Even submission must have been reluctant and treacherous where the bitter memory of fallen dignity, wealth, and power, must have united every passion and vice with many of the noblest virtues in a constant desire to recover an empire originally acquired by an extraordinary combination of falsehood, cruelty, and courage, and maintained for a long time with eminent policy and vigour, as well in its internal government as in its foreign relations.

You will observe that throughout this view of the subject, I have assumed the justice and necessity of the late war against Tipu Sultan, and consequently the right of conquest, under which I conceive the absolute disposal of the territory to have accrued to the Company and the nizam. In the exercise of this right, if I were to look to moral considerations alone, I should certainly, on every principle of justice and humanity, as well as of attention to the welfare of the people, have been led to restore the heir of the ancient rajah of Mysore to that rank and dignity which were arrested from his ancestor by the usurpation of Hyder Ali.

The long and cruel imprisonment which several branches of this family have suffered, the persecution and murder of many of their adherents, both by Hyder and Tipu, and the state of degradation and misery in which it has been the policy of both those usurpers to retain the surviving descendants of their lawful sovereign, would have entitled the representative of the ancient family of Mysore to every degree of practicable consideration. But it is also evident, that every motive must concur to attach the heir of the Mysore family, if placed on the throne, to our interests, through which alone he can hope to maintain himself against the family of Tipu. Something perhaps may also be expected from his gratitude, although that quality is not found among states in any part of the world, and seldom if ever among the native states of India.

For some time I doubted whether this arrangement, however desirable, could be attained in opposition to the mohammedan interest which I imagined to be firmly established in Mysore, but I am happy to be able to assure you that the jealous policy of Tipu, added to the brilliant and rapid success of the war, has left no mohammedan influence in Mysore from which any serious opposition is to be apprehended. I cannot better explain the actual state of the sultan's dominions in this respect than by quoting a passage of a letter received this day from Lieutenant-Colonel Close, which corresponds entirely with all the information which I have collected from other quarters.

'That Tipu loaded the departments of his government with dronish mohammedans cannot be denied, but the characteristic of his domination was to retain all power within himself, and to allow no hereditary claim or fixed offices that might in any shape oppose the dictates of his will. Individuals holding the principal offices of the state doubtless exercised authority, and from such cause possessed some influence, but of these, how many remain? Buchaun-ud-Din was killed at Sattimungalum, the Binky Nabob fell at Sedaseer, Syed Sahib, Mohomed Saduck, and Syed Ghofar at the storm of Seringapatam; Purneah is forthcoming and rests upon our will, Kummur-ud-Din rests upon our generosity, and is perfectly at our devotion. Where then is the mohammedan influence to embarrass us, or give a turn to our politics? Tipu's infantry are discharged, his sillahdar horse are dissolved, his killahdars pay us obedience, his asufs, if so disposed, have not means to resist us; the stable horse remain and look to our pleasure for subsistence; at best they are so many loose individuals connected by no head and kept apart by separate interests. They are ours for actual service at a nod.'

The rajah of Mysore will, therefore, be easily restored to the throne, and maintained on it under the protection of the Company, the nizam, and I trust also of the Marathas, who certainly all have a concurrent and common interest in the exclusion of Tipu's family, especially since the discovery that Tipu's alliance with France was directed not only against the existence of the British power in India, but also against the Marathas and the nizam, at least to the extent of recovering the districts ceded to those powers under the treaty of Seringapatam. It is my intention to draw the connection between the Company and the rajah as close as possible by a subsidiary treaty, under which I mean to retain the general power of garrisoning all his fortresses such as Bednore, Chittledroog, etc: and I will so clearly define our powers of interference with his internal government as to preclude (if any precaution can preclude) the embarrassments which have occasioned so much distress in the Carnatic, Oudh, and Tanjore.

Seringapatam, I shall retain in full sovereignty for the Company, as being a tower of strength, from which we may at any time shake Hindustan to its centre, if any combination should ever be formed against our interests. I shall not at present enlarge upon the advantages which are likely to be derived to the British interests from this settlement. They are too obvious to require detailed explanation.

The nizam will acquire such an accession of strength, as, with the aid of our subsidiary force, will enable him to maintain himself against the Marathas, while he will not only have acquired no strength which can render him formidable to us, but by our positions at Chittledroog, Seringapatam, and along the heads of the passes, together with the establishment of about 7,000 of our troops in the heart of his dominions, he will depend almost absolutely on our power. If this power be used with moderation, I think it must be permanent. We must abstain religiously from all interference with the nizam's government.

The Marathas will receive an accession of territory the value of which is considerable to them, but cannot render them in any degree dangerous to us or the nizam, while we retain the power of garrisoning the forts of Bednore and Chittledroog. As the Marathas have no claim of right to any share in this partition, I shall endeavour to connect the cessions made to them with some arrangements which shall tend to give additional strength to our interests.

The French influence in India, thanks be to God! is now nearly extirpated. Some adventurers, however, still remain in the service of the Marathas; and I shall endeavour to render the cession of territory to the Marathas the instrument of annihilating every remnant of a French party in that quarter. I must repeat to you my most earnest and anxious entreaty that you will never agree to the restoration of any part of the territories of France or Holland (while connected with France) on the continent of India. The papers found in Tipu Sultan's palace at Seringapatam will sufficiently prove the danger of allowing France to retain even the isles of Mauritius and Bourbon, and if the war should continue, I trust you will strike a blow against those prolific sources of intrigue in peace, and of piracy and buccaneering in war.

I transmit to you by this dispatch a set of the French papers found in the palace at Seringapatam. It might appear vanity in me to make any comment upon them, further than to request that you will compare them with the whole course of my communications with the court of directors, the secret committee, and yourself, previous to the war. I confess that in reading these papers I could not avoid trembling to reflect on the dangers which we have escaped, and which I trust are now effectually averted. If Tipu had obtained the aid of 2 or 3,000 French, there is not a doubt that he would have rushed into the Carnatic; and I refer you to all the communications from this quarter during the last summer for an estimate of the consequences of such an incursion. All the officers with whom I have conversed, who served in this campaign, assured me, that with 1,000 French Seringapatam would have been nearly impregnable, not only from the strength of its own fortifications, but from the difficulty of approaching it through that strong barrier which lies at the entrance of the tableland from the Carnatic in the neighbourhood of Kankanelly, Anicul, *etc.* Through the whole of that line of forest down to Sultan Pelt, a very small body of good French troops might have checked the progress of our whole army.

You will observe in the return of ordnance and stores taken at Seringapatam, the magnitude of the sultan's military preparations and resources. I have not yet received authentic accounts of the state of his military establishments compared with that of the last war, but I expect accurate information on that subject from the records found at Seringapatam. I understand that the sultan's horse appeared in larger bodies and manifested more discipline as well as boldness in this war than in the last; that his infantry appeared to be less numerous, but to be greatly improved in efficiency for service, and that it both attacked and resisted our European troops on several occasions with great vigour, firmness, and resolution. Under these circumstances, I confess that it was a matter of exultation and triumph to me to see the standard of Tipu Sultan flying under the colours of Fort St George on the 4th of June.

A little more eagerness than I could have wished has appeared in the army on the subject of the property captured in Seringapatam. The question would have been very awkward, if the amount of the property had approached the first statement which had been made by common rumour, and which extended to the enormous amount of 8 or 10 crores of rupees. The army conceive that as the place was taken by storm, they are, of right, entitled to what was found in it. This is certainly an erroneous opinion, and if the principle had been established, and so large a sum as that which I have stated had been seized by the army and distributed, it is impossible to calculate the mischievous effects which would have resulted to our military power in India. No regular return has yet been made to me of the amount of the property taken; but I have every reason to believe that it does not exceed in value thirty lakhs of pagodas, a sufficiently large sum. The official return has been withholden from an idea that the right is absolute in the captors, and that they are not bound to render any account under the peculiar circumstances of the assault. I shall endeavour to persuade General Harris to make an official return of the property, with a view to saving the rights of government and of correcting the erroneous opinions of the army; but I shall not hesitate to direct an immediate distribution of the treasure and jewels, as I am persuaded that in so doing I shall act conformably to your wishes and to those of the Crown, and the court of directors. The army would probably become a little impatient were I to propose to them to postpone the distribution until the orders of the directors and the King could be received. The question is rendered still more delicate by some orders of Lord Cornwallis, admitting the exclusive right of the army to all property captured in places taken by assault. The amount of the ordnance and military stores being very considerable, I shall endeavour to preserve them entire, until I can receive the orders of the court of directors and of his Majesty. I entreat you, immediately upon receiving this letter, to procure from the King and the court of directors full powers for me to dispose of the ordnance and military stores, either by granting them to the captors, or otherwise as I shall judge most expedient for the public service.

You will accompany these powers by a private letter from yourself stating your wishes on the subject, and I beg that you will dispatch these papers by express overland. My own opinion is decidedly that, unless the value of the ordnance and stores should amount to an enormous sum, this also should be given to the army.

I take this opportunity of requesting that you will take particular care not to permit any allowance, which I have found it necessary to make to any of the officers of this army, to be curtailed. A great effort was to be made, and it was essential to send the men of the first talents in the army into the field full of zeal and cordiality. For this purpose, I made a handsome allowance to Lieutenant-Colonel Close, the adjutant-general (a most able and excellent officer), and to others of General Harris' staff. To their efforts our success is to be attributed. If you reduce their appointments, it will be impossible to carry on government here in great emergencies.

The extension of our territory and revenue in the peninsula, as well as the command which we have now acquired over the central part of Mysore, will render a revision of the limits of the governments of Fort St George and Bombay absolutely necessary. My opinion has long been formed on this subject, for I never felt a doubt of the issue of the war.

Malabar has been miserably mismanaged by the people of Bombay, who are unquestionably the least qualified of any description of the servants of the Company in India to administer important concerns of revenue and government.

Malabar and Canara, together with Coimbatore and Davaporam, should be annexed to the government of Fort St George, which now will always have a ready and certain communication with the coast of Malabar overland.

I will add another opinion, which, if adopted, would save a very large sum of money. The governor and his council at Bombay, with all the apparatus of that expensive establishment, should be abolished, and Bombay reduced to a commercial factory, with a naval arsenal and a strong military post: the commanding officer to manage the whole of the government excepting the commercial details. Bombay should be subject to Madras, and the whole army of Bombay incorporated with that of Fort St George under one commander-in-chief. Ceylon, also, should be annexed to Fort St George. The saving would be great, and under an able and active government the general state of affairs would be improved. The charge is not more than one good governor with an efficient council might well manage.

You ought to endeavour to negotiate with Portugal the cession of Goa, for which you might give Malacca in exchange. This is an important point. The French look to Goa, and will labour to obtain it, either by force or intrigue.

Our artillery throughout India is very deficient. We should feel this severely in the event of a French invasion. Has it ever occurred to you that it would be a good plan to incorporate all the Company's European regiments into the artillery in India? I cannot too strongly press the necessity of attention to the artillery in India; if you do not send out ample supplies of proper men and officers for this useful corps, it will soon fall to ruin; it is already on the decay. Indeed, the whole army is alarmingly deficient in European officers: a larger annual supply of cadets, and a reduction in the annual export of writers, would tend to secure the commercial interests of the Company in India. I believe these doctrines are not popular in London; but if the efficiency of the army in India be once allowed to decline, the territory, revenue, and trade, will not long survive. We must either be a predominant military power, or we must be content to suffer the fate of those whose minds are unequal to the magnitude of their fortunes, and who are afraid of their own strength.

Believe me, . . .

MORNINGTON

PS. The account of revenue no. 1 has been found to be inaccurate. I do not, therefore, send it. In examining the paper marked no. 2, you will observe, that the rajah of Mysore's portion is not specified. It consists of whatever is not ceded to the nizam, the peshwa, or the English. I perceive that I have omitted to mention in its proper place, that a munificent allowance for Tipu Sultan's family and for all his principal sirdars will form a leading feature of the intended settlement.

M.

N.B. By a mistake, two *private* letters numbered *12* have been sent to you. This is therefore *16*, though numbered *15*.

XLIV

The Rt Hon. Henry Dundas to the Earl of Mornington

14 June 1799, Wimbledon
Private: no. 13

My dear Lord

I know not whether, by the present conveyance, I shall be enabled to write to you in detail upon many important subjects, nor, indeed, do I find that any particular one presses at the moment. The measures you are pursuing are so much in coincidence with every opinion of mine, of which you are already in possession, and have in most respects anticipated, that I feel no anxiety upon any of the particular objects you have under your care. When the end of the session of Parliament shall restore me to a little leisure and rest, it is my intention to go down to Walmer with my family, in the hopes of being able to make such an arrangement of my time as to completely do my business, without encroaching upon my quiet and rest more than necessary. I have had this winter an unusual pressure upon me, and my general health has not been quite so good as usual. I am now pretty well, and I should hope that the sea air will restore me to my usual habits of sleep, which I have not yet recovered. If I do not do it sooner, I will write you fully from Walmer Castle when I get there. At present, I only wish to touch upon one or two topics.

In the first place, as to your voluntary contributions, the accounts of them here have been received and regarded in the manner they ought. You have heard before this time that in place of the assessed tax bill we have now arrived at the completion of our financial wishes, and, by a direct tax upon income to the amount of one tenth, we are now relieved of every difficulty with regard to resources, and the war may go on as long as there is any occasion for it, without any inconvenience in that respect. When this measure was adopted here, it struck me to inquire what would be the amount of a tenth upon income in India, upon the same principles and modifications as those contained in the income tax bill. Any calculation on that subject must, from various causes, be obviously inaccurate, because we can make no calculation upon contracts or profits upon trade, besides many other difficulties; but I desired my accountant, as nearly as he could, to make out an estimate, proceeding solely upon the data of establishments, and I have thought it right to send you a copy of it, because it will suggest to you to consider, in concert with Lord Clive and Governor Duncan, how far some plan may not be adopted in India to contribute to the general welfare of the country upon a principle similar to that contained in the income tax bill. For as the ruin of our Indian interests seems to have been one great object of the hostility and animosity of our enemy, you will concur with me in thinking that our Asiatic subjects ought not to be behind those of Britain in the maintenance of our permanent interests and security.

I have reason to believe that there is a great disposition in a considerable part of the court of directors to oppose the measure of bringing home the private trade of India in India shipping, but the principle is so clearly right I trust you will persevere, without any hesitation, and you must rest assured of being completely supported. And you will likewise adhere to the principle of not augmenting our Indian debt for the purpose of investment, for the East India Company shall either curtail their trade, or they shall find resources at home for carrying it on.

Upon public matters, and the exertions of our allies upon the continent, I may comprise all in one sentence. The question is not now whether the French shall be driven from their conquests, but how soon they shall be so, and what steps shall then be taken for pursuing them at home and exterminating the usurpation, which has been so fatal to the peace and good order of the world.

Russia and the emperor of Germany are now making every exertion, and don't be surprised if my next letter should convey to you the accounts of a conjunct operation of the arms of Prussia and an armament from this country having proceeded to the recovery of Holland, and the restoration of the Stadholder.

Lady Jane desires to be kindly remembered to you, and,

I remain, . . .

HENRY DUNDAS

XLV

The Rt Hon. Henry Dundas to the Earl of Mornington

23 July 1799, Wimbledon
Private: no. 14

My dear Lord
In my last letter, I mentioned to you that I had a prospect of spending this autumn at Walmer, and when there I meant to give a great deal of my time to India, and should write to you from thence. I hope to go there in a few days, when I will execute my intention. In the meantime, I only think it

necessary to say that you will understand, that in the various opinions I have given to you on finance, trade, and politics, in the course of my correspondence this twelvemonth past, I adhere to them, and whatever difficulties and obstructions any of these opinions may meet, I am determined to follow them out. I allude particularly to what I stated of a firm determination to admit no more borrowing in India for the purpose of investment. The resources for that purpose must go from this. Connected with this subject is another material one, I mean opening to the Company's servants in India the trade of India, in order to give to Great Britain that portion of trade which at present is purloined from us by foreigners, in a great measure trading upon our capital. These principles will be combatted by the shipping interest of Leadenhall Street, but the argument is so clearly on the side of what I am stating, that I am sure it must prevail, and, of course, must lead to the continuance of the system you have countenanced of taking ships in India to carry the exports of India brought home on private trade.

Although it is not my intention to write to you at present in detail, there is one subject I must touch upon, I mean the specie sent out from this country for the purpose of investment either for India or China. In proportion as I will be tenacious in not allowing the debt of India to be increased by the governments abroad for the purpose of investment, exactly in the same proportion I must support the court of directors in the proposition of not diverting from their commerce for the purposes of war, the specie sent out from this country for the purposes of commerce. Indeed, it is most absolutely essential that this principle should be adhered to; for any material disappointment in the investment of the Company would bring upon them at home so much confusion and discredit in their affairs, as scarcely any prosperity abroad, or any military success, would in any degree compensate. It must, therefore, be held as a sacred principle that none of the money or resources sent out for commerce are to be diverted from that purpose. If the revenues of India are not adequate to the purposes of war, when we are engaged in war, the public must find the remainder in the same way as it does any other of its military expenses.

I have had several conversations with the chairman and deputy on the subject of the additional allowances to your brother. The governor's *private secretary* is one of those points, which, however absurd it may appear, has always been a sore point in the court of directors. It shall however be managed, somehow or other.

Our public situation is most brilliant in every respect, and I don't conceive it possible that the French monster can live much longer. The Russians, subsidized by us, have operated the deliverance of Italy. The conjunct force of Russia and Austria have nearly, and will soon totally, operate the deliverance of Switzerland, and when I go to Walmer next week, one of my amusements will be to witness the embarkation of twenty thousand infantry, and soon after, ten thousand cavalry, to co-operate with an army of Russians and Swedes from the Baltic for the deliverance of Holland, and probably ultimately the Netherlands, and, however *malgré lui*, Prussia will likewise be again obliged to come forward. Stocks are rising every day, and the omnium of last autumn is about 14 *per cent* premium, although it was got upon terms lower than ever known. I trust you will communicate the contents of this to Lord Clive, that he may participate with you in the satisfaction to be derived from the glory of our country. We have now forgot Bonaparte, who before this time is probably totally ruined.

Yours, my dear Lord, . . .

HENRY DUNDAS

XLVI

The Earl of Mornington to the Rt Hon. Henry Dundas

31 July 1799, Fort St George
Secret and Confidential: no. 9

My dear Dundas

By the *Sarah Christian* I forwarded to you a s[ecret] *and* c[onfidential] letter on the delicate subject of the leading characters at this place, particularly Lord Clive. Lest that letter should not have reached you (the absence of my brother at Seringapatam prevented me from taking a duplicate), I shall commence this with some observations on the same subject.

Every hour convinces me more and more of the utter inefficiency of Lord Clive, and of his total unfitness for this government, or indeed for any public station. I feel great concern in delivering this conscientious opinion, founded on accurate observation. We have lived ever since my arrival here on a footing of the utmost intimacy and confidence; and I have done all in my power to maintain him in dignity and influence, leaving all patronage and the ordinary business of his government entirely untouched. If I were to select a governor after my own heart, as far as relates to obedience and temper, I should choose him; but it is my duty to tell you in plain terms that he is entirely incapable of conducting this government; especially since the last prodigious increase of its territory and importance.

167

In my former letter, I advised you that Lord Clive's great reserve rendered it difficult to sound his understanding; and that his singular facility of writing was another veil to his incapacity. This will serve to account for my having been so long a time in forming a definitive judgement on his character. His understanding is the slowest I ever met; his memory is remarkably incorrect, and often entirely fails him. He has not the least idea of business, or of system for the dispatch of affairs, or for the allotment of time. He is totally deficient in firmness and vigour of mind; and the worst defect of all is, that he cannot raise his mind to view the patronage as a trust for the public, and not as an instrument of private favour or kindness. This circumstance arises from his ignorance of public affairs, and the consequent inability of his mind to conceive any extended notion. All his maxims and reasonings are drawn from private and domestic life; and he perpetually reverts to the events of his farm or park, never rising beyond the sphere of his regimental militia mess in his highest flights. Another unfortunate trait in his character is his extraordinary love of money, and consequent parsimony. This disgusting propensity has been discovered here, and it has lost him the respect of the settlement. The received opinion now is (and I cannot deny that I concur in it, although I dissemble my sentiments), that he actually remains in India principally for the purpose of saving money, and certainly his profits must now be enormous. His health is by no means good, and he leads a life that must ruin his constitution; excluding the air, lying in bed late in a morning, and never taking any exercise. Lady Clive is wretched here, and detests the country, as everybody must do who knows England, and has not some great object to occupy his mind. The children have suffered much in their health, and I believe Lady Clive will go home in December. He has never expressed any desire or intention to move: but now and then he has muttered a gentle sigh against the climate, which, this season, has been dreadfully hot. Now, my dear Dundas, let me implore you never to think of this good-natured but weak man for the government-general. Let me proceed one step farther, and entreat you to endeavour to find some handsome retreat for him from this government, to which he is unequal, not only in fact, but (what is perhaps as bad) in the opinion of every human being where he is to govern. If you should adopt my new scheme of government for India, according to my memorandum which accompanies this dispatch, you would then find an excuse for removing my good friend (for as such I shall ever esteem and love him); and a step in the peerage, with a red or blueish ribbon would be a just reward of his prompt obedience and conciliating temper in the late noble enterprise. You expect me to speak plainly to you on these subjects, and I therefore disguise nothing. You will observe that all my public language and conduct towards Lord Clive is respectful in the extreme. I must repeat that with all his *petitesses* I really love him, and I believe he does not dislike me.

Petrie is a *black* sheep. I am concerned to say he is universally despised here; and although he and I continue on the best terms, there is something about him which inspires distrust. It is evident that he is disappointed at my not having arrived here in a party frenzy, and not having excluded Webbe and all his friends. However, the falsehood of Petrie is notorious, and indeed transpires so plainly through all his manners, that I cannot confide in him. His present object seems to be to win the hearts of the court of directors by a thousand little mean tricks at the expense of Lord Clive, and perhaps at mine also. You must not suffer him to be at the head of the government here. He is a dangerous man. With respect to his talents, much discussion with him has convinced me that I overrated them extremely, having formed my opinion on his letters. I have entered very fully with him into the discussion of most of the arduous points which have lately come under my view, and I have found him a very little use. His manners are gentlemanlike to such a degree that I always lament his character; but be assured you must be cautious how you employ him in great affairs. I continue, and I shall continue, to receive him with great kindness and respect, and to discuss freely with him such matters as I think he cannot turn to any sinister purpose.

With respect to Fallowfield,[1] he is a true Indian councillor, whom you may dismiss or retain according to your caprice. He does nothing, says nothing, and writes nothing, so you may dispose of him as you will.

I must repair the injustice I had done to Mr Jos[iah] Webbe, the secretary to gov[ernmen]t, although I cannot acquit him of at least imprudent conduct in the summer of 1798. I have found him a most diligent and useful servant, with great knowledge of the details of this government. His understanding is very quick; not always quite correct: but he certainly possesses a considerable degree of genius. He has been well educated, is a tolerably good classical scholar, and perfect in Persian and Maratha. His integrity is unblemished, and he really is animated by a true sentiment of public spirit. This quality has rendered him peculiarly acceptable and useful to me during the war, in which he has contributed materially to our brilliant success by the wonderful celerity with which he has executed all my orders for the movement of the vast machine which we pushed to Seringapatam. His temper certainly is not good; and his manners are haughty, ungracious, and forbidding; but in these respects he improves daily. He is young and was spoiled by Hobart. I believe he feels his obligations to me for having corrected his familiarity without diminishing his

---

[1] Ernest William Fallowfield; member of council, Madras, 1793–1806; president, board of trade, 1800–6.

just influence. I should be guilty of great injustice, if I did not recommend him to you as one of the best informed, most able, most quick in business, and most honest, men I have found in India. If his manners were a little improved, he would be equal to the highest situations.

L[ieutenan]t-Col[onel] Close (whom I have appointed resident in Mysore) is by far the ablest man in the army of Madras, and few more able officers exist in the world. He was the life and soul of the campaign. You know perhaps the part he acted in the last summer. But I have forgotten it. Upon my arrival here last December, he entered with the utmost alacrity and zeal into all my plans, and I relied principally upon him for their execution. *He* commanded the army. Harris is a good old twodler, but a mere man of straw. In addition to Close's military talents, he is the ablest scholar in the Persian, and in several of the native dialects in India; and he is besides a man of extraordinary general knowledge and talents. He happened to be peculiarly conversant in the affairs of Mysore, and intimate with all the connexions of the ancient family. I therefore selected him as the fittest person to govern that fine country; and I flatter myself he will prove a better neighbour than Tipu to the Carnatic. His integrity is irreproachable; and he is a very amiable and pleasant man, with rather a warm temper. He must always be one of your main anchors in this quarter.

I have seen much of Cockburn (Thomas) since my arrival here, and I continue to think him in every respect the fittest man in this place for the council. Why do you not remove Fallowfield and put Cockburn into his place?

Kindersley[1] also is an excellent man. White[2] is (I believe) honest, but I hear he is a sour parliamentary reformer. Harington[3] is a good, but not an able man. Clerk[4] is a very sensible and worthy man.

I am concerned to inform you that the junior civil servants in general at this presidency are an idle, dissipated, and extravagant, set. I fear that Lord Hobart took no pains in this respect. Few of them know anything of the native languages; and notwithstanding all the lectures from home on this subject, they had not felt the real necessity of studying the languages until my arrival here. I have urged the matter so pointedly to Lord Clive, that I believe some improvement will soon be visible in this respect. The ignorance and stupidity of the old civil servants of the Company at this presidency, added to the scandalous corruption, and the idleness of the junior servants, had compelled the gov[ernmen]t to resort to the army for persons

---

[1] Nathaniel Edward Kindersley; collector of the southern division of Arcot, 1792–1800.
[2] Charles Nicholas White; member, board of revenue, Madras, 1795–1800; senior member, 1800–1.
[3] William Harington, senior; junior member, board of revenue, Madras, 1796–9.
[4] Robert Clerk; 2nd member, board of trade, Madras, 1799–1800.

competent to manage the revenues; and this plan has proved so successful in the Barahmahl and the ceded districts, that it had actually grown into a system to fill the civil departments in the branch of revenue with military officers. The effect of such a system must have been to destroy all emulation and extinguish hope in the civil service, and to convert the officers of the army into a band of collectors and clerks. It was my determination to urge Lord Clive to change this system as speedily as possible, consistently with the prosperity of the revenue, which the present civil servants of this presidency are really in general unfit to manage. When Mysore fell into our hands, it was necessary to appoint some new collectors, and I thought myself called upon in this instance to direct Lord Clive's choice, which, however, would, I believe, have fallen on the same persons even if I had not interfered. I selected three of the new collectors from L[ieutenan]t-Col[onel] Read's school in the Barahmahl. They are all three military men, and of considerable talents and knowledge in the languages. Their names are Captains Macleod, Graham, and Munro.[1] I appointed all the assistants from the civil service, choosing those who have manifested a desire to study the languages, and to attend to business. At the same time, I signified to the commander-in-chief that, for the future, no military officer would be appointed to the department of revenue, if a civil servant properly qualified could be found; and I annulled all such appointments of this description as had been made by the comm[ander]-in-chief during the war. I think with attention a spirit of emulation may be excited in the junior civil servants here; and Lord Clive is sensible of the necessity of exertion on this point. Three young collectors in the civil service now promise well: Mr Lushington, son in law to Gen[eral] Harris; Mr Hodgson, collector of the jaghire; and Mr Hardis, collector of Dindigul, to which I have added a part of the conquered province of Coimbatore. Mr Oakes,[2] an old civil servant, is said to be clever, and I believe him to be so: but he is entirely ignorant of the languages, and must therefore be in the hands of a durbash; and his character in point of integrity is not without blemish. In addition to this objection, he is of a very factious and intriguing spirit, of which some strong instances have come within my observation, since my arrival at this place. You will never, I trust, admit him into the council here. If you do, you will see some violent struggle, at least, if not some convulsion. My opinion is that your best civil arrangement for this presidency would be to recall Lord Clive honourably, and to place North in the gov[ernmen]t, annexing Ceylon to it; Cockburn in the council; and I believe Petrie, well watched, would do no harm.

[1] Capt. Thomas Munro (1761–1828); secretary to the Mysore Commission, 1799; governor of Madras, 1819–27.
[2] Possibly Thomas Oakes; member, board of revenue, Madras, 1792–5.

North is diligent, able, and spirited, and his rank will give him weight, as well as his knowledge and talents. In point of co-operation with me, there would be no difference, I believe, between him and Lord Clive. They are both (as I believe) really attached to me. North, I know, would willingly hold a *vice-presidency* under my new plan; for I have conversed with him on the subject.

With respect to military affairs, Harris, whose prize-money will amount to a noble fortune, will return home immediately. Braithwaite[1] of course will succeed: but, although he is far from being destitute of merit, he ought not to be fixed in the command. The other generals now on the staff here are all unfit for the chief command. Baird,[2] although a gallant soldier, has neither sense nor, I fear, correctness of honesty for such a situation. St Leger might be brought from Bengal, but I hope you will never trust this important stake, the key and arsenal of our empire in India, to such incapable hands. Stuart of Bombay, if you can persuade him to return speedily from England, whither he means soon to proceed, would be the best commander-in-chief here. Next to him I believe Craig must be the man (but heaven protect the poor governor in council!). I am very desirous that my brother, Colonel Wellesley, should be on the staff at this presidency, and should hold the command of Mysore. I need not make any excuse for my concurrence in the public opinion of his activity, talents, and integrity. On him I could safely depend in any trust, civil or military; and in my mind he is a person to whom you ought to look, as a well qualified candidate for the highest stations in this country. I have met no man so well informed with respect to all the details of an Indian army.

Braithwaite, I think, has not been very politely used. You ought to make him a baronet, or send him some honour. You know his case. Floyd is a great blockhead, tied to the petticoat of a midwife. He returns home this year.

You should not allow the directors to name to appointments in India, in the manner they have named Mr Dick,[3] although I believe him to be a good man. Such appointments from home extinguish the influence of the gov[ernmen]t on the spot. If this system is to be extended to Bengal, I shall have the pleasure of celebrating the fall of the house of Hyder in good claret at Wimbledon very soon. No man could undertake to govern India under such a degrading counteraction.

I mean to remain here for a month longer, in order to settle Tanjore, the Southern Polygars, the whole system of the permanent revenue and

[1] Maj.-Gen. Sir John Braithwaite (d. 1803); staff as Madras.
[2] Maj.-Gen. Sir David Baird; staff at Madras, 1798–1800; commander-in-chief, Egyptian Expedition, 1801–2.
[3] Mungo Dick; commercial resident at Vizagapatam, 1795–1800; member, board of trade, Madras, 1800–1; member of council, 1801–3.

courts of judicature, and the military establishments. The nabob has proved perfectly impregnable. I shall, however, try him again before my departure for Bengal. I do not think that our new acquisitions, vast as they are, will require any great increase of force. The enemy is destroyed, and many expensive garrisons are now become useless. My notion is to destroy most of the small but extravagant commands; and to canton the army in a few large bodies, of which Seringapatam shall be the central point, with ready communications between each. Our frontier line will now be from Bednore, by Chittledroog, Sera, and Nandydroog, to Punganoor.

The admiral is here: he is very tractable. But *I* must have the command of the fleet; for if a refractory spirit, such as Blankett, should succeed to the command, I could not enforce the protection either of the territory or commerce. I hope Lord Spencer will not leave Blankett here. He is a complete demon of discord.

Ever yours,

M[ORNINGTON]

PS. I wish you to understand that, notwithstanding my objections to Lord Clive's capacity, I do not believe that the government would go on so well as it does at present, although lodged in abler hands, unless the governor were equally cordial with me. The substitution of North for Lord Clive would be the best measure.

8 August 1799

Since I commenced this letter, my brother Henry is arrived from Seringapatam. Although it is very dreadful to me to be separated from him, I feel it to be a public duty to send him to you with these dispatches. He can give you a more just idea of the affairs of this government than it is possible to commit to paper.

A report has reached me that an idea is afloat of increasing the number of councillors at all the presidencies. If the measure be not irrevocably adopted, I must deprecate it most earnestly. Its operation must be to diminish the influence of the governor; embarrass the course of public business; and revive all the old system of intrigue, counteraction, and corruption.

XLVII

The Earl of Mornington to the Rt Hon. Henry Dundas

1 August 1799, Fort St George
Secret and Confidential: no. 10   [Abstract]

Character of the directors in India.

XLVIII

The Earl of Mornington to the Rt Hon. Henry Dundas

8 August 1799, Fort St George
Secret and Confidential: no. 11

My dear Dundas

The day on which I sailed from Cowes brought me a very kind letter
from you, in which you assured me, that you had confided the whole
honour and happiness of your public life to my hands, and that your future
peace of mind (as well as mine) would depend on my faithful and diligent
discharge of the duties of the important trust, which you had selected me
to fill. If I can trust to the testimony of my own conscience, and to the
public voice of India, I have been enabled to increase your honour and
happiness, since my arrival in India, beyond any expectation which you or
I could have formed at the time of my departure from Europe. That the
mere course of the late glorious and happy events in India has afforded me
an extraordinary degree of satisfaction, not unaccompanied with some
sensations of honest pride, I will not deny; and when you reflect on the
extent and intricacy of the political plan which it became my duty to frame
almost at the hour of my landing, its connection with more than one military
enterprise of an arduous and comprehensive nature, the difficulties of
finance, of counteraction, and despondency, as well as of indolence and
apathy, which were to be encountered, and the complete success which has
attended every part of the undertaking, you will pardon a natural emotion
of self-approbation; and you will not think it unreasonable, that I should
look to the gratitude and liberality of my country for a reward adequate to
the efforts which I have made in her service.

Relying with the most implicit confidence on your justice and public
spirit, as well as on your kindness and regard for me, I shall say no more

to you on this subject, than that it appears to me now to be in your power to gratify your own feelings, by restoring my family to the situation from which it was reduced by no imprudence of mine (unless respect for the memory of my father can be termed imprudence), and by raising me to a rank which I have pursued through no other paths than those of public honour and assiduous labour in the trying scene to which you called me.

You will learn from others to what degree the public opinion in this quarter of the world has raised my character (in which your own has been necessarily involved), and you will feel how essential it is to my interests, as well as to my honour, and to the vigour of this government and its influence among the native states, that (if my conduct should be approved by you) the marks of approbation should neither be delayed, nor circumscribed within limits unsuitable to the magnitude of our late acquisitions, and inadequate to the eminence of our present situation in India. You will exercise your judgement on these points with every disposition which I could desire, but if political expediency or any other embarrassment should occur to prevent your satisfying your own sense of whatever the occasion may appear to require, I hope you will not attribute it to vanity or presumption in me, if I express my anxious wish rather to remain wholly unnoticed, than either to receive an inadequate reward, or to be mixed in the crowd with others, who have no other merit than that of obedience, more or less reluctant, according to their respective tempers and situations.

My brother Henry will have many important public points to state to you. If you should think fit to advert to those which are personal to me, you will find him fully possessed of my sentiments on the subject of this letter.

Ever my dear Dundas, . . .

MORNINGTON

XLIX

The Earl of Mornington to the Rt Hon. Henry Dundas

14 August 1799, Fort St George
Private: no. 17

My dear Sir

My last *private* letter to you was *no. 15* [*recte 16*] dated the 7th of June. Since that time Mr H. Wellesley has written a letter to Mr Canning, dispatched from hence on the 5th of August, together with duplicate and

175

triplicate of a part of my dispatch to the court of directors of the 3rd of August,[1] containing a view of the final settlement of the late Tipu Sultan's dominions and copies of the new treaties of Mysore and Seringapatam.

The whole of the original of the same dispatch is now forwarded by the ship *Cornwallis*, and contains much matter too voluminous to transmit overland. The original dispatch is, therefore, much more detailed and full than those copies which were sent by that conveyance. To this dispatch is added a letter from me to the secret committee, dated the 14th of August,[2] to which I refer you; and also a packet from the Persian translator addressed to the secretary at the India House, which deserves your particular attention, especially the letters of Lieutenant-Colonel Kirkpatrick on the papers found at Seringapatam, and that of Mr Edmonstone[3] on the evidence of Tipu's designs, collected from those curious and interesting documents.

Referring you to these voluminous dispatches, I shall add nothing to their contents on the subject of the settlement of Mysore, excepting my assurance that it is likely to prove permanent; and that its numerous and almost boundless advantages have expanded to my view more and more every hour since the conclusion of the treaties.

The extraordinary nature of the late events in India, and the extensive and intricate questions which have been involved in every measure of my government since the hour of my arrival, as well as the important consequences which must result from the new order of things in this quarter of our possessions, appeared to me to require a degree of communication with you more particular and minute than could be obtained by any correspondence in writing, even if it had been practicable for me to devote for that purpose a sufficient share of my time and labours to my European dispatches. I have, therefore, thought it advisable to dispatch to England a person intimately acquainted with the whole course of my thoughts and actions, and master of all my present views, as well as of the actual state and condition of India. In endeavouring to select such a person, my choice was confined to the very limited number of those with whom I transact the most secret affairs of government; and I at length determined (whatever might be the personal sacrifice) to employ him who must naturally stand highest in my confidence and esteem, and who is, without question, most competent from his information, habits, and discretion, to communicate confidentially with you. I have, therefore, appointed Mr H[enry] Wellesley to take charge of my present dispatch, and I can safely refer you to him upon every point of importance which has arisen in my mind, or can arise in yours with relation to the government of India; as he is furnished by me with mem-

[1] *Wellesley*, ii, 72.
[2] I.O. L/PS/5/23, p. 249.
[3] Neil Benjamin Edmonstone; Persian translator to the supreme government, 1794–1801; secretary, secret, political, and foreign departments, 1801–7.

oranda upon every subject which has appeared to me material for your consideration.[1] I trust that you will enter without reserve into the most free communication with him, and that you will facilitate his return to India at the earliest possible period after your mind shall have formed a decision on the various points which he will submit to your view. Under this impression, and with this hope, I shall add nothing to this letter further than my acknowledgements for your satisfactory dispatches *nos. 6, 7, 8, 10, 11,* and *12* received on the 4th of August. On many of the points which they contain, you have already received my opinions by the *Eurydice,* or by subsequent dispatches. I trust that by the next ships from Bengal (whither I purpose to return in the first week of September), I shall be able to transmit full and satisfactory answers to such of your suggestions as have not before been under my particular consideration.

Believe me, . . .

MORNINGTON

L

The Rt Hon. Henry Dundas to the Earl of Mornington

6 September 1799, Walmer Castle
Private: no. 15

My dear Lord

A dispatch is going overland to inform you of our late glorious successes. It would take a longer detail than I have time for at present to tell you all the circumstances that led me to hope that I would be successful in bringing in and executing an act of Parliament for recruiting from the militia. The two *Extraordinary Gazettes* herein enclosed, will show you the fruits of that measure in its commencement. The happy consequences to result from what has happened, and the glorious footing on which it has placed us, I must leave to your self to fill up.

I remain, . . .

HENRY DUNDAS

---

[1] Mornington was also hoping that Henry's presence would increase his chances of a promotion in the peerage.

LI

The Earl of Mornington to the Rt Hon. Henry Dundas

22 September 1799, Fort William
Private: no. 18

My dear Sir

In pursuance of the determination signified to the court of directors in my letter dated the 3rd of September, I embarked from Fort St George on the 5th instant and arrived here on the 14th following, after a pleasant and favourable passage.

At the time of my departure from Fort St George, the state of affairs in Mysore was perfectly satisfactory. General Harris had arrived at the presidency from the army, to the charge of which Colonel Wellesley had succeeded.

Soon after my arrival at this place, I learned from Poona the failure of the negotiation which I had directed to be opened with the peshwa on the basis of the partition treaty of Mysore. It was broken off ostensibly upon the articles respecting the exclusion of foreigners from the service and dominions of the peshwa. To this article the peshwa would not assent, expecting under limitations which would have defeated my object in the stipulation. I am not satisfied that the ostensible was the real cause of the failure of the treaty. I suspect, either that the peshwa has been insincere throughout the negotiation, or that Sindhia has contrived to influence the peshwa against the measure. In consequence of this event, I have adopted immediate measures for dividing the reserved territory between the Company and the nizam, conformably to the stipulations of the 2nd separate article of the treaty of Mysore.

Although the issue of the late negotiation is unfavourable to my design of acquiring such an influence at the court of Poona, as should enable me effectually to hold the balance between the peshwa and the nizam, I apprehend no other serious disadvantage from it. The peshwa will probably regret the loss of a valuable territory, which he might have acquired on terms not only moderate and just but highly beneficial to him; and he will view with jealousy the transfer of that territory to the hands of the Company and of the nizam. But however his perverse temper may incline him to overlook the reason and justice of the question between us, the consciousness of his own weakness and of our strength affords us ample security against any rupture with the state of Poona on this occasion. I consider the same argument to be equally applicable to the probable conduct of Daulat Rao Sindhia.

My letter of the 3rd of September to the court of directors[1] will have apprised you of the ill success of my repeated endeavours to bring the nabob of Arcot to any arrangement of the affairs of the Carnatic. I shall soon furnish you with the details of my proceedings on that subject.

Before my departure from Fort St George, I had placed the affairs of Tanjore in such a train as will lead (I trust) to a speedy and favourable settlement. I left in Lord Clive's hands my plan for a new arrangement in the form of a treaty, which was to be immediately proposed to the rajah. The leading principle and object of this treaty is to secure an ample provision for the rajah, and to vest the government of the country exclusively in the Company.

I ordered the preliminary steps towards the introduction of a system of judicature and definite settlement of revenue into the Company's possessions on the Coast, and into the ceded and conquered districts, to be taken at Fort St George in the course of a few weeks.

Vizier Ali having effected his escape to Jynagur has been placed under personal restraint at my desire by the rajah of that place; who, I hope, will deliver the assassin into my hands.

I have the satisfaction to inform you that I have received accounts, which seem entitled to credit, that Zeman Shah has been under the necessity of moving towards Herat for the purpose of defending his dominions against the revolt of his brother Mahmud Shah and an invasion threatened from Persia. This danger the mission of Captain Malcolm to the court of Baba Khan will, I trust, serve to confirm and augment;[2] and in the meanwhile I hope to be able to effect such a reform of the nawab vizier's military establishments as shall afford us a reasonable degree of security against any future attempts which may be made by the shah to disturb the peace of India. I have already commenced my operations at Lucknow for this purpose with a fair prospect of success. The vizier has paid his subsidy with exemplary punctuality, not having left one rupee of arrear.

Before I left Madras, the finances of that presidency had reached a point of prosperity unexampled at that presidency since 1793; and I have now the satisfaction to inform you that the condition of the finances of Bengal, notwithstanding the heavy demands to which our resources have been subjected, is daily improving.

I enclose a copy of the address presented to me yesterday from this settlement. It was voted unanimously. I have received similar testimonies of goodwill from Madras and Bombay under the same happy circumstances of unanimity.

I mean to open the voluntary contribution here immediately for the

[1] *Wellesley*, ii, 113.
[2] For Malcolm's instructions, *ibid.*, v, 82.

current year. I shall subscribe exactly as I did last year, and I trust my example will be followed by most of the annual subscribers. I trust Mr Pitt will indemnify us against the operation of his income tax, by taking our annual subscription on account of our respective assessments. A clause to this effect would be flattering to India.

I remain, . . .

MORNINGTON

LII

The Rt Hon. Henry Dundas to the Earl of Mornington

27 September 1799, London
Private: no. 16

My dear Lord

Although the many ideas that are at this moment floating in my mind are too numerous and too extensive to be the subject of an overland dispatch, and it is my intention to write to you again immediately by the packet under orders to sail, both with regard to yourself and with regard to the public, I cannot allow the dispatch to go this day without in a few words expressing to you the genuine satisfaction I feel on the late arrival of the glorious news from India. We have the arrangement of that extensive empire now in our own hands, with the means of ensuring, I had almost said for ever, the peace and prosperity of that country. When I say that, I need say no more to satisfy your Lordship that I feel every sentiment with regard to you that either private friendship or public considerations can dictate. Probably you have made the arrangement finally before this reaches you, and, if you have, I make no doubt it will be such as I ought to approve of, altho[ugh] it may in some shades differ from what I might have wished. From what you have wrote to me, I feel confident that you have appropriated to this country everything below the Ghats on both coasts. If you have given any part of the Mysore country either to the nizam or the Marathas, I trust Seringapatam itself, with a proper garrison of our forces to be kept there and paid out of the revenues of Mysore, has been reserved to us. Indeed, if the Marathas and [the] nizam can be satisfied with pecuniary compensation for the aid you may have derived from them, my ambition goes so far as to feel that the whole Mysore country would be better in our hands than anywhere else. Next to that would be the restoration of the old Mysore family to a nominal sovereignty, but the real defence of the country to be in our hands and all its material operations subject to our control. If the circumstances which are now in your power should open the door for any new arrangement with the Marathas, I cannot help entertaining a longing wish for Diu and the Guzerat country, as affording a controlling boundary to the safety of the Malabar Coast, as affording the means of removing the great drain that is made by Bombay from Bengal, and as putting us in a situation to watch everything that is going on on the Indus, which is a quarter of India where I have always thought a great European power, wishing an influence in India ought to turn their attention more than they have hitherto done. This is, however, a larger chapter than I meant to begin upon, and to continue the discussion would far exceed the bounds of this letter. The newspapers will tell you that yesterday, in thanking some of our heroes by sea and land, I postponed those to you and my Indian friends till I should have such papers laid upon the table as should satisfy Parliament and the public, that our success was not only complete and brilliant, but the war which preceded it was just, necessary, and literally defensive.

I remain, . . .

HENRY DUNDAS

LIII

The Rt Hon. Henry Dundas to the Earl of Mornington

9 October 1799, Wimbledon
Private: no. 17 (Secret)

My dear Lord

By the overland conveyance of date 27th September, I wrote to your Lordship a few lines giving a very general outline of my sentiments respecting the final arrangement of the late conquest made of the kingdom of Mysore. I resume the subject under considerable difficulties, as in all probability your Lordship may have made an arrangement which it would be inexpedient to disturb. But my uneasiness arises from the immense importance I attach to the settlement of India at the present crisis. In the *confidential* letter I received from your Lordship dated [16 March 1799, *no. 6*], after the war commenced, you stated your intentions with regard to the objects of negotiation to be pursued under every contingency except the one which actually happened, *viz.* the complete overthrow of Tipu's power by the capture of Seringapatam. I confess I see no permanent peace in India if any of the descendants of Tipu are placed upon the throne of Mysore. Let them be curtailed in power and influence as much as you please, still there will remain the seeds of new hostility, perfidy, and revenge, which experience has proved to be inseparable from the continuance in power of that family. One would have thought that the severe lesson Tipu was taught, by the event of the war terminated by Lord Cornwallis, would have ensured the quiet of India for some time, by teaching him how incompetent he was to struggle with the power of Great Britain in India. But from the documents lately transmitted by you, he appears as early as 1797 to have resumed with redoubled animosity all his hostile intentions to the interests of this country in India. It may be true that, if the temptations of aid from France had not been held up to his view, he might have remained quiet, but he would only have done so till some fresh temptation was presented to him. Our situation in India never can be sustained, if its peace and security is to rest on such a precarious tenure. I need not enlarge on this topic, as I am persuaded your Lordship will feel the principle I am stating as strongly as I do, and if you do not apply it in the present occasion to the purpose of totally excluding the family of Tipu Sultan from either the reality or semblance of power in Mysore, your not doing so must arise from your Lordship not feeling as forcibly as I do the necessity of adopting that line of conduct as essential for the security of the British interests in India.

I have often heard an idea circulated that it would be an act of munificent generosity on the part of this country, if they would restore the old Mysore family, dethroned by the usurpations of Hyder Ali and his son. This is a refinement to which, I confess, I am not disposed to subscribe. I know not with any certainty that there is any such family. If there is, let them feel the generosity of the British nation in the exercise of its power, but don't let this be done by sacrificing or exposing to risk our own permanent interests. Such a measure could not be adopted without fettering and controlling him in such a manner as to render all his operations and transactions subservient to our own interests and safety. He must, of necessity, by a cypher on his throne, and I can only appeal to your Lordship's experience in the cases of Arcot, Oudh, and Tanjore, if we need much inducement to resort to that species of mixed and double government, which has hitherto proved as unpropitious to the happiness and prosperity of the governed, as it has to the safety, interests, and character, of the governors.

I distinctly state as my wish, that your Lordship may have seen cause to annexe the kingdom of Mysore to the crown of Great Britain, to be administered in the same mode, and by the same rules, as those which are applicable to the other British possessions in India. I know from the communications you have made to me, that under no circumstances your

Lordship would agree to allow the maritime parts of the Mysore country in the Malabar Coast to remain in any hands but our own, and I, likewise take it for granted, that you would not allow any part of the country below the passes, which enter into the Mysore country from the Carnatic, to remain under any government but ours. Holding these points as certain, I am at a loss to form any solid grounds for thinking that any reason can be assigned why that part of the peninsula, instead of forming an extensive, disjointed, and irregular, boundary to our interests in the Carnatic, should not be concentrated into one valuable and efficient possession, connecting together our territories on both coasts, of which Seringapatam itself would be the centre and capital. By such an arrangement, we would be impregnable from any quarter; we would have a productive revenue adequate to all our objects both political and commercial, and thereby relieve ourselves from the necessity of draining the revenues of our dominions on the Ganges for the support of our other settlements; we would be placed in a situation with facility and promptitude, either to check the first appearance of hostility on the part of the Marathas and the nizam, or to afford them our protection so long as they remained faithful to their engagements with us; in short, we would be enabled to preserve the peace and be the arbiters of India, and if we took care that in every act of our administration our justice should be as conspicuous as our power, I can see no reason why our Indian interests may not for ages rest upon a basis of impregnable security.

Under such an arrangement, I should doubt the necessity of having so many separate settlements. Bombay ought to remain a powerful military station, with a competent marine establishment; and all our other settlements on both coasts (including Madras and Ceylon) ought to be stations dependent on the government established at Seringapatam, where the great central army ought to be. Those different stations on the coasts would continue to be great commercial establishments, with as much military force as was necessary for their security; but my reason for saying that the great army of that part of India ought to be in the Mysore country is, that from its elevated situation it could watch over, not only our territories, but those of our neighbours from whom alone any danger could threaten us. An army situated there could at any moment march, either into the Maratha dominions or the nizam's country, or our own possessions on the coasts of Malabar and Coromandel, as circumstances might require.

In all this reasoning, I do not overlook the objection which naturally suggests itself for consideration, I mean the claims which our allies may be supposed to have to a share in the conquests we have made. Those allies can only be the Marathas and the nizam. The first do not appear to have any claim at all, for they have not in any respect borne a share either in our dangers or in our exertions, and in place of thinking of new acquisitions, they can only consult their interest by bestowing their attention on the management of those vast territories they already possess. The nizam certainly has a claim to attention, and after the situation in which we are now placed respecting him by your Lordship's masterly stroke in banishing French intrigue from his durbar, there can be no doubt of its being our interest to cultivate by every means the most cordial connection with him. Whatever difficulties there might have been in managing that connection, when we had to consult the jealousies both of the Marathas and Tipu, I do not think any such difficulty now remains. The Marathas must, from past experience, be sensible of our sacred attention to the faith of treaties, and, therefore, will feel it their interest and their inclination to connect themselves with us in the preservation of our common engagements with the nizam, the bases of which are purely defensive, and to which our guarantee must inviolably attach. If your Lordship feels that you have the option in your hands, I would rather prefer remunerating the services of the nizam by pecuniary compensation than by additional territory; but if you find that to be inexpedient, I have no hesitation in saying, that I would much rather gratify the nizam in his favourite wish to recovering the Circars, than I would break in upon that unity and connection of power and dominion which it is now in our hands to obtain by annexing the Mysore country to our territories. From the anxiety the nizam has never failed to feel and express on the subject of the Northern Circars, there can be no doubt he would feel such a concession on our part as an ample compensation for any proposition we may have occasion to make to him. If, in the course of such an arrangement, the Circars should return to the nizam, it will not escape your Lordship's attention to guard with the utmost precision against any chance of those territories being alienated to any other power whatever, without our special consent previously obtained. And under the circumstances by which we are now related to him, you will be under no difficulty in excluding all other powers from the ports in his maritime dominions, except with our consent and concurrence.

I refer your Lordship to the map of India for the boundary which this agreement would establish between the nizam and us. It would run from Innaconda to where the Tungebadra River touches the Maratha territories, and would bring the districts about Adoni and Cudepah within our boundary. But I understand that this is not a valuable part of the nizam's country, and the cession of the Circars would be felt by him as a full remuneration for those districts and the services he has performed to us in the course of the war.

If your Lordship has made, or shall make, such an arrangement as I have detailed, there arises an easy answer to the question your Lordship puts to me how far it is eligible that the nabob should take up his residence at

Arcot. I answer without hesitation in the affirmative. The only plausible reason why it has ever been stated that he ought to reside at Madras, is that we have thereby the means of watching over him, and preventing his intrigues with the French, with Tipu, or any other power in his neighbourhood. That reason, I trust, is at an end. The commanding situation we would possess gives the full means of every such precautionary attention, and to your Lordship, who by this time have probed to the bottom, and felt the pernicious effects of it to your government, I need not detail the incalculable advantages which would accrue to the interests, the morals, and the national character, if we could, by removing his durbar at a distance from our government and servants, annihilate that source of wickedness, intrigue, profligacy, and corruption.

In my letter of the [18th of] March [*no. 6*], I entered so fully into a detail of my sentiments on the situation and importance of the native powers in India, and with our relative connection with them respectively, it is not my intention at present to enlarge again on those topics. But the new situation in which India is now placed by the fall of Tipu, tempts me to look forward to a state of affairs beyond the present moment. The different modes of disturbing our power in India have been supposed to be, either by a direct attack on our territories on the Ganges, or by overwhelming us by expensive contests in the Carnatic by the union of European and native enemies.

As to the first of those modes, I can scarcely be looked upon as a probable, or indeed a possible event, unless the French were to be in possession either of Ceylon or the Mauritius, joined to a superiority at sea. This last is an essential ingredient; for altho[ugh] the French were to be able to collect a great military force at Ceylon or the Mauritius, and land it in the Bengal provinces, the army could not long maintain itself there unless reinforced and otherwise supported by the protection of a superior naval force.

The Carnatic, therefore, has hitherto been the chosen spot for annoying us; and this has been done in co-operation with a powerful native force, chiefly in the person of Hyder Ali or his son Tipu. If we improve the present moment as I trust we will, this mode of attack will be rendered so unpromising as almost to remove the apprehension of it. The Marathas or the nizam are the only native powers in that quarter to whom the French could apply for co-operation, but if the measures are adopted which I have detailed in the course of this letter, I think their own manifest interests to keep well with us, and the example before their eyes of the fall of Tipu, give us just ground to hope that our interests in the Carnatic rest on so sure a foundation as to exclude any alarm of danger in that quarter.

But in contemplating the local situation of Hindustan, and the nature of its inhabitants in the northern parts of it, we should act a very unwise part, if we did not keep a watchful eye on what is passing there. There seems no reason to doubt that Zeman Shah was implicated in the late combinations against us, and as his object is well known to be the recovery of the throne of Delhi, if he persevere[s] in that pursuit, it is impossible for the British power in India to be an indifferent spectator, or inattentive to the consequences of so powerful and restless a chief coming on the back of our territories. He would not long remain quiet, but the country of Oudh would be the immediate object of his ambition, and I need not detail to your Lordship the fatal consequences to our Bengal provinces, if ever he should be successful in such an enterprise. Such an attempt must be met and resisted in the first and in every stage, and if we are not remiss in our attention to the subject, I don't feel it to be attended with either difficulty or danger. Our own resources alone in the Bengal provinces would be sufficient for the object, and as the Marathas, particularly Sindhia, have so manifest an interest in the question, there seems no reason to doubt his cordial concurrence in the resistance to such an invasion. But I do not think even there it ought to be allowed to rest; for by keeping up a connection with the various tribes in the north-western parts of India, it is not a difficult matter to find him at all times business at home to prevent him from hazarding so dangerous an enterprise at so great a distance from home. With this view, allow me to direct your attention to the Indus River and those who inhabit the borders of it. I have always thought, that if any great European power had a view to destroy our interests in India, they would have acted a wiser part in directing their attention to that quarter than even to those which have more immediately attracted it. But be that as it may, if they are excluded by recent events from annoying us in those former quarters, it is reasonable to suppose they will now turn their eyes to that which seems to present a fair opening for that purpose, if we do not take care to shut the door against the danger of their intrigues. For this purpose the possession of *Diu* would be a most desirable acquisition. Even alone it would be so, as it would be the means of preventing its falling into the hands of France. The Portuguese are totally unable to keep it, nor do I know of what advantage it is to them to possess it. It cannot escape observation, that the Portuguese possessions on that side of India formed an essential part in the confederacy lately formed between the French and Tipu Sultan. Even now that Tipu is destroyed, depend upon it they will still remain great objects of importance to them to obtain. Goa and Diu would be valuable possessions to the French, if they direct their attention to intrigue with powers in the north-west. The Indus is navigable with vessels of considerable size the length of Moultan, and therefore in respect both of its valuable commerce, and in respect of the means it affords in forming connections with the various chiefs and tribes who border upon it, it opens prospects of extensive speculation to any power who may wish to rival the wealth, or overthrow the power, of Great Britian in India. The alliance which such a power would naturally cultivate would be that of Zeman Shah. He annually resorts to Moultan; the tribes who inhabit the border of the Indus from Moultan to the sea are tributary to Zeman Shah, and he would be well disposed to give them to any power who would aid him in his views in Hindustan. Every inducement of interest and hostility must excite in the breasts of the French the desire to concur in these views. By doing so they introduce a powerful invader upon our Bengal territories, in like manner as they tempted Tipu to be our inveterate enemy in the Carnatic. Zeman Shah is the natural enemy of the Marathas, and he would cordially concur with the French in the conquest of the Guzerat country. Thereby, they would be enabled to maintain a very considerable army, to act in co-operation with Zeman Shah in the establishment of their joint wishes of invading Hindustan and exterminating the British power in India.

Your Lordship will probably anticipate the conclusions I naturally draw from these observations. It is my wish that you should explain to the Marathas the deep interest they have to prevent the accomplishment of the views I have described. Their existence is implicated in the question, and if they are duly sensible of it, they will readily concur in the wish of our obtaining possession of *Diu* and *Goa* from the Portuguese, and of our maintaining a considerable force at their expense in the Guzerat, for the protection of it, and to be prepared to thwart and counteract any views which may be formed by a co-operation of France with Zeman Shah and the tribes bordering on the Indus. If we had a well-disciplined force at *Diu* and in the Guzerat, we could effectually watch over every operation which might take place on the Indus, and if Zeman Shah should at any time meditate hostilities against Hindustan to the eastward, we could, by moving a force up the Indus and co-operating with the Sikhs or other tribes hostile to him, recall him to his own territories by very hasty strides.

This letter has extended to a greater length than I proposed. I shall have occasions to write to you on other subjects, but I wished to confine myself at present to that which I have treated of in this letter; and I flatter myself I have made my ideas so intelligible to your Lordship as will enable you to act upon them so far as circumstances will now admit.

I have the honour to be, . . .

HENRY DUNDAS

LIV

The Rt Hon. Henry Dundas to the Earl of Mornington

16 October 1799, Wimbledon
Private: no. 18 (Secret)

My dear Lord

When your Lordship's letter on the subject of the Spanish settlements in Peru[1] first reached me, there was no occasion to give any particular answer to it, as the prospects of hostility then opening in India gave no room to look for any disposable force from that quarter. Even now I cannot give you any precise answer to the question you put. It is a very difficult and delicate question. The conduct of Spain to this country deserves no favour from us, and the exhausted state in which it appears with regard to every sentiment and feeling that ought to operate on a great monarchy, leaves little ground to hope that it can long maintain its rank among the nations of Europe; and the natural conclusion from all this which at first presents itself is that Great Britain ought to make use of the means in its hands to overturn the power of Spain in South America. A doubt, however, arises from the strange state of confusion and anarchy which the distracted principles of the French Revolution have disseminated in the world. If the effect of our attack on New Spain was merely to produce an unregulated independence, and that independence was to assume the form of democracy, founded on the principles of the French Revolution, no commercial benefit which this country could derive from it would compensate for the mischievous calamities which would result from such a revolution taking place in so large a quarter of the globe; and, if the question rested there, perhaps the wisest line of conduct we could pursue would be that of forbearance. This, however, is not the whole question. There is too much reason to dread that America does not act upon such principles, nor with a due attention to the dictates of sound policy, in the political sentiments by which they are swayed. If they can open to themselves a new market and a new source of commercial enterprise, it is too apparent that they do not much attend to the means of acquiring these advantages, or give much consideration to the risks at which they acquire them. If either with or without the concurrence of the American government, our interference could be so interposed as to direct and regulate the transition of South America from under the yoke of Spain into some other form of regular and legitimate government, the change would be productive of many important and beneficial effects to the commercial interests of this country. These

[1] The editor has been unable to trace the letter to which Dundas was replying.

advantages strike me so forcibly, I rather lean to the opinion that we ought to come forward and make use of the means we have in our hands to annihilate at once the small remnant of power still retained by Spain in South America. Very little exertion would be requisite for the purpose, and if the attempt on full consideration should be thought eligible, a material part of the force can act with great effect from the East Indies, and be better spared from that quarter of the world than from any other part of the empire. Of course, your Lordship would receive precise instructions from me. At present, amidst the doubts and difficulties which attend the question, I am not warranted to direct you to adopt any decided line of conduct. But as you have brought the question so pointedly under my view, I thought it right so far to put you in possession of the general ideas which are entertained upon the subject.

I have the honour to remain, . . .

HENRY DUNDAS

LV

The Rt Hon. Henry Dundas to the Earl of Mornington

16 October 1799, Wimbledon
Private: no. 19

My dear Lord

In my letter of 18th March last, I stated to you so much at length what occurred to me on the financial and commercial affairs of your government, I have little more at present to add, nor indeed till I hear from you the course of arrangements you have made subsequent to the conclusion of your contest with Tipu.

Altho[ugh] from the result of that war, I have reason to believe that our annual revenues will be considerably increased, I have the satisfaction to think that our establishments will not require any degree of proportional increase, at least of military establishment. For the just cause of alarm, which the rooted animosity of Tipu kept up, necessarily occasioned a constant watch to be kept over him, and to render that effectual a corresponding military force was essentially necessary. I don't expect this to be diminished beyond what was last arranged with the East India Company as a peace establishment. To keep up an idea of our power, and of our ability with promptitude to repel every attack and to avenge every insult, is essential to the preservation of our importance in India. Indeed, it would not surprise me if it was increased beyond that scale, if the ideas are acted upon, in the arrangement of peace, which I have so fully detailed to you in a letter which goes by the same conveyance as this.

As to the European military establishment, I have so often had occasion to explain myself, it is unnecessary to say, that at whatever scale it may under all circumstances be proper to fix it, it must be the same in peace and war. At such a distance from home, it is impossible to think of recruiting our armies when hostilities begin. The case is different with regard to the native force; it may be more expediently increased, and in the last arrangement with the East India Company, the establishment of officers and privates was placed upon a footing which, with regard to privates, admitted an increase without any necessary increase of officers.

I remain still distinctly of opinion, that the whole European force in India should be his Majesty's troops, and that the native force might, with great safety, remain on its present footing. After repeated struggles with the Company, their European establishment has now been reduced to four regiments. The Company are all alive to jealousy on the subject, and therefore I am not disposed to resume the contest again, unless there were any sufficient grounds to induce me to do so; but I think the public service would be greatly benefited if, in place of their four regiments of European infantry, the Company would substitute four or even six regiments of native infantry or cavalry. Their patronage would not be diminished by such a change, and their service, in my apprehension, greatly benefited. Be so good as [to] let me know what your real opinion is on this subject, and, if it strikes you, with better means of information than I have, in the same light it occurs to me, there would be a propriety in your stating that opinion not merely to me in a private letter but in some of your public dispatches.

I cannot omit on any occasion to inculcate upon you, both in a political and financial view, the anxiety I entertain that you should carry on as far as possible the system which is adopted at the nizam's court, of having large detachments of our troops in their territories, paid by the native powers. By such a system, we form with them the strongest political connection; we render them efficient allies; we keep up a large and efficient military force at a comparatively small expense; and at the same time it is a system of wise economy on their part, because they are eased of the expense of the great part of their own useless rabble, and substitute in the place of it a well-disciplined and efficient military force. It, at the same time, provides against the danger of European adventurers being introduced into their armies and forming cabals and intrigues prejudicial to our interests or the quiet of India. On all these grounds, and many others that could be suggested, I recommend the extension of this system to your particular attention.

Notwithstanding the hopes I entertain that the event of the war will add very considerably to the revenues of our Indian empire, I remain of the opinion I formerly suggested to you, that a proportional increase of it should not be made to the allotment for investment. The great and immediate object is a reduction of the debt which has been necessarily contracted. When that is accomplished, and the debt is reduced within a very narrow compass, we are placed beyond the danger of embarrassment; the credit of the Company in India is kept entire, and there is room to act on that credit when unforeseen exigencies render it necessary. But when the system goes on in time of peace, of gratifying the demands of the Company at home by a large investment, and of course a small impression is made on the debt, the smallest diminution of revenues and any sudden and unforeseen expense, from war or otherwise, creates every species of embarrassment, and it is with great difficulty the credit of the government in India can be supported or its wants supplied, even by loans at an extravagant rate of interest. I hope your Lordship will manfully set your face against any deviation from these principles, and lay down a system for the speedy reduction of the existing debt, and you may rely on the most cordial support from home.

The plan of giving encouragement to the private trade from India, and bringing the whole of it to the River Thames, has undergone a good deal of discussion and found its way to the general courts of proprietors, who seem favourably disposed to it. My opinion remains the same as when I last wrote to you on the subject, and I make no doubt in the course of the next winter the controversy will be arranged on some rational system. In considering the question wisely, it is necessary to guard against the extremes of both disputants. Viewing the subject merely as an abstract commercial question, there can be no doubt of the proposition, as an abstract one, that the more of the trade of India that is brought into this country for re-exportation, in place of going directly to foreign countries, so much the better. But as applicable to India, it is necessary to control this abstract proposition by another consideration, *viz.* the danger of allowing commercial agents or unlicensed persons of any description to settle themselves in India, either in reality or under the pretence of carrying on trade. Such persons, mixing themselves with the natives *ad libitum*, do incalculable mischief. They are guilty of various tricks, frauds, and abuses, and thereby diminish the respect for the European character, which is one of the strong holds by which we must hope to maintain our political importance. Add to this the danger that such a system, if not duly restrained and regulated, will ultimately lead to colonization in India, which would most certainly and rapidly lead to the dissolution of our Indian empire.

It does not occur to me that I have any occasion to trouble your Lordship further at present on any of these topics.

I am, . . .

HENRY DUNDAS

LVI

The Rt Hon. Henry Dundas to the Earl of Mornington

12 October 1799, London
Secret and Confidential: [*Unnumbered*]

My dear Lord

Altho[ugh] all my answers to your *very confidential* letters will be in my own hand, you must always take it for granted, unless it is indeed something very particular (such as your letter relative to Lord Clive), that they must be copied by one person; I mean Mr Cabell, for unless he was to do so, it would be impossible for me to furnish you, either with duplicates, which would be inconvenient, or to have any of them at any time put into cypher. You know, however, that Cabell is secret as the grave, and from him the torture would not extract anything that was committed to him in secrecy.

This is an answer to your letter of the 1st October 1798. Every one of the points treated of in this letter are certainly very delicate ones, and likewise difficult, from the circumstances that I cannot assign my reasons even to the chairs for several things I shall have to enforce, and, therefore, must bring them forward merely as a matter of authority from me. You are aware from observation in this country, that this is an unpleasant way of dealing with the court of directors.

The first point of this kind is your suggestions relative to council, in which I have two favourite points to combat. The first is the desire of the court never to depart from seniority, and the second is their aversion to grant pensions to their servants. Add to these two difficulties that both Mr Speke and Mr Cowper have powerful supporters in this country, and I have never heard that any of them have wished to come home, and, if they are to be brought out of council against their will, I feel with you that they must have pensions. However, I think it is for the interest of the public service that the measure should take place, and therefore I shall take early steps, which I could not for many reasons do sooner, to procure appointments to council for Mr Barlow and Mr Bebb, and the vacancies to result from thence must be filled by yourself, and therefore I need make no exertion relative to them. I don't think anything would induce Charles Grant to return to India.

Upon the subject of military command, I confess I am of opinion that you cannot be better than with Sir Alured Clarke. I believe Sir James Craig may be fully as good an officer, and he is a considerable favourite at home, but I have always stated to the duke of York that I was afraid of his temper, especially if introduced into council, where probably it is right that the commander-in-chief should be. In all respects of temper, industry, good intentions, and cordial co-operation, I take it for granted Sir Alured Clarke must be entirely to your mind, and you will be as well with him as anybody. If he wishes to come home, I should then recommend General Harris, and I am clear General Stuart is the best for Madras. There would, however, difficulty exist in that respect, for he is younger in rank than Sir James Craig, and the duke of York would not like to supersede Sir James Craig. That, however, must be combated, and Sir James' military talents may be of considerable use where he is. Indeed where he now is may, under present circumstances, be considered as one of the most important commands in India. In the event of General Stuart being called to Madras, I don't think he could do better than put Hartley[1] at the head of the Malabar army.

It does not appear to me that any Parliamentary authority is necessary for the regulations you propose respecting the sudder dewany and nizamut adaulat, and I believe you know that I am never desirous, except when compelled to do it, to introduce any Indian subject for parliamentary regulation. I shall, however, of course inform myself on the subject by legal aid and act accordingly.

The next points you state are more difficult than all the rest, I mean the authority you want over the army and navy. As to the army, the very example you give of the lord-lieutenant of Ireland, if mentioned, would be far to ruin everything ever of arrangement, for the authority of the lord-lieutenant with respect to the army in particular is one of the sorest points at St James's. I think the whole patronage of the British army in India must remain with the commander-in-chief at home, acting on the recommendation of the commander-in-chief in India. As to every movement or operation of the army, whether King's or Company, those of course must be thoroughly subordinate to, and remain under the absolute control of the government in India, and any particular instructions he may at any time require from home must come from the secretary of state. I don't recollect any orders going from the secretary of state to the commander-in-chief

[1] Maj.-Gen. James Hartley (d. 1799); staff at Bombay.

except, I believe, in the case of the Dutch possessions in India, and there was a doubt how far any orders on such a subject (which was somewhat anomalous) could go regularly through the Company's government. In the present moment, however, I should, without critically examining the legal powers, write directly to you, and I rather think I shall very soon have occasion to write to you on the subject of Batavia. To obviate difficulties of that kind, I think the suggestion of the governor-general having an authority likewise from the King as well as the Company merits consideration. I am not clear the Company would not be jealous upon the subject, thinking of it in a prospective view. That, however, must be obviated somehow or other, if on due consideration the measure shall be thought right.

I am happy in the accounts you give of Sir John Anstruther. From the temper he set out in, and his anxiety to secure an honest fame, by a meritorious exertion of his talents for the public good, I had no doubt of his doing well, and he may be assured that in doing so he shall be supported against all cabal.

There is nothing in your letter of the 12th January requiring any particular answer more than has been already done, except with regard to your wish for a naval authority, which I have reserved for consideration in answering this letter, where the suggestion is again repeated. Your Lordship knows that there is nothing that requires more delicate management (because there is nothing on which such jealousy exists) as the exercise of authority over the board of admiralty. It is such that there has very seldom existed a perfect understanding between the secretary of state and the first lord of the admiralty arising from that very circumstance. Lord Spencer and I are in perfect good habits, and will probably continue to go on well together, but every now and then there is something like a claim to executive authority in the board of admiralty, which certainly does not constitutionally exist there, and of course a danger of unpleasant collision when I have occasion to convey the king's commands. I am, therefore, very certain, if I was to propose to transfer from the admiralty to the governor-general the whole control or power of the fleet serving in India, it would be productive of very unpleasant consequences. I am, at the same time, perfectly aware of the convenience that would arise from the exercise of the authority by land and sea going on in perfect unison and understanding together, and therefore I shall endeavour to concert with Lord Spencer some arrangement for that purpose.

Your letter of the 21st February announces the change of conduct in the servants of Madras, of whom you had formerly complained. After so thorough a reformation, it became difficult to renew old sores by a rebuke which their first conduct naturally demanded. The truth is your letter of the 21st Feb[ruar]y came just in time to save them, for I had actually taken the steps for bringing the whole of them home without any exception.

Our last accounts from Egypt are in a French newspaper containing a letter from Bonaparte, in which he states his having got some considerable advantage at Aboukir,[1] but after the severe repulse he got at St John de Acre from Sir Sidney Smith,[2] and the former diminutions of his army, it seems impossible he can ever do anything of moment there. If, however, he should not soon die out of himself, and by the force of the country itself, it may be right to give him some help, by sending a force from the Mediterranean for that purpose.

The conduct of Vizier Ali in all its parts, and with all its consequences, will require your best attention on your return to Bengal. So extensive a conspiracy must have been hatching for some time past, and must now be thoroughly probed and the seeds of it completely extirpated. If Vizier Ali should be laid hold of, he must certainly be punished, but I should think the most efficient way of doing it would be on the spot where his wickedness was committed, and the authority of the new vizier may with great propriety be employed for the purpose. Lord Teignmouth furnished me with a perusal of the narrative sent over to him by Mr Edmonstone (sent also to the secret committee).

Your letter of the 16th March 1799 mentions Mr Duncan's wish of returning to Benares, if he could return reinstated in his former authority. I see no objection to his doing so, if it does not set aside any ameliorated system in a material degree, but if it does he certainly cannot. But I am at a loss to know precisely what his wishes are, for in one of his letters to me he expresses a wish to continue some years longer in his present situation at Bombay, and therefore I shall take it for granted that is his wish, unless I hear something decisive to the contrary, and then it may be proper to take his wishes into consideration.

You may rest assured that I have no disposition to return anything to the French anywhere in India, and I have as little inclination to restore anything on the continent of India to the Dutch, unless they show themselves in a situation to possess it totally independent of France. I do not mean to say that while they are permitted to trade there, they are not to be permitted a factory, or such establishment as may be necessary for commercial purposes.

There is nothing material in your letter of the 21st April to which I have not adverted. I advert to what you say respecting Petrie. I am sorry for it, as he is certainly an able man and most cordially disposed to support your government. When he was last appointed, I hung back and stopped it

---

[1] On 11 July 1799 he drove back into the sea 20,000 Turkish troops which had landed at Aboukir Bay.
[2] Capt. Sir Sidney Smith; commanding the blockade of Egypt, 1799–1800.

for some time, under an idea that he had not got all his fortune in a credit-
able way, but in having that matter fully investigated by our friend Scott
and others, and after having laid before me a very accurate statement on the
subject, I was perfectly satisfied he had been injured and consented in
recommending him to the court that his appointment might go forward.

If any arrangement of the nature you suggest should take place relative
to Ceylon, and a vacancy occur at Madras, I should have no objection
whatever to Mr North being appointed to that settlement.

Admiral Christian's family have not escaped my attention, but I believe
his family will not be in bad circumstances, in consequence of his share of
some prizes taken under his command at the Cape or St Helena.

I had almost omitted to mention your wishes respecting General
Hartley and Capt[ain] Kirkpatrick. There is such a request for ribbons and
baronets, particularly this last, from India, that I shall be obliged to be on
the reserve on the subject. But Capt[ain] Kirkpatrick stands on a fair
ground of superior pretension.

It does not occur to me that there is anything [else] to advert to in your
confidential letters of the dates to which I have referred in the course of
this letter, and I have only further to assure you that I remain, . . .

HENRY DUNDAS

LVII

The Rt Hon. Henry Dundas to the Earl of Mornington

16 October 1799, London

Most Private: [Separate]

I have received, and am truly embarrassed beyond expression by your
confidential unnumbered letter [dated 16 May 1799] on the subject of Lord
Clive. When I consider the many respectable qualities you attribute to
him, and recollect, that but one motive of the most honourable ambition
could have induced him to offer to serve in India, there must be some very
strange and uncommon persuasion in the structure and formation of his
mind and understanding, if so many valuable qualities, and such an
honourable ambition is incapable, by experience or advice, or adherence
to a plain system laid before him, to adhere to it, and to pursue it. At
present in this country, he stands, in character, extremely high; those who
are most intimate with him, speak most pointedly of the soundness and
directness of his understanding and integrity; and the late honourable, and

(under such circumstances) unparalleled co-operation with you in every measure that tended to your fame and glory, and which a little mind would have construed as taking from his own, are all features so prominent in the eyes of the public, that I am sure I could not do so disgusting a thing to the public feelings as to recall Lord Clive, if the proposition did not come from himself. I must still, therefore, hope that upon a further view of him, and his mind, animated by his exalted and important [station], he will be found to possess talents and energy to use them. Your letter shall certainly induce me to watch them with the most anxious solicitude, but unless something should occur in the conduct of his administration to suggest his recall, I do not, at this moment, see my way in doing so. No explanation could be given of it which I could support, by any ostensible fact, or any avowable cause, and, of course, the transaction would stand as a wanton exercise on my part, either of culpable caprice towards the son of the great founder of the Indian empire, or it would be branded with the imputation of unjustifiable partiality to whoever may be selected as his successor, if such a person could be found, whom I could, with propriety, select with a view to the supreme government, if at any time it should become vacant. In proportion as the supposed disgrace of Lord Clive would be reprobated, exactly in the same proportion would it be difficult to find a successor. After what I have stated to you in this letter, I need not tell you, that yours has left me in a state of real anxiety and solicitude.

I remain, . . .

HENRY DUNDAS

LVIII

The Earl of Mornington to the Rt Hon. Henry Dundas

26 October 1799, Fort William
Private: no. 19

My dear Sir

My dispatch of this date to the secret committee[1] will apprise you of the success which has attended the measures, which I directed Mr Duncan and Mr Uhthoff[2] to take with a view to the important object of establishing a British garrison at Goa.

[1] I.O. L/PS/5/23, p. 279.
[2] Joshua Uhthoff; assistant resident at Poona, 1786–98; 3rd member, Malabar Commission, 1798–9; envoy to Goa, 1799–1801.

It is my intention to augment that garrison without delay, but even at present it is sufficient to secure us against any possible attempt of an European enemy in that quarter. It will also operate as an effectual check upon the Marathas. You are already informed of my opinions with regard to the importance of the possession of Goa to our security and interests in every point of view, and I should hope that the present might prove a favourable opportunity for accomplishing the great advantage of obtaining the cession of Goa, either to the Crown or to the Company, in exchange either for Malacca or the Spice Islands, or for some equivalent pecuniary compensation. It appears to me, that the attempt to obtain this cession ought not to be delayed, and as I know you concur with me in my estimate of its value, I rely on you that the negotiation with the court of Lisbon will be immediately opened.

The claims of Portugal to any part of the Canarese dominions of the late Tipu Sultan are so obviously weak, that I do not think it necessary to trouble you further on that subject than to request you to advert to the length of time during which the places claimed by the Portuguese have belonged to the state of Mysore, and to the nature of the conquest which brought them under our power. The governor and captain-general's[1] pretension to be considered as an ally in the late war, appear to be founded principally on the share which his Excellency bore in issuing an order for a royal salute to be fired from Fort Alguada on the occasion of the fall of Seringapatam and of the death of Tipu Sultan. Although this claim is certainly more powerful than any which can be alleged by his Highness the peshwa, I do not expect, that, in the most liberal construction, this meritorious effort of the forward and active zeal of his Excellency the governor and captain-general will be deemed to entitle her Most Faithful Majesty to any proportion of our conquests. Even if the principle could be applied to cases of alliance in war, I doubt whether any degree of promptitude and alacrity manifested in rejoicing over the destruction of our late enemy could justify a claim on the part of the governor and captain-general to the rights of an accessory after the fact.

In my intended dispatches by the next ships, I shall give you a detailed view of the state of affairs in Mysore, at Hyderabad, and Poona.

At present, it will be sufficient to inform you, that the general aspect of affairs becomes every day more favourable in Mysore, that the whole of the country is now reduced to our authority, and to that of the rajah and the nizam, and that a seasonable fall of rain affords a prospect, that, even in this year, we may realize no inconsiderable part of our new revenue and subsidy without injury to the country.

With regard to the court of Hyderabad, its temper returns, and with it

[1] Don Francisco Antonio da Viega Chabral.

the establishment of an additional regiment of cavalry to the subsidiary force will soon be admitted. The court of Poona continues in the same state of weakness and confusion, and the distractions of the Maratha empire have recently been augmented by the hostilities which have broken out between the rajah of Kolapur and Pursuram Bhow. The latter is stated (by accounts which appear to be credible) to have fallen in an engagement with the former. Upon the whole, no apprehension appears to me justifiable by the actual state of the Maratha empire. For the present I have been compelled, by the perverseness of the peshwa's disposition, to proceed to carry the 2nd separate article of the treaty of Mysore into effect; but I shall anxiously watch any opportunity of renewing my proposals at Poona on their original basis, and I do not yet despair of success. I am afraid, however, that in order to improve our situation in that quarter, I must remove the present resident, who is to become too languid and inactive for such a station.

At Fort St George the whole state of affairs is astonishingly improved, and I am perfectly satisfied with the present course of that government. You will soon receive my new treaty with the rajah of Tanjore,[1] vesting the whole administration of his government and revenues in the Company. You will also, I trust, learn the success of the steps which I had ordered for disarming the Southern Polygars, who had begun to revolt even during the short period of the late war. We are now employed in framing a code for the introduction of a permanent settlement of revenue, and a system of judicature for the Company's possessions in the peninsula. I have ordered two members of the board of revenue to proceed immediately from Madras to Calcutta for the purpose of aiding in this salutary work; and I trust that its benefits will be extended in a short time over the whole of the Northern Circars, the jaghire, the countries under the Company's dominion ceded in the last war, and those conquered in this (with the exception of Canara), the countries of the Southern, Eastern, and Western Polygars, and the kingdom of Tanjore.

With regard to Bombay, I have already stated my opinions to you by former dispatches, and by Mr Wellesley. The necessity of some decision respecting Bombay is become so pressing, that I am compelled to urge you with the utmost earnestness either to adopt some plan on the subject, and forward it to me, or to furnish me with discretionary powers. I trust you will take one or other of these measures with every practicable degree of dispatch, and that you will forward to me sufficient authorities by express overland.

The annexation of Canara to the government of Fort St George has excited alarm among the civil servants at Bombay, who seem to imagine that they possess an exclusive right to the government of the western side of

[1] *Wellesley,* ii, 705.

the peninsula. My intention never was to exclude them from employment under the government of Fort St George. Even if an union of the two governments should not take place (as I anxiously trust it may), it would not be difficult to transfer a portion of the civil servants of Bombay to the establishment of Fort St George. But my wish is to effect a complete incorporation of all the establishment, civil, military, and commercial, of the two presidencies. Indeed, I am rather disposed to think, that an union of all the establishments of the three presidencies would be the most efficacious measure to extinguish all jealousies, and secure a consistent and vigorous system of government through India. Mr Duncan informs me by a private letter, that the civil servants of Bombay have had a meeting, at which they have voted a sort of remonstrance to me on my arrangements for the government of Canara. This is a most irregular and dangerous proceeding, which I fear I shall be compelled to reprove with some degree of severity. The fact is, that want of firmness has reduced the authority of government at Bombay to a very low scale. This remonstrance ought to have been checked by the government on the spot. The transaction, however, will I trust prove a powerful incitement to you to give an immediate decision on the questions which I have submitted to you relative to the government of Bombay; at least as far as they respect the administration of the affairs of Malabar and Canara. I found Bengal and the provinces in a state of profound tranquility: the effect of our success in Mysore has utterly annihilated the spirit of insubordination and contempt which for some time past has been gaining ground among our mohammedan subjects. I have commenced a negotiation with the nawab vizier for the reform of his military establishments. The resident with Sindhia has proceeded to Jynagur in order to receive from the rajah the person of Vizier Ali. I shall soon write to you in detail on the state of our courts of justice, and of the revenue and general finance, and of our commercial interests. With respect to finance, I shall only say, that, great and unprecedented as the effort has been which I was compelled to make within the last, and must make within the present year, our resources have corresponded with the exigency of the occasion, and public and private credit have improved to an astonishing degree, and are still progressively improving.

I think it necessary to apprise you of my intention to adopt without delay a plan for the improvement of the civil service at Bengal in a most important point. The state of the administration of justice, and even of the collection of revenue throughout the provinces, affords a painful example of the inefficacy of the best code of laws to secure the happiness of the people, unless due provision has been made to ensure a proper supply of men qualified to administer those laws in their different branches and departments. This evil is felt severely in every part of this government, and it arises principally from a defect at the source and fountain head of the service, I mean the education and early habits of the young gentlemen sent hither in the capacity of writers. My opinion, after full deliberation on the subject, is decided, that the writers on their first arrival in India should be subjected for a period of two or three years to the rules and discipline of some collegiate institution at the seat of government. In such an institution they might attain the groundwork of the several native languages necessary to their respective stations, together with the principles of general laws, those of the Mohammedan and Hindu codes, and the voluminous regulations enacted by the governor-general in council for the administration of justice in Bengal and the provinces. Other branches of knowledge also, suitable to their intended duties, might be acquired; and habits of activity, regularity, and decency, formed, instead of those of sloth, indolence, low debauchery, and vulgarity, now too apt to grow on those young men, who have been sent at an early age into the interior of the country, and laid the foundations of their life and manners among the coarse vices and indulgencies of those countries. I shall not pursue this topic further at present, intending to make it the subject of ample discussion at an early period. But I now wish to inform you, that I feel the mischief to be so pressing, that I intend, without waiting for orders from home, to proceed to found such an institution at Calcutta. I have already taken some steps towards the measure, and I hope to be able to carry my plan into effect with little (if any) additional charge to the Company.

I rely on your active and zealous support of this arrangement, in which I feel the greatest interest.

Ever, . . .

MORNINGTON

27 October 1799

I have received the address or remonstrance from the civil servants at Bombay, to which I have adverted in this letter. It is expressed very respectfully, but the substance of it is highly improper. The conduct of the government of Bombay on this occasion has been weak in the extreme.

I am sorry to inform you that General Hartley is dead. He died on the coast of Malabar on the 4th of October, and the intelligence was received at Madras on the 11th. You are also apprised of the death of General St Leger. We have now no King's general officer on the whole western side of India excepting General Stuart, who returns to Europe this season. Generals Harris and Floyd also return to Europe this season.

M.

There has been a skirmish in Soondah between our troops and some Maratha banditti, which I mention only because it may perhaps be made the ground of the rumour of a Maratha war. It was, however, nothing more than what I state, and my accounts received last night state all to be quiet at Soondah.

M.

LIX

The Rt Hon. Henry Dundas to the Earl of Mornington

28 October 1799, Whitehall
Private: no. 20 (Secret)

My dear Lord

In addition to the various letters I have already written to your Lordship by the present conveyance, I trouble you with these few lines merely to enclose [a] copy of a letter I have written to Lord Grenville within these few days,[1] in consequence of his Lordship having transmitted to me two papers received from the Portuguese ambassador,[2] suggested by our late successes in India, and expressive of an idea that his court has a claim upon the equity of this country on account of the injuries it supposes itself to have suffered from the late Hyder Ali, owing to its connection with Great Britain.

Having stated my sentiments at large on the subject in my letter to Lord Grenville, I content myself with referring you to a perusal of that letter; and will, from time to time, communicate to your Lordship what may further pass on the subject.

I enclose [a] copy of the two papers received from the Portuguese ambassador above alluded to.

I am, . . .

HENRY DUNDAS

[1] Add. MSS. 37274, f. 293.
[2] The Chevalier d'Almeida.

LX

The Rt Hon. Henry Dundas to the Earl of Mornington

1 November 1799, Wimbledon
Private: no. 21

My dear Lord

I send you an extract of a letter I have received from Governor Duncan respecting the recorder and one of the counsel who went recently from this country to practise as a barrister at Bombay; and I send you likewise a copy of the only answer I could send to him. And I am afraid, from what I have heard, and by the letters I have received from Sir Thomas Strange,[1] that the new establishments, which have gone out for the administration of justice at Madras and Bombay, meet with obstructions and difficulties in the outset of their duty. Of course, if it has come under your observation, or within your information to know anything of the sort passing, you will have interposed to give the proper check to whoever may be wrong. I have, since the arrival of the recent dispatches from India, had so much to occupy me, I have not been able to take under my consideration and decide on the voluminous statements Sir Thomas Strange has transmitted to me: but I shall do so at an early opportunity. In the meantime, if anything disagreeable occurs, I trust your discretion to apply the proper remedies. The judicatures must be supported against any improper cabal by those whom it is meant they should overawe, and punish if necessary; but on the other hand, they must not be permitted to entertain any idea of setting themselves up as a separate power, in opposition to the government where they reside.

I am, . . .

HENRY DUNDAS

LXI

The Rt Hon. Henry Dundas to the Earl of Mornington

1 November 1799, Wimbledon
Private: no. 22

My dear Lord

Your letter of the 7th June (*no. 15*) reached me. Previous to the receipt of it, I had wrote to you my sentiments at large on the subject of the Mysore

[1] Sir Thomas Strange (1756–1841); recorder of Madras, 1798–1800; chief justice, 1800–15.

country, and the terms on which I conceived it would be best to arrange it. Your letter, now before me, states those likely, with trivial alterations, to be adopted by your Lordship; and when those terms finally arranged arrive, I have no hesitation in assuring you that they shall receive my most cordial approbation. By my letter already referred to, you will see that I had wished for more, but the terms you have pointed out are highly honourable, and lay the basis of permanent security; and there are many will be of opinion that you do more for our security by the moderation of your conduct, than you would have done by those terms which my view of the question pointed out. It gives me much satisfaction to observe, that your Lordship on the spot have felt and acted on many of the leading considerations which weighed deeply with me in the sentiments I detailed in my letter of the 10th of October (*no. 17*). Your retaining the fortress of Seringapatam is a most important point; and is perhaps the one of all others I was most anxious about, because, in possession of that fortress with a large central force constantly stationed there, we must possess an overawing authority over every coterminous quarter. It is not my intention, in acknowledging this letter, to enter into any large consideration of any part of the subject I have already discussed. If opportunity should hereafter occur, you will not omit to pay due attention to any observations I have laid before you. One point, however, I must again recur to, I mean endeavouring if possible to make such an arrangement with the Marathas, as may ensure an efficient part of our army being in their pay and officered by our officers, to the exclusion of those of all other European nations.

In the letter from the secret committee, your Lordship will find the instructions you wish respecting the booty found at Seringapatam. I could not refer to your letter, nor to the information derived from it, because it was not offered, nor could I make mention of it, to the court of directors. Previous to the intimation which your letter conveyed to me, a belief was entertained by many, and chiefly on the authority of our friend Lord Macartney, that the treasure in the various forts would amount to fifteen or twenty millions. I could not figure the possibility of such an accumulation of wealth, when I considered the extent of his revenues, the largeness of his establishments, and the large sum he had so recently been obliged to pay in consequence of his treaty with Lord Cornwallis. I, therefore, not only myself discredited it, but did what I could to impress others with the same idea. Since such an erroneous idea had become prevalent in the army, as that which I have reprobated in the letter from the secret committee, it would have been extremely inconvenient if the treasure had amounted to such a sum as has been supposed. In every other view, it would certainly have been very comfortable if so large a share of the booty could have remained, as could have paid off the whole debt of the Company, and contributed at the same time a considerable sum to the expenses of the war at home.

You will see by my letters, that my ideas coincided entirely with yours as to Bombay, and Ceylon, being dependencies of one head government in the Carnatic. If such [a] plan is to take place, it will require a good deal of management to arrange it, and as, perhaps, it may not be speedily done, I shall be glad to have your ideas in detail upon it. I shall not, however, wait for them, if a favourable opportunity occurs in the course of [the] next session of Parliament, and I am not otherwise too much occupied. There is, however, another subject on which I wish, before taking any final step, to have your detailed sentiments. Not knowing exactly what may be the number and extent of your military positions under the treaty you have concluded, I am unable to form any accurate state of what ought to be our military establishments on the coasts of Coromandel and Malabar. I should hope that not much, if any, additional military force will be necessary in those quarters; at least, if it is any larger, it may be at less expense in consequence of the arrangements you may make for the payment of it by our allies. I have not a doubt, that the whole of the Company's European force should be in the shape of artillery, and that all the other European force in India should be King's troops, and I shall endeavour to bring about that arrangement. But in that point of view, it will be necessary for me to know what, under the new state of affairs, will be a sufficient number of King's regiments to be kept in India, taking them at one thousand or twelve hundred men per regiment. Whatever native regiments of infantry are necessary to be kept up, it has always occurred to me, that in time of peace, as well as war, the establishment should be complete in point of officers, and at such a rate of officers as would, in case of emergency, admit of an addition of privates to the establishment without any addition of European officers, which the distance between the two countries excludes the possibility of making in the requisite time.

I certainly have no objection to your settling the proper stipends on Tipu's family: but I should have been sorry indeed, for the reasons you give, if you had adopted the idea of placing any of his family on the throne of Mysore.

I am, . . .

HENRY DUNDAS

205

LXII

The Rt Hon. Henry Dundas to the Earl of Mornington

31 October 1799, Wimbledon
[*Private*]: *no. 23* (*Confidential*)

My Lord

Your Lordship had occasion to know before you left Great Britain, how much importance I attached to the conquest of all the colonial possessions of our enemies, and how pertinaciously I adhered to that system, notwithstanding the many difficulties it was necessary to encounter and overcome, and notwithstanding the clamour which circumstances gave rise to, particularly the loss of our troops from an uncommon degree of sickness in the West India Islands. Under such discouragements, nothing certainly would have justified a pertinacious adherence to such a system, but the rooted opinion then entertained, and to which I do now unalterably adhere, that Great Britain can at no time propose to maintain an extensive and complicated war but by destroying the colonial resources of our enemies and adding proportionately to our own commercial resources, which are, and must ever be, the sole basis of our maritime strength. By our commerce and our fleet, we have been enabled to perform those prodigies of exertion which have placed us in the proud state of pre-eminence we now hold. The French have for a long time been deprived of all their colonial resources, and of all their commerce, but still they have continued to derive considerable aid through Holland and Hamburg, in consequence of the trade of neutral nations being employed in conveying to Europe from the Dutch possessions, chiefly those of Demerara and Surinam, the produce of those rich and valuable colonies. These resources are now at an end, as far as the colonies of Demerara and Surinam are concerned, both of them being now in our possession. But a great source of wealth, conveyed to Europe in the same mode as the West India produce, still exists from the circumstance of Batavia still remaining in the possession of the Dutch. I need not dwell much on detailing the circumstances of that trade, as from your local situation your Lordship has the best means of being informed upon it, and in consequence of that information you must know what an enormous amount of the produce of Batavia, and the islands with which it is connected, is now brought home in neutral vessels, chiefly those of Denmark and America. Many of these vessels have certainly been captured, but a greater proportion escaped, and we are reduced to disagreeable questions with neutral nations in consequence of those captures.

The object of this letter is to convey to your Lordship the measures I wish to take for remedying this evil. I have no wish to possess ourselves of Batavia by force of arms. It would be scattering our Indian force; it would be exposing us to inconvenient expense; and from the unhealthiness which is imputed to the settlement in its present state, our troops would suffer more than even the importance of the object would, in my opinion, justify. But it appears to me that everything essential to our interest may be obtained without having recourse to military operations by land.

Your Lordship will, however, understand, that such military force as may give weight to your proposals and tend to facilitate the negotiation, by justifying, apparently at least, the compliance of the government of Batavia, would certainly be requisite. You will see by my instructions respecting Surinam, that the appearance of such a force was a necessary preliminary to the surrender of the colony. It has been stated to me from many quarters, that the settlement would be well satisfied to put itself under our protection, provided the fortunes and interests of individuals were secured to them. With a view to this, I herewith transmit for your Lordship's information the correspondence and other papers, from which you will perceive the mode and terms under which we obtained possession of Demerara, Berbice, and Surinam. Both from the information I have received, and from the example of these colonies (joined to the total annihilation of the naval power of Holland, by which they are deprived of any means of protecting their foreign possessions), I am hopeful, that similar measures applied to Batavia would bring that settlement under our protection, and secure the whole commerce of it being brought to the ports of this kingdom. For this purpose, your Lordship will select such persons as you conceive best calculated for this service, to go with a flag of truce to Batavia, and propose to the government there to follow the example of Demerara and Surinam, by putting themselves, and their property, and their commerce, under British protection. An examination of the papers I herewith transmit you, will furnish you ample materials for forming the articles of agreement, under which you call upon them to surrender themselves; and I leave it to your own discretion to make such alterations and modifications of the terms of agreement, as may not be inconsistent with the leading principles which govern the measure.

First: That the colony becomes a British colony and entitled to the privileges of other British colonies.

Secondly: That its whole trade must be brought to Great Britain in British ships, or ships licensed by the East India Company.

Thirdly: That its ports and harbours must be open to all the shipping of Great Britain, and shut to the ships of all its enemies.

I have communicated this letter to Lord Spencer, and instructions will be given to the officer commanding on the Indian station to appropriate such a naval force as may be necessary for the purpose, and it will be necessary that this force be kept constantly there till the settlement yields to the terms proposed, because if that is not the case, the great inducement to surrender will not exist. That inducement will arise from seeing that they have no chance of any of their property being conveyed away in neutral bottoms. If their harbours and ports are completely blocked up, this must be the necessary consequence, for by the law of nations we are strictly entitled to seize every ship, neutral or otherwise, coming from the settlement loaded with the colonial produce of a nation at war with us. This we are entitled to do without any regular intimation of blockade to those neutral nations, but if we shall superadd such an intimation, the consequence is that we are entitled to prevent neutral ships from at all entering the ports so blockaded. Some time after this, it may be proper to make such intimation of blockade, but it would be imprudent at this moment, as it would announce prematurely, and without sufficient cause the measures your Lordship is instructed to take by this dispatch.

I am, . . .

HENRY DUNDAS

LXIII

The Rt Hon. Henry Dundas to the Earl of Mornington

4 November 1799, Wimbledon
Private: no. 24

My dear Lord

In my letter of the 31st of October, I have detailed to you my sentiments regarding the settlement of Batavia, and the measures proper to be taken respecting it. I meant in sending that letter, that your Lordship, in possession of my sentiments, might act upon them by your own authority, without any official instructions. I was induced to rest for the present upon that ground, because I could not officially address you as governor-general, except through the secret committee of the court of directors, and there are reasons why I did not choose by that channel to detail the measures I wished you to execute. It has been suggested to me, that as it was meant to capitulate with the government of Batavia in the name of the King, and to take it under his Majesty's protection as a British colony, it would be best to convey his Majesty's instructions to you, not as governor-general, but in your individual capacity, which it is certainly competent for his Majesty to do. In that shape, accordingly, you will receive his Majesty's instructions, and it has further occurred to me, that it will be proper to send you a short letter through the secret committee, which, without entering into any details, will shortly refer to an intimation made by me as secretary of state, and, under that intimation, the secret committee will instruct the governments in India to co-operate with you, to the extent of any requisition you may make from them. By this means, you will technically, in due form, be possessed of the full powers of the India government to concur with you in the execution of the instructions you will receive from his Majesty. The enclosed is a copy of the dispatch through the secret committee,[1] which I will send them in the course of this day.

I am, . . .

HENRY DUNDAS

LXIV

The Rt Hon. Henry Dundas to the Earl of Mornington

4 November 1799, Wimbledon
[*Secret and Confidential*]: [*Unnumbered*]

My dear Lord

This letter, being of a nature perfectly personal and private, will not be copied even by Mr Cabell nor numbered, but *I* shall keep a copy of it, that I may send it in duplicate by a fitter conveyance, in case of any accident befalling this dispatch.

Your Lordship will have observed, that [al]tho[ugh] in several of your letters you mentioned Lady Mornington, with an earnest wish of her coming out to you, I have always avoided entering upon that subject. My reason was, that altho[ugh] I should certainly, if it had come to my decision, done whatever was necessary to comply with your wishes, I would have done it solely upon that motive, reluctantly, and contrary to my own judgement of what was most expedient for your own interests and that of your family. I need not, therefore, tell you, how relieved and gratified I was, when the speaker informed me that Lady Mornington herself had so forcibly stated to him her objections, and had taken the decided part of writing to you, to

[1] Finally dated 5 November 1799, I.O. L/PS/4/2.

induce you to depart from the idea. I need not, therefore, say more upon that subject, but I found it necessary, in candour, to say this much.

When the account of your final and brilliant success at Seringapatam arrived, Mr Bernard[1] called upon me, and stated, that previous to your departure for India, you had left with him a confidential memorandum of what were your wishes in case any of your services should induce his Majesty to advance you in the peerage. Mr Bernard, at the same time, mentioned to me that you had an anxious wish that the reversion to your Irish office should be granted to your son.[2] I, of course, laid all this before Mr Pitt, who, of course, will write to you himself. The title, he seemed to understand there would be no difficulty about, but doubted at present the King's acquiescence in the grant of reversion.

Leaving these points to others, to whom they with more propriety belong, I confess my ideas with regard to your family run in a different course, and, from the peculiar situation in which your children are circumstanced, it occurred to me, that the most substantial mark of friendship I could bestow upon your Lordship, was to direct my attention to consider by what means I could put under your power a large sum of money, which, in the event of any accident befalling yourself, would leave those children in a state of independence. I mentioned my ideas to Lord Grenville and Mr Pitt, both of whom were exceedingly pleased with my idea, and they both concurred in thinking, that in whatever way I could accomplish the idea, it must of all things be most gratifying to you. If the booty taken at Seringapatam had amounted to a sum so large as to render it improper to give it to the army, or if you had not promised it to them, my intention was it should be burdened with a large sum to be granted by his Majesty at your disposal. It would appear, however, by your last *private* letter to me of the 7th June [*no. 15*], that the amount of that booty was no more than what you thought it right to promise to the army.

In the dispatch which goes by this conveyance from the secret committee respecting the booty to be given to the army, your Lordship will observe an order given to ascertain the value of the military stores captured at Seringapatam, and to report to the court of directors for their further instructions. It has not been customary for the court of directors to pay for stores of that kind taken by their armies, and they will not be very willing, even in this instance, to commence the practice. They will, however, be induced to do it, but it will be done under the reserve of one hundred thousand pounds to be at their own disposal, and, after what I have stated in this letter, your Lordship will easily guess why that reserve will be made.

[1] Mornington's banker.
[2] Mornington's son Richard was illegitimate. The office was one of the chief remembrancers of the Irish Exchequer.

I have spoke on the subject to the chairman and deputy, and they enter warmly into my suggestions. In some shape or other the idea must be carried into execution. I certainly much prefer the ways I have hinted at, because in these ways it will come in one sum, whereas in any other mode it must be by instalments from the new acquired territories, which is more tedious and progressive in its effect, and, on that account, less valuable.

It does not occur to me that I have any more to trouble you with at present in this letter. I have been obliged to enter more upon topics of a delicate and domestic nature than I have been accustomed to do in any of my former correspondence with you, but the motive must be my excuse, as it was unavoidable.

I am, . . .

HENRY DUNDAS

LXV

The Earl of Mornington to the Rt Hon. Henry Dundas

29 November 1799, Fort William
Private: no. 20

My dear Sir

I have recieved your *private* letter *no. 13* [14 June 1799] by the *Asia*, and also the cypher which you sent by the *Charleton*, and which I now employ.

My letters of this date to the secret committee and to the chairman preclude the necessity of troubling you with a long dispatch; nor should I indeed have written to you at all by this occasion, had not one point required a direct application to you.

I find by letters from Bombay, that Mr Harford Jones conceives himself to be a more competent judge than me of the measures to be pursued with relation to the court of Persia, and to Zeman Shah. The zeal of Mr H Jones may possibly lead him to take steps at the court of Kabul entirely inconsistent with those I deem essentially necessary to the security of the objects which I have in view in Oudh. My conviction is, that a pacific embassy now sent to the shah would tend to revive his designs against Hindustan, which he has lately been compelled to relinquish, at least for the present season.

I shall, hereafter, explain more fully to you the principles of the policy which I have observed respecting the shah. At present I shall rest satisfied with enclosing you a letter (no. 1) which I have addressed to Mr Jones,[1] requesting you to enforce its contents. I do not know to what extent Mr Jones is under my orders, or whether he be so at all: if not, I trust he, and every other person who may be employed in Asia on any service likely to affect the interests for which I am responsible, may be immediately subjected to my general powers of control.[2]

The overland dispatch dated the 23rd of July has been lost on board the *Pearl*, taken by a French privateer. I trust you will in future direct all important overland dispatches in time of war to be forwarded in duplicate, and to be sent by two separate conveyances from Basra to Bombay.

I trust the *Swallow* may bring a duplicate of the last dispatch.

Some time since, the governor of Bombay under my orders established a resident in the district of Sind, with a view to obtain correct information of the motions and condition of Zeman Shah. This measure appears likely to effect all my objects in adopting it. Mr Crow,[3] who has been appointed to this station from Bombay, has manifested considerable activity and talents, and from him I have received more accurate and rational intelligence respecting Zeman Shah than has ever reached me since my arrival in India. I enclose a copy of the last letter (no. 2) which I received from him. The accounts which had been given to Mr Crow of the force of Baba Khan are certainly (as Mr Crow states) exaggerated. But I desire to call your particular attention to the fact that Zeman Shah is alarmed for his own safety, and that his mischief is diverted from Hindustan. Of this fact, Mr Crow's local situation enables him to form a more competent judgement than can be formed by any other British agent in Asia. I, therefore, trust, that you will not permit yourself to be disturbed by any false alarms from other more remote quarters, where it is not possible that the intelligence respecting Kandahar should not be vague and inaccurate.

I remain, . . .

MORNINGTON

Pray remember me kindly to Lady Jane.

M.

[1] Add. MSS. 13710, f. 34. He told Jones that this 'will exonerate you from any supposed responsibility with relation to any orders which you may receive from England'.
[2] He asked Grenville 'not to allow any of your tribe to interfere'. *Dropmore*, vi, 49.
[3] George Nathan Crow; envoy to Sind, 1799–1801, when he was expelled by the amirs.

LXVI

The Earl of Mornington to the Rt Hon. Henry Dundas

4 December 1799, Fort William
Private: no. 21

My dear Sir

The great pressure of business and the delay of our accounts from Madras, compel me to postpone my intended dispatches in reply to yours received by the ships of April and June down to *no. 13.* In the meanwhile, I send you a memorandum from the accountant-general (no. 1) on the subject of your last financial letter, and observations (no. 2) of the import warehouse keeper on the last sale of European imports, I have added (no. 3) several papers relating to an establishment formed under my directions in Sind.[1] By the ships of the season, I hope to be able to write you more in detail on a variety of subjects.

Believe me, . . .

MORNINGTON

LXVII

The Earl of Mornington to the Rt Hon. Henry Dundas

28 December 1799, Fort William
Private: no. 22

My dear Sir

You will naturally be anxious to know the state of my negotiation in Oudh, in consequence of the extraordinary proposition of the nawab vizier announced in my separate letter to the secret committee of the 29th of November.[2] It is, however, impossible at present to ascertain the result of this business. The nawab vizier's conduct has disclosed such symptoms of treachery and falsehood, as leave me in great doubt with regard to his real intentions. I have, however, taken such precautions as I trust will render it impracticable for him to frustrate the important object of establishing

---

[1] Memorandum by Kirkpatrick relative to the establishment of a factory in Sind. I.O.L. Film. MSS. 607.
[2] *Wellesley*, ii, 154.

(before the close of the present season) such a force in Oudh as shall render our frontier on that side nearly impregnable. By the next overland dispatch, I hope to be enabled to speak with more certainty on the affairs of Oudh.

I enclose two letters which will afford you complete satisfaction with regard to the state of Mysore, and will enable you to form a just estimate of the merits of Colonel Close. You are aware that Purneah is dewan to the rajah of Mysore, and was the principal financial minister of Tipu Sultan.

Some reports from Persia have excited an apprehension of the death of Baba Khan. I have written orders to Bombay for the purpose of suspending the departure of Captain Malcolm until the state of affairs in Persia can be better ascertained.

The accounts of Zeman Shah stated in my letter (*no. 20*) of the 29th of November have been confirmed from various quarters. The court of Poona continues in the same state of distraction and weakness; and the general confusion of the Maratha empire seems to increase. The court of Hyderabad appears to have recovered its temper. In consequence of documents found among the records at Seringapatam, implicating the leaders of the party adverse to our interests in treasonable correspondence with the late Tipu Sultam, the nizam has adopted measures which cannot fail to strengthen our connection with that court. I refer you to my dispatches to the court of directors by this packet for all points not touched in this letter.

Believe me, . . .

MORNINGTON

LXVIII

The Earl of Mornington to the Rt Hon. Henry Dundas

25 January 1800, Fort William
Secret and Confidential: [Unnumbered]

My dear Sir

In this letter I have enclosed a memorandum relating to several points in my former *s[ecret]* *and* *c[onfidential]* letters to which I have not yet received answers from you. The marginal notes to the memorandum will serve to show what variations (if any) have taken place in my opinion since the date of my former letters.

Since my return from the Coast, I have discovered several features in Bebb's character which have entirely altered my opinion of his fitness to sit in council. He is now going home in a state of health which probably will never admit of his return to India; but it may still be prudent to warn you of the defects of his character. I knew him to have been deeply tainted with the new philosophy and a friend to the French Revolution; but I flattered myself that he had sincerely recanted his errors, and that he had become a convert to the true faith. He is, however, a Jacobin at heart (I say it with grief); he has not a principle of religion; is very loose in his maxims of morality, and entirely unsound in his notions of government. He has not subscribed to the voluntary contribution: he refused to do so, on the principle of not supporting the war. I leave the conclusion to your judgement. His temper is both violent and morose, and his prejudices absurd and invincible on many subjects. His obstinacy renders him utterly untractable in business. Add to these faults that he is under the dominion of his wife, and that his opinions with respect to characters cannot be safely received, as they often proceed from complaisance to his wife, and from a wish to advance her friends. I advise you by no means to admit him into the direction, he will give you much trouble; and I trust that you will never send him into council here.

Myers[1] is a much better man in every respect, but he is not fit for council. He would, however, make an excellent director. He is zealously attached to you, and to all your Indian systems.

In fact, no Company's servant, whom I have met (with the single exception of Barlow), is fit to be a member of the executive gov[ernment] at any of the presidencies, even under the present large powers of the governors in council. Their education, habits, and manners, all tend to disqualify them from a situation in which general knowledge, and extended views of policy, as well as dignity of character and conduct, are required. They must, therefore, either be absolute cyphers (and in that case, their existence as component parts of the government tends to degrade it), or, if they are active, their ignorance and prejudices will prove a great embarrassment to the public service. Even with all your knowledge of India, I am concerned to tell you, that you have no adequate conception of the scarcity of able and well-informed men in the civil service. It is a lamentable fact, that I have not found two men in all India, whom I would trust to write a common dispatch without accurate revision. Under the present law, a refractory councillor might render the progress of the public business so slow and difficult, as to frustrate the activity of the boldest and most active governor. My opinion is, that the council as now constituted is a useless, if not a dangerous, expense. The governor should have the power of summoning a privy council, and should act in it as the King or l[or]d-l[ieutenan]t of Ireland in council: but neither the executive nor legislative power should be

[1] Thomas Myers; accountant-general, Bengal, 1796–9; then home.

supposed to be parcelled out among the councillors, although the governor ought to be compelled to record all his acts. His privy council should be avowedly nothing more than a court of registry and record. The councillors now assume a certain state, and affect to consider themselves to be in too elevated a station to condescend to pay the marks of respect due to the person invested with the supreme power, such as attending his levées, being present at all ceremonies, *etc.* This tends to distract the obedience and respect of the people for the government, and gives it more the character of an aristocratic republic than of a monarchy. The commander-in-chief also has no business in council excepting when called to assist in military affairs. Soldiers, particularly in India, are miserable statesmen; but commanders-in-chief are very fond of displaying their political science. Sir J[ames] Craig, I know, is a *profound* statesman. According to the present constitution, the commander-in-chief is a fixture at Calcutta, holding levées and collecting attendance about him, and hardly ever sees the army. If the commander-in-chief were placed on the same footing as he is in Ireland, the army would see more of him, and he would be less troublesome to the government. I desire not to be understood to reflect on Sir A[lured] Clarke, whom I really esteem but he, too, possesses great notions of his independent privileges, and perhaps might give trouble to another governor-general.

On the whole, I think that the civil members of the council and the commander-in-chief should be reduced to the mere rank and relative station of privy councillors in England and Ireland. If the salaries must be maintained on the same scale (that of the commander-in-chief certainly must), they might be annexed to the office of chief justice of nizamut adaulut, and president of the privy council. These suggestions, with the addition of a lieutenant-governor (from England) at each presidency, would redouble the vigour and efficiency of our Indian administration.

The judges of the supreme court entertain idle notions of their controlling powers over the government itself; and the act of Parliament, giving rank to the chief justice next to the governor-general, countenances the idea of a greater approximation of their respective stations than is consistent with propriety. This should be corrected. Between Anstruther and myself the utmost cordiality and kindness subsists; but the system is defective. I do not like to say to him, what I now say to you, that in my conscience I think, after full consideration, the supreme court an expensive nuisance, as now constituted. It is not true that the superiority of the civil service in Bengal to that of the other presidencies is to be ascribed to the operation of the supreme court: it is to be ascribed to the example and precepts and institutions of Lord Cornwallis' government. Perhaps the most profligate period in the whole history of India is from the date of the institution of the supreme court to that of Lord Cornwallis' accession to the government; and is it possible to ascribe his system to the control of Sir Robert Chambers,[1] Sir William Jones,[2] Mr Le Maistre and Mr Hyde? Add Sir William Dunkin— *hoc est, oleum adde camino*. Two more corrupt personages than Sir Robert and Sir William have seldom doubled the Cape of Good Hope. I shall write to you more largely on this subject. In the meanwhile, you ought to place the governor-general in such a station, that no rank should at all approach his: he ought to be the representative of the King; and his person should be inviolable in India. Anstruther (I am grieved to say) has acquired the character of a most intemperately passionate man. His ungovernable impetuosity sometimes has discovered secrets which it is not useless to know. During my absence on the Coast, he was provoked into one of these fits of fury by a man of some honour (Colonel Gordon, aide de camp to Clarke), when he declared that he was superior to every man in this settlement or in India; that he represented the authority of the Crown; that he possessed the power of committing to gaol not only Sir Alured Clarke, but the governor-general himself, and that he would not shrink from the exercise of that power, whenever the occasion should demand it. This harangue was pronounced at a card assembly before fifty or a hundred people. You know the fact to be, that, if a proper story could be fabricated, the law does subject the person of the g[overno]r-gen[era]l to the supreme court: is this safe? Is it right? I know not where you picked up your Sir Henry Russell.[3] He is a vulgar, ill-bred, violent, and arrogant, brute; he gives universal disgust. I hope you will never allow him to be chief justice. I confess I have great fears for Anstruther's health (whom I really esteem). He visibly declines, and last summer he was at the point of death. If he should unfortunately die, I hope you will name no successor until you shall have fully considered the question of a new constitution for the court itself; at all events, do not place that brute Russell in a station which his manners and conduct will disgrace. At the same time, I believe Russell to be a very honest man, and a pretty good special pleader.

I was sorry to observe, in one of your letters, that you had adopted the opinion of the directors, that bullion or other funds sent hither for commercial purposes must never, even in time of war, be diverted to any other purpose whatever. The execution of this order appears to us all in India utterly impracticable. It requires an extreme case to justify any diversion of the funds destined for the Company's trade; but when such a case shall exist, no choice may be left but to divert their commercial funds, or to hazard the loss of territory, revenue, and commerce, together. Such was the case when

[1] Sir Robert Chambers (1746–1803); chief justice, Bengal, 1791–8.
[2] Sir William Jones (1746–94); judge of the supreme court, Bengal, 1783–94; founder of the Asiatic Society of Bengal, 1784.
[3] Sir Henry Russell (1751–1836); judge of the supreme court, Bengal, 1798 1807; chief justice, 1807–13.

I *made a catch* (as Mr Bosanquet expressed it) at the bullion destined for China. Do you really mean that in the event of sudden war, the gov[ernmen]t in India is not (like every other gov[ernmen]t in the world) to consider the security of its military resources as the paramount object of its attention? Is not this principle impossible in practice? I admit that nothing short of a real exigency can justify an invasion of the commercial funds, but I really tremble at the interdiction menaced in your letter of [23 July 1799, *no. 14*] overland; as it would bind this government down to the earth in the event of unforeseen war.

Bebb, I know, has a notion of sending out bullion or specie direct from England to the board of trade, to be applied by them without the control of the gov[ernmen]t in India, whom he would restrict absolutely from touching the commercial funds. This would throw a large share of the gov[ernmen]t of this country into the hands of the board of trade, which I presume you would not permit. Indeed, this doctrine would lead to a state of warfare between the sovereign and mercantile characters of the Company; and I must say, that it more resembles the maxims of a merchant, than those which become a sovereign. I refer you to Myers on these points.

Pray receive my aide de camp Major Davis with kindness. He is a very worthy man.

Your letter of the 27th September [*no. 16*] reached me on the 13th January 1800. I was exceedingly pleased with the reception given to the dispatches by the *Sarah Christian*. I hope that the arrival of my brother Henry with the treaties of partition and subsidy has satisfied your anxiety respecting the settlement of Mysore. It would have been impossible to have retained more of the territory without throwing the nizam absolutely into the counsels of Poona: but if you will have a little patience, the death of the nizam will probably enable me to gratify your *voracious appetite for lands and fortresses*. Seringapatam ought, I think, to stay your stomach a while; not to mention Tanjore and the Polygar countries. Perhaps I may be able to give you a supper of Oudh and the Carnatic, if you should still be hungry.

I think my dispatches by various occasions, and my brother Henry's arrival, must have given you my ideas on most of the subjects touched in your letters. I shall, however, reply regularly to your letters by the last ships of this season.

Ever yours, . . .

MORNINGTON

I wish you would prevent the directors from naming persons to offices or reversions in India. The master attendancy of this port requires an able and active man, and I conclude they will name some unfit person to fill it from England. Mr Baird, whom they have sent to Prince of Wales' Island, is absolutely a madman, as will appear by his correspondence with Mr Counter. These appointments injure the authority of the gov[ernmen]t on the spot.

Destroy this letter when read.

LXIX

Memorandum of Points Hitherto Unanswered by Mr Dundas*

12 August 1798, Secret and Confidential, no. 1

Mr Lumsden would also answer tolerably well.

New arrangement of council: removal of Messrs S[peke] and C[owper] and appointment of Messrs B[ebb] and B[arlow], or eventually of Messrs Barlow and H[arington].

Certain alterations in the judicial department of government; and the expediency of new laws for the purpose of removing the doubts with regard to the power of the gov[ernor]-gen[eral] in council to constitute courts of sudder dewany and nizamut adaulat, either by adding assistant judges to sit with the council, or by appointing judges to be entirely separate from it.

Sir J[ames] C[raig] and I are on very good terms; but every hour convinces me more, that if he sh[oul]d ever be made c[ommander]-in-ch[ief] (under the present constitution of that office) while I am in India, he will compel me to return to England. I know he publicly

The appointment of Sir J[ames] C[raig] to the chief command of the army on the departure of Sir A[lured] C[larke] earnestly deprecated.

* This is the slightly fuller draft version.

219

declared, he, if comm[ander]-in-chief, w[oul]d not have submitted to my active interference on the occasion of the rupture with Tipu. Had the least obstacle (of the kind Sir J[ames] C[raig] declares he w[oul]d have made) been thrown in my way, my whole plan might have been frustrated. Is such a man a proper c[ommander]-in-chief?

I continue to be decidedly of opinion that the gov[ernor]-gen[eral] ought to have the supreme and efficient conduct of the King's army in India, in such a manner as that both the fleet and army sh[oul]d consider the gov[ernor]-gen[eral] as the full representative of the King in India.

Deficient state of the Company's European troops recommended to *early and serious attention.* Deficiency in *European artillery,* particularly noticed, and a considerable increase of that establishment stated to be *essentially necessary.*

Necessity of rendering the governor-general in council the centre of all authority within the British possessions in India strongly urged; and the expediency of the admiralty's carrying on its correspondence with the naval commander in India through the supreme government, or at least in communication with the government, stated. Similar recommendations on the subject of the King's force in India strongly pressed.

The expediency of granting to the governor-general, in addition to his commission from the Company, a *concurrent commission from the Crown,* suggested as the best remedy for the defects set forth.

Presses for an answer to all these points *by the ealiest opportunity,* and expresses hope of receiving it before the end of June 1799.

Requests in the most earnest manner some immediate mark of the King's favour to be conferred on Gen[eral] Harris.

12 November 1798, Secret and Confidential, no. 3

I continue to be of this opinion.	Earnestly requests a most pointed censure of the 10th July and 3rd of August [1798] dispatches from Fort St George to the governor-general to be transmitted to India *by the earliest possible opportunity overland and by sea.*
I continue to be of this opinion.	Requests a similar censure to be passed on the political and secret letters of the 15th Oct[ober] 1798 from Fort St George.
I am quite concerned that this has not been done already. I entreat it may not be further delayed.	Expresses a desire that the resident at Hyderabad may be created a baronet.
This applies to the case of my absence from Bengal. A good lieut[enant]-governor; a new sudder dewany adaulat; a well-constituted secretary's office; and the power of calling into the privy council every man of ability in the settlement; would be the best provisions in the case supposed. You will observe by the public dispatches of this season, that I have endeavoured to strengthen the sec[retar]y's office by calling in fresh assistance. I must proceed to appoint a new court of sudder dewany adaulat. The rest remains with you.	*Repeats* a wish that the suggestions respecting the supreme council in Bengal may be answered without a moment's delay; *as everything may depend on the arrangement of that business.*

12 January 1799, Secret and Confidential, no. 4

They are still necessary, but sh[oul]d not proceed beyond censure.	All faction at Madras stated to be now dispelled; but the necessity of the censures from home (recom-

mended in *nos. 2 and 3 s[ecret] and c[onfidential]*), with a view to the prevention of future mischief *still insisted on.*

Suggestions respecting the changes in council and the royal commission renewed.

4 September 1798, Private, no. 8

This ought to be established by two modes:

1st: Regular packets sh[oul]d sail every month from India and England. They might take small cargoes. The places of departure in India might vary according to the season.

2nd: The overland dispatch ought to be established.

Suggestions relative to the great utility of regular monthly advices being dispatched to India.

LXX

The Earl of Mornington to the Rt Hon. Henry Dundas

27 January 1800, Fort William
Secret and Confidential: Unnumbered

My dear Dundas

In addition to my *secret and confidential* letter of the 25th ins[tan]t, I wish to call your attention to two or three points.

Mr Mackenzie,[1] Lord Loughborough's[2] friend, who was formerly in high office here, and was strenuously recommended to Lord Teignmouth, is a violent and absurd coxcomb, utterly unfit for any high station. I hope in God you will never allow him to be sent to the council here. His temper remains unsubdued even by all his misfortunes.

A letter has lately been sent from the King to the peshwa, of which I

[1] John Mackenzie; 3rd member, board of revenue, Bengal, 1786–9, removed by Cornwallis; salt agent, Bengal, 1791–4.
[2] Alexander Wedderburn, Lord Loughborough (earl of Rosslyn, 1801); lord chancellor, 1793–1801.

have received no copy, and am utterly ignorant of the contents. Mr Duncan has forwarded it to Poona with extraordinary ceremony and honour, and the resident has presented it. All this has been done without any previous reference to me. Duncan and Palmer will receive a *flagellation* from my pen; but I trust to you to prevent such proceedings in future at any of the native courts. I leave it to you to judge what might be the effect on our influence in India, of letters from the Crown, delivered with extraordinary pomp and uncommunicated to the government-general, the legitimate channel of war, peace, and negotiation. Such letters might effectually frustrate every operation of the Indian government. I should certainly have stopped the delivery of the letter in question, until I could have learned its contents, if the precipitancy of Mr Duncan and of Colonel Palmer had not precluded me from taking any such step. On this subject, I must observe that any distinction in the manner of presenting the letters from the Crown leads to most mischievous consequences. The native princes should be taught to look up to the Company and its governments as the regular authorities for the administration of Indian affairs. Their respect should never be distracted by the interference of the Crown: or, if the Crown be to interfere, let the interference be effectual, and the government at once made Royal. It is impossible to calculate what effect the King's letter may produce in the present critical state of affairs at Poona. Palmer has no copy of it. I believe Duncan has none: at least, he has transmitted none to me. The letters from the prince of Wales to the nabob of Arcot have occasioned infinite mischief. You ought to check his Royal Highness. Sir J[ohn] Macpherson[1] is his evil councillor on such occasions. The nabob despises the prince, and believes his only object to be to obtain presents.

Great disgust has been occasioned here by the little, or rather no, notice taken of our address to the King and voluntary contribution. The court of directors and his Majesty have not signified a syllable of approbation or feeling on the subject. The consequence is, that nobody will subscribe this year. I have sent my subscription; but the spirit of the settlement is really extinguished by the unaccountable neglect of the directors. The *Eurydice* arrived in England the 12th of April; and the last ships sailed from thence the 18th June 1799; and not one line of applause, or even notice of the astonishing effort made in Bengal by the loyalty and zeal of the British and native subjects.

By this dispatch, I have forwarded to the court of directors a particular expression of my sentiments respecting Sir Alured Clarke. He is wounded to the soul, and really deserves great praise. I make it my most anxious request to you, that you will obtain a vote of thanks for him, and ultimately

[1] Sir John Macpherson (1745–1821); governor-general, 1785–6; M.P. for Horsham, 1796–1802.

a peerage of the same rank as Harris'.[1] Pray have the goodness to state this matter to the King as my most cordial wish. I shall consider his Majesty's compliance as a great personal mark of favour towards myself. I refer you to my letter of this date to the court.[2]

Ever, . . .

MORNINGTON

LXXI

The Earl of Mornington to the Rt Hon. Henry Dundas

29 January 1800, Fort William
Private: no. 23

My dear Sir

Your kind letter of the 27th September 1799 (*no. 16*) reached me on the 13th instant, together with those of the 23rd July (the duplicate *no. 14*) and of the 6th September (*no. 15*).

I need not say how happy I feel in the honourable reception given to my packet by the *Sarah Christian*. It was peculiarly satisfactory to me to perceive that the motion of thanks to me was postponed, until the whole circumstances, causes, and conduct, of the war with the sultan could be fully before Parliament. I am very anxious, however, that you should cause distinguished notice to be taken of the services of Sir Alured Clarke. They are particularly enumerated in my separate letter by this dispatch to the court of directors. I sent a copy of my letter to Sir Alured after I had it made up for dispatch, and I enclose a copy of his answer to me, which reflects the greatest honour on his character. You will really oblige me by obtaining a peerage for him, and I wish you to state the application to the King as a personal request from me.

My dispatches in various departments for these last eight months have nearly anticipated the answers to all your letters: and I trust in God that before this time my brother Henry's arrival in England has satisfied your expectations respecting the settlement of Mysore. To have retained the whole territory for ourselves would have raised such a flame, both at Hyderabad and Poona, as could hardly have been extinguished without another war. Henry will have informed you of the difficulties which

---

[1] Clarke was not mentioned in the resolutions of the houses of parliament.
[2] *Wellesley*, ii, 200.

delayed even the settlement as ultimately effected at Hyderabad. The nizam's pride would not have been satisfied without a considerable cession of territory; and territory is more acceptable to his Highness' ministers, as affording a larger field both for patronage and peculation. Money and jewels accompanying territory would also have been acceptable no doubt; but, distinct from territory, would not have contented the nizam, and as they would have passed directly into his private coffers, and would have been inaccessible to his ministers. The present settlement is more gracious, and as effectual in point of real power, as that which seems to have formed the extreme point of your wishes.

I shall hope to be able to answer your letters in detail by the last ships of this season.

The affairs of Oudh continue in the same uncertain state; but advantage will certainly flow from what has passed.

The private tonnage this season has given me much trouble. It is difficult to decide such a question permanently on principles supposed contradictory to the orders of the court of directors. I shall endeavour to proceed at least so far as to prevent the trade from taking a bent towards foreign European markets in this year; and you ought, in justice to my situation, to decide the question at home.

Referring you to my dispatches to the court and committee,

I remain, . . .

MORNINGTON

LXXII

The Earl of Mornington to the Rt Hon. Henry Dundas

30 January 1800, Fort William
Private: no. 24

My dear Sir

I think it necessary to request your immediate and particular attention to the novel circumstance, which has recently occurred, of a Danish frigate entering the River Hoogly. She is said to be designed to protect the homeward-bound trade of the Danish nation from Bengal. Under the same pretext, a squadron of ships of war might be introduced into this river. The same pretext might equally be applied to serve the purposes of other neutral and friendly nations; all of whom might suddenly become our enemies. Hitherto, the frigate in question (owing probably to a strong suggestion which I conveyed to the chief of Serampur) has not attempted to proceed higher than Kedgeree; but I wish to know from you how this government is to act in the case of a foreign ship of war attempting, without permission, to pass Fort William. Considering the value of our commercial fleets, which remain for a great part of the year in Saugur Roads, or at Kedgeree and Diamond Harbour, it becomes a question, whether the privilege of the river to any extent, however limited, ought not to be placed under very strict regulations in the case of foreign ships of war; and particularly during a period of war in Europe.

Among the regulations on this head, one might be, that no foreign ship of war, the destination of which had not been formally announced to the government in India by the government at home, should be at liberty to enter this river. In the present instance, the only intimation which I have received respecting the Danish frigate has been from the government of Serampur.

You already know how injurious Tranquebar has proved to our interests during the whole of the present war. I assure you, that the Danish settlement of Serampur is, in some respects, a still greater evil. Its vicinity to the seat of government in Bengal renders it peculiarly obnoxious. Adventurers of every nation, and Jacobins of every description, swarm at Serampur; and it is the asylum of all our public defaulters and debtors.

These circumstances cannot fail to have the effect of occasionally unsettling the notions of many of our native subjects with regard to the extent and source of the authority of this government: and this impression is assisted by the affectation of importance and state sometimes assumed by the chief of this paltry factory, which, as it happens, is placed exactly opposite to the cantonments occupied by the garrison of Fort William.

You are not perhaps apprised, that Colonel Bie is *governor and commander-in-chief of all the Danish dependencies in the provinces of Bengal, Bihar, and Orissa:* and that he announces himself in this high character through the channel of the public newspapers.

I will conclude with assuring you, that you would render a most important service to our national interests in this part of the world, if you could devise any means of annihilating the whole of these petty European states throughout the continent of India; but above all, those of Tranquebar and Serampur.

I remain, . . .

MORNINGTON

LXXIII

The Earl of Mornington to the Rt Hon. Henry Dundas

5 March 1800, Fort William
Private: no. 25

My dear Sir

My last *private* letter to you was numbered *24* and dated on the 30th of January; and my last *secret and confidential* letter was numbered *11* and dated in August. I annex to this dispatch a memorandum of all the letters which I have addressed to you since my arrival in India, and of the several conveyances by which they were respectively dispatched. I also annex a memorandum of all the letters which I have received from you.

Although most of the points touched in your several dispatches have already been anticipated; either by my letters to you, by the communications which, I trust, you have received through Mr Wellesley, or by my dispatches to the secret committee and the court of directors; I propose in this letter to reply regularly to such of your communications as have not already been directly answered by me.

No. 5: 29 December 1798
The last of your letters which I answered directly was *no. 5* dated the 29th of Dec[embe]r 1798; the receipt of which was acknowledged by me in my *secret and confidential* letter dated the 19th of May 1799, of which one copy only was made and transmitted by Mr Wellesley.

No. 6: 18 March 1799
I received with the greatest satisfaction your approbation of the treaty of Hyderabad. Subsequent events have abundantly confirmed the justice of the expectations which you formed upon the first view of that treaty. It was indeed the source of all our recent successes in India; and even if it has in any degree aggravated the characteristic jealously of the Marathas, it has furnished ample compensation in establishing an impregnable barrier against their power. The system on which the treaty of Hyderabad was founded would certainly be most effectually completed by the conclusion of a similar engagement at Poona, and I am resolved never to lose sight of that most desirable object.

The various instances in which the jealousy of the Maratha state has lately been disclosed are rather to be attributed to the peculiar character of that nation, and to the singular disposition of the present peshwa, than to any formed aversion to a nearer connection with the British power.

The influence of Sindhia has also contributed to frustrate my proposed measures; because their necessary effect must have been to restore the peshwa to a certain degree of credit and power, and to reduce Sindhia in the same proportion. I have no reason to believe that Sindhia would be averse to a separate connection with us; but not perceiving any possible advantage which could arise from such a connection, under all the circumstances of the present moment, I have taken no steps to cultivate it, while I have avoided any manifestation of an unfriendly disposition.

The distractions of the Maratha empire must continue to increase until they shall be checked by foreign interference. No power in India, excepting the British, now possesses sufficient strength to interpose with effect in these dissensions; and I shall not be surprised, if ultimately the subsidiary force which I am so anxious to establish at Poona, should be required with equal anxiety by the Maratha state, as the only means of restoring order, and of saving the whole of that country from plunder and desolation.

Mr Colebrooke[1] has now resided several months at Nagpur, and I have every reason to believe that the rajah of Berar will prove well inclined to support whatever plan the British government may ultimately adopt with regard to the affairs of the Maratha empire.

With respect to the views of Zeman Shah, the papers found in the palace at Seringapatam have completely justified your opinion of Tipu's disposition to obtain the assistance of that prince, and of Zeman Shah's to afford it. Although I am far from despising the strength of Zeman Shah, the best information which I can collect leads me to believe that the accounts of his talents, military force, and pecuniary resources, transmitted by Mr Jones at Baghdad, are much exaggerated.

For some time to come, I trust that Zeman Shah will be too much occupied at home to admit of his turning his arms against Hindustan; and I am inclined to think that the encouragement of divisions in his own government, and of hostility between the contiguous state of Persia and his dominions, is the system of defence against Zeman Shah, on which it is most safe to rely under the present circumstances of affairs in India.

The profligacy of Sindhia's character, the distracted state of his councils and armies, and the distress, or rather ruin, of his finances, preclude the hope of effecting a secure or useful alliance with him.

The establishment of a subsidiary force at Poona would compel Sindhia to return to his own dominions; and, in that event, it might not be difficult to convince him, that his best security would consist in imitating the example of the nizam and the peshwa, and in placing himself under the immediate protection of the British power.

I entirely concur with you, after full consideration, in your opinion of the

[1] Henry Thomas Colebrooke; resident at Nagpur, 1799–1801.

impolicy of involving Russia in any branch of our Indian alliances or affairs. At the time when I stated that suggestion, the danger arising from the designs of the French, of Zeman Shah, and of Tipu Sultan, appeared to be so urgent as to justify a temporary departure from our general principles of policy, with a view to obtain an effective aid against the immediate pressure of the moment. No such exigency now exists. I understand that the court of Persia entertains considerable jealousy of the views of Russia; and that it would be extremely difficult to persuade the Persians to enter into any concert with the court of Petersburg.

My various dispatches have so fully submitted to you the whole course of my thoughts and proceedings with respect to Tipu Sultan, that I shall add nothing on that subject.

With respect to the general system of policy to be adopted by us in India in consequence of the conquest of Mysore, I shall review all the important considerations connected with that extensive question in a separate dispatch, addressed, by some future opportunity, either to you or to the secret committee.

I conclude that the power of the French is either already extirpated, or that you will continue the war until that indispensable object shall be completely effected. Notwithstanding the present proud and commanding predominance of the British power in India, we cannot expect an uninter-rupted continuance of tranquillity while France shall be permitted to maintain a powerful establishment in Egypt.

Since I wrote the preceding paragraph, I have received dispatches from Lord Elgin,[1] dated the 22nd of December 1799, by which it appears, that Kléber[2] remains in Egypt with 15,000 men; and that Bonaparte is at the head of a new government in France. Lord Elgin presses the utility of a powerful diversion from India through the Red Sea, for the purpose of accelerating the evacuation of Egypt by the French; but after a full dis-cussion of this subject with General Stuart, I am satisfied that it would be an useless waste of treasure and blood to attempt such an expedition on a large scale, unless the whole plan of co-operation from the Mediterranean had been previously concerted. Desultory operations against any places retained by the French on the shores of the Red Sea may be advantageous: they would neither be perilous, nor expensive.

In discussing, towards the close of your letter *no. 6,* some of the separate points stated in my former dispatches, you suggest a doubt of the importance of Tipu's maritime possessions in Canara, with a view to our security and to the means of preventing his communications with the armaments of France.

[1] Thomas Bruce, 7th earl of Elgin (1766–1841); ambassador-extraordinary to Constantinople, 1799–1803; famed for his marbles.
[2] General Kléber succeeded Bonaparte as commander-in-chief in Egypt in August 1799. He was assassinated on 14 June 1800.

I am aware that your reasoning is not applicable to the case which actually exists, in consequence of the death of Tipu and the total destruction of his power; but I am persuaded that the papers discovered at Seringapatam, and subsequent information, will have convinced you that Mangalore is not the only harbour on the coast of Canara at which the French might have landed. You will have observed that one of Tipu's plans was formed with a view to their landing at Mirjaun; and I believe that they might have effected a landing on other parts of that coast. You are already apprised of my entire coincidence in your opinion respecting the importance of Goa; and I trust that you will be enabled to give full effect to the measures which I have adopted for the purpose of rendering that possession an additional source of strength to the British empire in India. I also consider the possession of Diu to be a most desirable object; particularly with a view to the coercion of the piratical states on the north-western coast of the peninsula of India.

No. 7: 18 March 1799

The memorandum which I transmitted to you (in my *private* letter *no. 21*) from Mr Myers, late accountant-general in Bengal, contains the substance of all my sentiments respecting the state of our financial affairs in India. Referring to that memorandum, I shall add some remarks tending to confirm the truth of the general principles on which the reasonings therein are founded.

Notwithstanding the large import of bullion during the present season, the expenses of the war, and the considerable amount of the 12 per cent securities coming in course of payment within the current and succeeding year of accounts, have compelled me to continue the system of adding to the debt in India, in order to secure a considerable commercial investment for the ensuing season. I have, however, the satisfaction to assure you, that every symptom has concurred to confirm my opinion, that the debt in India is likely to become more manageable in every succeeding year. The loans which I have opened at this presidency during the current year have been made at a rate of interest much more favourable than that of any loan which has been raised since the year 1796, as will appear by the terms of the loans of this year, which I annex to this letter. Although the second loan on the same terms is open, the state of the public securities is now—

5 March 1800

	Buying	Selling	
6%	13–0	14–0	
8%	5–8	6–8	
10%	10–8	9–8	}Premium
12%	1–8	2–0	

Having been at the corresponding period in the preceding year—5 March 1799.

	Buying	Selling	
6%	24–8	25–8	
8%	14–8	15–8	
10%	—	—	
12%	0–2	0–6	Discount

The distress for specie has gradually vanished and private credit has proportionately been improved; and I have been able to send home with valuable cargoes every regular ship belonging to the Company in India, while, on the other hand, I have employed the whole tonnage, which the port of Calcutta could furnish since the month of Dec[embe]r, to carry to the port of London nearly the whole of the goods of individuals, which had been tendered for exportation previous to that month, over and above the 3,000 tons, which the Company is bound by law to furnish.

The regulations under which the private trade has been shipped are fully explained in the proceedings of this government now before the court of directors, and in the commercial letter dated the 1st instant. Any further explanations which you may require on that subject can be furnished by Mr Bebb, who returns to England on board the *Earl Howe*. I have extended these regulations to Madras, from whence I expect several ships laden with private goods to proceed to London during the present season.

In my dispatches to the court of directors and to the secret committee, I have fully discussed the expediency and facility of furnishing an effectual supply to the treasury in China through the medium of Indian produce. The experience of every hour convinces me that my opinions on that subject have not been erroneous, and I do not feel it necessary to add any further observations upon it, entertaining a confident expectation that you will carry into complete effect my repeated suggestions for discontinuing the annual export of bullion to China, and for increasing that to India in the same proportion. This measure will operate as a considerable aid to the finances of India, and will be sensibly felt through every branch of the public and private credit.

The finances of the government of Madras have improved in a still greater proportion than those of Bengal. At that presidency, they have opened a loan (of which I enclose the terms) under which they have been enabled to raise a large supply. The great augmentation of the resources of Fort St George under the subsidiary treaties of Hyderabad and Seringapatam, together with the improvements in the revenues of Tanjore and the country of the Polygars, will render the finances of that presidency an object of the highest consideration. It may also be expected, that industry, population, and manufacture, and all the sources of public and private credit, will take a new spring in our possessions on the peninsula of India, in consequence of our increased security in that quarter. To these pregnant causes of progressive prosperity, it is reasonable to add the benefits which cannot fail to accrue from the extension to that part of our empire of the system of judicature and revenue under which these provinces have attained so eminent a degree of opulence and internal tranquillity.

I trust that the 8 per cent loan now open in Bengal will be rapidly filled, and will enable me to provide for all the services stated in my several estimates, and I expect hereafter to be able to borrow money at 8 per cent under the former system of repayment of the public securities according to priority of date.

Notwithstanding these favourable expectations, I continue to concur with Mr Myers' opinion, that the surplus revenue of India is not likely to afford any considerable or certain resource. The increasing magnitude of our empire in India, and the continual expansion of every branch of our numerous and complicated interests, must preclude any considerable reduction of our permanent charges, civil, military, or commercial. More cannot be hoped from the utmost exertion of vigilance, integrity, and ability, in any persons to whom the government of this empire may hereafter be entrusted, than to check, by a seasonable and diligent system of revision, that tendency to excess and abuse, which is the inherent vice of all great establishments. On the other hand, it is my decided opinion, that the growing resources of India will keep pace with the demands upon them. In the course of this month and April, I propose to enter into an accurate review of the whole of our resources, and I shall furnish you with the result at the earliest possible period.

With respect to the resource which you expect to derive in India from bills drawn upon the East India Company under the plan of remittance, the best consideration which I have been able to give to that subject has served to strengthen the opinion expressed in Mr Myers' memorandum. The prosperous state of public credit in England and in India will co-operate to render that resource of little avail. The state of the public funds in England will diminish the desire of remitting private fortunes to England from India in proportion to the increase of the public prosperity at home; and the high degree of security which our Indian empire has acquired, by the success of the late war against Tipu Sultan, has inspired so general a confidence in the stability of the British power in India, that individuals will think their capital equally safe in India, where it will certainly be more productive than in England.

These circumstances, added to the vast increase of the export of goods from India to England, will probably detain much capital in this country, and retard the operation of any plan of remittance which could be devised. Private merchants, for commercial purposes, will always offer more advantageous terms than the Company; and in time of public prosperity, the bills of individuals of undoubted capital will be received by many in preference to bills drawn on the Company, on terms less favourable. The same causes will naturally tend to maintain, if not to increase, the present high rate of exchange upon bills on England, and while the natural current rate of exchange shall be so much higher (as it is at present) than that allowed by the plan of remittance through the Company, it is not to be expected that individuals will resort to that plan to such an extent as shall furnish any important financial resource.

That the export of British manufactures to India, under proper regulations, might be extended to the amount of a considerable resource, I entertain no doubt; but I must observe, that, before such an effect can be expected, an entire reform must take place in the conduct of the East India Company's exports to India. On this subject, I transmitted a paper to you in my *private* letter *no. 21*; and I must recommend it to your most particular attention. The leading points which require minute and diligent care in the management of this branch of the Company's affairs appear to me to be, first, that the goods should be of the first quality; secondly, that they should be invoiced at a reasonable and just price; and thirdly, that they should be assorted in a manner suitable to this market, conformably to the indents sent from hence.

Under the present system, the quality of the goods is frequently defective. For the last two years, the invoice price has been considerably increased, without any correspondent improvement in the quality of the goods, and the assortments have been injudicious, and contrary to the indents sent from hence, by those officers, who are best acquainted with the nature of the market.

As connected with this subject, in one point of view, I desire to call your particular attention to the defective and unserviceable state of the arms annually exported to India for the use of our troops. This is a disgraceful evil, and of a most pernicious tendency. I am apprehensive that the whole system of the Company's exports to India is rendered subservient to private interests at the expense of the public.

I entirely concur with you in the whole of your reasoning respecting the private trade of India. In my commercial letter in council of the 1st instant, I have detailed the grounds of my proceedings on this subject; which, you will remark, have been directly opposite to your sentiments and to my own; but, at the time of writing your letter *no. 7*, you do not appear to have adverted to the orders of the court of directors of May the 25th 1798, which absolutely preclude the renewal of the arrangement of the 5th of

October 1798, as well as the adoption of any plan founded on similar principles. If you had relieved me from the restraints imposed by the letter of the 25th of May 1798, I should have immediately opened the port of Calcutta on the most liberal principles; but, in a point purely commercial, I conceived myself to be absolutely bound by the order of the court of directors. However, I lament the necessity under which I found myself placed, to act in contradiction to your opinion and to mine, I flatter myself that the discussion contained in my commercial letter will produce the beneficial effect of establishing those opinions beyond the possibility of future controversy; and that the important question at issue will immediately be settled for ever by the authority of the government at home.

Mr Pitt's bill for the reduction of the duties upon imports to and from India has grievously disappointed the expectation of the commercial part of the community. The duty imposed by that bill upon the sugars, particularly on the coarser sort, is much too high; and the object of inviting the trade of India to the port of London, will, I fear, not be effected by the general scale of duties adopted in that bill. On this subject, I shall write to you more in detail hereafter.

I have annexed to this dispatch a letter from Mr Udny (whom I have lately introduced to the board of trade), which will serve to throw considerable light on the question relative to private tonnage, which I was compelled to decide during the present season.

I think it necessary in this place to observe, that I have every reason to believe, that none of the servants of the East India Company have any concern in foreign or illicit trade from India to Europe.

No. 8: 19 March 1799

The animosities and divisions among the court of directors, having occasioned public discussions at the East India House of a most indecorous nature, produced a mischievous effect in India. Such scenes tend to degrade the character of the government, as well as to weaken its energy. I return you many thanks for the papers which you transmitted to me on this painful subject.

No impartial man can entertain any other opinion, than that the attack upon Mr Scott was a most unwarrantable proceeding. I have always esteemed Mr Bosanquet's honourable and pure intentions; but his correspondence with me affords abundant proof, that his judgement is incorrect, his temper precipitate, and his knowledge of Indian affairs neither accurate nor extensive. Notwithstanding these defects, the same correspondence manifests an honest zeal for the public service. I need not mention my opinion of Mr Scott. You know my sincere esteem and regard for his character. The general opinion here, as far as I could collect it, was essentially in his favour. In my situation, it is a duty to abstain from all political discussions, and to discourage them at my table or in my presence. This duty became more urgent in proportion as the question at issue related more immediately to the character of that body, which is the direct channel of the government of this part of the British Empire.

No. 9: 21 March 1799

I have not yet been able to discover the author of the curious paper transmitted by Mr Liston to Lord Grenville; but I take this opportunity of calling your attention to the state of this government with relation to the powers of banishing Europeans from the British possessions in India. I have no hesitation in declaring, that those powers appear to me still to be too limited.

The number of persons (not in the Company's service) resident in these provinces, as well as in all parts of the British empire in India, increases daily. Among these are to be found many characters, desperate from distress, or from the infamy of their conduct in Europe. Their occupations are principally, either the pursuits of commerce or of intrigue in the distant parts of these provinces and of Oudh, or, at Calcutta, the lowest branches of the law, the establishment of shops or taverns, or of other places of public entertainment, or the superintendence of newspapers and monthly registers. At Calcutta, no less than seven different weekly newspapers are published. Amongst all these persons, but particularly the tribe of editors of newspapers, the strongest and boldest spirit of Jacobinism prevailed previous to my arrival in Bengal. Since that period, this spirit has not been active; a circumstance which I cannot attribute to any sincere reform in the minds of the disaffected, and which, I flatter myself, is still less to be ascribed to my popularity among any class or description of Jacobins. I have sent home one or two libellers; not for libels upon myself, but for having attacked, with indecent disrespect, some of the public officers employed under the government. One example was made in the person of a most audacious and turbulent demagogue, named McLean.

I have also placed all the newspapers under the inspection of the secretary to government; and I never permit a line to be published which has not been previously sanctioned by him. I have established the same regulation at Madras, and mean to extend it to Bombay. Previous to my arrival, the newspapers had been made the vehicle of every doctrine and statement which could tend to subvert our establishments in this country. An insidious attempt of this nature (made at Calcutta during my absence on the Coast) was the immediate cause of my subjecting all publications to the previous inspection of the secretary of government.

At Madras, the evil resulting from Europeans not in the Company's service is still greater. The advisers of the nabob of the Carnatic, as well as the principal instruments of his opposition to the British government, and of his oppressions over his own subjects, are almost exclusively to be found among that class of Europeans.

The covenants granted to persons not in the service of the East India Company operate as a protection against the general power of banishing from India. These covenants require so long a notice to be given to the offending party, as would, in many instances, entirely defeat the object of the banishment.

Persons who have been long established here are also supposed to acquire certain rights of continuance from the mere circumstance of their establishment; and the barristers and attorneys, with the whole tribe of lawyers, are supposed to possess the same rights under the protection of the supreme court of judicature at Calcutta; and at Madras and Bombay under that of the recorder's court. In the case of Mr McLean (whom I had confined in Fort William, in consequence of his not being able to give security for his embarkation to Europe), a fictitious suit of debt was instituted in the supreme court, and Sir Robert Chambers issued a writ *re exeat regno*, which was served upon the town major. I executed this writ, by embarking Mr McLean on the evening on which it was served, and by conveying that gentleman on board the *Busbridge* Indiaman. I had the satisfaction to learn his safe arrival at the Cape of Good Hope, through the channel of a libel which he published against me at that place. I shall be happy if a similar intimation should acquaint me of his arrival in England; and in this expectation, I take the liberty of recommending him to your attention. It may not, however, at all times be expedient or practicable to remove obnoxious persons with as much expedition as Mr McLean; and I therefore request, that you will, without delay, extend the power of remitting persons to England so largely, as to exempt the government in India from any other restriction, than its responsibility to the government at home.

In the observations stated in the foregoing paragraphs, I do not include the respectable merchants and shipowners established at Calcutta, as constituting a part of the grievance of which I complain; but I confess that I see no means of exempting them from the general authority of government to banish all Europeans, which would not involve innumerable difficulties.

No. 10: 21 March 1799—Internal Administration of Bengal
The increasing arrears of the land revenue of Bengal occupied my attention immediately after my arrival in India; and you will find my opinion upon that subject stated in some detail in my minute of the 12th of June 1798. After full consideration, I passed a law for the purpose of remedying the increasing evil of accumulating balances. You will find this law in the

printed regulations, under the title of regulation no. 7, 1799. The beneficial effects of it have already been felt to so great an extent, as to warrant a confident expectation that the stipulated jumma will hereafter be paid with great regularity. I enclose an account calculated to bring under your view the operation of the law in question. I have been principally indebted to Mr Harington, whom I have lately placed at the board of revenue, for the suggestions on which this arrangement has been founded.

My judgement and experience coincide entirely with your opinion, that the system adopted by Lord Cornwallis has proved, and must continue to prove, a fruitful source of happiness, wealth, industry, and population, to this flourishing country. That system, however, has still to encounter some avowed, and many secret, enemies; nor have its benefits been yet fully realized. It has not yet been carried into execution with a cordiality, zeal, and energy, proportioned to its merits. It has received no aid from collateral institutions, calculated to furnish a supply of men properly qualified to fill the several stations of judicature and revenue; nor has a due and impartial selection been uniformly made of the persons best qualified, in the actual state of the service, to fill such stations as have progressively become vacant; nor has the administration of justice throughout the provinces been superintended with a sufficient degree of vigilance and care.

I have nearly matured a plan with a view to these salutary objects. The principal measure, on which it will be founded, will be, first, the institution of a court of sudder dewany and nizamut adaulat, distinct from the council, but of which the chief justice shall be capable of sitting in council, if appointed from home to a seat in council. The province of this new court shall be, not only to receive and judge appeals, but also to superintend the administration of justice and the general state of the police in all the courts, branches, and departments, of the judicial institutions.

It is my intention to constitute this court of those persons who bore a principal share in framing the system so happily adopted by Lord Cornwallis. Their talents, integrity, and experience, as well as the peculiar propriety and dignity of their manners, render them the fittest to hold this distinguished station; to which it is my intention to annex the highest rank which the law enables me to grant.

The chief justice of this new court may hereafter become a member of the council, in which event he will still continue to preside in the court. In the meanwhile, I wish to be empowered by law to give a rank to the chief justice of the sudder dewany and nizamut adaulat, which shall place him, as nearly as possible, on a level with the chief justice of the supreme court of judicature.

Secondly, the institution of a college or university at Calcutta, in which the writers shall be subject to the rules of collegiate discipline for the first two or three years subsequent to their arrival; and shall study the languages, history, laws, manners, and customs, of India, the laws enacted by the governor-general in council, and such rudiments of the laws of England, as are necessary to enable the judges, throughout these possessions, to administer the laws of India in the spirit of the British constitution.

Thirdly, I propose to pass regulations subjecting all persons appointed to offices of judicature or revenue to a public examination in the several branches of knowledge requisite in their respective stations, before they shall be entitled to receive the emoluments of the office to which they may have been appointed.

Fourthly, in the several stations of revenue and judicature throughout these provinces, many public officers are to be found avowedly incompetent to the due discharge of their duties; some from ignorance, natural incapacity, or fixed habits or indolence and dissipation; others from age and infirmity. Such persons have been suffered to retain their stations under the orders of the court of directors, prohibiting the grant of pensions of retreat to the civil service. This prohibition is contrary to true principles of economy. The inevitable operation of it has been to fix incapable persons in stations requiring efficiency; and the loss sustained by their negligences or errors infinitely overbalances the expense of providing for them at the public charge. The application of this prohibition to persons who have grown old or infirm in the public service is illiberal and cruel, as well as impolitic. On the other hand, it may perhaps be questioned, whether those whose ignorance, natural inability, or other defects, disqualify them for the public service, can be entitled to any compensation from the state which has already supported them at a considerable expense, under the presumption of their sufficiency to discharge the duties for which they receive emolument?

But viewing the actual state of the civil service at this presidency, I know, that many persons do not, and never will, render justice to the public in the stations which they now hold; although it would appear an act of great harshness and rigour to remove these persons, without making some provision for them. Their number is not very considerable: it bears no proportion to the mischief occasioned by their evil administration, and by the dangerous example which their conduct affords to the younger branches of the service. My intention, therefore, is (without waiting for orders from home) to remove from efficient office all persons of any of the descriptions to which I have adverted; and to provide for them by adequate pensions for life, payable to their agents in India, on condition of their returning to England. The present allowance of the Company's servants out of employment, being payable only to such as reside in India, would not answer the purpose proposed. Among the servants now out of employment, but residing in Bengal, few, if any, are qualified for efficient office. The amount of the pensions to be paid, under the new plan, must bear a just proportion to the period of service, as well as to the offices actually enjoyed at the period of removal. It will be for the government at home to consider whether any permanent plan of pension for civil servants retiring from the service in India shall hereafter be adopted. The measure, which I propose to carry into effect, is more immediately applicable to the actual state of the civil service in India; but the principles on which it is grounded may furnish the foundation of a permanent system, which shall for ever secure this government against the evils of inefficiency, ignorance, and negligence, in the subordinate branches of the executive administration.

The accounts which you will have received this year of the revenue on salt will be highly satisfactory to you; and you will have observed, with peculiar pleasure, that the revenue arising from the sale of opium has been completely restored by the improved system of agency, by the extreme care applied to the manufacture of the drug, by the due proportion now preserved between the quantity manufactured and the current demand, and by the measure, which I have uniformly carried into effect, of publicly destroying all such opium as has been declared to be adulterated. The produce of the two last sales of opium (which include the whole annual quantity for the last season) has exceeded that of the most favourable sales of that drug ever experienced in Bengal; the net profit to the Company upon the two sales in December 1799 and February 1800 having amounted to more than 23 lakhs of rupees. I have little doubt, that this branch of revenue will continue to flourish under the same judicious system vigilantly administered. The public is greatly indebted to Mr Fleming, second member of the medical board, for his careful inspection of the opium, as well as for his various able suggestions, by which the manufacture has been placed under improved regulations.

You will observe with great satisfaction the considerable increase which has taken place in the government customs at Calcutta since my arrival in India. This is to be attributed entirely to increased care and vigilance in the business of the custom house. I found myself under the necessity of removing Mr Foley, the late collector, not for any irregularity or defect of integrity, but for negligence and absolute incapacity to discharge the duty of his office. The customs were placed for some time under the management of Mr Haldane, a member of the board of trade, who was principally aided by a young gentleman of the name of Twining[1] in restoring order to the business of the custom house. Mr Twining has distinguished himself

[1] Thomas Twining; deputy collector of customs, Calcutta, 1798–1801; collector of Shahabad, 1801–3.

very much in this transaction: he is at present too young in the service to be placed in the enjoyment of a salary adequate to his merits; but I shall take the first opportunity of promoting him. In the meanwhile, I have appointed Mr Dashwood[1] to the collection of the customs. I can rely on his diligence and integrity and Mr Twining will act under him.

It is necessary to observe, that the right of the governor-general in council is questioned by the lawyers here, in the present indefinite state of our powers of legislation.

An improvement of the tax upon spiritous liquors and intoxicating drugs is now under my consideration; and I have little doubt, that this branch of the revenue may be much increased. But here again I feel myself embarrassed by the anomalous constitution of this government. Under the construction given to the laws for the government of the British possessions, it is a received doctrine, that the governor-general in council cannot legislate for the town of Calcutta. Therefore, the capital city of this empire must be exempt from the operation of any law imposing additional duties on the articles above-mentioned; unless I can contrive to pass such a law under the pretext of an improvement of the duties appropriated to the support of the police. I am disposed to hope, that sources of just and moderate taxation may be discovered on other articles of general consumption; but this measure must be adopted gradually and with great caution. I must here also observe, that, although Calcutta must necessarily be the place of the greatest consumption, as well as that where any new tax would be less sensibly felt, than in the country, the supposed restrictions on the law, and the strange conflict of authorities, between the supreme court of judicature and the government, preclude the possibility of my applying any system of taxation on articles of general consumption to the town of Calcutta. I trust you will, without delay, relieve this government from a predicament so embarrassing. The police at Calcutta is now in a deplorable condition; and if speedy measures be not adopted, the town will soon relapse into its ancient state of filth, and unhealthiness, and will again become fatal to European constitutions. It is my intention immediately to proceed to improve the drains and roads, to widen the streets and avenues, to clear the jungles, and remove the tanks, and other nuisances situated in the neighbourhood of the town. These improvements will necessarily occasion expense, but it is an expense which the Company must incur, or forfeit every title to the character of a wise and munificent sovereign. In aid of this expense, it would be just to levy an assessment on the inhabitants of Calcutta; but I have already stated that measure to be impracticable in the limited state of my powers. Various other regulations of police are

[1] Thomas Dashwood; superintendent of stamps, 1797–1800; custom master, Calcutta, 1800–1.

requisite for the preservation of the peace and order of the town. Even these I shall find it difficult to enforce, until my right to legislate for Calcutta shall be rendered indispensable by act of Parliament.

Oudh

Of the two general heads under which you have stated the objects of your anxiety with regard to the situation of Oudh, I trust that the second is now nearly accomplished; namely, the substitution of an efficient military force, under the Company's authority, in place of the nawab vizier's dangerous and indisciplined army. This reform has not been effected without great reluctance on the part of the vizier, whose character has been displayed on this occasion in the genuine colours of Asiatic treachery and falsehood. I have nothing to hope from any quality in his Excellency's mind, excepting his acknowledged pusillanimity; which I flatter myself will induce him to submit to the introduction of such a portion of the British authority into the management of his country, as is indispensably necessary to the just and pure administration of the government, to the accurate collection and economical expenditure of his revenue, and to the relief of his people from the extortion, cruelty, and oppression, under which they now suffer. I shall, hereafter, submit to you a detailed view of my proceedings in Oudh; at present, it may be sufficient to say, that I consider the reform of the vizier's military establishment to be far advanced; and that, in consequence of the success of that preliminary step, I entertain a sanguine hope of being able to carry the same spirit of reform, with vigour and effect, into every other branch of his affairs.

Government of Fort St George

I am happy to be able to express my entire concurrence in your opinion with regard to the progressive improvement of the administration of affairs at Fort St George; and I have no doubt, that the same system will continue to be pursued by Lord Clive, and by the persons who now constitute his advisers at that presidency. My long residence at Fort St George, and the cordiality, temper, and honour, of Lord Clive have completely identified the two governments; and I find no more difficulty in governing our extensive possessions on the Coast, with all our recent acquisitions of territory and influence, than in regulating any of the collectorships in Bengal. You will observe by the public proceedings, that I have lately transmitted to Fort St George detailed orders for introducing into the possessions under the immediate government of that presidency the same system of internal administration, under which these provinces have so happily flourished. I entertain no doubt, that, under the present government at Fort St George, any orders will be carried into effect with the utmost degree of honesty, alacrity, and zeal. The execution, however, of those orders must necessarily be imperfect, unless accompanied by the application, to the civil service at Fort St George, not only of all those subsidiary improvements still requisite in Bengal, but of other remedies more peculiarly demanded by the state of the service at Fort St George. My present inclination is to render the court of sudder dewany and nizamut adaulat in Bengal the supreme court of appeal from all the Company's possessions; and to vest in it the general superintendence of the administration of justice, and the regulation of police, throughout the British empire in India. This arrangement appears to be well calculated to secure uniformity, consistency, and purity, in the conduct of all the subordinate courts of justice, and in every institution of police. I do not apprehend that it will be necessary or expedient to establish any intermediate court of appeal at Fort St George, between the sudder dewany adaulat in Bengal and the ordinary courts of circuit and appeal to be instituted on the coast of Coromandel. I am also inclined to think that the writers destined for Fort St George may advantageously pass the two first years of their residence in India at the university of Calcutta; where proper professors may be established for their instruction in the languages peculiar to the territories subject to the immediate government of Fort St George.

The adoption of a plan for pensioning public officers incapable of service is required at least as much at Fort St George as in Bengal. But the peculiar evil now inherent in the constitution of the service at Fort St George is not only unknown in Bengal, but directly contrary to the principle on which Lord Cornwallis rested all his plans for amending and purifying the administration of affairs in these provinces. He prohibited all indirect and secret emoluments, and all mixture in pursuits of commerce, or of other affairs incompatible with a due attention to the public service; and he established the allowances of the public officers on so liberal a scale, as might enable them not merely to subsist during the period of their public labours, but to realize, with due economy, a competent provision after a moderate period of service.

This system is not founded on any principle exclusively applicable to the characters, habits, or interests, of the public servant in Bengal: it is founded on a just and correct knowledge of mankind. For no proposition can be more self-evident, or of more universal application, than, that the best security against the temptation of illicit profit is to annex liberal emolument to honest labour. It is, therefore, difficult to conceive on what ground an expectation can be formed, that the public service at Fort St George should be as pure and correct as that in Bengal, while the civil servants of Fort St George shall be permitted to mix in pursuits foreign to their public duties, and while the general scale of allowances at Fort St George shall remain as low, as to preclude those prospects of honest profit deemed necessary in Bengal for securing the integrity of the public servants. I am aware that this remark does not apply with so much force to the commercial, as to other branches of the Company's service at Fort St George. Some of the commercial allowances have been increased at that presidency on the very principle of rendering them so ample, as to preclude the temptation of irregular profit; and yet the irresistible application of the same principle to other branches of the service at the same presidency has never been admitted in practice, however it may have been acknowledged in argument. For it can never be supposed that the Company can deliberately deem it to be a more incumbent duty of government to secure the honest discharge of its commercial concerns, than to preserve its revenues from peculation, and the administration of its laws from corruption and oppression. It is possible that the limited and precarious condition of the revenues of Fort St George, and its state of insecurity, during the existence of the contiguous hostile power in Mysore, may have retarded the due consideration of this subject. But in the present increased, and, I trust, progressive state of the prosperity and security of that valuable possession, no such obstacle exists to a reform, urgently demanded by every principle of humanity, policy, and justice.

I am convinced, that the continuance of the present inadequate allowances of the public servants at Fort St George would prove an insuperable bar to the improvement of the revenues, and to the due administration of justice, in that part of our empire. At present, the public servants at Fort St George, in most of the offices, can find no alternative between poverty and corruption. Is it the part of wisdom or honour in any government to reduce its servants to such an alternative? During my residence at Fort St George, a most respectable member of the board of revenue, Mr Harington (to whose labours I have been much indebted for the groundwork of my late orders to that presidency on the subject of their revenue and judicature) resigned his seat at the board, because his salary did not afford him the hope of providing a competent maintenance for his family at the expiration of his service; and he entered into a commercial house of agency, withdrawing from the Company's service talents, integrity, and zeal, which had already proved highly useful, and might, in the present crisis, have been exerted with increased benefit to their affairs. I know that Mr Cockburn (whose abilities, knowledge, and integrity, are not surpassed by any person in India) entertains similar intentions of retiring from the Company's service; and it must be evident to your comprehensive view and long experience of public affairs, that this evil will be aggravated in proportion to the increased magnitude and importance of the interests entrusted to the management of the public servants at Fort St George; and that, ultimately, a service so defective must be deserted by all who are not disposed to take advantages of its abuses.

The consideration of all these circumstances has induced me to call Lord Clive's particular attention to the scale of allowances at Fort St George; and it is my intention to accompany the institution of the new courts of judicature at that presidency by a general review of the salaries of their civil service; the result of which will, I trust, enable me to place all their allowances on a proper level.

The delay attendant upon the expectation of orders from home, and the urgent pressure of the evil, will, I trust, sufficiently justify my determination to apply, with all practicable dispatch, such a remedy as shall appear to my judgement to promise the most speedy, beneficial, and permanent, effect.

I entertain little doubt that the revenues under the management of the government of Fort St George will be considerably improved in all their branches; and that the additional expense of providing for the important objects stated in the preceding paragraphs will be far overbalanced by the consequent amelioration of all our resources in that quarter.

The double government of the Carnatic is a difficulty which continues to present the most serious and alarming obstacles to every attempt at reform. The expectation of favourable opportunities of negotiation with the nabob of Arcot, and of the effects of conciliation towards him, will, I am convinced, be ever disappointed by the event. You recollect with what sanguine hopes I looked forward to the result of measures adopted in a spirit of mildness and persuasion; but I have found them entirely vain and fruitless. Nor can I cherish the slightest ray of hope that such a course can ever prove successful during the life of the present nabob. His Highness is surrounded by European advisers of the most dangerous and profligate character, whose interests are deeply involved in the perpetuation of the abuses of his government; and who (amongst other means of perverting his councils) labour to inspire him with the notion of a distinction of interests and powers between the Royal government and that constituted by act of Parliament for the administration of the British empire in India. In all his conversations and correspondence, he studiously distinguishes his Majesty's government from that of the court of directors; uniformly treating the latter with disrespect, and even with ridicule and contempt. In my last conversation with his Highness, he plainly declared to me that he considered his Majesty to be his father, friend, ally, and protector; but that the court of directors desired to *obtain his country anyhow.*

The principles of this distinction are encouraged in his Highness' mind by the letters and embassies which have occasionally reached him from his Majesty, through channels not only unconnected, but avowedly at variance with the British government in India. All such letters and embassies have the most pernicious tendency to withdraw the confidence and respect of the natives from the governments in India and to fix their attention on his Majesty's naval and military officers; or on such persons (of whatever character) as may accidentally be the bearers of his letters. The frequent letters which his Highness the nabob receives from his Royal Highness the prince of Wales greatly aggravate the same evil; and it is with the utmost concern, that I feel myself bound by my public duty to request that you will take an opportunity of representing to his Royal Highness, that his correspondence with the nabob of the Carnatic has produced an effect entirely contrary to his Royal Highness' wishes and interests; and has been highly injurious to the public service in India.

Few, if any, of the Company's servants at Madras are now directly engaged in the intrigues of his Highness' durbar. The principal and most mischievous agents and counsellors of his Highness are to be found among persons who have been the bearers of letters to his Highness from England, and among the attorneys and low practitioners of the law, who notoriously conduct his Highness' correspondence with the government. Nor can I entertain any expectation that the newly established judicature at Madras, under its present constitution, will in any degree assist the government in repressing the intrigues and corruptions of the durbar. My experience, during my residence at Fort St George, leads me to believe, that the powers of the court of the recorder will prove entirely inadequate to the detection and punishment of the usurious and corrupt practices which the court was intended to repress; while the establishment of such a court will tend to confirm the audacity of the tribe of pettyfoggers, which now infests the Carnatic, and governs the nabob's durbar. I confess that I cannot concur with you in ascribing the purity of the service in Bengal to the influence of the supreme court of judicature at Calcutta. The most corrupt period in the history of Bengal, or perhaps in that of any of our foreign establishments, is to be dated from the institution of the supreme court to the arrival of Lord Cornwallis; a period of time, during a considerable portion of which, that court exercised its powers to their utmost possible extent. The purity of Lord Cornwallis' personal example, and the integrity and wisdom of his institutions, the increase of the regular and avowed public allowances, the separation of the legislative, judicial, and executive, powers of the government, and the consequent subjection of the government itself to the control of its own laws, were the real foundations of the reform at this presidency. This constitution was the source, and its operation has been the security, of that reform. Neither the design, nor the execution, of the amended system of administration in Bengal, was in any degree aided by the co-operation, influence, or example, of the supreme court. During the administrations of Lord Cornwallis and Lord Teignmouth, the supreme court teemed with abuses of every description; and would have afforded a much fitter subject, than an instrument of reform. Respectable and honourable as the person is who now presides in that court, and eminent as his public services have been, in the detection and remedy of the abuses abetted by his predecessors, I cannot discover in what manner the influence or authority of the supreme court now operate to preserve the purity of the service of government.

The public servants look exclusively to the person in whose hands the government resides, and to the practical result of that constitution which he is bound to administer. Under that constitution, he possesses ample power of reward and punishment; and the due exercise of those powers constitutes the vital principle of the public service, and the sole spring, from which the purity or corruption of the subordinate officers must ever flow. The responsibility of the governor-general in council to the government at home, and the conspicuous station in which he is placed, sufficiently secure that due exercise of his arduous functions

The supreme court possesses no power of rewarding the public servants; and with respect to their punishment, it can never proceed rigorously and efficaciously without the co-operation of government. Even with that co-operation, the powers of the supreme court must always be limited by the difficulties of obtaining legal proof of malversation; and even where such proof can be obtained, the species of punishment which the supreme court can inflict, can neither be so speedy nor so formidable to the public servants, as the powers of suspension, and subsequent prosecution at home, vested in the government. Wherever punishment in the form of public prosecution may become requisite, I am convinced that it would be much more effectually inflicted, if the prosecution were always to be instituted in England. With regard to petty cases, every useful purpose would be answered by a tribunal independent of the government, but placed towards it in the relation of a mere interpreter of the laws of England, modified by such as may be enacted by the governor-general in council. The supposed control of the supreme court over the person of the governor-general never can be exercised without occasioning a convulsion in the government. It is, therefore, either useless, or dangerous, and every trace of it ought to be abolished. The extreme cases in which the crimes of the governor-general may require the control of a superior authority, cannot be provided against in India, without the application of a remedy infinitely more perilous than the supposed evil, the existence of which is scarcely within the verge of possibility. The remedy of such cases should be left on the same ground as it stands on in Ireland with relation to the possible personal crimes of the chief governor, exercising the sovereign executive power. No power in

India should appear to be co-ordinate with the government, and still less to rival or control it.

I shall hereafter address you more in detail on the present constitution of the supreme court of judicature; particularly on such points of it, as have proved practical impediments to the exercise of the control of this government over its own native officers, civil and military, and native subjects. But it would have been uncandid in me to have passed without notice a passage in your correspondence, relating to so important a subject, in which I have the misfortune not to concur in your opinion.

I cannot conclude this subject without adding my cordial testimony in favour of the moderation, discretion, and propriety, with which the present court, under the direction of Sir John Anstruther, has uniformly exercised its powers, not only without a symptom of jealousy, but with every possible attention to the dignity, vigour, and efficiency of the government: but a power radically dangerous ought not to find protection in the temporary forbearance of those hands in which it is vested; and I am satisfied that some of Sir John Anstruther's brethren entertain notions very different from him, and, that, if they were not controlled by his authority, they would break forth into the most troublesome excess.

The duty of communicating to you, without reserve, my sentiments on the subject of the utility of the supreme court of judicature, has led me to digress from the actual state of the Carnatic.

I am thoroughly convinced that no effectual remedy can ever be applied to the evils which afflict that country, without obtaining from the nabob powers at least as extensive, as those vested in the Company by the late treaty of Tanjore. At the death of the present nabob, such a treaty might easily be obtained from his successor; if, after that event, it should be thought advisable to admit any nominal sovereign of the Carnatic, excepting the Company. A young man resides at Chepank, who is treated by the nabob as his Highness' son. This young man is certainly the son of a dancing woman, who has resided for some time in his Highness' house; and the nabob declares himself to be the father. Numerous legitimate descendants of Wallajah are in existence. The whole question of the succession will therefore be completely open to the decision of the Company, upon the decease of the present nabob. The inclination of my opinion is, that the most advisable settlement would be to place Umdut ul Umrah's supposed son on the musnud, under a treaty similar to that which was lately concluded with the rajah of Tanjore. It will, however, be expedient, that you should immediately consider, whether it might not be a more effectual arrangement to provide liberally for every branch of the descendants of Wallajah and Umdut ul Umrah, and to vest even the nominal sovereignty of the Carnatic in the Company.

247

On this subject, I request your immediate instructions; which you will frame with reference to the following most important and interesting considerations.

During the whole course of the late war with Tipu Sultan, the conduct of all the nabob's officers, without exception, amounted nearly to positive hostility, in every part of his territories through which the British army, or that of the nizam, marched; or even in which supplies were ordered to be procured or collected for their use.[1]

When complaints were stated to his Highness, he promised redress; but never afforded it in any instance. I was compelled to seize the persons of some of his principal officers, and to bring them down to Fort St George from districts in which our force was not sufficiently considerable to furnish an effectual check to their treasonable practices. In all districts so circumstanced, his Highness' officers did not scruple to proceed to open violence for the purpose of obstructing our supplies.

During this arduous crisis, his Highness frequently endeavoured to anticipate my complaints by alleging pretended grievances to justify the conduct of his officers; but, upon examination, his Highness' complaints uniformly appeared to be utterly devoid of foundation.

At the most critical period of our military preparations, when every European and native at Madras emulated each other in aiding the public service by loan and contribution, his Highness could not be induced to advance (even on account of his acknowledged debts) any assistance to the public treasury. He, indeed, with much reluctance, under the apprehension of a cessation of all friendly intercourse between him and me, engaged to advance a sum on account of his new cavalry debt: but, after the most solemn protestations of punctuality, he broke his faith, with every circumstance of infamy and dishonour; at a moment, when this violation of his engagements might have proved fatal to the progress of the army, if I had suffered myself to be so far the dupe of his repeated assurances, as to have relied in any degree on their performance for the pecuniary supply of the troops in the field. During the whole of this period, I have every reason to be confident, that his Highness possessed the ready means of satisfying a much more considerable demand than I had deemed it expedient to make upon him. It was perfectly evident, during the progress of our success, that his Highness derived no satisfaction from the triumph of our arms; and it is remarkable, that he never appeared in public at the celebration of any of the rejoicings occasioned by the glorious termination of the war.

Whatever suspicions of his Highness' personal disaffection to the British government might have been warranted by all these combined

[1] The British had the right, if they wished, to take over the administration of the Carnatic in time of war.

circumstances, I was rather disposed to attribute them to the weakness of his government, or to the corruption and intrigues of his advisers, than to any spirit of positive treachery in his own disposition: but the records of the late Tipu Sultan, which fell into our hands after the capture of Seringapatam, have furnished me with the most authentic and indisputable evidence, that a secret correspondence, of a nature the most hostile to the British power, was opened with Tipu Sultan by the late Nabob Wallajah, towards the close of his life, through the agency of Umdut ul Umrah the present nabob.

Umdut ul Umrah appears to have been extremely zealous and forward in the conduct of this secret intercourse during the life of his father; and no question can be entertained, that the late nabob, as a principal, and Umdut ul Umrah, as an agent, were guilty of a flagrant violation of the 10th article of the treaty of 1792, as well as of the fundamental principle of their connection with the Company. Umdut ul Umrah was a party to the treaty, and on that circumstance founds all his present rights. Sufficient proof appears that Umdut ul Umrah, after his accession, manifested a disposition to maintain the correspondence, which had been commenced by his father through him; and I entertain no doubt, that his objects in that correspondence were of the same hostile and treacherous character, as they had been previous to the death of his father. The proof arising from written documents of his overt acts of hostility since his accession is not so full and distinct, as that which relates to his former agency. But this defect may be supplied by oral testimony, as all the necessary witnesses are alive and in our hands. I annex to this letter a summary review of the whole evidence, drawn up with his usual ability by Mr Edmonstone, the Persian translator, under my directions, together with some of the documents found at Seringapatam. I propose, hereafter, to transmit all the necessary papers to the secret committee, with my detailed sentiments upon this extraordinary, and in my judgement providential, discovery.

No doubt exists in my mind, that the British government would now be completely justified, in depriving the nabob of all power over his country, and reducing him to the state of a mere pensioner.

The only questions which remain for decision are, the time of carrying this measure into execution, and the amount of the provision to be made for the nabob, for his descendants, and for those of Wallajah. As soon as you shall have received this letter, I request you to dispatch an express to me with your opinion; although mine is so decided, that I shall not wait for the communication of yours, if the season should appear to me to be favourable for the great measure, which is now become indispensable on every principle of justice and policy.

With respect to Tanjore, the treaty,[1] which I framed previous to my

---

[1] *Wellesley*, ii, 705.

departure from Fort St George, and which has since been carried into effect by Lord Clive, will, I trust, place the administration of the affairs of that country on an improved foundation. The difficulties which I encountered, in obtaining a correct and consistent account of the state of Tanjore, are scarcely to be described or imagined.

After a most tedious inquiry, I brought the several contending parties to a fair discussion (or rather to a bitter contest) in my presence; and, after an argument, which lasted three or four days, I proceeded to review the whole case in a regular manner, adverting to every fact and argument on both sides of the question. At length the contending parties unanimously concurred in the expediency and justice of the treaty, in the form in which it has been concluded.

A question will arise with respect to the unregistered debt of the late rajah of Tanjore. I am inclined to believe, that some branches of that debt, as well as of the unconsolidated debt of the nabob of the Carnatic, are at least as well entitled to consideration, as any part of the debt sanctioned by Parliament. The subject merits your attention. I shall not feel myself at liberty to act upon it without orders from home; but I am satisfied, that you will find many cases of great hardship among many rather deserving prosecution than payment.

The Northern Circars, according to the report of the board of revenue at Fort St George, are now in a state to receive the same principles of government, with some local modifications, which have been applied to Bengal. The new settlement now about to be introduced upon the Coast will therefore include that vast tract of country.

It may be convenient to observe to you in this place, that my determination (stated in my letter in the judicial department by this dispatch) to render the new settlement of the land revenue on the Coast perpetual, without previous reference to the court of directors, was founded on intelligence from Mr Cockburn, that the terror of such a reference would render all settlement impracticable, and above all, would entirely frustrate the sale of the Havelly lands.

The condition of the coast of Malabar has been so entirely changed by the conquest of Mysore, that the principles stated in your dispatches to the government of Bombay, and in General Stuart's letters to you, are no longer applicable to the actual circumstances of that district. The conquest of Mysore will, I trust, enable us to settle Malabar and Canara on a systematic and durable plan of government. The subject is now under my consideration. One principle, however, I am persuaded will appear as evident and incontrovertible to your mind, as it does to mine; that, whatever may be our ultimate determination with respect to the power of the several rajahs, it must appear to flow from the generosity, justice, and power, of the British government; and not to be derived from a timid sub-mission to the refractory spirit of any rebellious tributary.

If you should not think fit to incorporate the government and services of Fort St George and Bombay, I shall proceed to introduce, at the latter, all the improvements, which I have declared in this letter my intention to apply to the former. But if you adopt my system of union, the whole reform will be effected through the authority of the government of Fort St George.

No. 11: 23 March 1799

This letter requires no particular answer. I have received the cypher which you were so good as to send to me. It may be useful to remark in this place, that my intelligence respecting Egypt, and the transactions in the Mediter-ranean, has been uniformly tardy and defective.

Mr Jones (apparently a man of talents and activity) is not in a position to acquire speedy or correct information. My most useful sources of intelligence have been Constantinople, Aleppo, Basra, and our own squadron in the Red Sea. I must repeat in this place my most earnest and anxious entreaty that the dispatch overland from England may be estab-lished on a proper foundation.

If the war with France should be protracted, and Bonaparte continue at the head of affairs, I am persuaded that some attempt will be made by France against our Indian empire. A regular monthly dispatch overland from London to India will, in that event, be of the utmost importance. Indeed, under any circumstances, a speedy and certain communication between England and India appears to me to be an object in which the interests of both countries are deeply involved. My opinion is, that, in addition to the dispatch overland, monthly packets should be established to sail regularly both from Europe and India. They might carry small cargoes and passengers, which, with the profits of postage on letters, would more than defray their expense.

No. 12: 25 March 1799

This letter merely enclosed a rough draft of Mr Pitt's bill for reducing the duties on Indian imports.

No. 13: 14 June 1799

I was extremely concerned to hear of your indisposition, but flatter myself your recovery is completely established.

A tax upon income in this country on the principle adopted in England would either produce so inconsiderable a sum as to furnish no important resource of revenue, or would interfere essentially with the fundamental principle on which the purity of the public service in India must ever be grounded. Such a tax would form so large a deduction from the annual profits of the Company's servants, as would leave the mass of them without hope of honestly accumulating even moderate fortunes within any reasonable compass of time. I need not enlarge on the mischievous effects of such a measure. I refer you to Mr Myers on this subject.

A voluntary annual contribution in this country, on the principle of the income tax, might have succeeded, during the war, if the court of directors had received our public-spirited exertions with common attention. But although the dispatch by the *Eurydice*, conveying our address to the King, and our first subscription, reached England in April 1799, no notice whatever has yet been bestowed upon it. This neglect has produced the worst effects in Bengal, and entirely damped the ardour of the former subscribers.

You do not appear to be aware that my present limited powers of legislation (the perpetual theme of my complaint) would not admit of my levying a tax upon the British subjects resident in India.

The answer to the remainder of your letter *no. 13* has been already anticipated in this dispatch.

No. 14: 23 July 1799
I have already anticipated all the topics contained in this letter in former dispatches.

I repeat the declaration of my inability to conceive how a line of separation can be drawn between the commercial and military funds of the government in India, in time of war, without divesting the Company of its character of sovereignty.

The conduct of the chairman and deputy, with respect to my brother Henry,[1] may serve as a caution to my successors against the perils of indiscreet candour, sincerity, and public zeal.

I take this opportunity of observing, that I have been able to effect a very considerable improvement in the revenues and management of the post office; and that I hope to be able to extend those improvements still further.

I highly applaud your able measure of recruiting from the militia. Although my last advices from Lord Elgin relate the unpropitious news of the retreat of the duke of York's army from Holland, I still trust that you will derive all the benefits which you expected from your late spirited plans for the augmentation of your disposable force.

No. 16: 27 September 1799
I have already replied to your letter of this date.

---

[1] The East India Company refused to sanction the allowances Mornington wished to pay his brother.

In reviewing your correspondence, I have not thought it necessary to return any particular replies to your several letters of recommendation. The receipt of them is noted in the annexed memorandum. Being in possession of your principles with respect to recommendations, I do not think any further explanation necessary.

Believe me, . . .

MORNINGTON

LXXIV

The Earl of Mornington to the Rt Hon. Henry Dundas

9 March 1800, Fort William
Private: no. 26

My dear Sir
I avail myself of the present overland dispatch to transmit to you the copy of a most interesting and important paper, the original of which (together with all the documents referred to in it) has been forwarded to you by the *Lord Thurlow* Indiaman, now dispatched for England.[1] I refer you to my *private* letter (*no. 25*) by that conveyance for my reflections on the transactions to which this paper relates.

I am, . . .

MORNINGTON

LXXV

The Earl of Mornington to the Rt Hon. Henry Dundas

9 March 1800, Fort William
Secret and Confidential: [Unnumbered]

My dear Dundas
Although my health continues unimpaired, and the state of this government and of its vast dependencies is in every respect flourishing and prosperous, my separation from my family and friends becomes every day more painful to me, and frequently reduces my spirits to a state of melancholy, which is the more oppressive, because it must be concealed, and can-

---

[1] Edmonstone's memorandum about the conduct of Umdut-ul-Umra. *Wellesley*, ii, 740.

not be indulged, or even disclosed, without injury to the public service. Under this pressure, I trust I have not yet betrayed any symptoms of a declining spirit; but having lost all hope of seeing Lady Mornington in India, and having even abandoned the wish of exposing her to all the perils of the voyage and climate, I am destitute of every ray of domestic comfort, while no resource of society can be obtained here to supply the void. I can truly say, that it is not the weight of the business of my office which oppresses me; my only happy hours are those of the most intense labour; and the moments of relaxation to others, bring to me nothing but painful recollections, and intolerable regret. I am aware that the strict letter of my commissions, combined with those of Sir Alured Clarke, admit of my returning to Europe, whenever I may feel disposed to leave this government; but I am also sensible, that I could not take such a step consistently with any principle of honour, justice, or public duty, before I had given a seasonable intimation of my intentions to you. I confess also, that I feel great reluctance to abandon this government before I shall have carried into effect various plans of improvement in all its branches, founded in the spirit of the subsisting institutions, but calculated to give them additional vigour, and to establish the permanency of our empire on the most durable foundations. I am still more unwilling to suffer the favourable opportunities of the two or three next years to pass away unimproved, under any weak or inefficient government. However, I flatter myself, that much has been done during the two years of my government towards the accomplishment of all these important objects; and unless my health should fail, I may entertain a just expectation of forwarding them still more effectually in the interval of time between this season and the month of January 1801. My wish is to be at liberty to return to England at that time, if the state of my mind and spirits should render me unable to continue in India. You may be assured that I will use every exertion to continue longer in this arduous charge, if you should earnestly press it; but I hope you will leave me at liberty to use my own discretion on the subject; and that you will rely on my determination never to relinquish my post, if any crisis or alarm should arise. My happiness, however, depends on my speedy return to my family and friends; and I cannot say what effect a longer absence from them might produce on my health.

I have a favour to ask of the court of directors, which I think they might grant to me, after all that has passed; that they will send me an order, empowering me to occupy such one of their regular ships, as I may choose, in any season, to the exclusion of all other passengers, excepting such as I may admit; and that they will indemnify the captain for the expense of my passage. The latter condition I do not urge earnestly, although, if I quit India in January 1801, I believe I shall be the poorest governor-general that ever left Fort William for Europe. This order might be given to me, applicable to any time when I might find myself unable to remain in India.

I am persuaded that your good nature and your kindness towards me will induce you to answer this letter by express overland as soon as you receive it, and that you will by the same occasion endeavour to send me the order which I request.

Believe me, . . .

MORNINGTON

I have received from Constantinople English newspapers to the 25th Oct[ober 1799]. My disappointment at our failure in Holland,[1] and our reverses of fortune in Switzerland, was great. No details appear of news from London beyond the 25th Oct[ober]. Some of the foreign *Gazettes* have apprised me of the d[uke] of York's actual return to England, and of the new revolution at Paris.

I request you not to mention the contents of this letter to Lady Mornington. I never propose to give her any previous notice of my embarkation for Europe.

It is necessary that you should know, that Mr Cowper, member of the supreme council, has announced to me formally his intention of returning to Europe in December next.

LXXVI

The Earl of Mornington to the Rt Hon. Henry Dundas

25 March 1800, Fort William
Secret and Confidential: no. 12

My dear Dundas

I request you will take care that the enclosed letter is delivered to L[ieutenan]t-Gen[era]l Stuart, late commander-in-chief at Bombay, on his arrival in England. Let me also avail myself of this opportunity to renew my earnest recommendation of that excellent officer and most worthy man for some mark of favour of the Crown and of the Company. If his health should permit, he would make the best possible commander-in-chief for India.

Harris is returned to Europe in a passion. He thought fit to authorize a

---

[1] *Vide* A. B. Piechowiak, 'The Anglo-Russian expedition to Holland in 1799', *S.E.E.R.*, xli (1962–3), 185.

most dangerous and indecorous address to the army from General Floyd and the committee of prize. A reference to me from Lord Clive necessarily compelled me (in the secret department) to express my entire disapprobation of Harris' conduct. I need not observe to a person so conversant with arduous affairs as yourself, that it is not possible for a man in my station to discharge his duty to the public without some occasional pressure on individual feelings. Harris has left an absurd minute behind him, which I shall answer at my leisure. When you have fathomed his understanding (which you will accomplish in about five minutes), you will not be surprised at what has passed. It may be useful to apprise you, that my letter (in answer to Lord Clive's reference) was transmitted to his Lordship as a private letter, with liberty to record it in the secret dep[artmen]t, if he should judge it necessary for the public service to enter it on the records. It is attested by the chief secretary to the gov[ernmen]t, according to a practice which I have recently introduced, with respect to all such separate letters, as it appears to me to be proper to frame, with a view to *eventual* record: but the letter had not been recorded here, and never would have been recorded at all, if Lord Clive had not judged it necessary to record it at Madras. I think his Lordship's judgement was right. So scrupulous have I been respecting addresses to or from the army in India, that I have not even admitted any addresses from that body on the subject of the late war, although there was not a military station in India, which was not desirous of addressing me. Harris' conduct can be palliated only by the weakness of his understanding.

I have not received a line from you, or from England, since the 27th September 1799. I am most anxious to learn the state of affairs on the continent of Europe, and in Ireland, and also to receive your instructions on the points stated in my dispatch overland of the 7th June 1799 [*no. 15*].

Believe me, . . .

MORNINGTON

LXXVII
The Rt Hon. Henry Dundas to the Marquis Wellesley

15 April 1800, Wimbledon
Private: no. 25

My dear Lord

I was in hopes by this conveyance to write to you more in detail, but I find I would do it incompletely without more materials than I at present possess.

I write this, therefore, merely to say that I [am] in forward preparation to carry into execution some of the more essential points which have been in correspondence between us. I mean particularly the plan of forming the Coromandel and Malabar Coasts under one presidency, and the plan of connecting your situation more completely with the executive government at home, [by] a royal commission on [the] principle of the lord lieutenant of Ireland. It is now under the consideration of the law friends, to what extent it is necessary to have the authority of the legislature to these and other propositions. It is certainly right to do it all at once. The packet goes tonight, and I could not refrain writing to you these few lines before it goes.

On Thursday next, we have the Irish Union before the house of commons, it having now returned from Ireland. Lady Jane joins me in every good wish to you and,

I remain, . . .

HENRY DUNDAS

LXXVIII
The Rt Hon. Henry Dundas to the Marquis Wellesley

18 April 1800 [Wimbledon]
Private: no. 26   [Abstract]

Private trade and India-built shipping: Copy of a letter to the directors enclosed.[1] The principles recommended therein will probably be adopted.

LXXIX
The Marquis Wellesley to the Rt Hon. Henry Dundas

29 April 1800, Fort William
[*Private*]: [*Separate*]

My dear Sir

This letter will contain my answer to your very kind *private letter of the 4 Nov[ember 17]99*, relating to my domestic and personal interests. Your

[1] Add. MSS. 37275, f. 27.

257

judgement respecting Lady M[ornington]'s visit to India coincides w[it]h my deliberate opinion: and altho[ugh] I feel her absence grievously, I am satisfied that I sh[oul]d expose myself to still greater misery, if I were to induce her to come here. The climate is remarkably adverse to persons of her constitution; the society is worse than the climate; and her separation from my children w[oul]d be a continual source of alarm and vexation to us both. Had it been possible to establish her here in safety and comfort, my continuance in India might have been much prolonged. It must now be shortened, which I most sincerely regret, because I feel every hour the increasing advantage of the situation in which our late successes have placed us, and I am conscious that I c[oul]d within a few years establish the most extensive and impregnable system of improvement in every branch of our Asiatic interests. But I have not the vanity to suppose myself to be the only person capable of accomplishing so great and glorious a work: and altho[ugh] the prosperous course of my admin[istration] to the present time has placed singular advantages in my hands, I confess that, I feel those advantages to have been in a very great degree impaired by recent events in England; and I am confident that my successor might prosecute the benefits of my success with at least equal prospects of securing the public interests, and of promoting all the objects which I had in view. Perhaps, indeed, the reports which I can submit to you personally in England upon my return, w[oul]d prove more serviceable than any exertion which I am likely to make here.

With respect to the reward which the King has (I understand from Mr Pitt) conferred on me by creating me an Irish marquis, as you state that such points do not properly fall within your care, I sh[oul]d not have troubled you on the subject, had not his Maj[esty]'s mode of accepting my services appeared to me to lead to consequences, which must be interesting to your particular department, and which w[oul]d be uncandid in me to conceal from you. A step in the Irish peerage was an honour to which I thought I might without vanity have aspired in the ordinary course of my gov[ernmen]t; and I had occasionally talked over the idea with Bernard, who is my banker. But I confess that I little expected that the King w[oul]d have thought a step in the Irish peerage a proper ostensible mark of his Maj[esty]'s gracious acceptance of services, of which both houses of Parl[iamen]t have spoken in the terms of the reso[lution]s which I have had the honour and happiness to receive. I am ready to appeal to the unanimous voice of all India; to the civil and military service; to our native subjects and dependents; and to our allies; and to rest on their testimony, whether the honour conferred on me by his Maj[esty] be in any degree adequate to the magnitude and importance of the occasion. Being sensible that the public opinion here will be, and indeed is, that the title granted to me in Ireland is a proof that his Maj[esty] does not deem *me* a proper object of those honours which are appropriate to such services, I feel my new dignity as a mark rather of deprecation than of honour,[1] and I know that it will be so felt throughout India, where the scale of British and Irish honours is well understood: and I really despair of being able, under such circumstances, to serve the public with the same efficacy and spirit, which under a more cordial encouragement from his Maj[esty] I might have hoped to manifest through the remaining period of my admin[istration]. I, therefore, am induced with addit[iona]l earnestness to express my anxiety to return to Europe; and although I assure you, that I will use every exertion to aid you in the execution of your wise, comprehensive, and noble, plans for the glory of this empire until the last moment of my continuance here, and that I will endeavour to retain my station, under all its present disadvantages, as long as possible, I cannot flatter myself with the possibility of remaining here to any good purpose (in my present circumstances) after the month of December next. I, therefore, hope that you will release me from my now painful and humiliating position by an express overland as soon as you shall receive this letter.

I cannot express to you how strongly I feel the almost parental kindness of the principle on which you have recomm[ende]d it to the c[ourt] of d[irectors] to frame a pecuniary grant to me. Your judgement has been equal to your friendship in concluding that a disposable sum of money w[oul]d be more advantageous to me and to my children than any pension; and altho[ugh] the whole of my estate in Ireland, and whatever accumulation of savings from my official salary may have accrued, are secured to my children, and w[oul]d leave them under any circumst[ance]s in a state of perfect independence, I am naturally most anxious that every accession to my property sh[oul]d be turned to their benefit. The principle, therefore, of your kind intention is most acceptable to me, and I receive your zealous and cordial exertion on this occasion with all the gratitude which it demands. Having stated my sincere feelings on this part of the subject, I am persuaded you will not deem me fastidious or capricious when I express an objection to the fund from which (if I understand the suggestion of your letter) this bounty of the E[ast] I[ndia] C[ompany] is to proceed. I understand that, if the reserved part of prize taken at Ser[ingapatam], consisting of stores and ordnance, sh[oul]d come into the possession of your c[ommittee], it is their intention to grant the whole to the army, reserving £100,000 to be hereafter granted to me. I am satisfied that upon reflection you will perceive, that my acceptance of such a grant w[oul]d place me in a very invidious and humiliating situation with respect to the army. The

---

[1] 'I will confess to you openly,' he told Pitt, 'that as I was confident there had been nothing *Irish* or *Pinchbeck* in my conduct, or in its result, I felt an equal confidence that I should find nothing *Irish* or *Pinchbeck* in my reward.' P.R.O. 30/8/188, f. 109.

army w[oul]d feel that I had been rewarded at their expense: and they w[oul]d view the transaction with perhaps aggravated jealousy and contempt for my character when they recollected the effort, which I made in the face of their prejudices and popularity, to reserve these very stores for the ostensible purpose of saving the rights of the Crown. It w[oul]d be said that my view of the transact[ion] had been personal and ungenerous: and I sh[oul]d lose all influence and consideration with the mil[itar]y branch of the service. But independent of any question of my character, or of the dignity and vigour of my gov[ernment], I sh[oul]d be miserable if I c[oul]d ever feel, that I had been enriched at the expense of those who must ever be objects of my affection, admiration, and gratitude, and who are justly entitled to the exclusive enjoyment of all that a munificent King and an admiring country can bestow. If, therefore, the independence of my family were at stake (which I thank God it is not), I never c[oul]d consent to establish it on an arrangement injurious to the conquerors of Mysore. Even any appearance of such an arrange[men]t must affect my character; and I therefore trust that if my services sh[oul]d appear to merit a pecuniary reward from the Com[pany], your friend[ship] will be employed to direct their liberality thro[ugh] some channel wholly unconnected with any prize taken by the army. Various other modes might be pointed out. Perhaps the most advantageous to me and to my family, and the easiest to the Company, w[oul]d be to order the gov[ernmen]t of Bengal to issue to my order gov-[ernmen]t securities to the amount proposed in any of my loans. The decennial (10 per cent) w[oul]d be the most favourable to me; or to open a loan to the same amount chargeable on the revenues of the conquered countries. In short, I cannot object to any mode which shall not diminish the fair reward of the army's service, and shall not bear the appearance of being a reduction from their prize money. You will excuse these observations. I think my delicacy is not false; and I am sure it does not in any degree impair my deep sense of your kindness.

You will find that I thought it my duty not only to promise but actually to grant the treasure and jewels found at Ser[ingapatam] to the army, reserving all ordnance and mil[itary] stores. I believe the amount divided and remaining to be divided of the granted prize is about 26 or 30 lakhs of pagodas, which is equal to the sum stated in the letter from the s[ecret] com[mittee] received by the *Morn[ington]*. I cannot yet state even a rough calculation of the value of the reserved prize. When I can ascertain it, I shall give you a private estimation of my opinion whether it ought to be granted in the first instance to the Com[pany] or to the army, and whether the Com[pany] ought in any event to regrant any part of it to the army. The present inclination of my opinion is rather that the army have had money enough. Perhaps the best application of the fund arising from the stores, would be the pensions of Gen[eral] Stuart, Gen[eral] Baird, the family of L[ieutenan]t-Col[onel] Montague of the artillery, *etc.*, but certainly not to provide for any Irish marquis.

Be assured that I am fully sensible of the friendship of those motives which induced you to enter so fully into my private affairs in the letter to which I now reply, and that,

I am, . . .

M[ORNINGTON][1]

LXXX
The Marquis Wellesley to the Rt Hon. Henry Dundas

29 April 1800, Fort William
Most Private: [*Separate*]

My dear Sir

I am anxious to reply to your letter superscribed *most private*, and dated the 16th October 1799, because mine, *confidential and unnumbered*, which you received by the *Sarah Christian*, appears to have distressed you very much.

I continued to the hour of my departure from Madras to entertain the opinions relating to character stated in that letter, and I still retain precisely the same opinions, founded on letters from the best-informed, ablest, and worthiest, men in that settlement. The arrangements, however, which I made on quitting Madras have greatly relieved my mind, and will relieve yours, from some of the most painful of the apprehensions stated in my letter by the *Sarah* [*Christian*]. With Lord Clive's cordial approbation, I gave my implicit confidence to a select number of the ablest and honestest men at Madras, and induced him to call them near his person as a sort of cabinet council, and to use their active assistance in the whole administration of the gov[ernmen]t. This system has worked extremely well since my departure from Madras; and I hope it may continue to be serviceable while I shall continue in India. Between myself and Lord Clive the freest intercourse subsists on all occasions, and not a step is taken at Fort St George without my direct authority: so that I think I can now answer for the safety of affairs at Madras. How far this scene would change, if I were to leave India, is a subject of more dangerous speculation. This gov[ernmen]t in

[1] In protest, Wellesley refused on this occasion to use his new title.

other hands than mine might not be so cordial with Lord Clive or with his cabinet as I am, and am resolved always to remain, while Lord Clive shall remain at Madras. On the other hand, with all my real affection and esteem for Lord Clive, I am conscious that he is not equal to conduct any government in his own person, and that he must always act under some influence. What this influence might be, if he were to succeed me, or how far any man not accustomed to act for himself could succeed in governing this empire, I cannot determine. I can only say that I am satisfied Lord Clive's intentions would be honourable; I hope also that he would seek for the best advice, that he would be disposed to attend to any general system, which I might propose to him on leaving the gov[ernmen]t in his hands, and, I flatter myself, that he would repose his confidence in those whom I think worthy of mine. But I fear that his personal influence and powers of personal exertion would scarcely be found equal to the daily difficulties of this station, and above all to that of crushing all intrigues and opposition. However, I really think him preferable to any other member of the present council of Bengal, and still more superior to Sir J[ames] Craig. In the prospect, therefore, which my present communications will open to you of my speedy if not immediate return to Europe, I recommend on the whole that you should immediately appoint Lord Clive my provisional successor, and state it to be done at my desire. Such an appointment will not accelerate my return, and certainly will not cause any jealousy between Lord Clive and me. Having thus recommended an arrangement which I certainly do not think the best imaginable, not by any means exempt from danger, but which appears to me to be the best easily attainable under all the circumstances of the moment, I must add a word for the peaceable life of my successor, and eventually for my own. Sir J[ames] Craig must not come into council, unless you mean to employ your governor-general in debating and minuting, in place of acting with vigour and effect. Lord Clive entertains precisely the same dread of his contentious qualities, which I have repeatedly expressed; and you may rely on it that such a man at the head of the army here would throw your gov[ernmen]t into confusion under its present constitution, which I perceive you do not intend to amend, according to my earnest entreaty.

I hope this letter will relieve you from immediate anxiety respecting Madras. I cannot, however (would to God I could), retract the opinions on most of the material points of character, which excited your alarm.

Believe me, . . .

WELLESLEY

As connected with the subject of this letter, I must remark that Sir Alured

Clarke has intimated to me his intention of going home, and probably will go home next December. Mr Cowper has made a similar communication to me. I trust you will have received my suggestions respecting Mr Bebb, who is gone home, in time to prevent your placing him in the council according to my first idea. I wrote to you on that subject by the *Earl Howe*, and I shall send a duplicate by the *Mornington*.

LXXXI
The Marquis Wellesley to the Rt Hon. Henry Dundas

1 May 1800, Fort William
Private: no. 27

My dear Sir

The *Earl of Mornington* packet imported here on the 20th of April and brought me your several dispatches from *no. 17* to *no. 24* inclusive, together with various other communications of a *secret and confidential* nature from you.

As it is my intention to dispatch the *Earl of Mornington* to Europe within the course of a few weeks, I shall defer, until that period, my answer to the several suggestions contained in your dispatches, contenting myself at present with assuring you, that my attention will be carefully fixed on the important objects to which you have directed it.

By the same conveyance which brought your letters, I received, from the speaker of the house of commons, an attested copy of the resolutions unanimously voted by that house upon your motion on the 4th of October 1799. I cannot close this dispatch without expressing to you, the cordial assurance of my high sense of the distinguished honour conferred upon me, by that part of the resolutions which repects my conduct in the discharge of the duties of my station, from the period of my arrival in India until that of the fall of Seringapatam; and I trust that the settlement which I have effected, of our extensive and splendid conquests, will have been found answerable to your expectations and to those of the house of commons. It was a great satisfaction to me to find that the house of commons entertained a just sense of the eminent services of Lord Clive, Mr Duncan, Lieutenant-General Harris, and the officers and troops employed under him in Mysore.

By this dispatch I forward to the secret committee a letter upon the subject of the Nabob Umdut ul Umrah's conduct. I request your particular attention to that letter and to its enclosures, especially to Mr Edmonstone's report and to the several translations annexed to it, as all these papers have been altered in some degree since copies were transmitted to you by the *Lord Thurlow*, and overland in my *private* letters numbered *25* and *26*.

I have the satisfaction to inform you that our tranquillity and prosperity in India continue undisturbed. The reform of the nawab vizier's army advances regularly towards completion; and the number of our troops established in his country is increasing according to my intended plan. This important measure has hitherto proceeded without producing any commotion; and I have every reason to believe that it will be completed in the same tranquil manner.

I transmit to you by this opportunity a copy of a letter from Purneah, the dewan of Mysore, which will furnish you with a satisfactory view of the state of that country, as well as of the character of the person who now administers its affairs.

I am, . . .

WELLESLEY

LXXXII
The Marquis Wellesley to the Rt Hon. Henry Dundas

8 June 1800, Fort William
Secret and Confidential: [*Unnumbered*]

My dear Sir

My dispatch of this date to the secret committee[1] will apprise you of the general state of political affairs in India. By the *Mornington* packet, which I propose to dispatch in the course of the month of August, I hope to be able to reply fully to all your communications received by that ship.

I trust it will be a matter of satisfaction to you to observe that I have never overlooked the advantages to be derived by obtaining from the nizam the line of boundary stated in your dispatch *no. 17*, dated October 9th 1799; although your opinion and mine have so far differed, that I should have thought it at all times more advantageous to have gained such a cession by a commutation of the subsidiary payments, than by the cession of the Circars; a measure, which, for reasons hereafter to be stated to you, I am convinced your deliberate judgement would never approve.

[1] *Wellesley*, ii, 266.

If my depending proposition should succeed,[1] your utmost wishes will be accomplished, without any sacrifice either of territory or of money: unless indeed you attach any importance to the establishment of a nominal power in Mysore, under the conditions by which that power is limited. By the *Mornington*, I shall explain to you the reasons which rendered it absolutely necessary to adopt the expedient of introducing an intermediate partner between us and the nizam, for the purpose of reducing his Highness' claims within reasonable limits. I hope, however, that my brother Henry, and the documents transmitted by him, have already satisfied you on this point.

The evils which I have constantly apprehended from the defective power of the governor-general with respect, as well to his right of acting independent of the council, as to his authority over the army, are likely to produce the most dangerous effects, unless you should determine to apply some speedy remedy, according to my repeated and earnest suggestions. It is with grief and concern, not unmixed with indignation, that I inform you, that the disappointment and jealousy occasioned in Sir Alured Clarke's mind by the success of the late war, and by the fame which has attended those concerned in its plan and conduct, have entirely destroyed whatever he possessed of temper or discretion. He has plainly informed me, that he considers the governor-general as *nothing more than the first member of the government*, and he has *recently*, for the *first* time, manifested the most captious disposition with respect to the mode in which I have conducted the government *uniformly and without variation* since the first hour of my arrival in Bengal. He has particularly manifested his ill humour in several points of form relating to trivial military questions. You are already apprised that I have given him the most unlimited powers over the patronage of the army; and even thrown into his hands many branches of it jealously reserved by my predecessors. I am concerned to say, that on this occasion he has disclosed the most unequivocal symptoms of a false, mean, and frivolous, mind. He has not entered into any open opposition, and disclaims all such intention. You may rely on my determination not to suffer his caprice and envy to change the even tenor, or to impair the vigour, of my government. But I most earnestly entreat you not to lose a moment in placing both the civil and military authority of the governor-general on such a basis, as to preclude all rivalry in India; and to prevent any possibility of an attempt from any quarter to participate in those powers, which cannot be divided without being weakened, and which have been exercised by me with success, from this *sole* cause, that the practice of my administration has concentrated them exclusively in my own hands. I conceive my practice to be strictly con-

[1] Wellesley had reopened negotiations with the nizam for a revised subsidiary treaty; in which the nizam was to cede territory instead of paying a subsidy.

formable to the true spirit of the laws for the government of India. If I should prove to be mistaken, I must resign a charge, which I cannot hope to hold with advantage to the public on any other terms, than those of undivided power in India, subject to no check or restraint on the spot, but open to the most severe scrutiny of the authorities constituted in England for that purpose. I have no hesitation in declaring my conscientious conviction, that the vigour, energy, and dispatch, of this government would be utterly extinguished, if the principles stated to me by Sir Alured Clarke should be admitted in practice. Under this impression, I am induced to renew with great earnestness my anxious request that Lord Clive (whose opinions are very different) may immediately be appointed my provisional successor; and that his appointment may be sent out to me by an express overland. It would be very satisfactory to me if it could be expressed in the body of the appointment, that it had been made at my particular solicitation.

I retain the most anxious desire to be furnished with permission to return to Europe in the month of January next; although I trust that your knowledge of my disposition, and your view of the present dispatches will satisfy you, that I am neither inclined to relax my exertions in the prosecution of your laudable views for the public service, nor to desert my post by a premature or capricious resignation. Since the date of my last letter to you, I have suffered more from indisposition (having experienced more internal disquietude and vexation of mind) than at any period since my arrival in India. At this moment, however, I am in tolerably good health.

Although I have received no dispatches overland of a later date than the 27th September 1799, nor by sea than the 18th November, English newspapers down to the 7th January 1800 have reached me. The public notification of my Irish honours has produced in India precisely the effect which I anticipated. I will add nothing to my former observations on that painful subject. His Majesty's gracious grant of an honourable augmentation to the arms of my family, produced a singular contrast with the Irish titles to which it was annexed; and the distinguished terms in which that grant is expressed have rather increased the public surprise at the nature of my promotion in the peerage.

I shall hereafter write to you fully on the subject of Batavia. At present, I think it sufficient to inform you, that I lost no time in issuing such orders as appeared to me necessary for carrying his Majesty's instructions with regard to that colony into effect.[1] The military force which I have been able to allot for this service is inconsiderable, but the mere possibility that Lord Clive may eventually be obliged to replace it (for I have ordered it in the first instance to be furnished from Ceylon) has excited some alarm at Madras.

[1] On 9 May 1800. Add. MSS. 13751, f. 48.

Lord Clive's nervous disorder (which I hoped the war had cured) has returned with the appearance of Dhoondhia Jee on the frontier of Mysore. I think no cause exists to justify uneasiness on this account; I have committed the principal conduct of the expedition to Batavia to Admiral Rainier,[1] and I have appointed Colonel Champagné[2] to the command of the land forces. The conduct and correspondence of this officer, while in the command of the troops in Ceylon, and in the temporary charge of the government of that settlement, have impressed me with a most favourable opinion of his abilities and temper; and induced me to select him as the person best qualified on the whole to co-operate cordially with Admiral Rainier in the execution of his Majesty's orders. I should have preferred Colonel Wellesley, but Lord Clive will not allow me to withdraw him from Mysore. The expedition will probably depart from Madras in the course of next month: but a squadron of his Majesty's ships of war will precede it (and perhaps have already sailed), for the purpose of blockading the port of Batavia.[3]

Believe me, . . .

WELLESLEY

I dictated this letter to Mr Barlow, in whose secrecy, and honour, I place the greatest confidence. The severe heat, and my present state of health, did not admit of my using my own hand. I observe that I have not stated to you with sufficient force, that Sir A[lured] C[larke] has plainly intimated his expectation, that I should refer *all*, even the most minute details, political as well as others, to the council before I proceed to act in any instance; adding with *great politeness*, that it was *not unnatural that I should err*, and insinuating that his sapience might prove a salutary correction of my errors.

The fact is, that he cannot sleep for Harris' laurels. My kindness and attention to him have been unbounded; but he is unfit to hold this government, and he shall not render it as weak in my hands as it would be in his own. His character is a composition of low pride, and ridiculous vanity; but I request that you will not on account of this letter relax your efforts to obtain for him the honours which I formerly solicited in his favour.

[1] Wellesley was not prepared to allow Rainier to send Blankett instead; because 'although I have great confidence in Admiral Blankett's naval skill and activity, I confess I am not equally satisfied that his temper and discretion are such as to warrant' such a command. *Ibid.*, f. 71.
[2] Lt-Col. Champagné was lieutenant-governor of Ceylon, and acting governor, April–September 1799, while North was away at Madras.
[3] Rainier sent Captain Ball with three frigates.

LXXXIII

The Rt Hon. Henry Dundas to the Marquis Wellesley

27 June 1800 [London]
Private: no. 27

My dear Lord

I think it right to send you a copy of a letter I have recently wrote to the chairman of the East India Company,[1] and which I make no doubt will be adopted by them as the basis and principles of the subject which it treats of. Where there are so many adverse and jarring interests, there must be delay, and I cannot expect unanimity; but I am so satisfied of the soundness of my own principles, that I shall insist on the adoption of them, and I trust you will keep the same principles in view in your decisions. Indeed, I was in some hopes that you have acted upon them decisively in consequence of my former correspondence, and that perhaps would have been as good a way as another for introducing a final decision of the question by an approbation of what you had done.

I remain, . . .

HENRY DUNDAS

LXXXIV

The Rt Hon. Henry Dundas to the Marquis Wellesley

11 July 1800, Wimbledon
Secret [and Confidential]: [Unnumbered]

My dear Lord

Your Lordship cannot fail to anticipate the very great regret and embarrassment which the receipt of your *secret and confidential* letter of the 9th of March has created to me. I now write with your brother's knowledge and approbation, and under a conviction that your Lordship has taken up your resolution under the depression of spirits which dictated your letter, and to which I am more disposed to attribute the contents of it, than to any steady resolution formed after a deliberate consideration of all the circumstances, which ought to have suggested themselves in considering the effects of such a communication. No man can be more disposed than I am to con-

[1] Apparently, another copy of his earlier letter.

template with lively satisfaction and hope the state of our affairs in India; but I know too much of the subject not to feel and say, that perhaps upon the administration of those affairs during the next two or three years depends whether those hopes are ever to be realized. Successive treaties may be ably devised, and the relative interests of the different powers well poised and arranged, so far as human foresight can be supposed to operate; but I will venture to assert, that by experience only any man is able to judge how far the assortment of such various and complicated interests has been so happily accomplished as to preclude the occurrence of new difficulties. Upon the most superficial view of the question, it must occur to everybody, that the Marathas are dissatisfied and that Zeman Shah will ever probably continue to be restless; and it would be an over degree of confidence for any man to pretend to decide what new jealousies and hostile combinations may arise out of such a state of affairs. Are you even certain that the late approaches to the court of Persia may not create more extensive jealousies amongst all the Mohammedan powers (extending even to Constantinople), of which more than one power may be disposed to take advantage? These topics are too extensive for the contents of an overland dispatch, but I will explain myself more at large to your brother, and likewise to yourself by more convenient conveyances than the present offers for such a purpose. I feel confident in stating, that whilst the war continues in Europe, and all former interests and connections remain as much disjointed in this quarter of the globe as they now are, he must have a very superficial view of the subject, who will pronounce with exultation that our interests in India are in such a state, as to justify repose and relaxation from watchfulness on our part.

I need not, however, for the purpose of the present letter, have recourse merely to probable or future contingencies. I could call your attention to objects of immediate pressure, amongst the first of which is the amount of our debt and the absolute necessity of the speedy reduction of it, if we are to look upon India as a source of great annual addition to the wealth and capital of the country, instead of considering it (as many are apt to do) as large provision for great numbers of civil and military servants, existing upon its establishments. I have no occasion to enlarge upon this topic. I have only to refer your Lordship to your own statement of the 23rd of January last,[1] the result of which is a surplus of only nine lakhs of sicca rupees, after defraying the expense of the establishments and the interest of our debt. This is not the proper time, or mode, of making observations on that statement, but I refer to it as exhibiting not a state of despondency, because, by good management, I see clearly an effectual remedy to the inconveniences which must result from such a state of Indian finances, if not as soon as

[1] *Wellesley*, ii, 185.

possible materially changed. For this purpose, however, vigour and vigilance are absolutely necessary. In addition to that, allow me barely to remind you, that the state of affairs in Oudh has always been felt, from its lamentable situation, to be rather a weakness than a strength to our territories. I am aware that the steps your Lordship is taking will ultimately produce, I flatter myself, a happy and comfortable change in this material article of [our] Indian interests, but I am sure you are much too sanguine in supposing, as you seem to do, the work to be performed in a few months. The whole mischief must be probed to the bottom, and the cure administered when the disease is perfectly understood, but no sooner. We must not expect that your revolution can be in a moment accomplished, when the inveterate habits, prejudices, and vices, of the people, and of their ruler, have taken as deep a root as they have done in the country of the vizier of Oudh. It has unfortunately been, and still is, the interest of too many to foster and cherish those vicious habits and prostitutions, and the difficulties of eradicating them must in proportion be greatly increased. And here again, I must be permitted to observe, that we shall judge rashly indeed, if we suppose that this or any great work of the kind is finished, merely because the principles of it are detailed upon paper or in a treaty. Experience alone can elucidate whether the case is radical, or whether the wound is only skinned over, to break out in various other shapes and modes. And if in this, or any other quarter of India, such occurrences should happen, I need not observe how essential it is, that the same authority should watch over the events and complete the cure, which may be further necessary to administer to such unsuspected occurrences.

The same conveyance which brought me the letter to which I am now replying, likewise brought me the very extraordinary discoveries made at Seringapatam respecting the conduct of the late and present nabob of Arcot. Did it not occur to your Lordship, at the moment you was meditating your retreat from India, that probably at the very moment you was putting your foot on board of the ship that was to convey you home, events might occur, and measures be on the line of execution, which might change the whole complexion of our Indian interests? This, surely, is not the moment when your Lordship could wish to be retired and at a distance from the scene of so material a transaction. It would, however, be endless to run over in detail every particular, which at this moment presents itself to my imagination. There is not one spot, from the one end of India to the other, or one interest in it, that anyone intelligent in the subject can contemplate without feeling that vigour, prudence, and, above all, established authority, are ingredients in the government of India essentially requisite for the final consolidation and arrangement of the British interests in India for several years yet to come. When the interests of Europe are arranged, and the

Indian machine set smoothly a-going, less energy, and less talents, may be necessary to keep matters in their proper fortune; but he must be short-sighted who thinks that period is yet arrived.

I have stated enough to convince your Lordship, what I must have severely felt when I received your intimation that the government of India was likely to be thrown loose a few months hence, without either the time or means afforded to me of applying the remedy. In no former letters had I ever received from you the most distant hint of such an idea floating in your mind, and you surely cannot have forgot the very confidential communications of your opinion I have received, relative to the person whom I should naturally have looked to as your successor? All of which must still further convey forcibly to your mind the feelings which have agitated mine on the receipt of your letter. But even if the circumstance I have last alluded to had not existed, your Lordship knows enough what I think of the Carnatic, and the difficulty of administering well our affairs there, not to be sensible that a governor of Madras, extended and complicated as that presidency must now be, is not a person to be found in every street where one may choose to look for him.

After the description I have given of the ingredients essentially requisite in the government of India for these two or three next years, what I am now to write certainly exposes me to the imputation of arrogance, but I contemn the affectation of either feeling or saying, that the experience I have had of the affairs of India does not qualify me for that duty, perhaps more than many others of far more excellent qualities in every other respect; and at least, if I was in that situation, I should feel that I had undertaken a task on the success of which my heart and soul must be engaged, because upon its success my happiness and fame are both embarked. I must be destitute of every particle of public virtue or honourable feeling, if I was not ready to make every sacrifice for such an object. My resolution was speedily taken, and would have been executed so as to set your Lordship at liberty soon after the period you have mentioned, notwithstanding the doubts of those whose opinions I am bound most to value, and who, over-rating (I really believe) any services I can perform at home, think that in the present state of Europe, not improved by recent events, and even with a view to the government of India itself, my presence in this country was of some use. I confess that those doubts did not alter the conviction I had formed, that, if I could be of use anywhere under all the circumstances of the present crisis, India had the preferable call upon me, and whatever considerations of a personal nature at my time of life might operate against the decision, I don't pretend to be perfectly disinterested on the subject. However anxious I may be, after a period of thirty-eight years' laborious exertions, to enjoy a few years of domestic repose, I am conscious to myself such repose would afford no comfort, to me or to my family, if it was disturbed by the reflection that my presence in India would have prevented any of these evils, which I augur from an abrupt dissolution of the present government of India. When I contemplate the example of Lord Cornwallis, who, without any personal object to induce him, embarked for India at a late period of life, offered to do so a second time on the mere suggestion of its necessity, and is now, without a single temptation or inducement but the feelings of a virtuous mind, devoting the remaining years of his life in the execution of a public trust attended with many unpleasant and uncomfortable circumstances, I should be ashamed, if I was to allow any sentiments to operate upon my mind, but those which at this moment guide the conduct of that much-valued friend.

From the description I have given you of the motives which have activated me in the determination I had formed, your Lordship must perceive, that I had only a choice of difficulties, and, therefore, I am happy, after a minute conversation with your brother, to feel myself at liberty to suspend any further proceeding for the present, as he is convinced, that your resolution must have been formed under a momentary state of feelings, which, however laudable in themselves, you would not permit yourself to act upon, the moment you began to reflect upon all the consequences. I, therefore, feel myself warranted to confide in his judgement. I likewise observe, that in your letter you express yourself so as to convey to me, that an urgency on my part for your stay would decide your doing so. I certainly do not mean to make any ungenerous use of that concession, both because it would not be fair to interpose any what may be supposed authority to counteract what seems to be the dictates of feeling, and because I know well service, either undertaken or continued without the heart going along with it, cannot be attended with that degree of energy which is peculiarly necessary in the arduous affairs in which you are now engaged. I have put your brother in possession of all my feelings on the subject, which he of course will communicate to you. I do, however, feel myself entitled to hope, that no abrupt resolution will be executed, and that you will not leave India till I am enabled, by your reply to this, to know your final resolution, that I may take my measures so as that the government of India may not be left under an interim governor-general.[1] You allude to the commission of Sir Alured Clarke, but your Lordship must be aware, that his commission is only meant to obviate in reality the event of your sudden death or bad health, but was never meant to be acted on as a matter of course. Besides, your Lordship likewise knows that Sir Alured Clarke has intimated, that

---

[1] Dundas told Grenville that, 'I cannot think it possible he will come away abruptly; if he does I will never forgive myself for not carrying my own intentions into immediate execution'. *Dropmore*, vi, 272.

he only awaits a successor to enable him to return home, and upon that ground it is in contemplation to send General Lake[1] to India.

I make no apology, my dear Lord, for the length of this letter, or the terms in which I have expressed myself. The public service of the country is too deeply implicated in the subject of it to admit of reserve. I likewise hope, that I am not mistaken when I feel that every sentiment I have uttered is mixed with a feeling of genuine friendship for you, and that the day must come when you will thank me for the fair and candid exposition I have laid before you.

I have not thought it necessary to make any reply to the concluding part of your letter, because, long before this time, your Lordship must know that there is no room for the supposition on which it is wrote.

I remain, . . .

HENRY DUNDAS

LXXXV
The Marquis Wellesley to the Rt Hon. Henry Dundas

13 July 1800, Fort William
Private: no. 28 (Secret)

My dear Sir

The representations which I have lately received from Fort St George, relative to the reduced state of his Majesty's regiments of infantry serving at that presidency, have suggested such serious considerations to my mind, as render it my indispensable duty to direct your immediate and unremitting attention to this most important subject.

It would be superfluous to detail in a letter to you the reasons which demonstrate that the security of our interests in India requires the European force, which may be deemed necessary for the different establishments in India, to be maintained as complete and efficient as possible. The total number of European troops to be maintained for the general service of India may admit of some variety of opinion. My own judgement is, that the augmentation of our European force should always bear a due proportion to the increased value and extent of our possessions in India; since in every arduous crisis we must principally depend, for the preservation of those

---

[1] Lt-Gen. Gerard Lake (Lord Lake, 1804); commander-in-chief, India, 1801–5.

possessions, on our European troops. If, therefore, previous to the late war in Mysore, the European establishment of India did not exceed the requisite proportion, that establishment must be deemed inadequate to our present extended dominions, as well as to the increase which it has been unavoidably necessary to make in the native part of our Indian army. Considerations of prudence, as well as of military convenience, demand that every augmentation of our native troops in India should be accompanied by a due augmentation of our European force, artillery as well as infantry. The conquest of Mysore, by diminishing our danger in India from the native powers, may appear to diminish the necessity of augmenting our European force: but if the extension of our dominions and of our alliances has rendered an increase of our native force indispensable, the same reasons demand a proportionate augmentation of the European part of the army. In addition to these considerations, it must be observed, that, while the war in Europe shall continue our empire in India must constantly be exposed to the attempts of the French, although that danger is certainly much diminished by the fall of Tipu Sultan.

It is unnecessary to observe to you, that no augmentation of our European force has taken place since the late war in Mysore. But I desire to call your particular observation to the alarming diminution of our European force in India since that period. The casualties of the several corps have necessarily been numerous: and the supply of recruits from Europe has either totally ceased, or been extremely inconsiderable. The number of his Majesty's regiments of infantry in India continues indeed to be the same; but, instead of consisting of 1,200 rank and file, according to the establishment, those employed under the presidency of Fort St George are stated to be reduced to an average of about 500 rank and file fit for duty. The regiments belonging to the establishment of Bombay, and those on the island of Ceylon, are also very incomplete. His Majesty's three regiments of infantry at this presidency do not exceed 2,400 rank and file; or about 800 men each. The Company's European artillery are everywhere extremely weak. The fixed establishment of this corps is defective at all the presidencies: and the numbers wanting to complete even that defective establishment are now so considerable, that I intend without delay to reduce one of the Company's European regiments in Bengal for the purpose of augmenting the artillery of this presidency; and I shall probably carry into effect a similar measure at Fort St George and Bombay. From a statement which I have received from the commander-in-chief, it appears, that the sixteen King's regiments of infantry, now in India, consisted, on the 1st of May 1800, of about 11,000 rank and file; the deficiencies amounting to about 8,000 men. The Company's four European regiments may be reckoned at 2,500 rank and file, the Swiss regiment de Meuron at about 600, making the total European infantry in India, King's and Company's, about 14,000 rank and file. But, as these numbers include the sick, from this amount must be deducted at least one-fourth in calculating the numbers now ready for service; which would leave the total number of Europeans actually able to take the field in the British empire in India about 10,500 men.

This European force is far inferior to the strength of that which ought to be constantly maintained in India in a condition of field service. In Bengal alone 6,000 European infantry should always be ready for active duty: and the establishment of Bengal, in order to be enabled, at all times, to furnish such a disposable force, ought to consist at least of eight regiments of the present nominal strength of 1,200 rank and file each.

Eight thousand European infantry should always be ready for service on the coast of Coromandel including Mysore; and at least 4,000 for the service of Ceylon, Bombay, and the coasts of Canara and Malabar. To furnish constantly 12,000 efficient men for these different points would require an establishment of at least 20,000 rank and file.

I would therefore propose, that the European infantry for India should be fixed at twenty-five regiments of the present establishments and strength (1,200) (making altogether 30,000 rank and file),[1] [which] number according to past experience would be requisite in order, at all times, to furnish a force of 18,000 for field service. This calculation, however, supposes an improved degree of attention to the regular supply of recruits from Europe.

The whole of this European infantry should consist of King's troops; and the Company's European regiments in Bengal, Fort St George, and Bombay, should be converted into artillery, as far as the men might be found serviceable for that branch of the army. The remainder might be drafted into his Majesty's regiments or returned to Europe.

I am not of the opinion, that it will be necessary, that the European regiments of the Company, which I propose to be reduced, shall be replaced by new regiments of native infantry raised merely for that purpose. The course of subsidiary engagements, and the extension of dominion to which they are likely to lead (by means of the commutation of subsidy for territory), will necessarily require some increase of the native infantry, and consequently afford sufficient means of disposing of the officers belonging to the reduced European corps. But whatever augmentation of the native infantry may hereafter be requisite on account of our new subsidiary engagements, and the augmentation of our territorial resources, you will observe, that the expense will not prove any additional burden to the Company, but will be defrayed, either in money, or by cession of territory,

---

[1] In 1800 Dundas could not provide more than 27,000 troops both to defend Portugal and to invade Egypt.

by the state for whose service or protection the additional troops shall have been raised.

An augmentation of our European cavalry is scarcely less necessary than that of our infantry. I am of opinion, that we ought to maintain at least eight complete regiments of dragoons. Of the additional regiments, two should be stationed in the peninsula of India, and two in the province of Oudh.

I have already stated the alarming deficiency of our artillery throughout India; and the expedient to which I intend to resort for the remedy of this serious evil. But the best remedy which I may be enabled to apply will be insufficient, on account of the great deficiency of officers of artillery. Some companies have now no more than one commissioned officer doing duty with them. This deficiency proceeds in a great measure from the original inadequacy of the establishment in point of commissioned officers. Defective as it is, nearly one-third are either on furlough or employed in staff offices, which preclude them from the performance of regimental duty. One additional subaltern, at least, should be posted to every company of artillery; and I most particularly request your attention to the necessity of sending out to India, without delay, both an ample supply of artillery men and of cadets for the artillery corps.

As connected with the subject of artillery, I beg leave to call your particular attention to the declining state of the foundry at Fort William, which, owing to the ignorance of those in charge of that department, is no longer able to supply the ordnance required for the use of this, and of the other presidencies. This failure has made it necessary, that we should apply to England for supply of field ordnance, and I earnestly entreat you to adopt requisite measures for enforcing an early and complete compliance with the indent of the military board for this purpose. I also most particularly recommend to your immediate consideration the absolute necessity of sending, as soon as possible, to Bengal one or more scientific persons properly qualified to conduct the foundry at Fort William. This is an evil which requires the most serious attention and the most prompt remedy.

I remain, . . .

WELLESLEY

LXXXVI

The Marquis Wellesley to the Rt Hon. Henry Dundas

13 July 1800, Fort William
Private: no. 29 (Secret)

My dear Sir

My *private* and *secret* letter *no. 28* of this date will prove to you the great difficulty, amounting nearly to an impossibility, of our making any effort from India, on an extended scale, to dislodge the French from Egypt.

In my *private* letter *no. 14*, dated 16th May 1799, I stated that if the French should be established in Egypt, it might be advisable to consider whether an expedition might not be fitted out from India to co-operate by way of the Red Sea with any attempt which might be undertaken from the Mediterranean. I added that I could not venture to prepare any such expedition without orders from England; but that, if I received them, you might be assured that they would be executed with activity and diligence. You will observe, that, although at that period of time I declared my determination not to undertake any expedition to Egypt without special orders for the purpose from home, I did not intimate any doubt of my ability to prepare such an expedition, if it should be judged expedient by his Majesty's ministers. During the residence of Lieutenant-General Stuart at Fort St George, my conversations with him induced me to entertain serious apprehensions, founded upon the professional sentiments and communications of that experienced and intelligent officer,[1] that any enterprise from India against Egypt would be attended with great difficulty and danger. Within this last month, a full disclosure of the actual state of our European force in India had confirmed the doubts raised in my mind by the opinions and statements of Lieutenant-General Stuart, and completely convinced me, that by detaching to Egypt such a proportion of our reduced European force as could alone be expected to produce any beneficial impression, we should incur a much greater, as well as a more immediate, hazard, than any which could result to our security in India even from the absolute establishment of the French in Egypt, much as that event is to be deprecated. The naval superiority of Great Britain, and the general state of her resources in Europe, authorize a hope, that she will be enabled to accomplish the expulsion of the French from Egypt, by exertions from the Mediterranean, before they can become formidable from that point to our possessions in India. But were we to detach from the protection of our Indian dominions (so much extended since the late war

[1] Memorandum by Stuart for Wellesley, 6 July 1799, W.O. 1/357, f. 319.

277

with Tipu Sultan, and increased as they may soon be by new relations with the nizam and the Marathas), a large proportion of our present European force, the consequences might be fatal to our existence in India, and certainly would deprive us of all the benefits of the late settlement in Mysore, as well as of those which we may expect from further arrangements at Hyderabad and Poona.

For these reasons, I am persuaded, that, if an attack on the French in Egypt from India, in concert with one from the Mediterranean, be thought advisable, it is indispensably necessary, in order to enable the government of India to take an efficient part in the expedition, without immediate and imminent hazard to all our most valuable interests in India, that additional troops from Europe or from the Cape of Good Hope should be dispatched instantly in order to replace without a moment of delay any European force which it may be determined to send from hence for this service. In my judgement, it would be advisable, that the additional regiments should actually have reached India before the expedition from hence shall take place.

It may be thought that our native troops might be employed on this service. I am of opinion that some corps of them, acting with a large European force, would be extremely useful; but highly as I appreciate the valour, discipline, and attachment, of our sepoys, it is my duty to declare, that, unless they should be powerfully supported by Europeans, I should not be sanguine in my expectations from them when they came to be opposed to the veteran troops of France, in a remote country and an unfavourable climate. If an expedition from India to Egypt is to take place, I am decidedly of opinion, that it ought to be formed principally if not exclusively of European troops.

You will be apprised by Lord Elgin's correspondence with me, that his Lordship had called my attention to the measure of co-operating from India with the Turkish army. You would also learn, from the same correspondence, that Mr Morier[1] (the agent of Lord Elgin with the grand vizier) has positively encouraged the Turks to look for early assistance from India. I need not state to you, that Mr Morier had no authority directly or indirectly from me to give any such assurance to the grand vizier. For my farther sentiments on this subject, I take the liberty to refer you to the enclosed extracts of my letters to Lord Elgin and to Sir Sidney Smith.[2]

Our European force in India being reduced to so low a scale, as I have stated in my letter *no. 28*, the intentions of the enemy being uncertain, and our internal situation in India, although on the whole highly prosperous,

---

[1] John Philip Morier; private secretary to Elgin; on 22 December 1799 sent on a mission to the camp of the grand vizier. *Vide* Add. MSS. 13791, f. 46.
[2] Add. MSS. 37282, f. 214.

being in some parts, and particularly in our recent acquisitions, rather un-settled, I have deemed it an indispensable duty to suspend for the present all preparations for the expedition against Batavia.[1] You will easily conceive the reluctance with which I have relinquished this design: a con-scientious conviction of the serious evils which might result from the diversion of any considerable proportion our naval and European force to so distant a point as Batavia, has induced me to suspend the execution of his Majesty's commands for the present. If a favourable change of cir-cumstances should take place, you may depend upon my making the attempt. I enclose for your information extracts from my letters to Admiral Rainier signifying my determination on this subject.[2]

I remain, . . .

WELLESLEY

LXXXVII

The Rt Hon. Henry Dundas to the Marquis Wellesley

15 July 1800, Wimbledon
Private: no. 28

My dear Lord

Although I must reserve all details to be transmitted to you by your brother, I cannot omit the present opportunity of expressing to you the anxiety I feel on the extent of the military establishments in India, and the little prospect hitherto held out of such a reduction as to give a prospect of any substantially useful surplus from the revenues of India. It is with me an object of the most essential moment, that the debt in India, which has increased to an amount hitherto unknown, should be reduced as speedily as practicable. If we should be involved in another expensive war there, before our debt is greatly reduced, we will be in a very critical situation. I am open to conviction, but I cannot help feeling, that the alteration in our situation, by getting rid of such an enemy as Tipu, should enable us to secure our possessions, new and old, without such expensive military establishments as under other circumstances our extended dominions might require. Upon this principle, my idea, and which I have stated to the court of directors, is that of the seventeen King's regiments now in India, three ought to be brought home; that the whole of the Company's European infantry ought

---

¹ On 21 June 1800.
² Add. MSS. 13751, f. 77. *Wellesley*, ii, 311.

to be reduced, but that out of the saving thence to arise, an immediate addition of one subaltern and ten privates should be made to each company of artillery; that three native regiments should be reduced at Bengal, that the same number should be reduced at Madras, and that two native regiments should be reduced at Bombay. The enclosed memorandum will point out at one view what would be the amount of our strength in India, more efficient than at any former period, and I should think fully adequate to the security of our own dominions, including the subsidiary force to be furnished to our allies. The chief doubt I may entertain in that respect, arises from the great force to be kept up in the vizier's country, according to the arrangements you are making with him. But on the other hand, if there is a large force in the vizier's country, there seems from thence fair grounds to conclude that it is so much a security for our own Bengal territories as to render so large a separate force unnecessary in those territories. But be that as it may, I take it for granted, that the whole of the great additional force to be kept in the vizier's country is to be paid by an additional subsidy from him, so that at no rate our own military expense will be increased from that arrangement. On the contrary, it gives me confidence in hoping that the reduction proposed in our own expense and establishment may be done with the greatest safety. I likewise flatter myself that the great force to be kept in the vizier's country will give occupation to all our officers who otherwise, by being reduced and supernumerary, might bring a considerable expense upon us.

I remain, . . .

HENRY DUNDAS

LXXXVIII
The Rt Hon. Henry Dundas to the Marquis Wellesley

15 July 1800, Wimbledon
Private: no. 29

In my other letter of this date, I have mentioned to you my idea of reducing totally the Company's European infantry. It would certainly be a great saving and a great improvement in our force. At the same time, you are aware, that it has always been a sore point in Leadenhall Street, and they will endeavour to resist it; but I dare say I shall prevail. The point they will take up is, that I am reducing their European infantry at the same time that I am proposing to keep up a King's force exceeding the limitation of the acts of Parliament, which restricts the King's force to between ten and eleven thousand. It is not true that the acts limit the *number*, but they only limit what is to be *paid* from the revenues of India, and, therefore, if the point is started, it is easily obviated by keeping the supernumerary King's force either in Ceylon, to be paid from the revenues of that island, or in the vizier's country, to be paid out of the Oudh revenues. I thought it right to mention this to you, and at the same time to add, that, if more than fourteen European regiments of infantry are requisite, on account of the force to be kept up and paid in Oudh, it would lead to not bringing home the three King's regiments mentioned in my other letter.

I remain, . . .

HENRY DUNDAS

PS. I send you an extract of a letter I have received a few days ago from Lord Clive, which will show you how much his ideas of the military force of the Madras Presidency exceeds all ideas I have on the subject. General Harris is arrived, but I have not seen him yet.

LXXXIX

The Marquis Wellesley to the Rt Hon. Henry Dundas

10 August 1800, Fort William
Secret and Confidential: Unnumbered

My dear Sir

You will be glad to learn by this letter, that my health is nearly recovered from the shock it had received. The nature of my illness is not reckoned by the physicians to have been at all serious or dangerous, or to indicate that the climate of India has produced any alarming effect on my constitution.

I have received letters from my brother Henry, dated on the 12th of March, by which I was highly gratified to find, that you had given so much time to him, and that you were determined to adopt the leading measures which I have recommended for the improvement of the gov[ernment] of India. Your early attention to my suggestions, and your uniform kindness and zealous support, require that I should employ every exertion both of mind and body to secure and improve the interests of which I received the charge, as a sacred trust of honour and friendship from you. I am, therefore,

281

determined to remain in India as long as it shall be possible for me to discharge the duties of my station with any degree of benefit to the public; and I am even resolved to sacrifice every personal feeling, and to expose my health and even my life, if requisite, rather than subject you to any embarrassment by a premature resignation. It will, however, be advisable that you should name Lord Clive, or General Lake, if he should be appointed commander-in-chief, to be my provisional successor in the event of any accident.

My *Irish* honours have produced precisely the effect which I expected. I wish Pitt would relieve me from my disgrace (for such it is in effect), but whatever he may do, you may be assured, that I will not fail in my duty, while I retain the power of discharging it. The grant of money from the Company, if connected in any degree with the prize taken at Seringapatam, will distress me exceedingly. Surely it would not be difficult to relieve me from this distress also. Will it not be a cruel turn of fortune, that my rewards both from the Crown and the Company should have been so formed as to degrade my personal consideration in India?

I bespeak your most cordial support to my college at Fort William, an institution from which I expect to derive the greatest advantages to the general administration of the affairs of this empire, especially in the judicial branch. Without some institution *in India* of the nature founded by my late law, I have no hesitation in saying, that the whole of Lord Cornwallis' admirable and benevolent system must have dissolved in the insufficiency of the instruments employed to administer its benefits to the native subjects of the British government in India.

I refer you on all other points, relating to the actual state of affairs in this quarter, to the dispatches which accompany this letter.

Believe me, . . .

WELLESLEY

XC

The Marquis Wellesley to the Rt Hon. Henry Dundas

18 August 1800, Fort William
Secret and Confidential: no. 13

My dear Sir

I enclose a copy of my letter to the chairman on the subject of the foundation of a college at Fort William. It is unnecessary to recommend such an institution to your support.

The principal object of this dispatch is to request your assistance in filling some of the professorships. The annexed memorandum (A)[1] will explain to you my intentions, and will enable you to make proposals to the persons in my contemplation, if you should approve them.

The professorships of English law, ethics, civil jurisprudence, and the law of nations, might be advantageously united. This professorship, with its necessary reference to the Mohammedan and Hindu codes, and to the laws enacted by the governor-general in council, would form the fundamental part of the course of study applicable to the administration of these governments. It is, therefore, the most important of all the professorships in my college; and I am anxious to fill it respectably and efficiently. The name of Mr Mackintosh (author of *Vindiciae Gallicae*) must be familiar to you. He was a follower of the false principles of the French revolution; but I understand that the natural vigour of his own mind, and the experience of the last three or four years, have restored him to a just sense of the sound principles of government. I have seen a plan of lectures which he had commenced in London, drawn with a most correct and able hand. If his conversion be sincere, I am inclined to think that he would suit my purposes, and those of this empire, admirably in this professorship; and accordingly (if you should concur with me) I request you to offer it to him, on the terms stated in the memorandum. If he should accept, embark him as soon as you can. Whether he finds me, or Lord Clive, or anybody else here, I will ensure him an honourable reception.

I wish you to press Rennel to accept the professorship of geography. His coming to Bengal only for two or three years would give great alacrity to the institution, as he is a man of general knowledge, and zeal for its extension. He has a son here, who requires his attention. I would willingly give Rennel the full pension at the end of three, or even two, years, merely with a view to the brilliant opening of my plan.

The professorship of the history and antiquities of Hindustan and the Deccan, I request you to offer to Mr Maurice, who has distinguished himself by many valuable works on these subjects. If Mr Charles Grant should come to India, I shall request him to undertake the branch of political economy, *etc.*

I know you will feel a pleasure in forwarding the object which I have in view, and I therefore trouble you with these commissions.

Believe me, . . .

WELLESLEY

[1] S.R.O. GD. 51/3/2/39.

XCI

The Marquis Wellesley to the Rt Hon. Henry Dundas

22 August 1800, Fort William
Secret and Confidential: no. 14

My dear Sir

At Lord Clive's desire, I transmit to you the enclosures of this dispatch, which will serve to explain his private letters to you nos. 14 and 15, dated 30th of June and 1st of August.

A motive of extreme delicacy towards my secret correspondence with his Lordship was the cause which prevented him from, either communicating to you, or referring to the dispatch, which forms the enclosure of this letter, without my express authority.

Believe me, . . .

WELLESLEY

XCII

The Rt Hon. Henry Dundas to the Marquis Wellesley

4 September 1800, Cheltenham
Private: no. 30

My dear Lord

I have recently received three letters from you. I received the duplicate of *no. 25*, dated 5th March, about a month ago, and the other two, dated the 25th and 27th January *unnumbered*, have reached me here two days ago. Your brothers Gerald[1] and Henry are with me at present, the latter on his way to India. We agreed that he should stop here for a few days in order that we might have our last unreserved conversation immediately before his departure. This letter, therefore, you will consider rather as a catalogue of memorandums on subjects whereon he is in possession of all my sentiments, and will detail them where necessary more at large. At the same time, I mean it should be an answer to every point that requires one previous to the date of it.

[1] Rev. Hon. Gerald Wellesley; 3rd son.

Egypt

We stand in an awkward predicament with regard to that business. Under an anxiety that the French should not send back their Egyptian army to take part against our allies on the Continent, we did not take advantage of the moment when we might have got them out of the country.[1] I was in Scotland at the time the resolution was taken. I have always doubted the wisdom of it, and, if we get into negotiation, the evacuation of Egypt will be the great stumbling-block. If the war continues another year, I rather think it ought to be the primary object of our share in the war, and I agree with you that co-operation from India can only be of material avail in the event of our acting vigorously from the Mediterranean.

Goa and Diu

The copy of my letter to Lord Grenville, wrote to Lord Grenville since I came here, and to be communicated to you by your brother, will show you how that business stands.[2]

Loans in India

I have explained myself fully in that subject to your brother in many conversations, and he will communicate to you some ideas which I have communicated to Mr Pitt. I am very sanguine on the subject, and I was happy to find that Mr Pitt was no ways alarmed at the idea, but as it is not yet matured, nor the finances of India in a state as yet to render my plan a completed one, I mean not to say anything of it as yet. I am anxious above all other things speedily to reduce the debt. Unless that is done, I am sure we shall find ourselves, in the event of another storm from any quarter bursting out in that country, unable to sustain our credit, and if we are ever obliged to have recourse to the public treasury to maintain a conflict in India, India will then lose much of its glory, and half of its estimation in the general feelings of the public here. I have given your brother a copy of a letter I lately wrote to the chairman on that subject, and on the subject of their military establishments.[3] From the perusal of them, you will perceive how much I am impressed with the importance of reducing our debt. Since I came here, I have received a letter from the chairman, begging my permission not to make any use of those papers till he and the deputy have an opportunity of conversing with me again. They are afraid to bring forward the subject of reducing their European infantry, as it is a sore point with the court of directors and proprietors, and if, upon further conversation with them, I find that it is likely to bring on any quarrel with the

---

[1] He is referring to the British refusal, on 28 March 1800, to carry out the convention of el Arish (24 January 1800) for the evacuation of Egypt.
[2] *Dropmore*, vi, 312.
[3] Dated 21 August 1800. Add. MSS. 37275, f. 168.

court, or to lose the authority of the chairs with the court, I shall not think the point worth contending for at that expense. In like manner, if they shall be able to satisfy me, that adopting my proposed dispatch relative to the reduction of the debt is likely to affect their investment too abruptly, it may admit of some modification; but on the general principles of the dispatches I shall remain very inflexible, and make them trust more for their investment by provisions to be made for it at home, in place of exhausting without mercy their credit in India. In the meantime, however, you will consider the papers I send you merely as private sentiments of my own, and not as official papers which have as yet been before the court, far less as what has received their sanction.

Private Trade

I suppose you received the copy of a letter I wrote to the chairman on that subject in the month of April last. It produced a very long and elaborate paper from Charles Grant full of useful information. Agreeing with him in most particulars, but not seeing some of his doubts as strongly as he did, I wrote him a letter with my observations on his paper. If these papers are copied and sent here to me before your brother leaves me, I will send them with him. If they do not arrive before his departure, I will send them by the first sea conveyance. They are much too bulky for a land dispatch.

Bullion to China through India

That subject is under the consideration of the court of directors, and if upon mature consideration they are fully satisfied, that there is no danger from it of any interruption to the certainty of their China investment to its full extent, they cannot have a doubt of the propriety of adopting your suggestions.

Europeans to be Sent Home

It did not occur to me, and I have not the acts of Parliament here to refer to, that your power of sending home Europeans of every description was not as ample as you could wish, but I shall take care that these laws be carefully revised, and, if there is any material defect in them, it ought to be corrected; for my ideas on that subject, and the danger of indiscriminate residence of Europeans in India, are as strong as you can figure or desire.

Sudder Dewany and Nizamut Adaulat

Upon your statement of the benefits to be derived from the proposed institution, I must be disposed to think well of it, but there is no forming a decisive judgement without seeing the plan more in detail, and in the present moment, I am sorry to add, we must look accurately to expense.

Colleges

I confess I have considerable doubts about this suggestion. The court of directors ought to be attentive, and I trust they are daily becoming more sensible of inquiring into the education of the young gentlemen whom they send out as writers. The knowledge of the Persian, to a very considerable degree, is to be got in this country, and, if the directors will only resolve that such acquisition of languages is essential to their being appointed, the parents and friends would feel the necessity of attending to so essential a requisite. With the exception of languages, and such other acquirements as young men of education generally receive before they arrive at the age of nineteen, I doubt if any of the other accomplishments for Indian business are to be attained so well in any seminary of education, as by experience and that progressive knowledge of business which is only to be got on the spot. But I likewise confess to you, that my chief objection to such an establishment arises from a consideration of the danger attending the collection of literary and philosophical men, which would naturally be collected together in consequence of such an institution. I would not be surprised if it should ultimately resolve itself into a school of Jacobinism, in place of a seminary for education. I hate Jacobinism everywhere, as I know you do, but in India I should consider it as the Devil itself, and to be guarded against with equal assiduity.

Pensions to Civil Servants

I am aware of all you say on this subject, and that there is both policy and justice in extending the benevolence of the Company to worn-out servants, or even to those whose places might be better supplied by more able and efficient men. But I own I dread such a provision as an established system. The remedy may be occasionally interposed as the disease is discovered, but it must be done with a sparing hand, and not held out as a general expectation. For if it is, you may rest assured, it will before long degenerate into a system of profuse indulgence and extravagance on frivolous pretences, and bring on the finances of the Company an inordinate expense, without any adequate benefit resulting from it. These are the thoughts which have on the first consideration suggested themselves to me.

Power to Tax Calcutta

Till the receipt of your last letter, I had not fully understood what was the defect complained of, and, on that ground, I agreed to strike a clause out of the bill lately introduced, understanding that there were some doubts entertained as to the propriety of the provision, and not choosing on that account at the close of the session to endanger the other parts of the bill. I shall now cause the subject to be more closely investigated, and apply a remedy if necessary.

Permanent System of Land and Judicature at Madras
Very great doubts were entertained on this subject in Leadenhall Street, and on the first consideration of it, I was staggered at the idea of allowing the subject to get totally out of our hands, without the power of any final control or correction, but I resolved to spend some days in going through the voluminous collection of papers that had come home on the subject, and particularly the very able and luminous report prepared by the board of revenue at Madras; and I became perfectly satisfied, that no substantial benefit could arise from the delay of waiting for final approbation from home, and that much mischief might arise from it, if it was to create any idea of distrust in the natives with whom we were to treat. I accordingly put my ideas into the shape of a dispatch, and sent them to the chairman the day before I came here, in order that he might in that shape bring it before the direction. If the copy of that draft comes here before your brother leaves me, I will send it to you by him. I trust the same opportunity will be taken to put the allowances of the revenue servants at Madras on a compatible footing; and when I cast my eyes on the past labours of such men as Mr White, Mr Cockburn, Mr Harington, Mr Kindersley, and some others, I think they will meet with injustice, if, in providing more liberally for future servants, no retrospective attention is paid to the past exertions of such meritorious servants as those I have named. Don't believe your brother Henry, if he should tell you that Mrs White's eyes, which I saw at the well this morning, have any influence in the suggestion I am now offering.

Double Government in the Carnatic
This has long been a distressing subject, but my mind is now completely made up upon it. Indeed, the dispatch approving your taking the most vigorous measures would have gone by the present conveyance, but when I left town the ship which contains the proof of his (the nabob's) treachery had not arrived, and altho[ugh] the statement made up by Mr Edmonstone, and transmitted in your overland dispatch, is very satisfactory, it is better on such a delicate subject to be able to give the final orders after a complete examination of all the materials. I am surprised the chairman has not sent them down to me, if they are arrived, for your brother, who came from town later than me, tells me the chairman had expressed to him great anxiety that I should send out orders upon the subject as quickly as

288

possible. If the papers come within a day or two, I shall draw the dispatch here, and send it up to be forwarded through the secret committee, which is the proper channel for such a dispatch.

Supreme Court at Calcutta and Recorder's Court at Madras

I am much obliged to you for the candid exposition you have given me of the grounds of your difference in opinion with me on the subject of the supreme court at Calcutta, and which I am aware applies equally to the recorder's and new judicature introduced at Madras by the late act. It may very probably be, that my opinions are biased by ancient prejudices, but having been an eyewitness of all the controversies which took place in Parliament near twenty years ago on the subject of the Royal court at Calcutta, and having seen every man without exception, who either was corrupted by Indian rapacity, or suspected of being so, united together in one confederacy to destroy the credit and existence of that court, I could not resist the conclusion naturally resulting from such a combination, that they did not feel the institution favourable to the continuance of those evils, which that institution was calculated, or at least intended, to correct. And the only return I can make to your candour on the present occasion is to state to you, that I am by no means satisfied by your reasoning that your judgement is correct on this subject. I am the more encouraged to adhere to my own opinion by observing, that you seem to rely to a considerable degree on the expectation and opinion that prosecutions at home will be more effective for the punishment of Indian delinquents than prosecutions carried on upon the spot. Unfortunately, every day tends more and more to convince me, that, if we trust to prosecutions at home, where the distance from the scene of action and the seat of evidence gives such advantages to those who wish to procrastinate, we will be foiled at least nine times out of ten in bringing the most notorious delinquents to punishment. Witness the case of Mr Holland from Madras, who, having settled with his infamous fortune abroad, is laughing at our prosecution. But it does not require actual proofs of my opinion. It is apparent, from the circumstances which I have already referred to, joined to the delays and shields which the forms of law have interposed for the protection of innocence, but of which guilt must likewise have the benefit, that a prosecution in England, for an offence committed in India, must in general be unsuccessful, and even where it happens to be otherwise, the punishment must come so long after the offence as to lose half its effect. Under the impression of those opinions, you will naturally suppose that I must be very unwilling to subscribe to the reasoning you have laid before me, for I am afraid, if it is well founded, and that likewise my opinions are so, the only practical conclusion to be drawn from such premisses is, that Indian delinquents must be exempt from all prosecution, because a competent court cannot be found for trial of them. I shall struggle hard and make many experiments before I shall sit down quietly under such an opinion, and when I look around to the state of jurisdiction in every country and part of the world where any happiness exists, we shall find the principle recognized and acted upon, that there should exist a judicature for the administration of justice independent of the executive government of the country. This was the principle on which the supreme judicature was established, and it is difficult to figure a country which in a manner more peculiar than any other calls for such an institution. The executive government must, from the nature of our connection, be vested in a few strangers over vast numbers of natives. Should it not be a solecism in such government, if you was not to present to them a judicature so constituted as to inspire them with a confidence that, if they met with oppression or injustice, from any of the subaltern instruments of the government which has started up in the country (for in that light they must naturally look upon every European in India), the same country which planted those Europeans has provided a suitable redress and recompense for such evils by an uncorrupt tribunal, to which they have immediate and ready access. I say *incorrupt* for I must assume that supposition in my argument; for if, either in the first foundation of the judicature, or in the selection of judges to fill it, there has been either negligence or abuse, these are no objections to the institution, however much they may justly merit attention on the part of those now entrusted with the government of India, either at home or abroad. I confess to you, that I cannot see the ground of giving so much just praise to the system of native judicature, in the separation of the functions of collectors and judges in the provincial courts, unless upon the very principles which convince me that there would be a manifest defect in our system of Indian government, if there was not a supreme judicature held out to the country, to which every European was amenable, if the natives conceived themselves aggrieved by them.

Viewing the supreme court in this light, I must likewise remain unconvinced by your statement that Indian delinquencies may be more effectually prosecuted in Britain than in India. I am sure, so far as example is of use, one promptly made on the spot must operate tenfold to one at a distance and after long delay. When to this you join the comparative facility of finding and bringing forward the evidence and supplying any defects of it in the course of the prosecution, I cannot easily satisfy myself, that, upon a review of your opinion, you will not concur with me in thinking, that the only real chance of obtaining justice against Indian delinquency, is by a speedy and zealous exertion of the talents of the servants in the law department, acting under the authority and support of the government in the conduct of prosecutions. And it does not seem to me, there is any rational ground for concluding, that the supreme court of judicature is not a competent and efficient judicature to sit in judgement on such prosecutions.

You mention that the supreme judicature has no power of distributing rewards. Neither ought they to have any such power. They ought not to have any means of either rewarding or punishing, except such punishments as belong to them ministerially to inflict, as the chosen instruments for the execution of the law.

Not having before me the acts of Parliament, I do not accurately recollect what are the powers, or the extent of them, in which it may be supposed that even the government-general may be personally implicated. I agree with you, that the authority of the governor-general ought to be paramount to every other whatever in the country, and in truth responsible solely at home for the abuse of his power, and if there is anything in the acts of Parliament that encroaches upon that principle, I think it is wrong, and I certainly should not have put such provisions in the act, if I had been the author of it. If, however, they are there, and have not been attended with any *practical* inconvenience, it may be matter for the exercise of sound discretion how far it would be wise to start such delicate questions of government merely as a theory, unless some real inconvenience, either had arisen, or was likely to arise from the law as it presently stands in the dead letter of it. I am sure you will agree with me in thinking, that any loose or idle discourse, which may have been reported to have dropped from the mouth of any chief justice, would not be ground sufficient to proceed upon for so important a consideration.

As everything I have said respecting the court of judicature at Calcutta applies equally to the presidency of Madras, you will not be surprised, that partly on my own judgement, and partly on the recent investigation of the government under Lord Hobart, I thought it proper to establish a Royal court at that settlement; and it gave me infinite satisfaction to hear from the mouth of Mr Kindersley (one of our most respectable servants from Madras) a few days ago, that the recorder's court at Madras, and the administration of it under Sir Thomas Strange, had been esteemed one of the greatest blessings that could be conferred upon the settlement. I trust they will have more ground to think so, now that I have relieved it from the mayor's court and put it entirely on the footing of the court at Calcutta. I am not sure if I fully comprehend what you say as to the mischief created by the protection which these courts of law give to the residence of many of your worst subjects in India. I don't recollect anything, either in the acts of Parliament, or the charters of justice, which enable them to afford any such protection. If there is, I am sure it should not be there, and I shall cause the whole to be examined with that particular view. When a person is licensed to act as a barrister or solicitor at law, his license is a valid authority so to practise, but it is incompatible with any idea of authority in government, that such license should be held a protection against any exercise of the functions of executive government.

I have troubled you at some length on this head, because, it being the only subject so far as I recollect on which we have very materially differed, I owed it to you, on every principle of the connection which subsists between us, to put you in possession of the grounds of my opinion upon it.

Nabob [of Arcot] and Rajah of Tanjore's Debts

I approve very much of all you have said and done on this subject. Mr Fordyce, as agent for the creditors, has wrote to the directors making a proposal founded on the letter which you wrote on that subject. I herewith send you a copy of that proposition. I don't know if it has come under the consideration of the court, but I have had some conversation with the chairman and deputy upon it, and their chief difficulty seems to be a doubt, how far you have not estimated at too low a state the amount of the debt still due by the nabob to the Company. But if that turns out to be the case, it does not vary the principle, and I dare say when it is seriously taken up and decided upon, it will be arranged in the principles you have chalked out. It is perfectly clear, that if we in any shape take the nabob's country into our own hands, it must be with such a due attention to the interests both of his family, and those who have just claims upon him.

The Coast of Malabar and Canara

In consequence of your opinion concurring entirely with my own as to the propriety of joining the new conquests to the Fort St George presidency, I made Parliamentary provision to enable the court of directors to make the arrangement. They have it under consideration, and it will require a good deal of detail, principally on account of the condition of the servants to be removed from the one settlement to the other. It would have been more economical to have reduced Bombay to a residency, but the suggestion of it seemed to give great alarm to all those who are either directly or indirectly interested in the large property vested at Bombay. If the court of directors participate in that sentiment, or the measure of annihilating the government at Bombay is found to be unpalatable, I don't mean to push that point, and in that case Bombay, with all to the northward of it, will remain a settlement by itself, and regulated according to the nature and extent of its government and resources. But all to the southward, including the Canara country and the Malabar Coast, must be united with the presidency of Fort St George.

Overland Dispatches and Sea Packets

The monthly overland dispatches are pretty well established. The directors complain loudly of the expenses of frequent packets, but, if by the means you suggest that objection can be removed, I dare say every other objection will be done away, and I shall, the first convenient moment, turn my attention to it.

Tax upon Income
I think your objections to a tax upon income as applicable to India are unanswerable, but, from the Parliamentary notice taken of the contributions from India, you will be satisfied, that due value was placed upon their public-spirited exertions in the cause of the parent state.

I think to the best of my recollection, I have adverted to every particular that might seem to require an answer in your long letter of the 5th March [*no. 25*], which I received first. The others, of the 25th and 27th January (which I have only received within these last few days since I came to this place), I shall advert to tomorrow morning, and as your brother has received intimation of the *Georgiana* packet being ready for his reception at Plymouth, I shall endeavour to dispatch him by Sunday morning, and certainly not later than Monday.

6 September 1800, Cheltenham
I have, agreeably to my intention of yesterday, looked over carefully the contents of your letters of the 25th and 27th Jan[uary, *unnumbered*], and in so far as these letters (which is the greatest part of them) go to a discussion of characters and persons, they require no other answer but that I have received your communications, and, if the occasions present themselves for doing so, I shall not be unmindful of the precautions you have suggested to me. Sir James Craig is a great favourite with very high authorities in this country, and it would have been very palatable to them, if I had made choice of him for the superior command in India. But the suggestion of your brother, confirmed to me by the authority of Lord Cornwallis, decided me to recommend General Lake, who accordingly is appointed, and sails with the present fleet. I really believe Sir James to be a good officer, and from all I can learn correct in other respects, but I have heard so many doubts stated of his temper, I have not been able to get the better of the apprehensions resulting from that circumstance. It is unlucky that the vacancies at all the three presidencies have happened at the same time, for, if none of them are filled by the Company's officers, they will be apt to look upon it as a systematic proscription of them from such situations. That is very nearly a settled system; at the same time it is not one that can ever be avowed, and it is a great doubt with me at present whether it would not be right to appoint old Braithwaite to the command at Madras. General Stuart told me a few days before I left town, that altho[ugh] he was not

able to take an active command in the field, he doubted not to give his opinion, that in the regular details requisite in the command of an army, he would not be found inefficient. Unless he is fixed upon, I don't see I have any other choice but Sir James Craig.

Some of the general suggestions in your letters now before me, and in other parts of your correspondence, render it necessary, that I should bring under your consideration some topics which may not be familiar to your recollection *at a distance*, but as necessity and due attention to the character and stability of government at home render it essential that I should never lose sight of them *at home*, I must so far interfere between your suggestions and that consideration, as to warn you of the propriety of applying in a particular manner to the government of India the old maxim, *that we must look rather to what is practically best, than to what in theory we think so.* There is another principle equally true in government and in legislation, and essentially necessary to be attended to in the administration of great concerns. *We must legislate and regulate public affairs, not on the hypothesis that the instruments of government are always to be the ablest, the purest, and the best, of men, but we must take mankind according the general run of human nature, some better some worse, some able some less able,* and we must recollect, that in the general currency of human affairs the rulers and governors of India, like all other public men, must occasionally be selected from the heterogeneous mass of which the world consists.

If we could suppose, that the governor-general of India was always to be a perfect being, whom no provocations could ruffle, whom no power could intoxicate, and whose mind was proof against both the open attacks and the more concealed approaches of intrigue, ambition, avarice, and every other bane of good government, we might with great tranquillity acquiesce in any idea of despotism and unlimited power that any man could suggest; and, however paradoxical it may appear to be, I have no hesitation in saying, that the best men would be the most likely to suggest such an unlimited form of government in India, because they would do it under a consciousness that they meant to make the best possible use of the power so possessed. But then it must immediately occur that the successor of the same virtuous governor might be a person of a different complexion of character, to whom controls and restraints were necessary to be applied, in order to preserve him from deviating into a crooked, corrupt, or feeble, system of administration. The conclusion I wish to impress upon your mind from this reasoning is, that altho[ugh] unlimited powers might at times enable a good governor-general to do unlimited good, the same powers would enable a bad governor-general to do unlimited mischief, and would, in the hands of a feeble governor-general, enable him to allow the whole functions of government to fall asleep. I remember well, during the first five years after the establishment of the board of control, I fancied often to myself, that if I was relieved from the trammels, the vexation, and altercation, necessarily at first resulting from the nature of the new institution, I would be able to act with more energy and to do good with more rapidity. This, however, was but a theory. The pause sometimes essential in great measures, and the reconsideration which opposition and difference of opinion often produced, tended greatly to mature business in its progress, and to ascertain with precision that propositions were not rashly and prematurely adopted. In support of what I am now saying, I could even refer to the turbulent and factious government which prevailed in India, when Clavering, Monson, and Francis,[1] were sent out from this country to check Mr Hastings. The acrimonious discussions which took place at that time may even now be resorted to with much utility, as containing elaborate and able reasoning on all the great subjects of Indian policy. I admit that these altercations went to a degree of personal animosity incompatible with the conduct of anything resembling government, but I do conceive, that the very great and independent powers which have since been conferred on the governor-general, were intended and do in fact operate as a very substantial remedy to that mischief.

Allow me further on this subject, my dear Lord, to remind you, that the present government was formed on the basis of maintaining that the administration of our Indian affairs was capable of being carried on without annihilating the form of its government through the medium of its ancient channel the East India Co[mpany]. In the maintenance of that conflict, we were supported by the East India Co[mpany], who cordially concurred in the control that was established over them; we were supported by the independent voice of the country; and we have had the satisfaction of perceiving, that under a system so framed, our Indian affairs have been brought to a degree of prosperity beyond our most sanguine expectations. It cannot fail to occur to you, that almost all the suggestions of change which you have transmitted are founded upon an enlargement of the direct power and patronage of the Crown, and a proportionate diminution of the importance of the East India Co[mpany] and all their servants. I dispute not the plausibility, or, if you please, even the justice of your theories, but depend upon it, the experiment would be a dangerous one, and the risk resulting from it would far outbalance any good that may be imagined to flow from it.

I believe in the course of this letter, I have exhausted all the topics of importance noted in the memorandum enclosed in your letter of the 25th January. A very few at least remain.

---

[1] Gen. Sir John Clavering, Col. George Monson, and Sir Philip Francis, were named supreme councillors in the Regulating Act of 1773.

New Council

Your brother will explain to you the steps taken with that view, and I am not without hopes that Mr Charles Grant and Mr Barlow will soon become your coadjutors. I send you a copy of a letter I have received from Mr Grant on the subject since I came here.

King's Fleet and Army

The Royal commission which goes out to you is the utmost length I can propose to the King [as] an authority in the governor-general over his army,[1] and to obtain any direct authority from the admiralty over the fleet is so impossible as to be idle to attempt it. The utmost that can be hoped for is pointed instructions to co-operate in their proceedings with the supreme civil government of the country.

Resident at Hyderabad a Baronet

I think this should be done, and, since you press so much, I will urge it. I have explained myself at full length to your brother on the subject of honours and rewards, all of which he will communicate to you.

Royal Correspondence with the Nabob [of Arcot]

I agree with you perfectly on this subject. I have kept very much aloof from it, because if I was supposed to know anything about it, I must have taken some strong step upon it. I hope the nabob will soon be put into a state to render his correspondence a matter of very little moment, but I think I may in the meantime take some way of conveying your sentiments to the proper quarters as to the mischievous consequences of it. I know not what you mean by the letter you write about as having gone through the government of Bombay to the peshwa. I recollect some complimentary letter coming to the King through Sir Charles Malet, and I think after too long a delay some answer was wrote to it, but what the answer was I really cannot recollect. I am sure it could contain nothing of any moment, otherwise I would have sent you a copy of it. But I really cannot attach to Governor Duncan the blame which you do, and I don't think his nerves are of a nature to require too much to be checked.

I remain, . . .

HENRY DUNDAS

[1] *Wellesley*, ii, 466.

XCIII

The Rt Hon. Henry Dundas to the Marquis Wellesley

11 September 1800, Cheltenham
Private: no. 31

My dear Lord

I write you these few lines in addition to the long letter you will receive from your brother, chiefly with the view of stating to you the very sincere satisfaction I have received from the various communications and interviews I have had with your brother during the time he has been in this country.[1] I am aware that he has been detained much longer than you expected, but it has been unavoidable. The various interruptions our communications have met with, partly from the multitude and variety of great objects which have pressed for these twelve months past on the time of all public men, and partly from the tardiness which attends all proceedings in which great bodies of men are sharers, has been the cause of much more procrastination than I expected, and certainly much more than I wished. But to return for one sentence more to the subject of your brother, I cannot allow myself to part with him without assuring you, that in the course of my life I never met with any person with whom I have had more satisfaction in transacting business than with him. He joins together one of the most amiable tempers to one of the soundest judgements I ever met with, and I trust opportunities will occur to enable him to prove to the world that my judgement of him is not erroneous.

Within these two days, we have been joined here by General Stuart, and latterly by Mr Myers. I have had conversation with both of them. In the course of the one with General Stuart, I have derived considerable satisfaction from the hopes that his health is getting so rapidly restored as to make me believe that, by accepting the chief command at Madras, he will relieve me from the embarrassments I have stated in my letter.

Mr Myers is the distinct and intelligent man you represent him, and I will often have occasion to resort to him on the subject of finance. He was not able to give me any hopes of any such surplus as will operate on the reduction of our large Indian debt. That, however, is an object so deeply and impressively rooted in my mind in all my future prospects of security in India, I can never allow myself to lose sight of it.

When I return to town, I shall immediately resume the subject of your

---

[1] Grenville thought sending Henry was unnecessary. He remarked that he did not 'imagine he has brought any other ideas than those of the Mysore conquest, which I presume are more, and probably better detailed in Wellesley's own dispatches'. Buckingham, iii, 57.

military establishments with the chairman and deputy. If it should end, as is likely, in their not being able to persuade their colleagues to depart from their absurd notions about a European infantry of the Company in India, still it will not alter the extent of the King's infantry which I have stated in my letter to them. It may alter the distribution somewhat, and my opinion is that they should collect all their European infantry at one settlement, probably Bengal, and then the King's regiments would be distributed, seven under the Madras government, five of the King's and the Company's whole European infantry at Bengal, and two King's at Bombay. I propose three of the King's regiments for Ceylon. After this appropriation, there will remain still two of the King's regiments in India. These two will be to be brought home, or to be stationed and paid for in the vizier's country; and I have only to suggest for your consideration, that, if the Company will be obstinate in maintaining their European infantry, you will at least take care that the whole European force placed in the vizier's country shall be King's troops, and if, for that purpose, or for the stations of Goa and Diu, any more European troops are necessary, more King's infantry will be sent from this country. Altho[ugh] these are mere outlines of what is now floating in my mind, I thought it right in this manner to put you in possession of them, before you hear the final result of further consideration in an official form.

I have wrote a private letter to Mr North to inform him of what is nearly decided in my mind. I mean to take the government of Ceylon again into the King's hands, and separate it from the government of the Company. The junction has done no good, and a good deal of mischief. I would have carried this idea immediately into effect, if I did not think that we were tending fast to negotiations for peace, and, if that should be the case, there would be an absurdity in making a new arrangement of a country when entering upon a negotiation, one of the essential points of which would be whether we are to keep it or not. You will not suppose from my saying this, that I entertain any doubts what ought to be the result of any negotiation on that subject, but still I will not expose myself to the ridicule which would attend any new arrangement of the government of Ceylon, made at a time when there might be at least a chance of others differing with me on that point.

We separate today. Your brother sets out for Plymouth, where the *Georgiana* packet waits for him.

I remain, . . .

HENRY DUNDAS

XCIV

The Rt Hon. Henry Dundas to the Marquis Wellesley

25 September 1800, Wimbledon
Private: [*Separate*]

My dear Lord

I last night received your Lordship's *most private* letter of the 29th April last. I need not enter into any detailed observations on the contents of it, as your Lordship is already prepared for my feelings on the receipt of what I wrote to you on the 11th July in answer to a former letter. I pass over altogether the grounds of discontent with which you are impressed, and which you describe as generally felt in India. I should, however, be un-candid, if I was to mislead you so far as to flatter you with an idea that any such feeling exists in this country, as that your Lordship's services had not been duly felt and acknowledged. It was not, however, to dwell on that topic, or combat your sentiments upon it, that I took my pen. You have wrote to Mr Pitt on the subject, and, if there is to be any further discussion upon it, it can only be with his Majesty, or those who advise him on the distribution of honours. It is the public interest connected with the depart-ment over which I preside, that I must particularly attend to, and I have lived too long in the world not to know, that, be the cause what it may, no person in a state of mind discontented with his situation, can discharge long the duties of it with energy, and therefore I do not press you to resist the inclination you feel to return to Great Britain. At the same time, I have a perfect confidence that after what I have stated to you in my former letter, you will not abruptly leave your situation, without giving me a reasonable time to make some proper arrangement. In that respect, I am even more embarrassed than I was when I wrote to you in July last. Some proceedings have lately taken place, and are now under consideration, pointing to negotiation between this country and France.[1] If these negotiations end in peace within a few months, and the peace is such as to give me confidence in the security of India, there will remain no public reason why I may not follow out the intention stated in my former letter of proceeding to India, and, however distressing the resolution may be on account of some private and domestic considerations, these cannot on such an occasion be allowed to operate. If peace does not take place, or is concluded on terms that would in my judgement render my administration of India a matter of little moment, which I would feel if the peace was an insecure one for that

---

[1] Dundas is referring to the project of a naval armistice, of which he strongly disapproved. S.R.O. GD. 51/1/548/6.

country, I shall then suggest some arrangement to the court of directors, the best that occurs at the moment. It is necessary that I should trouble you with this explanation, the result of which, however, amounts only to an expression of my confidence, that you will not leave India in such a manner as to deprive me of the power of making an arrangement, so as not to expose India to the inconvenience it always experiences under an interim administration, and I think that consideration of so much importance as to induce me to trouble you with this letter by an overland dispatch.

I remain, . . .

HENRY DUNDAS

XCV

The Marquis Wellesley to the Rt Hon. Henry Dundas

4 October 1800, Fort William
Secret and Confidential: Unnumbered

My dear Sir

Being apprised of your disposition to manifest every mark of respect and attention to Lord Bute's family, I think it necessary to inform you, that his Lordship's son, Lord Herbert Stuart,[1] applied to me some time ago for permission to resign the Company's service and to proceed to England on account of the bad state of his health. I could not refuse my assent to either of his Lordship's requests, and he accordingly returns home on board the *Princess Mary*.

It is not usual for me to enter into any explanation of my motives for withholding or granting promotion to any of the Company's servants subject to my authority. All such questions necessarily involve considerations of a complicated and delicate nature, which it would be always difficult, and sometimes impossible, to detail. The judgement of the public and of those authorities to which I am subject will be exercised on my conduct in the discharge of this, as of every other branch of my public duty. It would be an endless labour to attempt to meet every possible case of personal disappointment, or of individual expectation. My respect, however, for the high rank and birth of Lord H[erbert] Stuart induces me to transmit to you

[1] Hon. Herbert Stuart; assistant register, court of circuit and appeal, Calcutta, 1794–7; assistant to collector of Purnea, 1797–1800; register of the zillah adaulat, Murshedabad, 1800.

the enclosed letters, and to state to you the particular motives which have governed my conduct in his Lordship's case.

Under the peculiar circumstances which preceded Lord Herbert Stuart's appointment to the Company's service, and which were well known to me at the time of my departure from England, I should have deemed myself guilty of a gross violation of the arduous trust which I hold, if I had appointed his Lordship to any station of eminence in the Company's service, without having previously satisfied myself, that he was actually qualified to discharge the duties of such a station.

It was therefore my wish, as soon as the public business admitted, and a proper vacancy opened, to station his Lordship in the vicinity of the presidency, for the express purpose of ascertaining by personal knowledge, whether I should be justified in entrusting the interests and happiness of any portion of the Company's subjects to him.

Accordingly, on the first practicable occasion, I offered to him the first regular step of promotion towards the higher offices either of judicature or revenue, and I proposed to have placed him at Murshedabad, with immediate permission to proceed to the presidency, and to state his views and objects to me.

The office of register to one of the zillah courts is the first regular step towards a collection of revenue; and it is not dispensed with, except in cases of extraordinary merit, wherein the candidate for a collection, by some accidental circumstance, may already have been in the temporary charge of a collection, and may have had the opportunity of proving his qualifications for that office. This exception has applied to the case of Mr Ernst,[1] and of some others.

His Lordship declined the office to which I had appointed him, and stated his intention of proceeding without formal leave to Calcutta; conceiving himself to be no longer in office; and the official channels of communication with me to be closed by his refusal of the office to which he had been appointed. As he intimated in the same letter his intention of having a personal interview with me immediately upon his arrival at the presidency, I passed over without notice his Lordship's transgression of the established rules and discipline of the service, in relinquishing his station at Purnea without a regular permission from the governor-general in council.

When his Lordship arrived at Calcutta, I was confined to my room by a severe indisposition; but upon my recovery, I held several levées, and gave repeated private audiences, without having had the honour either of seeing his Lordship, or of hearing from him; nor was I apprised of his actual

---

[1] Thomas Henry Ernst; assistant to Persian translator, Bengali translator to board of revenue, Bengal, 1797–1800; collector of Midnapur, 1800–3.

arrival at Calcutta, until the secretary brought me his Lordship's public letter of resignation of the service.

His Lordship continued at Calcutta for several weeks, and although repeatedly pressed by his friends to apply for an audience from the governor-general, I am informed that he rejected their instances, being determined to quit India without seeing me. I refer you to the accompanying letters, and particularly to those of Mr Egerton,[1] a very worthy young man, in whose house his Lordship resided during his continuance at Calcutta.

You are at full liberty to communicate this letter, together with its enclosures, to Lord Bute, provided the communication shall be understood to be merely a matter of personal respect to his Lordship's high rank and honourable character.

In any other view, such a communication would be irregular and of dangerous precedent.

The distribution of the offices through which the government of this extensive empire is administered; the qualifications requisite for the due discharge of these various and arduous trusts; the rules of selection, applicable to the dispositions, talents, and acquisitions, of the numerous candidates for employment in India; constitute one of the most difficult and invidious branches of the governor-general's authority and duty.

To the court of directors, to the commissioners for the affairs of India, and to Parliament, I shall always be ready to submit myself for judgement on my conduct in the discharge of this great and sacred trust; but I do not hold myself answerable on any of these important questions to any individual, however exalted by rank or character; although my general desire of manifesting personal civility and consideration to those who deserve both, will render me at all times ready to afford any explanation tending to satisfy the anxiety of the respectable parents or connections of any public officer subject to my authority.

Believe me, . . .

WELLESLEY

Most Secret

There is one subject on which I am very anxious that you, and all my friends likely to have any influence in naming my successor, should be fully and seasonably apprised of my sentiments.

I understand that Lord Hobart is using every effort to secure the succession to me in this government, and has declared his determination never to be satisfied, until he shall have recovered his station in India, and been appointed governor-general.

---

[1] William Egerton; accountant to board of trade, Bengal, 1796–9; accountant, marine department, 1799–1800; deputy accountant-general, Bengal, 1800–3.

I must enter my protest against his appointment to succeed to me, and I ground my objections on reasons both of public expediency, and of private justice. Lord Hobart's temper, prejudices, and reputation in Bengal, disqualify him for this government. He will overturn the whole system of this establishment, and he never will be respected here. As far as he is capable of forming any regular plan, he appears to have formed one diametrically contradictory to mine in every respect. He will, therefore, overthrow all my institutions, and frustrate all my plans. He will be the more inclined to this violence from his natural temper, as displayed at Madras, and from his personal resentment against me, and his jealousy of my reputation. All the best men here dread the appointment of Lord Hobart, a few of the worst would rejoice at it. He now corresponds with the famous Mr Bristow, and with others whom I know to be adverse to me.

On private grounds, inseparably connected with those of a public nature, I think I may claim from the justice and merited gratitude of my country, that my most bitter and implacable enemy, whose hatred is derived from the consciousness of his own base ingratitude and flagrant injustice towards me, should not be my immediate successor. Either I am unfit for my office, or he cannot wreak his revenge on my memory without injury to the public service. If Lord Clive should not succeed me (of whose integrity, honour, and correct principles of Indian government, I entertain the highest opinion), I make it my earnest request to all my friends, as they tender the public interests and my honour, not to suffer Lord Hobart to be introduced into my place. I sincerely wish him success wherever he can be employed without hazard to the public. Whether my career in India should terminate by my return to Europe, or by my death, I rely on the justice and affection of my friends to keep this request in remembrance.

WELLESLEY

XCVI

The Marquis Wellesley to the Rt Hon. Henry Dundas

6 October 1800, Fort William
Private: no. 30

My dear Sir

It is my intention to dispatch the *Mornington* packet in late November, when I propose to reply regularly to your letters received by that ship, and to such as have since reached me. My official letters to the secret committee, and to the court, are so full on this occasion as to leave scarcely any point of importance for this letter.

I request your particular attention to the necessity of large and seasonable remittances of bullion to Bengal, to my plan for the provision of funds for the treasury at Canton, and to my orders relative to the private trade in ships built in India.

The deficiencies of the revenue collected on salt in Bengal may occasion alarm in England, but I trust that we shall be able to discover and correct the evil which has caused this temporary defalcation.

In all other branches, the state of the revenue is highly prosperous and flourishing.

Referring you to the letters to the court and committee, and to my intended dispatch by the *Mornington*.

I am, . . .

WELLESLEY

XCVII

The Marquis Wellesley to the Rt Hon. Henry Dundas

7 October 1800, Fort William
Secret and Confidential: Unnumbered

My dear Sir

I request your attention to my correspondence with Sir George Yonge,[1] transmitted by this occasion to the secret committee. My accounts from the Cape all concur in representing that government to be in a state of great confusion. The imbecility and ignorance of Sir George Yonge entirely disqualify him for his situation, which ought to be placed in hands of some degree of strength and skill. The importance of the Cape in its relation to India increases every hour; and the connection between the settlements becomes more intimate in every view of our military, political, and commercial, interests. If the war with France should continue, I trust you will in the next year, enable me to take the islands of [Ile de] France and Bourbon. This might, I believe, be effected at any time, by means of an addition of five or six thousand Europeans distributed between India and

---

[1] Sir George Yonge, Bart. (1731–1812); governor of the Cape of Good Hope, 1799–1801; recalled by Dundas to face an official inquiry.

the Cape. At present it is provoking to know, as I positively do, that if I could spare 3,000 Europeans from India, the fall of the Isle of France would be certain. But you are already apprised that I cannot venture to make such an attempt in the reduced state of our European force in India.[1] In the meanwhile the Isle of France covers our coasts with privateers, and infests every track of the trade of India.

Sir George Yonge is employed in founding theatres and masquerade rooms with an activity and zeal which would merit the laurel of the piazza, the lane, and the market. Heydegger was a Methodist compared to this exorbitant master of the revels. He dances with more perseverance and graceful gravity than Lord Keeper Hatton;[2] and the fame of his brawls has not only reached the kaffirs, and animated every kraal from the Cape to the desert of Sahara, but extended to the Indus and the Ganges. I tremble upon my musnud: I dread the conflict between the theatre at the Cape, and the college in Bengal. Without further metaphor, I really apprehend serious evil to the King's army and to our civil and military service here from the ridiculous and absurd encouragement extended with so much zeal at the Cape to the idle practice of acting, dancing, singing, and playing in public *under the immediate eye and sanction of the government.* The younger branches of the King's army, those of the Company's civil or military service who may touch at the Cape in the passage between India and England, or who may remain at the Cape for the recovery of their health, may be infected by the contagion of this dissipated example; and all the pains, which I have taken to lay the foundations of industry and activity in this empire, may be frustrated by the follies of my neighbours. I enclose an extract of a private letter from me to Mr Barnard, which will explain to you my ideas on this part of the subject.

On the whole, my opinion is, that the government of the Cape ought speedily to be placed in better hands, and that it ought to be rendered subordinate to the governor-general, or lord-lieutenant of India. Such an union would greatly invigorate the local administration in Africa; and in Asia, would afford the means of applying at all times the military and political resources of the Cape to the security of this empire; of regulating the commercial intercourse between Africa and Asia; and of combining their reciprocal commercial interests on those principles most beneficial to both settlements, and most safe to the Company's trade. The governor-general should have the power of visiting the Cape as he now possesses that

[1] In fact, Wellesley was preoccupied with the chance of negotiating a subsidiary alliance with the peshwa.

[2] Sir Christopher Hatton (1540–91); lord chancellor, 1587–91; famed for his dancing. Wellesley told Scott that Yonge 'was playing the fool founding theatres and masquerade houses, and violating your charter as if it were nothing better than an opera ticket'. Add. MSS. 27282, f. 186.

of visiting Fort St George or Bombay; neither his powers, nor his emoluments, nor his dignities, should cease until he shall quit Africa on his return to Europe. This arrangement would consolidate and concentre all our force and all our advantages of every description in Africa and Asia. It would be no inconsiderable encouragement to the governor-general or lord-lieutenant (in the hours of dejection, to which this climate occasionally subjects all European constitutions) to feel, that such a climate as the Cape was always within his reach, that he could there recruit his declining spirits and strength, not only without injury, but with benefit to the public service; that he might return to India with renewed alacrity and vigour; and that by these occasional visits to a better climate (within the reach of a voyage of six weeks) he might hope to be able to extend his administration in India to a period of time, which might admit of his becoming the witness on the spot to the success of his own plans and institutions, and of his bringing to some degree of perfection under his own immediate superintendence a uniform, consistent, and harmonious, system of government for the preservation of our extensive empire in India. If you concur with me in these sentiments, you will greatly relieve the anxiety of my mind, by extending my powers in the manner suggested. I apprehend that a mere order from the Crown would be sufficient to subject the government of the Cape to the government-general: but an act of Parliament would be requisite for the purpose of empowering the governor-general to repair to the Cape, and to exercise all his powers from thence, enjoying all his dignities and emoluments. A power should also be given to him of naming an acting governor-general in Bengal, subject, however, to the orders of the governor-general himself from the Cape. If you wish my administration of affairs in Asia to be prolonged, I know no circumstance so likely to enable and encourage me to hold my station, as the adoption of the plan which I now describe. In the meanwhile, I think you should not delay the change of government at the Cape; and you should call Barnard into some more forward station in the government. He is an honourable and industrious man. If you mean to act on my suggestion, I hope you will not delay it. The arrangement cannot operate on my intentions with respect to my continuance in India, unless adopted without a moment's delay after the receipt of this letter. It is probable that I shall pass the next year between Fort St George, Mysore, and Bombay, for the purpose of consolidating our new empire, and of uniting all its dispersed and disjointed parts; as well as of introducing the Bengal system of internal government. Oudh does not require my presence yet, nor can I accomplish any useful object by visiting Lucknow, until my plan of reform for the vizier's military establishments shall be absolutely completed. That period is not remote. In the meanwhile, the residency is in the hands of one of the most able, firm, intelligent, and honourable, men in India,[1] who adds to these great qualities a most ardent zeal, and a most enterprising spirit of just and rational ambition.

Believe me, . . .

WELLESLEY

XCVIII

The Rt Hon. Henry Dundas to the Marquis Wellesley

9 October 1800, Wimbledon
Private: no. 32

My dear Lord

I think it right to trouble you with these few lines to state to you, that although I remain satisfied of the necessity of reducing our military establishments in India the first moment we can, it will be impossible to do it at a time when we are making such great calls on our Indian force for Batavia [and] the Red Sea, and it is more than probable we shall not be able to do it while the war continues. I must, therefore, at present, content myself with urging the [Company] to find other means for providing their investment than loans in India, for we must at least take care not to allow our debt to increase, if we have not the means of diminishing it at the present moment.

I remain, . . .

HENRY DUNDAS

XCIX

The Marquis Wellesley to the Rt Hon. Henry Dundas

25 October 1800, Fort William
Private: no. 31 (Secret)

My dear Sir

The dispatches of the *Princess Mary* packet were finally closed on the 6th instant, and that vessel was on the point of sailing, when the appearance of the enemy's privateers at the mouth of the river, rendered it necessary to

[1] Lt-Col. William Scott; resident at Lucknow, 1799–1804.

postpone her departure, until a vessel could be armed to afford convoy to her and to the *Anna*.

The detention of the packet enables me to inform you, that on the 15th instant, I received the most alarming accounts from Basra and Constantinople of the progress of the French, both in Egypt and on the continent of Europe.[1]

The impression made on my mind by these accounts, and the measures which I have adopted in consequence of this unfortunate change in the state of affairs, will appear in the enclosed copies of my dispatches to Vice-Adm[iral] Rainier, Rear-Admiral Blankett, Vice-Admiral Sir Roger Curtis,[2] and Sir George Yonge.[3] It would occasion a considerable detention of the packet were I to delay her departure until I could add to these documents copies of the instructions which I have dispatched to the governments of Fort St George, Bombay, and Ceylon, in consequence of the plan of measures which I have framed with a view to meet the approaching exigency. The tenor of my letters to Admiral Rainier will afford you a sufficiently accurate knowledge of the general scope of those instructions.

The most pressing object of the present dispatch is to impress you with the urgent and indispensable necessity of augmenting without an hour's delay our European force in India to the extent demanded by the situation of this empire.

In my letter of the 13th July 1800 [*no. 28*], I represented to you in the most urgent and anxious terms the perilous weakness of the European force in India; and I earnestly entreated you to complete it with all practicable expedition to the extent of twenty-five efficient regiments of infantry and eight regiments of dragoons. If the war between Great Britain and France should continue, the late events in Europe and Egypt sufficiently indicate that the theatre of action must be transformed to India and Egypt. The necessity, therefore, of an early augmentation of the European army in India, to the extent proposed in my dispatch of the 13th of July, is not only become more urgent, but the increased probability of an active war in this quarter of the globe requires an augmentation beyond the amount proposed in that dispatch.

My immediate wish is, that you should complete the corps in India to the strength proposed in my dispatch of the 13th of July without delay, and at the same time that you should embark for the Cape of Good Hope as large a reinforcement as possible, instructing the government of the Cape to comply promptly with every requisition which I may at any time make for troops from that colony.

[1] Wellesley is referring to the Austro-French armistice at Alessandria.
[2] Vice-Adm. Sir Roger Curtis, Bart. (1746–1816); flag officer in command, Cape of Good Hope, 1800–3.
[3] *Wellesley*, ii, 399, 405, 406.

You will recollect, that in the event of my succeeding during the ensuing months of January or May in my design against the Mauritius, a considerable body of Europeans will be required to garrison that island. Such a deduction from the European force necessary for the protection of our Indian empire has not entered into any of the estimates which I have hitherto formed on this subject; and consequently the reinforcements to be sent to India should be calculated with a view to the probable additional demand of a strong garrison for the Isle of France, and of another for Batavia, since the reduction of Batavia would necessarily follow that of Mauritius. The garrison of Mauritius ought not to be less than two thousand Europeans, nor that of Batavia than one thousand.

An early and extensive augmentation both of our naval and military force in India is further necessary with a view to the conquest of the Philippine Islands, which certainly ought to be undertaken with the least possible delay, especially if the theatre of war should be likely to be transferred from Europe to this quarter of the globe. France is reported to have opened a negotiation with Spain a few years past, for the exchange of the Philippine Islands, and it may be reasonably supposed that she has not relinquished her views upon those valuable possessions, which, in the hands of the French, would prove the destruction of our trade with China. But even if this object should not be entertained, our naval force requires immediate augmentation, especially in the department of frigates. Without a considerable increase of the number of our frigates, the protection of the trade of India against privateers, or rather pirates, will become impracticable. The reduction of Mauritius would indeed destroy the present resort and haunt of the most formidable force of piracy in these seas; but other stations might possibly be substituted by the indefatigable activity and enterprise of French, American, Danish, and Irish, adventurers. The capture of the *Kent* will, I trust, induce Lord Spencer to condescend to pay some attention to my urgent entreaty, stated in a letter written to him soon after my arrival in India. In that letter, I declared my opinion, that an insult offered to the British flag at the mouth of the Ganges ought not to be felt with less indignation than an insult offered at the mouth of the Thames. In this sentiment, I know you will concur with me, but unless you act upon it with resolution and system, the audacity of the enemy will increase in the Indian seas, the confidence of our native subjects in our naval superiority will be extinguished, and the trade, both of individuals and of the Company, will be materially interrupted, if not seriously injured.

Believe me, . . .

WELLESLEY

C

The Marquis Wellesley to the Rt Hon. Henry Dundas

26 October 1800, Fort William
Private: no. 32

My dear Sir

I have the pleasure to congratulate you on the final conclusion of my treaty
with the nizam, of which the substance has already been communicated to
you. A copy of the treaty is forwarded from Captain Kirkpatrick overland
by this dispatch to the secret committee.[1] The treaty does not seem to
require much explanation; but I shall soon transmit a full discussion of its
principles and objects. The boundaries of our empire in the peninsula are
now, the Tungebadra, the Kistna, and the sea. I must repeat, in the most
earnest manner, my anxious recommendation of Captain Kirkpatrick for
some distinguished mark of his Majesty's favour.

Believe me, . . .

WELLESLEY

CI

The Marquis Wellesley to the Rt Hon. Henry Dundas

12 November 1800, Fort William
Private: [*Separate*] (*Secret*)

My dear Sir

Your *private and secret* letter of the 11th July 1800 reached me on the 5th
instant. The difficulty of the cypher which you employed, and in which my
secretary is not yet expert, has delayed my reply until this day. As you have
referred me, however, to my brother Henry, whose arrival may be soon
expected, I shall postpone any detailed answer to your letter, until he shall
arrive, contenting myself with a short statement of such considerations as I
judge necessary to bring before you without delay, for the purpose of
apprising you distinctly of my former and present intentions with respect
to my continuance in India.

My letter (*Secret and Confidential*, 9th March 1800) was written under

[1] *Wellesley, ii,* 709.

the first attack of sickness which I have felt in India; and although that attack was not at the moment extremely severe, it was of a nature to create apprehensions of more serious indisposition. This state of health was aggravated by the depression of my spirits, which had suffered considerably from the prospect of a long separation from my family, and from the absence of my brother. Under the apprehension of being rendered less equal to meet the exigencies of my public duty by the combined and progressive effects of sickness and grief, I thought myself bound to give you the earliest intimation of my actual situation and of its probable consequences. I could not give you more timely notice, because I could not foresee the attack which occasioned my letter of the 9th of March. My silence until that period of time is a sufficient proof of my desire to remain in the public service as long as my health might permit. After the arrival of the *Morning-ton* packet (on the 20th of April 1800), the intelligence of his Majesty's unfavourable acceptance of my services aggravated the bad state of my health, and inclined me still more anxiously to desire to be relieved from a station, which I apprehended that I could no longer hold with private honour or public advantage. And, accordingly, in my letters of the 29th April addressed to you and to Mr Pitt, I expressed my wish either to be restored to that consideration in India, which had been impaired by the nature of the mistaken reception of my services in England, or to be permitted to relinquish my charge. But neither in March or April did I intend to express any idea of abruptly resigning the government, nor any suggestion of the possibility of my relaxing any exertion of mind or body which I could employ in the discharge of my public duty.

During a great part of the summer my health was much affected, principally indeed by the vexation and mortification which I suffered in consequence of the unaccountable conduct of my friends in England, and of its humiliating and pernicious effects on those subject to my government in India. In June, however, I still expressed to you my determination to await your pleasure, and to continue my unabated efforts for the public service.

On the 10th of August 1800, having received intelligence of your intention to improve, enlarge, and strengthen, the powers of this government in my hands, and deeming the operation of the measures, which you had agreed to carry into execution, to be likely to counteravail any injurious effects which could be apprehended from the apparent depreciation of my services, as already described; I resolved to hold the government at all hazards, and to sacrifice every personal feeling to the object of accomplishing the final settlement of this empire with my own hands. I refer you to the enclosed extract of my letter of the 10th of August. In the meanwhile my health had been recovered, with a prospect of its continuance.

At present, it appears sufficient for me to add, that I remain in the resolution of holding this gov[ernmen]t, as long as my health shall permit, or until the state of affairs in Europe and Asia shall render my charge less difficult and laborious. Recent events in Europe, and the state of the French power in Egypt, have confirmed my resolution; and you may be assured that the approach of public difficulty or danger will never be the signal for my retreat. You shall always have the earliest notice, which I can give, of my intention to return to Europe. It is now evident, that I must remain here until the next season for sailing from Bengal, in December 1801 or January 1802: whenever the time of my departure shall arrive, it must be in the months of December or January. My present views of continuance in India are not limited to any precise period of time, but must be determined by the state of my health and of public affairs. I agree with you, that unless my health should require it, my departure from hence may not be advisable before the year 1803, or at the close of 1802. With regard to the alacrity or success of my administration since the settlement of Mysore, I refer you to the public records and to my correspondence. They will exhibit the proofs of my services; and, if you desire to know what sacrifices I make of personal feelings and interests, you may visit my family and inquire of them.

You seem to be under some apprehension of the increase of the military establishments in India, and you state your expectations of a reduction, and even intimate that you have actually proposed such a measure to the court of directors. I have never encouraged the hope of a reduction of our military force in India; on the contrary, I have ever stated to you and to the court, that some augmentation of it would be necessary in consequence of our conquests and treaties. But I have also stated, that the augmentation of our military expenses would bear no proportion to that of our new resources. I enclose a paper which I trust will satisfy your anxiety on this subject. I cannot, however, refrain from entreating you not to attempt to weaken our force in India, until you shall have received ample details from me with relation to that most important branch of my government. Surely I may claim with justice this degree of confidence; and I may rely with equal security on your care not to suffer a fallacious and illusory clamour for investment to impair the foundations of this empire in the very crisis of our fortunes in the East. If the court of directors will listen to my suggestions respecting the supply of China, and will leave me unfettered by positive orders, and undisturbed by ignorant, crude, and hasty, schemes of commerce and finance, formed without local knowledge or circumstantial detail, I entertain no doubt of bringing their revenues and expenses to a satisfactory proportion. But time must be allowed to mature the fruits of our conquests, and to give full operation to our treaties. The late neglect of sending bullion for the purchase of the current investment has nearly ruined public and private credit here, at the moment when a timely arrival of the promised supply of bullion would have enabled me to have surmounted the last financial difficulty which I expect to meet, and to have raised the 8 per cents to par. When I recur to the passages which I enclose of your various dispatches on this subject, I look with confidence to your immediate and active exertion in dispatching a large supply to Bengal without the delay of an hour after the receipt of this letter.

I shall write more fully by the *Mornington* (now under dispatch), and by other conveyances, on all the topics which appear to be afloat in your mind. In the meanwhile be not alarmed at my nine lakhs of surplus revenue, but look at the other side of the account, and consider what has been the amount of supplies to the investment from India, to China, to the Spice Islands, *etc.*; expect also the effects of the treaties of Mysore and of the last treaty of Hyderabad, as well as of the reform so far advanced in Oudh.

Believe me, . . .

WELLESLEY

CII

The Rt Hon. Henry Dundas to the Marquis Wellesley

30 December 1800, Wimbledon
Private: no. 33

My dear Lord

A few days ago brought me your overland dispatch in cypher, dated 13th July last; and I conceive it is so material to put your Lordship in immediate possession of the impression it has made upon me, it is my intention to suggest to the chairman of the East India Company the propriety of dispatching this letter by an overland conveyance.

In our various private correspondence I have had, occasionally, an opportunity of stating to your Lordship the deep importance I attach to the necessity of such a steady and regulated system of economy, as may enable us to reduce the great load of debt, by which our affairs in India are encumbered. And unless we are able to accomplish that important object, all our ideas of boasted prosperity are mere delusion; and the bubble will burst the first moment we are again involved in any severe struggle for the protection or security of our Indian interests. For my part, I consider the overgrown and unwieldy load of Indian debt as our only mortal foe. Our debt, even at its present amount, is of so formidable a nature as to blast every prospect of future prosperity, if it is permitted to remain at that amount. I must, therefore, fight it down and unless that most dangerous of all enemies is subdued, the fall of Seringapatam, and the acquisition of Mysore will only be found ultimately to increase our weakness, by having extended our establishments beyond our means of maintaining them. From the close of the former Mysore war, down to the commencement of the present, I had the satisfaction, year after year, of detailing to the public, through the medium of my Indian exposition, the gradual diminution of our debt, and the gradual amelioration of our Indian concern at home and abroad. Neither was I in any degree alarmed by the rapid progress of debt which the late war in India has produced. But my reason for not being alarmed was, that if our debt in India was not permitted upon the whole to exceed about 14 millions sterling, I saw clearly before me the means of a rapid reduction of it, the moment that peace was restored in Europe; and there ceased to be any such exigency of affairs at home as to render any further loans necessary on the part of the public. But every idea I entertain of seeing a rapid reduction of our Indian debt is bottomed on the foundation of believing that the restoration of peace in India would be productive of such a state of our finances there, as would enable us at least to have a large surplus for the discharge of the principal and interest of our debt, after defraying every necessary establishment. If such is the state of our finances, we know, by experience, that the provision of investment and the discharge of our Indian debt can be made mutually and beneficially subservient to each other. And I have greatly deceived myself if I have not formed a plan by which, on the restoration of peace in Europe, that system of combining the reduction of debt and the provision of investment may be improved upon in a degree hitherto unpractised. But I repeat again to your Lordship, that this plan, and every other, for the solid and permanent prosperity of India, must prove abortive if, at that period, we shall find the state of our finances in India such, as that our large revenues in that quarter are found inadequate even to the discharge of our establishment.

I have contented myself with giving your Lordship this general sketch of my ideas, without troubling you with detailed explanations because I am so confident in my opinions, and in the certainty of the propositions and conclusions I have stated, that neither your Lordship, nor any other man equally conversant with you in the affairs of India, can entertain a doubt of the truth of anything I have stated. I have, therefore, only to refer your Lordship to the facts as they exist, and the application of them is too obvious. I refer you to the statement prepared by Mr Myers under your own authority, and transmitted by your Lordship for my information. I refer you to the statement of the India budget, as last prepared and transmitted to India for your perusal: and upon examining the statements therein contained, founded upon the data, as I thought myself then warranted to assume them, you will perceive how much upon a level our revenues and establishments appear to be, and what a pittance only of surplus revenue is there held out in expectation. But even at that time additions appear to have been made to the establishments, of which I was then ignorant, and which, when brought forward into calculation and statement, you will find to absorb and exceed every existing revenue.

With these feelings operating upon my mind, your Lordship will not be surprised when I profess myself truly alarmed by the extent of establishment, which your Lordship's letter of 13 July recommends to my adoption. I lay entirely out of view all considerations of a collateral nature, and, therefore, do not enlarge upon the topic, how far the population of the country, amidst all the other calls upon it, could easily bear such a drain for the maintenance of its European establishment in India. I wish at the present moment to consider the subject merely upon the footing of finance, and in that view I should be without hope indeed, if I could be persuaded that so great an establishment, especially of a European description, was necessary to be kept up for the security of our Asiatic possessions. I should be without hope, because in the present state of our finances, or under any near prospect of what they may arrive at, it would be impossible for us to pay such an establishment without having recourse to the finances of this country, and in so far, making our Indian empire a burden upon the mother country. I am sure your Lordship would be as sorry as I could be, to see such a new circumstance arise out of the events which have recently taken place in India; but it is altogether unnecessary to dwell upon such speculations, for I can venture to assert, that if such a contingency was to occur, the disappointment and chagrin of the country would soon put an end to any value they have recently been accustomed to attach to our Indian Empire.

In considering this subject, I have made a comparison of the establishment at a former period with that which would be the amount agreeable to the letter to which I am now replying. With this view I have referred back to the establishment as settled in 1796: this was a period when the establishments underwent a revision, and when the power of Tipu Sultan, and the danger resulting from it, were fully before us. And yet, including artillery, cavalry, and infantry—European and native—the establishment does not seem to have exceeded 80,000 men. Since that time, and particularly since the end of the late Mysore war, it has been increasing by rapid strides, and if put upon the scale recommended by your Lordship's letter, it would, notwithstanding the fall of Seringapatam and the Mysorean power, amount to no less than 142,600 men. The addition of expense is enormous in proportion, and the addition alone which your Lordship recommends of European forces, would, as nearly as I can conjecture upon a rough guess, amount to about £500,000 sterling *per annum*. I am sure, when I bring the particulars so pointedly before you, you will consider both your own time and mine as usefully employed, when we enter upon calm discussion, how far there can be a utility, far less a necessity, for such an overgrown establishment.

In the first place, I greatly doubt, if upon re-examination of the particulars of your letter, your Lordship will find yourself accurate in the data on which you proved you rest your opinion of the European and infantry establishment necessary for India, on the following principle, *viz.* that whatever be the number actually borne on the army returns, one-fourth must be deducted for the number probably sick or otherwise unfit for duty. On this principle, your Lordship argues, that an effective force for Bengal of 6,000 r[ank] and f[ile], will require 8 reg[iments]: or 9,000 r[ank] and f[ile]. And that an effective force for Coromandel, Bombay, Malabar, Ceylon, *etc.*, of 12,000 will require 20,400 r[ank] and f[ile], or 17 reg-[iments]. Taken together, that to furnish 18,000 effective men will require an establishment of 25 reg[iments] of 1,200 each or 30,000 r[ank] and f[ile].

Even if the principle be allowed to be correct, the calculation does not appear to be so: 9,600 men or 8 reg[iments] less by $\frac{1}{4}$ will leave 7,200 instead of 6,000, or $\frac{1}{5}$ more than you reckon upon; and 20,400 men or 17 reg[iments] less by $\frac{1}{4}$ will leave 15,300 instead of 12,000, being above a quarter more than you reckon upon. Take both together, 30,000 men or 25 reg[iments], as proposed by your Lordship, less by $\frac{1}{4}$, will leave 22,500 men, or more than the force wanted by your Lordship's statement by 4,500, or $\frac{1}{4}$.

Admitting the principle to be just, *viz.* that whatever the establishment is, one-fourth must be deducted for non-effectives and that the strength required in effective men is, as stated by your Lordship, 18,000; the number of reg[iments] necessary to furnish that force is twenty or, at 1,200 r[ank] and f[ile] each, 24,000 men. Deduct $\frac{1}{4}$ and we have 18,000: the strength required, and five reg[iments] less than proposed by your Lordship will be sufficient for the purpose.

But the deduction of one-fourth of the number on the army returns for the sick does not correspond with the actual state by the returns from Madras and Bombay, in which alone the distinction is made; however as the greatest number of European reg[iments] are stationed at those presidencies and their dependencies, (*viz.* 16 out of 21), it may be sufficient in a general view to take the calculation from those returns.

At the end of 1799, the number of King's infantry r[ank] and f[ile] at

Madras was 5,941, of which sick or invalids, 853, little more than $\frac{1}{7}$. The Company's infantry r[ank] and f[ile] were 1,286 of which sick, 109, about $\frac{1}{12}$. Both together, 7,227 sick, *etc.*, 962—rather more than $\frac{1}{8}$.

At Bombay the King's infantry r[ank] and f[ile] were 3,837, of which sick, *etc.*, 448, not $\frac{1}{8}$; the Company's 754 of which sick, 65, not $\frac{1}{11}$: both together, 4,591, of which sick, *etc.*, 513 or about $\frac{1}{9}$. Take both establishments together, the total rank and file are 11,818: of which sick, *etc.*, 1,475, or $\frac{1}{8}$.

It appears from what is above stated that an allowance of $\frac{1}{8}$ for sick would be sufficient and the force required to furnish 18,000 effective men would, therefore, be about 17 reg[iments], of 1,200 rank and file, each making 20,400. Deducting $\frac{1}{8}$ leaves 17,850, or 150 short of the complement.

But as the returns from Bengal do not specify the sick and as they may be more in proportion there than at the other presidencies, in order to make an apparently ample allowance let the deduction be stated at $\frac{1}{6}$. In this case, to furnish 18,000 effectives will require 18 reg[iments] of 1,200 each, or 21,600: deduct $\frac{1}{6}$ or 3,600 and we have the exact number of 18,000.

In the above observations your Lordship will perceive that I have proceeded upon the supposition that your proposition, of having at all times a force of 18,000 men for field service, was necessary for the security of India, but you have not laid before me any detailed data by which to judge of this as a military proposition. If I judge from past experience, and some general maxims which I have often heard stated upon that subject, I should be disposed to doubt if such an extent of European establishment were necessary.

Your Lordship's opinion upon this subject seems to rest upon two general grounds of reasoning. In the first place you state that our establishments ought to increase in proportion to the extent of our territory, and, secondly, that our European establishment should increase in proportion as we increase our native.

Upon the first of those propositions, I must beg leave to pause, and to substitute another criterion as more applicable to the subject. The criterion by which that question ought to be decided is rather by the relative power of our supposed enemies, than by our own extent of territory. I am perfectly aware that the internal peace and the security of a newly acquired territory may require an addition of establishment to a certain extent, but if, at the same moment, we acquire that territory, we have narrowed our former frontiers, and subdued a restless, hostile and enterprising neighbour, it does by no means follow that our new territory is to receive an establishment in proportion to our old one. The application of this principle to our present state in India is so obvious I need not consume your time by an illustration of it.

Your second proposition I admit to be true, in so far as to agree that there must be a certain proportion of European force corresponding to the number of native troops maintained upon the establishment. But still the question recurs, what that proportion ought to be. Some military men have stated a fifth of the whole to be sufficient. None with whom I have conversed have ever stated more than a fourth to be necessary. When your Lordship examines the extent of European establishments, as detailed in the orders which I hope the court of directors will send out without delay, and as more particularly to be stated in the sequel of this letter, I believe your Lordship will find that the European force, consisting of artillery, infantry, and cavalry, amounts to about a fourth of the whole military establishment which can with any attention to economy be maintained in our possessions in India.

Upon the best consideration, therefore, I can give to the subject, I do not find myself at liberty, consistently with any attention to necessary economy, to authorize an establishment of 25 European reg[iments] of infantry. I am satisfied that 17 is adequate to every purpose, even with a view to our subsidiary treaties, unless in one event: *viz.* that of a permanent arrangement being made with the Portuguese for retaining the possession of Goa. In that event two more would be necessary. But even in that case, it would be six short of what your Lordship proposes. I would propose six King's regiments at Bengal for the service of our own provinces and the vizier's country. I would propose six King's regiments at Madras for the purposes of our former territories together with our new acquisitions upon the coasts of Canara and Malabar; and to enable us to perform our engagements with the governments of Hyderabad and Mysore. I would propose two King's regiments for the protection of Bombay and its dependencies as now regulated.

These upon the whole amount to 14 reg[iments], which together with our Company's European infantry regiment at each settlement, would make the whole 17 regiments.

I have deliberated much in my own mind how far it would not be expedient to urge the directors at the present moment to give up totally their European infantry and to rest the whole of their European strength upon their artillery, which, I agree with your Lordship, ought to be put on the most respectable footing. I hold a well-regulated artillery and a highly disciplined cavalry to form our most solid and permanent pre-eminence for the preservation of our military superiority in India. You'll observe that I have proposed to get rid of one regiment of the Company's European infantry in order to make good a part of the expense necessary for the artillery. If I had been to consult my own judgement only, I should have urged the court of directors to get rid of their whole European infantry with the view of a still further immediate addition to their artillery, and I feel my reasons for the measure to be so forcible, I think I should have been successful in persuading the court of directors to acquiesce in my judgement. But as it has been stated to me, from quarters too respectable to be resisted, that it is essential for preserving the strength and connection of their different establishments, that there should be a proportion of European infantry from which their non-commissioned officers must be drafted for their native troops, I do not feel myself at liberty to be pertinacious in my own opinion, but acquiesce in the propriety of keeping up and recruiting at each of the settlements, one European reg[iment] of infantry under the immediate authority of the Company.

I have another objection to the proposal of sending out such a multitude of reg[iments] to India, for if ever any storm should arise in the north of Europe to threaten our Indian possessions, or if ever that menace should become more formidable by an union between any great European power and the northern tribes of India, it is not likely such a confederacy would be so sudden as not to enable us to take the necessary precautions. Against any combination that is not of a tremendous size I hold the proposed establishment perfectly adequate to our security; but if from any such causes as I have suggested it should become a necessary policy to increase our European force, your Lordship will agree with me in thinking that it is always a matter of great importance to study how far you can add to your military strength without increasing the number of officers which, not only from the expense of their establishment, but from the contingent charges attending them, add greatly in proportion to the expense of a military establishment. If, therefore, at any time it should be necessary to add to our European force, it should be done not by additional regiments with additional field officers, but by additional companies to the 17 I have already mentioned. Two companies to each regiment would at once add a European force of above 3,000 men and so, in proportion, even if four companies were, in case of urgency, to be added, they could on a short warning, be got from the army at home and would, when added to the 14 King's reg[iments] established for India, make each regiment consist of not more than 2 battalions of 800 men each.

By adhering to the system I have mentioned the expense and inconvenience of sending men and raw regiments would be avoided and the addition made to your European infantry, when required, would have the advantage of being engrafted on old-disciplined and well-seasoned reg[iments].

The same principle ought now to be applied to the other parts of the service in so far as there is just ground for the augmentation of any part of it. I entirely agree with your Lordship that the present artillery is inadequate to the great additional services now to be performed by that valuable corps; and I likewise agree with you in thinking that the great extension of territory, and the fulfilment of the subsidiary treaties must render an addition to our cavalry strength absolutely necessary. But in both those cases it does not appear to me that there is at present any occasion either for new battalions of artillery or for those additional reg[iments] of European cavalry which your Lordship's letter suggests. The court of directors I make no doubt will approve, as a temporary expedient under a pressing exigency, of the measure you have resolved to adopt of completing your artillery establishments by drafts from their European infantry: but besides completing that corps up to its former establishment, it is necessary to make an addition to it and for the present this should be done by adding two companies to each battalion and each company to have an additional Lieut[enant] Fireworker and 10 additional mattrusses.

With regard to the cavalry, there are at present four European reg[iments], and in place of adding to the number of the regiments, the addition should be made to the strength of the existing reg[iments]. This can be speedily and effectually done by adding two troops and twenty men to each reg[iment]; whereby a very considerable addition of strength would be obtained at a moderate expense of officers, namely one field officer and the officers necessary for the additional troops; whereas by additional regiments the expense is enhanced beyond all necessity by an addition of no less than 5 field officers besides all the others of inferior rank.

This reasoning equally applies to the native cavalry. By adding two troops to each regiment, you will, in like manner, at a moderate expense, comparatively speaking, make an addition to your cavalry strength both at Bengal and Madras of not less than 12 troops at each.

Upon the principles I have detailed I have resolved to recommend to the court of directors a revision of their establishments, making every economical deduction where circumstances will admit of it, and at the same time making such additions to some branches of their service as necessity dictates: but even in those additions, consulting economy in every instance, and adopting that mode, which gives the additional strength at the least possible expense.

In the detail I have given, it will not escape your observation that I have taken no notice of Ceylon. It is because I have formed a decided opinion that the protection of that island cannot be left as a burden upon the revenues of India. Indeed, at present those revenues cannot afford it. But independent of that consideration, I am fully satisfied that the measure of connecting the administration of that island with the governments of India was prematurely and inadvertently adopted. The possession of Ceylon I conceive to be of the least importance to the permanent security of India, but the principles by which it is to be governed and the establishments by which its affairs are to be administered, cannot be formed on this model of our Indian establishments. The European part must be very limited in point of number, and their establishments, such as they may be settled, must be upon a scale of expenses and allowances far inferior to the establishments upon the continent of India. I wish not to dwell upon the mischief which has already happened from blending the service of Ceylon with that of Madras. There may certainly be some exceptions to the observation, but as a general proposition I am fully satisfied upon a minute examination of the subject for some months past, that as on the one hand it would be unwise and inexpedient to admit only the Indian servants to the charge of affairs at Ceylon, so, on the other hand, it would be unreasonable to expect that the servants on the Indian establishment of superior talents would be induced to come to Ceylon, with the very limited prospects which the service there would afford to them.

For these and various other considerations unnecessary for the present purpose to be detailed, I shall submit to his Majesty my opinion that Ceylon be restored to the state of a royal government and administered on the same principles as the government of the Cape is now conducted.

In the perusal of your Lordship's letter I have not been inattentive to what you state as to the deficiencies in the present establishment of our European force and the inadequacy of the supply of recruits which latterly have been sent to India. And your observation is true in point of fact, that since the late war in Mysore, no augmentation of our European force has taken place. But your Lordship will recollect that on the first suspicion which arose in my mind of the probability of a war in India, I sent near 5,000 of the flower of the British army to the assistance of our Indian establishments, and that valuable force arrived in due time to perform most important service. And this very circumstance will fully account to your Lordship why there has been such a scanty supply of recruits from that period to the present. The defence of India was to the greatest degree pressing and, therefore, the force I have referred to, was sent there in preference of every other service. But your Lordship knows enough of the state of Europe at that time and ever since; and likewise of the state of Ireland, and our extended distant possessions, not to be aware how sensibly every other pressing service was affected by that great reinforcement sent to India. And, therefore, when the immediate danger of India was at an end, and its safety ensured by the brilliant issue of the contest, it was natural and wise to appropriate all the recruits we could collect to supply the deficiencies in other quarters. I have only further to observe that this inconvenience would not have been remedied if there had existed in India an establishment consisting of the number of regiments which your Lordship's letter suggests. The number of recruits for the service of India could not have been larger than it was, and the only consequence would have been an immense additional expense without any additional strength. I have had a full communication with the commander-in-chief upon the subject and I trust effectual means will be concerted for maintaining complete the European establishments to the amount I have mentioned in this letter, and which will be more accurately detailed in the official orders which will be sent without delay from the war office, and from the court of directors.

It only remains for me to advert to the concluding part of your Lordship's letter. I never before heard of the defective state of the foundry at Fort William, which your Lordship describes as no longer able to supply the ordnance required for the use of Bengal and the other presidencies. Your Lordship may rest assured I shall, without delay, call the attention of the court of directors to the subject, and an immediate and radical care must be administered to so serious an evil.

As your Lordship's letter was confined to the subject of military establishments, my reply is, of course, confined to the same topics. But I am sure, when your Lordship adverts to the foundation of a deep-rooted anxiety which I entertain upon one branch of our expenditure, you will so far concur with me in that feeling as to extend the same principles to every other species of expenditure. I am well aware that valuable improvements may still be made upon many of our Indian concerns; and I know that many of those improvements will likewise lead to expense. I am likewise aware that it is natural for men of ardent minds to wish the rapid execution of improvements which they reckon to be valuable and important, but in the present state of our finances, I have no hesitation in being of opinion that we had better for some time remain stationary and postpone for a while even desirable improvements if they are to lead to immediate expense. In short, my present creed with regard to India is, that nothing new is to be attempted without weighing well every rupee it will cost.

I have troubled your Lordship with a long letter, but when you consider the importance and extent of the subject I have been under necessity of discussing, your Lordship will be satisfied that I could scarcely compress the subject within a narrower compass.

I have the honour to be, . . .

HENRY DUNDAS

CIII

The Marquis Wellesley to the Rt Hon. Henry Dundas

7 March 1801, Fort William
Private: [*Separate*] (*Secret*)

My dear Sir

My brother Henry arrived here on the 22nd of February in good health. I shall reply to your several letters received by him, and also to all other unanswered letters from you, by the *Georgiana* packet in the course of a few days.

The dispatches forwarded overland under date the 30th September and 10th Oct[ober] have reached me in safety.[1] My official letter of this date contains a view of my proceedings with respect to the various military operations which have been in my contemplation, as well as with respect to the departure of the armament for the Red Sea.[2] Concluding it to be your intention, that I should hereafter correspond officially with you under the operation of the King's commission (at least as far as relates to the management of the army), I have commenced my new system of correspondence by this dispatch. I could have wished that the commission had been so framed as to have admitted a similar correspondence with relation to the civil affairs of this empire. On this point I shall hereafter state my opinion more fully to you.

The satisfaction which you have expressed in my brother Henry's judgement and temper is highly grateful to me. My motive for employing him as the channel of my late communications with you was the conviction, that no other man in India possessed equal qualifications for such a duty; and I am most happy to find that, in so important a transaction, I have met your wishes. The personal sacrifice which I made was very severe, and can scarcely be appreciated by any person, who has never been placed in the sole government of an extensive empire, at the distance of half the globe from his native country and family, and without the aid of one private and personal friend in any confidential communication. My brother informs me, that you suggested to him the possibility of your turning your selection towards him, in the event of a vacancy in the gov[ernment] of Fort St George. He at the same time understood, that you entered into no engagement whatever on the subject, but merely expressed your favourable opinion of him, and the prospect of its future effects. Certainly no arrangement could be more acceptable to me under any circumstances. My letter

---

[1] Instructions to send an army to Egypt.
[2] Add. MSS. 13457, f. 66.

of the 12th November will have apprised you that I have no idea of quitting India; my views at present indeed are extended to a much more protracted residence here, than had ever before entered into my contemplation; and I desire you to understand that (as far as my own wishes or ideas are to be consulted by you) I am inclined to hope, that I may be enabled to hold this government until all financial difficulties shall have been overcome; all political and external relations secured; all internal systems of judicature, revenue, and police, improved and extended; the great questions of private trade and public investment finally adjusted; and the military establishment placed on a basis equally connected with the stability of our power, and with the just economy of our finances. I entertain no apprehension of meeting any of these questions; if sufficient time be allowed for the operation of the innumerable causes of prosperity, which the success of our arms in Mysore has put in motion; and if reasonable assistance be afforded from England for two or three years, by remittances of bullion, and by funding a small proportion (even a fourth) of the Indian debt at home. *With such aids*, my present opinion is, that we shall realize a considerable surplus revenue at the close of four or five years from this time. I shall state this opinion to you in detail hereafter by the *Georgiana*. In the meanwhile, I have entered into a revision of the civil and military charges; and although I cannot concur in the possibility of a reduction of the army, I entertain no doubt of effecting a considerable reduction of charges, particularly in the military branch.

With these views (unless my health should be disturbed, which is now perfectly good), I see no near prospect of my resigning this government either to Lord Clive or to any other person for several years. And if Lord Clive should quit Fort St George, my brother Henry's establishment in that government would certainly be a great source of confidence and satisfaction to me. Lady Clive returns to Europe this season, and I suspect that Lord Clive will not remain long after her. The prospect of my succession may indeed prolong his stay; but if my health should continue, I shall think it a duty of friendship to inform him of my intention not to resign this charge for some years.

You will perhaps imagine that this state of my mind has arisen from the removal of some of those impressions which I stated to you in my letter of the 29th April. But I assure you that my sentiments remain unchanged, and after full consideration, I believe them to be immovable with respect to the manner in which my services have been acknowledged at home. I know my opinion on this painful topic to be the general sentiment here; and pardon me when I declare to you, that (notwithstanding your authority, and although no such opinions may have reached you) *I know* the same sentiment to be general in England. It prevails among some of *your* best friends as well as *mine*, who have plainly and distinctly signified it to me by letter, and otherwise to my family at home. By the *Georgiana* I shall write my *last words* on that subject; after which liberation of my wounded spirit, not a sentiment of that nature shall ever again reach my lips or my pen. In this dispatch, however, I cannot close my letter, without expressing my regret, that you should deem me capable of suffering any emotion of personal dissatisfaction to impair the energy of my public service in the arduous charge committed to my hands. Hereafter, I must take the liberty of offering with perfect frankness my remarks on the justice of such an apprehension, when applied to my character. At present, I am satisfied to rest the defence of my energy, on the reduction of 22 battalions of the vizier's infantry and of one-third of his cavalry; on the annexation of Surat to the Company's possessions; on the campaign in Mysore against the insurgent Dhoondiah; on the annexation to the Company's possessions of all the nizam's acquisitions in both wars with Tipu; and lastly on the anticipation of the King's commands for an armament against Egypt. These measures comprise the history of about six months, during which time I plead guilty to the charge of dissatisfaction to the fullest extent to which it can be urged: but I cannot admit the justice of your inference, that every mind must be weak which is sensible to public neglect; nor am I disposed to suffer my present sensations to induce any degree of oblivion of the affection and gratitude which I owe to my friends, or of the duty which I owe to my country.

I cannot seal this letter without again reminding you of the indispensable necessity of an early and large remittance of bullion to India. Without it, the Company must not expect investment: with it, interest will fall, credit will revive, and I shall be able to attack the debt with vigour and effect.

Ever, . . .

WELLESLEY

Inform David Scott that I find Captain Salmond a most useful retrencher, and that we are going to work very briskly upon several objects of reform, particularly in Oudh.

I enclose two private letters which passed between me and V[ice]-Admiral Rainier.[1] They could not be enclosed in my official dispatch.

On reading this letter, I observe an expression respecting Lord Clive which might be construed into a desire that he should quit India earlier than he might have intended for the purpose of admitting Henry at Madras. I therefore am desirous of assuring you, that I entertain no such desire, and that no person can be more acceptable to me at Madras than

[1] *Wellesley*, ii, 753–9.

Lord Clive, with whom I trust I shall ever maintain the most friendly and cordial intercourse. My intimations to him of my intention to remain in India (if you should approve of my continuance) will only be made, if I should observe that he was waiting for my departure, and if the state of my health and public affairs should render my long continuance probable. But nothing could ever induce me (not even the prospect of my brother's advancement) to throw out any suggestion which might shorten the period of Lord Clive's government at Madras.

It occurs to me to observe, that I read with great concern a passage in one of your letters by the *Georgiana* stating your objection to the institution of a system of collegiate education in India for the civil service. My letters, which must have reached you before this time, will show how little I expected any such objection; especially on the ground which you have stated, that any such institution might favour the introduction of Jacobinism into India. You are aware that the Jacobin principles had already made considerable progress here both in the army and the civil service; and I confess my expectation to be, that an early corrective of the first habits contracted by the writers and cadets in India, would prove the most effectual barrier which could be opposed to that most dreadful of human calamities. I trust that the notes which I have sent to you will have satisfied you on the necessity and utility of the college at Fort William. At all events, I am confident, that you will not suffer such an institution to be disturbed, until you shall have received further advices from me, and shall have discussed the subject with me in the most ample detail.

CIV

The Rt Hon. Henry Dundas to the Marquis Wellesley

16 March 1801, Wimbledon
Private: [*Separate*]

My dear Lord

By the time you receive this, you will hear many unexpected changes in the administration of this country. Mr Pitt, Lord Grenville, Lord Spencer, Mr Windham,[1] and myself, have resigned our respective situations in his Majesty's service. The chancellor likewise has resigned, not for the same reason but from a wish to retire. We have parted from his Majesty on the

---

[1] William Windham (1750–1810); secretary at war, 1794–1801.

most cordial terms, and mean to give a decided support to his new government. We differed with his Majesty in opinion upon the subject of the Irish Catholics. His five servants whom I have named, were of opinion that the union with Ireland gave a fair opportunity to relieve the Catholics of that country from the disenfranchisements to which they are still subjected, but his Majesty had been advised that his coronation oath was irreconcilable with such a concession. The lord chancellor, the duke of Portland,[1] Lord Westmoreland,[2] though not upon the same ground with his Majesty, concurred with him as to the policy of the measure. Lord Camden,[3] who was in the cabinet without an office, concurred with us, and has likewise retired: and for the same reason Lord Cornwallis gives up the lord-lieutenancy of Ireland.

Mr Pitt is succeeded by Mr Addington, the late speaker, whose chair is filled by Sir John Mitford; Lord Grenville is succeeded by Lord Hawkesbury;[4] Lord Spencer, by Lord St Vincent; Mr Windham by Mr Charles Yorke; myself in the war department, by Lord Hobart; and in the board of control by Lord Lewisham.[5] For his sake, and at his earnest request, and for the sake of keeping my own principles from going to wreck, I have allowed my name to remain as member of the board of control, and mean to give to the department every assistance in my power. Lord Eldon[6] succeeds the chancellor; Lord Hardwicke succeeds Lord Cornwallis in Ireland. There are some changes in the subordinate situations of government; but none of Mr Pitt's friends or mine have retired, so far as by our influence we could prevail upon them to stay; and as I have already stated, we will give every support to keep down a Jacobinical opposition, and to keep out a Jacobinical government.

I remain, . . .

HENRY DUNDAS

[1] William Henry Cavendish Bentinck, 3rd duke of Portland (1738–1809); home secretary, 1794–1801.
[2] John Fane, 10th earl of Westmoreland (1759–1841); lord privy seal, 1798–1806, 1807–27.
[3] John Pratt, 2nd Earl Camden (marquis of, 1812) (1759–1840).
[4] Robert Banks Jenkinson, Lord Hawkesbury (2nd earl of Liverpool) (1770–1828); foreign secretary, 1801–4; prime minister, 1812–27.
[5] George Legge, Viscount Lewisham (3rd earl of Dartmouth) (1755–1810); president of the board of control, 1801–2.
[6] John Scott, 1st earl of Eldon (1751–1838); lord chancellor, 1801–6, 1807–27.

CV

The Marquis Wellesley to the Rt Hon. Henry Dundas

10 May 1801, Barrackpore
Private: no. 33

My dear Sir

The object of this dispatch is to intimate to you my sentiments on the plans which you appear to have in contemplation relative to the permanent government of the island of Ceylon, if that possession should remain in our hands after the peace.

The present civil establishment is certainly a heavy burden on the finances of the Company in India: and as far as relates to them, it would be a relief to throw the burden of the civil government of Ceylon on the Crown. With respect to the European force to be maintained for the defence of that island, I think it might be provided without any addition to the number of 18,000 effective infantry, which I proposed in my letter of the 13th July 1800, for the whole of our present Indian empire, continental as well as insular, including Ceylon, the Moluccas, Malacca, and Goa as a British garrison.

The revenue of Ceylon is not adequate to the payment of the necessary establishments under a separate royal government; nor can I think, that the revenue of that island will be found answerable to its necessary expenditure under a separate government, if ever, for many years to come. The deficiency must, therefore, be provided from home, if Ceylon be entirely separated from the general government of India. To meet this charge at home, the cargoes of cinnamon, and the investment of Ceylon, might possibly be taken by the Crown. Still, however, an advance must annually be made by Parliament for the expenses of Ceylon, to be balanced by the sale of its investment, as the charges of our colonies in the West Indies may be balanced by the duties levied on the produce of those colonies. But I rather suppose, that the Crown would take no direct concern in the commercial investment, but would leave that trade, either to the East India Company, or to private traders under certain regulations, and that the Crown would levy duties on the trade, as a more natural and proper mode of drawing a resource from the possession of Ceylon.

The transfer of the civil and military expense of Ceylon to the Crown, would render that part of our Indian empire a charge on the public of the United Kingdom, and would be substantially the same measure which you so earnestly deprecate. For the direct operation of such an arrangement necessarily must be to render that part of our Indian empire a burden upon the mother country, and to have recourse to the public finances at home for the payment of that branch of our Indian establishments.

In this view of the subject, therefore, the account between the British Islands and India would stand, precisely the same as if aid were to be granted by Parliament, to a similar extent, in the shape of direct assistance to the finances of the East India Company, holding Ceylon as a territorial possession, and defraying the general charges of that possession together with those of the continental empire of India.

In this case, as in the separate case of Ceylon, if annexed to the Crown, the public would be remunerated by the duties derived from the trade, and by other collateral benefits resulting from the extensive power of Great Britain in the East.

It appears to me, however, to be a perfectly just and reasonable statement in taking a general view of the expectations which you have held out at various times to Parliament respecting India, to exclude from the account altogether, the charge of Ceylon, and of our possessions acquired from the Dutch in the Eastern Seas, of Goa, and perhaps of all our acquisitions in the East obtained from European powers during the present war.

But the same benefit must in reason and justice be allowed to the government of India, and to the credit of the Company's finances; and with this allowance, after having excluded the charges of those acquisitions, a large surplus revenue would certainly accrue applicable to the combined purpose of reducing debt, and of maintaining commercial investment.

As far as the questions of expense and finance are to be viewed distinctly from other branches of political consideration, I am convinced that the revenue of Ceylon would be infinitely better administered, and more productive, and that its expenses would be much more moderate, if it were permanently annexed as a province to the government of Fort St George, than if it be retained as a separate and distinct government under the Crown.

The permanent annexation of Ceylon to the Crown, while the continent of India shall remain under the government of the East India Company, is, however, a measure more important in my estimation with respect to its political, than to its financial operation.

It is essential to the vigour of this empire, that the administration of all its parts should be uniform, framed upon the same system, combined by similar principles, and directed to similar objects and views. Unity of power, and an invariable correspondence of system and action throughout the whole fabric of our government, are the best securities which can be provided against the dangers to which we are necessarily exposed in India, by the vast extent of our possessions, and by the variety of interests which they embrace. If to the natural principles of division and discord, resulting from the remote position of our provinces, and from the differences of local prejudice and conflicting interests, be added the establishment of distinct authorities, different in substance and in form from the general government of the empire, and exempt from its control, the weakness of overgrown dominion must ultimately fall upon us, and in every arduous crisis our power will be found inefficient in proportion to its normal magnitude and extent.

Whatever, therefore, may be the nature of that government which the wisdom of Parliament may permanently establish for India, I hold two principles to be indispensable to its permanent efficiency and vigour.

First, that every part of the empire in India, continental as well as insular, shall be subject to the general control of one undivided authority; which shall possess energy in peace, to maintain order, connection, and harmony, between all the dispersed branches of our dominion, and to extend equal benefits of good government to every class of our numerous and various subjects; and in war, to direct every spring of action to similar and correspondent movements, to concentrate every resource in an united effort, and by a systematic subordination, to diffuse such a spirit of alacrity and promptitude to the remotest extremities of the empire, as shall secure the co-operation of every part in any exigency which may demand the collective strength of the whole.

Secondly, that the constitution of every branch of the empire should be similar and uniform; and above all, that no subordinate part should be so constituted, as in any respect to hold a rivalry of dignity even in form with the supreme power.

The distinction between the Royal power and that of the Company is perfectly understood by the natives of India, and more sensibly felt by them than by any class of persons in Europe. Even by Europeans in India a degree of respect is attached to the representation of the Royal power, which they either boldly refuse, or reluctantly yield, to the Company's government.

The application of these principles to the case of Ceylon would lead me to submit most seriously to your consideration, the absolute necessity of preserving the control of the governor-general in council over the government of Ceylon, entire and in the fullest efficiency. Without this control, the possession of Ceylon, instead of being as you justly estimate it, the great bulwark of this empire, may become nearly as useless to the common cause as it it were in the hands of a neutral power.

An independent governor of Ceylon, acting in the King's name, might prove the source of the most dangerous confusion and distraction in the bosom of our dominions. In the next place, I should feel it my duty to represent to you, that if the governor of Ceylon shall permanently hold a commission, civil and military, from the Crown, the governor-general should hold a commission, civil and military, from the same authority. Without this arrangement, I doubt whether it would be possible permanently to maintain an efficient control over Ceylon when annexed to the Crown.

An anxiety for the good government of India, being the common sentiment of your mind and of mine, will be my excuse for having submitted these ideas to you. You will use them according to your discretion.

I remain, . . .

WELLESLEY

CVI

The Marquis Wellesley to the Rt Hon. Henry Dundas

30 September 1801, Monghyr
Private: [*no. 34*]

My dear Sir

Your letters of 16th March did not reach me until the 28th instant, having been detained at Basra on account of the defect of a safe conveyance. The reports of the late most extraordinary change of administration reached me many months ago, and necessarily occasioned the greatest distress to my mind. In the state of suspense respecting the nature and effects of the change, which the silence of my friends occasioned in my mind, I was at a loss how to conduct my official correspondence, and even how to regulate some material branches of our political relations. Nor was I by any means satisfied from the current reports of the causes and consequences of the change, that I might not deem it to be my public duty to resign my office. Your letter of 16th March has afforded very little information to assist my judgement, and contains no expression, from which I can derive any new light on that most astonishing event.

On the whole, however, I trust that I have acted conformably to my duty towards the public and towards my friends, in adopting the course stated in my dispatches by this conveyance, and in my private letter to Lord Lewisham, of which I enclose a copy.

I have not yet been able to obtain from the Coast, and from Bombay, the necessary information to enable me to return full replies to your unanswered dispatches. I must, therefore, delay my replies to them until the next packet.

With respect to the armament which I prepared in October 1800, and to my views against the Mauritius and Batavia, I refer you to my official dispatches. I acted to the best of my judgement after full deliberation; and I must leave my cause to the wisdom and justice of the authorities who are to judge me; yourself first, and next to you, such of the ministers and of other authorities as are competent to understand the subject. I shall for ever lament that it was impracticable for you to advise me at an earlier period of time of your designs against Egypt. Had I been certain in the month of December of those designs, I would have enabled you to drive the French from Egypt with as much rapidity, as you drove the Danes from the Sound.[1] I cannot express to you my concern for your old friend Sir Ralph Abercrombie;[2] but the glory of his death was a noble termination of such a life.

In former letters I have expressed a disposition to prolong my administration in India to a late period of time. You must be aware, that many circumstances have since occurred, which must incline me to return home, as soon as my public duty will admit. You will not, therefore, deem my letter by this conveyance to the court of directors[3] in any degree inconsistent with my former declarations on the same subject. But no provocation shall ever induce me to resign this charge abruptly; and you have never required more from me, than a sufficient notice of my wish to retire. At present, you will observe that my request is limited to the nomination of a provisional successor. I shall not avail myself of that nomination, unless I should be satisfied, that I can leave India with perfect security to the public interests, and that no essential public advantage can arise from my continuance here.

I have learned with concern and surprise the cruel indignities which are meditated against Lord Clive. A change in his council would be a very wise measure, if wise men be brought near him by the change. Mr Dick is an excellent man, Mr Cockburn still better. They would form an extremely useful council. I saw no objection to Mr Petrie while I was on the Coast, excepting his former connections, and his total want of the respect of the settlement; these defects will render him a dangerous governor. Mr Chamier[4] is an idle, silly, and ridiculous, coxcomb. How such a man could recommend himself to my friend David Scott, I cannot imagine. With respect to Mr Webbe, I *know him* to be one of the most able, intelligent, industrious, and honest, men in the world; and the persecution (which I

---

1 Wellesley is referring to Sir Hyde Parker's victory at Copenhagen on 2 April 1801.
2 Lt-Gen. Sir Ralph Abercrombie (1734–1801); commander-in-chief, Mediterranean and Egypt, 1800–1; died of wounds at Alexandria.
3 *Wellesley*, ii, 576.
4 Deschamps Chamier; chief of Vizagapatam, 1795–1801; chief secretary to government, Madras, 1801–3.

perceive to be commenced against him in Leadenhall Street, on the foundation of private reports and of secret intrigues of persons interested in his ruin) is in the highest degree unjust, and will prove ruinous to our affairs in the Carnatic. Mr Webbe, like most men whom I have seen, is neither exempt from passion nor error; but he has since my arrival in India been a main instrument in the preparations for the war against Tipu, in the settlement of Mysore, in the settlement of Tanjore, in the acquisition of the Carnatic, and in the new code of laws now preparing for that possession. He was completely erroneous, and almost criminal, in his conduct immediately subsequent to my orders for the assembling the army in 1798; he was then suffered to pass not only unpunished but unreproved. I forgave him when he saw his error and returned to his duty; and I know his conduct since that period to have produced the utmost public advantage. I cannot conceive the ground or object of the measure of removing him for the purpose of introducing Mr Chamier; but I know that the consequence will be the triumphant restoration of every species of corruption and intrigue at Fort St George. Nothing can repress this system but a bold and firm governor. I understand, however, that boldness and firmness are *now* deemed defects in a governor of India. I am afraid, my dear Sir, that the fatal effects to be apprehended from your resignation of the supreme control of India already begin to operate; and I dread every hour the symptoms of a rapid relapse into the distracted, weak, condition in which you found the government abroad. I need not tell you, that the first shock in India may be destructive; and never was a crisis known at Fort St George, which required a stronger hand. Lord Clive, I believe, is now going home in consequence of Lord Powis' death. At all events, I conclude that Mr Webbe's removal will send him home. If you do not provide an active and able successor with full confidence and power, the empire upon the peninsula will not last six years. But how can any governor be powerful with a secretary (Mr Chamier!) named from home, and bearing a provisional appointment to council.

I derive the greatest satisfaction from Mr Barlow's appointment to Council here. Mr Udny is also very respectable. I entertain the strongest hope of a great improvement in the conduct of business.

Amidst all the gloomy circumstances in the public prospects of England, I received the greatest degree of satisfaction from perceiving that the public has been just and grateful towards you in your retirement from the cabinet. My respect, gratitude, and affectionate regard, will ever attend you in all situations; and I trust that I shall ultimately be able to render a good account to you of this charge, which in my honour and conscience I think, owes more to you, than to any individual, whose conduct has ever influenced its prosperity or decline. Wherever difference of opinion may have arisen between us on a few points of detail, we concur in the main foundation of the principles by which this empire is to be maintained; and while I retain the power of public service, I will never abandon the cause of this flourishing empire, in the prosperity of which I shall always feel the deepest interest.

Referring you to the dispatches for the state of public affairs.

I remain, . . .

WELLESLEY

FINISH

INDEX

64, 66, 85, 98, 99, 105, 116–17,
122, 125, 128, 140–1, 155, 157,
229, 312; British expedition to,
150, 277–9, 285, 308, 323, 325,
332
El Arish, convention of, 285 fn.
Eldon, John Scott, earl of, 327 fn.
Elgin, Thomas Bruce, earl of, 229
fn., 252, 278
Elphinstone, Hon. William, 135 fn.
Emperor of Germany, 155, 165
Ernst, Thomas, 301 fn.

Fallowfield, Ernest, 169 fn., 170
Fath Ali, shah of Persia, 104, 179,
212, 214; *see also* Persia
Fathigur, 99
Finglass, Mr, 17, 31
Floyd, Maj.-Gen., 172, 201, 256
Foley, Mr, 239
Fort St George, 1, 2, 53, 67, 74, 80,
82, 86, 87, 88, 89, 90, 91, 92,
96, 97, 99, 100, 104, 106, 107,
108, 109, 112, 144, 152, 161,
162, 178, 179, 199, 200, 221,
241, 244, 245, 250, 251, 261,
274, 275, 277, 292, 306, 308,
323, 324, 333
Fort William, 1, 113, 226, 276, 282,
322, 326; *see also* Calcutta
France, 14, 18, 19, 20, 21, 22, 26, 31,
32, 36, 40, 41, 43, 46, 53, 54,
55, 57, 58, 59, 61, 62, 63, 76,
77, 82, 91, 92, 95, 100, 101, 102,
103, 107, 110, 111, 115, 118,
121, 123, 129, 130, 149, 150,
159, 165, 166, 206, 251, 274,
277, 278, 299; *see also* Egypt
Francis, Sir Philip, 295 fn.
Futteh Hyder, 149, 150

Ghazipur, 1

Gholam Mohammed, 98
Goa, 99, 100, 130, 163, 186, 187,
197, 198, 230, 298, 318, 328, 329
Gordon, Lt-Col., 217
Govind Kishen, 93 fn., 94
Graham, Capt., 171
Graham, Thomas, 73 fn., 84
Grant, Charles, 74 fn., 193, 283,
286, 296
Grenville, William Wyndham Gren-
ville, Lord, 47 fn., 48, 101, 111,
122, 136, 202, 210, 235, 272 fn.,
285, 297 fn., 326, 327
Guntur Circar, 92–3, 107
Guzerat, 8, 181, 187

Haldane, Mr, 239
Hamburg, 206
Hardis, Mr, 171
Harington, John, 74 fn., 75, 76, 219,
237
Harington, William, 170 fn., 243,
288
Harris, Maj.-Gen. George (Lord
Harris), 45 fn., 46, 53, 80, 86,
87, 88, 91, 93, 96, 107–10, 121,
124, 143, 146–50, 153, 161,
170, 172, 178, 193, 221, 224,
255–6, 263, 267, 281
Hartley, Maj.-Gen. James, 193, 196,
201
Hasilby, Mr, 69
Hastings, Warren, 11 fn., 295
Hatton, Sir Christopher, 305 fn.
Hawkesbury, Robert Jenkinson,
Lord (earl of Liverpool), 327
fn.
Herat, 179
Hobart, Robert, Lord (earl of
Buckinghamshire), 1 fn., 7, 20,
21, 35 fn., 87, 89, 138, 142, 153,
169, 170, 291, 302–3, 327

338

Mahmud Shah, of Herat, 179
Malabar, coast of, 35, 39, 43, 55, 62, 91, 95, 96, 97–8, 99, 124, 125, 139, 149, 155, 181, 183, 205, 250, 257, 275, 292, 316, 318; commission, 162
Malacca, 163, 198, 328; straits of, 82
Malartic, Anne, Cte de, 46 fn., 52, 63, 64, 100, 124
Malcolm, Capt. John, 12 fn., 100, 121, 179, 214
Malet, Sir Charles, Bart., 110 fn., 296
Malta, 117, 140, 141
Malwa, 33
Manesty, Samuel, 12
Mangalore, 54, 56, 82, 129, 230
Manila, 135; proposed expedition to, 35, 66
Maratha Confederacy, 2–3, 6, 8, 23–8, 32–4, 56–61, 93–6, 124, 126, 129, 140, 156–7, 160, 178, 184, 227–8, 269, 278; see also Sindhia, Baji Rao II, Poona
Masulipatam, 2, 18, 80
Maurice, Mr, 283
Mauritius, 4, 8, 46, 52, 53, 54, 56, 63, 65, 82, 114, 128, 147, 160, 185, 305, 309, 332
McLean, Mr, 235, 236
Mediterranean Sea, 66, 116, 117, 118, 128, 150, 251, 277, 285
Meuron, Charles, Cte de, 274
Minorca, 117, 141
Mir Allum, 121, 150
Mitford, Sir John, 327
Mohammed Ali Khan Walajah, 17 fn., 249
Molucca Islands, 328
Monson, Col. George, 295
Montague, Lt-Col., 261
Monthly bulletin, 66–7, 140, 147,

222; see also Overland dispatches
Morier, John Philip, 278 fn.
Mornington, earl of, see Wellesley, Marquis
Moultan, 113, 186, 187
Mozambique Channel, 155
Munro, Capt. Thomas, 171 fn.
Myers, Thomas, 215 fn., 218, 230, 232, 252, 277, 314
Mysore, 3, 5, 6, 13, 94, 95, 178, 250, 260, 274, 312, 314, 318, 321, 325; partition of, 123–5, 129–30, 157–60, 180–3, 203–5, 229–30; rajah of, 159, 163, 182, 214

Nana Fadnavis, 30, 32, 57, 93, 103
Naples, 47, 117
Narpilly, 17
Nelson, Rear-Adm. Sir Horatio (Lord Nelson), 47 fn., 101, 114, 116, 117, 128, 140, 141
Nile, battle of the, 101, 103
North, Hon. Frederick (earl of Guildford), 144 fn., 153, 171, 172, 173, 196, 298
Northern Circars, 2, 23, 80, 138, 139, 184, 250, 264

Oakes, Thomas, 171 fn.
Ongale, 17
Onore, 137
Opium, 63, 137, 239; see also China
Orissa, 1, 226
Oudh, 2, 7, 10, 13, 14, 34–5, 38, 39, 49, 76, 99, 122, 137, 186, 211, 213, 218, 225, 235, 241, 270, 276, 280, 281, 306, 313; see also Saadat Ali Khan, Vizier Ali Khan

Overland dispatches, 66, 222, 292–3; *see also* Monthly bulletin

Paangul, treaty of, 31
Palchautcherry, 124
Palmer, Col. William, 6, 27, 58, 59, 61, 92, 93 fn., 94, 95, 223
Parker, Vice-Adm. Sir Hyde, 332 fn.
Pattle, James, 69 fn., 70, 85–6
Paugah Party, 36
Perron, Pierre, 28
Persia, 43, 127, 179, 211, 214, 229, 269
Peru, 186, 188
Peshwa, *see* Baji Rao II
Petrie, William, 89 fn., 90, 108, 109, 113, 144, 152, 153, 169, 171, 195, 332
Philippine Islands, 309
Piron, M., 17 fn., 58, 63, 115
Pitt, William, the Younger, 1, 84, 101, 118, 133, 141, 149 fn., 155, 180, 210, 234, 251, 258, 282, 285, 299, 311, 326, 327
Plymouth, 293, 298
Polygars, 23, 172, 199, 218, 231
Pondicherry, 123
Poona, 13, 17, 23, 27, 30, 31, 33, 34, 36, 37, 39, 56, 58, 59, 60, 61, 87, 93, 94, 103, 127, 146, 178, 198, 199, 218, 223, 224, 227, 228
Portland, William Bentinck, duke of, 327 fn.
Portugal, 10, 13, 47, 48, 130, 163, 186, 275, 318
Pringle, Rear-Adm. Thomas, 29 fn., 57
Prussia, 117, 165
Purnea, 301
Purneah Dewan, 150, 157, 159, 214, 264
Pursuram Bhow, 33, 199

Pyche Rajah, 35, 39

Rainier, Vice-Adm. Peter, 82 fn., 96, 155, 267, 279, 308, 325
Rajputs, 127
Raymond, Michel, 17 fn., 18, 20, 21, 22, 23, 24, 25, 27, 28, 31, 57
Read, Lt-Col., 171
Red Sea, 97, 98, 105, 121, 146, 148, 150, 229, 251, 277, 307, 323
Rennel, Mr, 283
Rivers:
    Ganges, 185, 225, 305, 309
    Indus, 8, 181, 186–7; *see also* Zeman Shah
    Kistna, 310
    Thames, 134, 191, 309
    Tungebadra, 184, 310
Roberts, Lt-Col., 102, 103, 107
Robinson, Capt. George, 81 fn., 85
Rohilkhand, 2, 98, 99
Rosebery, Archibald Philip Primrose, earl of, 13
Russell, Sir Henry, 217 fn.
Russia, 43, 104, 117, 127, 141, 165, 166, 167, 229
Rykottah, 150

Saadat Ali Khan, 7, 34 fn., 60, 99, 126, 179, 213, 241, 270, 280–1, 298, 318, 325; *see also* Oudh
St Helena, 196
St Leger, Maj.-Gen., 172
St Vincent, John Jervis, Adm. the earl of, 105 fn., 327
Saldanha Bay, battle of, 81
Salmond, Capt. James, 142 fn., 325; wife of, 142 fn.
Satara, rajah of, 3
Saunders, Mr, 108, 153
Scott, David, 10 fn., 135, 142, 234, 305 fn., 325, 332

White, Charles, 170 fn., 288; wife of, 288

Wickham, William, 53 fn., 62

Wilson, Capt. Samuel, 122 fn.

Windham, William, 326 fn., 327

Wynaad, 40

Yonge, Sir George, Bart., 304 fn., 305, 308

York, Frederick, duke of, 48 fn., 193, 252, 255

Yorke, Charles, 327

Zeman Shah, 4 fn., 6–7, 13, 25–7, 35–6, 39–40, 43, 49, 60, 65, 85, 95–6, 98–9, 104, 113, 123, 126–7, 179, 186–7, 211–12, 214, 220, 228–9, 269

Personally I cannot o[f]
St George more satisf[y]
in every respect; I [be]
lieve; & I never met
I conceived more prue[?]
short an acquainta[nce]
correct the numerous
[w]hich require a vigor[ous]
& above all great p[?]
What may be my fa[te]
trust in God you wi[ll]
circumstances, send
[i]f you do, the whole sys[tem]